UNIVERSITY BODIES:
A SURVEY OF INTER- AND SUPRA-
UNIVERSITY BODIES AND THEIR RECORDS

Adrian R. Allan

Archives Unit
University of Liverpool

To the memory of

Geoffrey A. Dyer,
Archivist, Sheffield University Library
and the Centre for English Cultural Tradition
and Language, 1976-1982,
who instituted this survey.

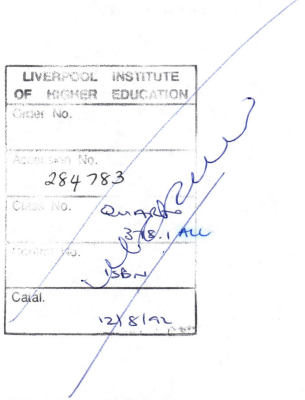
(c)   Adrian R. Allan and contributors, 1990

ISBN 0 907156 02 9

Printed in Great Britain by
Antony Rowe Ltd, Chippenham, Wiltshire

CONTENTS

Page

Survey : Entries for International Bodies

iv

vii

Introduction and Acknowledgements

How to use this book

This book originated in a survey of the archives policies of inter- and supra-university bodies but as now presented provides, in addition, (a) information about the history and publications of many of these bodies and (b) a general bibliography, introducing books, journals, and guides to information sources relating to higher education which should be found of use by those with a more general interest in the history of higher education as well as those particularly concerned to find out more about a particular country, body/organisation, or subject. Thus the book serves as both a survey and a guide.

The survey section of the book is in two parts. The first part (pages 9-248) provides full entries for 87 UK and 18 international bodies. The entry for each body provides an address and contact; a history of the body; details of publications about the body (bibliography); a note on the body's own publications; and a note about the body's records, their coverage, whereabouts, and availability to researchers. In some few cases it did not prove possible to provide details under all of these headings for some of these bodies. The second part of the survey section (pages 249-274) provides briefer details about further bodies, over 80 in all (principally in the UK): the name and address of each body, usually supplemented by some further details about the body's history and role. In the case of some, but by no means all, of the bodies covered, it should prove possible to find some reference to them (if only an address) in one of the periodically revised directories or year books which are listed in the bibliographical section of the book (pages 278-82).

The bibliography section of the book (pages 275-305) provides (a) a list of reference works (through the use of which readers can obtain further information about a particular body); (b) a select list of published guides to information sources and to archive repositories; (c) an introduction to the wealth of information about higher education to be derived from UK Government and Parliamentary publications; (d) a select list of books and journal articles on the history of university education in the UK, principally in the 19th and 20th centuries; and (e) a list of (and an introduction to) the principal indexing and abstracting journals and also the journals (over 40 in number) which cover higher education in whole or part.

There follows (pages 306-12) a glossary of abbreviations and acronyms, over 110 in all, which one might expect to come across in the higher education world, and also a select list of dictionaries of abbreviations which should assist in elucidating the other acronyms and abbreviations one may encounter.

The index of the book covers all the entries relating to the bodies (and countries, named reports, etc.) referred to in the text, but does not cover subjects. The index should be used in addition to the list of contents in order to ensure that all references are picked up, not just the main survey (or other) entry.

Origins of the survey

At the Society of Archivists' Annual Conference held at Leicester in April 1979 sixteen of those present met informally and agreed to establish an informal 'National, University and Specialist Repositories Forum' (NUSR Forum) and in discussion it was, amongst other things, agreed that a working party be established to try to evolve a common policy towards retention schedules in universities. The minutes add that 'an important factor would be to have proper information on the archives policies of inter and/or supra university bodies such as UCCA (Universities Central Council on Admissions).' The need for such information had been felt for some time by those archivists working in universities and my colleague Michael Cook had recently publicly voiced the subject in a letter to the editor published in the Society of Archivists' Newsletter, No.8, January 1979.

Conduct of the survey

The task of ascertaining the archives policies of inter- and supra- university bodies was initially undertaken by the late Geoffrey Dyer, assisted by Michael Cook (who undertook a visit to UCCA and USR (Universities' Statistical Record) and who joined Geoffrey in a visit to the CVCP (Committee of Vice-Chancellors and Principals)) and by Adrian Allan. In his letters to the bodies approached, Geoffrey asked them 'whether you have made any provisions for those records of permanent value (minutes, reports, correspondence relating to policy, etc.) to be kept whereby university archivists might safely dispose of many of the files from your body...which we receive. I would be most grateful for any information which you could provide in order that a comprehensive and consistent policy may be established within university archives towards the records of your body.'

In April 1980, at a Forum which the Specialist Repositories Group (as the NUSR Forum had become) organised in London, an interim report was submitted by Adrian Allan on the two dozen bodies which Geoffrey Dyer, in the main, had been in correspondence with or which (as in the cases of the CVCP, UCCA, and USR) had been visited. Work progressed thereafter until the death of Geoffrey in February 1982, at the tragically early age of thirty-two. His quiet, unobtrusive efficiency and his kindness and diplomatic approach had been much appreciated by those with whom he had worked, in the University of Sheffield, the archive profession, and in the other societies and bodies with which he was associated: his loss was profoundly felt.

Adrian Allan 'inherited' the survey work and working files of Geoffrey Dyer. That it has taken so long to produce this survey he would attribute to several factors - the pressure of other work, which those who have worked in the under-resourced British university system over the last decade will readily appreciate and which has determined that most of the work on the survey has had to be undertaken outside of 'office hours'; the wider scope which the survey adopted; and the desire - unrealised as yet and perhaps unrealisable - to produce a work whose accuracy and relative comprehensiveness could be relied upon by its users. The scope of the survey was broadened to provide the following additional details for each body : a brief history; details of any book or journal article containing an account of its work; and a list of its publications (or principal publications) with dates of first issue. As regards the bodies' records, the dates of commencement of individual classes of record or of the records as a whole was sought, a note being made of records of individual bodies housed other than with the body (e.g. in a record repository or library). Enquiry was also made whether bona fide researchers might by

2

appointment consult these records, perhaps after a fixed period of years in the case of unpublished material. The information obtained and reproduced in this survey is in most cases an amalgam of information provided by the body and of information culled from a large range of secondary sources. The survey's scope was also broadened to encompass a host of professional and other, non-government funded bodies in the UK and an attempt made to cover a few of the major bodies with international interests in tertiary education. The picture revealed by the survey keeps changing (with changes in titles, responsibilities, etc.) and growing bigger, and so without further delay in unveiling the canvas it is now presented for inspection, incomplete as the picture is.

Inclusion in the text of a list of abbreviations and acronyms, and a bibliography (see pages 275-312)

'Non minima pars eruditionis est bonos nosse libros' states the inscription above the entrance to Bishop John Cosin's Library on Palace Green, Durham.

In the course of compiling this survey a number of reference works and journals have been used both in tracing bodies and in finding out more about their objectives, achievements, and current programmes. Inasmuch as this survey does not cover all the bodies which might come within the scope of 'inter- and supra- university bodies' it was felt that it would be useful to include a list of such reference works and journals, so that researchers might be assisted in their search for information about a body not covered. In addition, a number of these reference works are periodically revised, so that if, for instance, a body covered in this survey changes its address or secretary this fact may be noted in a later edition of the reference work. A wide range of reference works have been listed for it was found that a number of bodies were not to be found in what one might assume to be comprehensive specialist directories. Reference is not made in such directories to a number of the bodies covered in the survey - evidence of the bodies' existence (or past existence) being initially derived from such sources as copies of publications amongst the deposited papers of graduates and former members of staff of the University of Liverpool, press reports of a conference, the forthcoming events listings in the Times Higher Education Supplement 'notice board' column, a reference to a hitherto unknown acronym in a higher education text, and the British Library's Catalogue.

Likewise it was felt that it might be useful to provide not only a list of the principal relevant dictionaries of and guides to abbreviations but also a list of those referred to in the text. Surprisingly, some abbreviations and acronyms of some prominent educational bodies do not appear in some of these dictionaries. With the changes in title of bodies and the creation of new bodies such dictionaries can, of course, never be up to date. At the time of writing, the sustained campaign by the universities against the Government's 'great' Education Reform Bill, 1987, had given rise to the popular, disparaging reference to 'GERBIL'.

The list of books (pages 291-4) about aspects of the history of universities reflects the natural bias of this survey to developments in the 20th century, and in particular to those dating from the rapid expansion of the British university system. The majority of the bodies covered originated in this era, particularly during the 1960s and 1970s, but some, such as SERC, took over bodies which had been established for many years, inheriting the records of these predecessor bodies. These bodies are a by-product of this expansion and a response to the problems and opportunities which were presented by a larger and more complex system in which a greater degree of specialisation in administrative (and academic) posts was possible and was encouraged. The 'barriers' between those in separate individual institutions who share similar interests may be broken down by such bodies, as well as through their membership of learned societies; and more recently within individual universities 'barriers' are being breached by the formation of institutes and centres bringing together specialist staff from a variety of separate departments to promote the study of a subject which benefits from a multidisciplinary approach. Co-operation on a regional basis has extended beyond the regional Management Services Units to cover use of computer, library, research and other facilities and, most recently, has been fostered in the new university-based SERC-funded Interdisciplinary Research Centres (each generally drawing upon staff within individual departments in several universities). With the disappearance of metropolitan county councils and the changing role of local authorities, universities are further developing their roles in regional co-ordination, promotion and development, in communication of information and expertise, and in joint ventures with 'outside' bodies, public and private. Where once a vice-chancellor might have been the chairman of a Settlement and of a Council for Social Service he might nowadays, perhaps in addition, chair a project for a regional library and information plan, and be a member of a Development Corporation.

Some Comments on the Survey and its 'findings'

(a)   Records

1.   Except in the case of the CVCP, MRC, UCCA, and USR, most of this survey has perforce had to be conducted by correspondence and by research based on secondary sources and such papers of the bodies as have already been deposited in university and other record repositories. My own experience in directing a MSC-funded regional field survey of hospital archives and artefacts emphasised the fact that there are no adequate substitutes for field surveys for reaching and revealing records which would otherwise not be revealed! The time and funds to undertake a field survey in this case were not available, and I am conscious that many records must yet remain to be located.

2.   There are very few bodies whose records are classified as 'public records' and are subject to the provisions of the Public Records Acts. They include the ABRC, ACARD, the Computer Board for Universities and Research Councils, and the UFC. The records of the Research Councils are not subject to the Public Records Acts but, for instance, the ESRC has (as noted) an arrangement with the Public Record Office whereby research grant files are deposited in the PRO; NERC makes its non-current records open to public inspection at its offices on the same basis as records in the PRO once they are thirty years old; MRC is to deposit some of its non-current records in the PRO; and SERC in fact adheres to the Acts, conducting First and Second Reviews. The records of other bodies are subject to no such Acts and the 'protection' they confer but several of the bodies covered are registered charities and/or companies limited by guarantee and in such cases are subject to legal provisions governing records, and one may expect to find copies of the governing instruments and the annual returns/reports and accounts of most of such bodies at the offices of the Charity Commission and of the Companies Registration Office respectively.

3.   Very few indeed of the bodies employ or designate someone specifically as records officer/archivist. Exceptions include the Conference of University Administrators, the British Association of Academic Phoneticians, and the British Association of Health Services in Higher Education (which has a designated Librarian and Archivist). It is clear that problems are presented upon the change in the post of Honorary Secretary of some of the smaller bodies when someone has not already been specifically assigned with responsibility for the records of the body. It appears that not all the records held by an Honorary Secretary (or other officer) migrate to his or her successor.

4.   "Field surveys of archives have a certain value as recording what existed at a certain point in time, but their value is greatly enhanced if they are the prelude to swift action to arrange deposit", I wrote in respect of the Mersey RHA hospital archives survey and as I write a number of the records of two Merseyside hospitals which, over five years after the survey, it has now been agreed may be deposited in the appropriate local record repository cannot now be found (A.R. Allan, 'Undertaking a Regional Survey', The Continuing Saga of Medical Records: Proceedings of a one-day conference, S.W. and South Wales Region, Society of Archivists, 1986, pp.50-58). Some bodies are themselves able to make adequate provisions for the selection, preservation and exploitation (by bona fide researchers) of their records, in some cases through deposit of the records with a record repository.

5.   A problem which confronts many of the bodies covered is that there is no 'natural' home for their records. There are specialist record repositories which particularly cater for certain sectors, most notably the Modern Records Centre, University of Warwick Library, in the industrial relations field (with its holdings of the records of trade unions, employers' associations, etc.) In cases where the body has or had strong links with a Government department and its work there may be a possibility of deposit in the Public Record Office - as happened with the records of the General Nursing Council. But in many other cases there are no 'natural' homes in this country for the records of the bodies surveyed and whilst, if the financial situation permitted, one might wish to see developed a record centre based in a university which has a particular research interest in higher education, in which the records of such bodies might find a 'natural' and productive home, in the meantime it is surely sensible to arrange deposit in a record repository, to ensure initially the future safe custody of the records. The example, for instance, of SCONUL (with its London office) in depositing its earlier records at the Manuscripts Department of University College London's Library is one which might be followed by other bodies. Perhaps other universities and university colleges with adequate facilities and staffing might 'adopt' one or more bodies and offer to administer their non-current records?

In certain cases the past existence of defunct bodies is revealed not by surviving records but by printed material, journals, the odd annual report, pamphlets, etc. The Holloway Collection of Contemporary Culture Records at the University of East Anglia Library, which has a large collection of printed material about cultural activities in the United Kingdom, might be considered as one of the potential homes (in addition to a record repository) for copies of some of the published products of bodies.

6. A few of the bodies surveyed, such as the Conference on University Purchasing and the Conference of University Registrars and Secretaries, do not have 'central' records, the records of each individual annual conference etc. being maintained by the office of the member responsible for hosting the conference, etc. Particular care in the disposal of such papers thus needs to be exercised.

7. Perhaps a case might be made out for an inter- and supra- university bodies liaison committee (ISUBLC) covering bodies based in the United Kingdom, one of whose roles might be the exchange of information and expertise in the field of records management? Overseas one can name such bodies as the Council of Europe's Non-Governmental Organisations Liaison Committee (established in 1976) performing a liaison role.

(b) Research

1. There is clearly considerable scope for the use of the records of these bodies for historical, political, and other research and it is perhaps significant that where there has been research for higher degrees based on the records of such bodies it has been mainly in those cases where the records have already been deposited in a record office, a particularly notable example being the National Association of Teachers in Further and Higher Education whose records are deposited at the Modern Records Centre, University of Warwick Library (see p.111-2). The information given here is presented with a view to facilitating the process by which a greater knowledge of the subject might be achieved.

2. Research into higher and further education has increased over the last two decades, fostered by international initiatives such as OECD's CERI and in the UK particularly by individual university departments and by the Society for Research into Higher Education (established in 1964 and now based at the University of Surrey, Guildford) and its conferences and publications. The study of the impact of inter- and supra-university bodies on national policy making and institutional decision taking and administration is still relatively undeveloped, and more recently published histories of individual universities still generally have relatively little to say about such bodies apart from, in the British context, the UGC and, to some degree, the CVCP and the NUS. (The draft of this book was entitled Para-Educational Forces: A Survey of Inter- and Supra- University Bodies and their Records!) The full impact of the increasingly international nature of trade, finance, and professional life has yet to be felt and taken into account. To what extent has the increasing uniformity of universities, their government and administration, been encouraged by work of the various bodies? What influence have they had on national policy making bodies? What role has been played this century by international bodies in the creation (? recreation) of a cosmopolitan academic community and common culture unbounded by national and linguistic boundaries? The active development of overseas links and the increasing awareness on the part of UK tertiary institutions of international funding and support bodies has been more pronounced over the last few years. We know about such co-operative projects between British industry and universities as the current Alvey Programme on information technology, about European collaborative programmes in industry and in space exploration, and about the role of co- operative research associations in British industry and their relationship to Government, but know relatively little about such co-operative ventures, past and present, within tertiary education.

Acknowledgements

It is hoped that this survey will be found of some value by the creators, custodians, and users of the records it briefly describes, and that it will ease the task of those archivists who have to determine whether or not to retain copies of the records (e.g. minutes) or correspondence with such bodies as they are offered by a member of staff of their university (or other employing authority) or by a member of such a body. The compiler of this survey is very conscious of its inadequacies, and in order that a revised and more comprehensive edition, or perhaps a supplement, might be produced in several years time, would welcome constructive comment and information in order both to correct and 'complete' the entries which appear and to facilitate the construction of entries for some of those bodies which are as yet unrepresented. It may be that such a revised edition could be produced on computer discs or the text made available on-line.

What merits this present survey has are very largely due to those many officers and members of staff of the bodies described who devoted time and effort to providing information, in several cases providing a complete entry for their organisation. Unfortunately, it did not prove possible to obtain a response from several bodies, despite several enquiries, whereby the entries for the same are unavoidably incomplete : these bodies principally comprise the Association of University Teachers of Economics, the Council of Europe, the International Union of Students, the National Institute of Adult Continuing Education (England and Wales), the National Union of Students, the Standing Conference on University Teaching and Research in the Education of Adults, the Universities Safety Association, and World University Service. I have also benefited from the assistance of those members of staff of the University of Liverpool who are members of some of the bodies covered; from the help of fellow archivists (amongst whom I must particularly mention my colleague Michael Cook, University Archivist; Mrs. Alexandra Nicol and Dr. Alfred Knightbridge her successor as Liaison Officer, Public Record Office; the Scottish Record Office; Richard Storey, Archivist, Modern Records Centre, University of Warwick Library, who has also kindly permitted me to make use of his descriptions of the relevant records in his care; and Miss Ruth Vyse whilst she was Assistant Archivist, Oxford University Archives); and from the services of librarians (notably in the Liverpool City Libraries and the University of Liverpool's Sydney Jones, Education, and Continuing Education Libraries). None of them can be held responsible for the 'final' product and the inevitable sins of omission and commission which the compiler will, so far as possible, bear responsibility for. Perhaps one might agree with the words attributed to Samuel Johnson, that 'dictionaires are like watches; the worst is better than none, and the best cannot be expected to go quite true'.

The text of the draft of this volume was completed in April 1989 and submitted in July to the Publications Committee of the Society of Archivists. The Committee's 'imprimatur', given subject to certain alterations being made in the presentation of the text, was received in May 1990 and an endeavour (not entirely successful, given constraints on time and manpower) has been made to update the text to cover developments over the intervening year. I am very grateful for the valuable comments of the Committee's reading committee and for their general support.

I owe a particular word of thanks to our Secretary, Mrs. Andrea Owens, for coping so cheerfully with my handwriting and for considerably improving the presentation of the text. She was assisted in the early stages by Mrs. Margaret Wearing.

Adrian Allan
University Archives
University of Liverpool
P.O. Box 147   June 1990
Liverpool L69 3BX

Tel: (051) 794 5423/4
Fax: (051) 708 6502
Email via JANET:ARCHIVES @ UK.AC.LIVERPOOL

ADVISORY BOARD FOR THE RESEARCH COUNCILS

<u>Address and</u>
<u>contact</u>
Advisory Board for the Research Councils,
Elizabeth House,
39, York Road,
London,
SE1 7PH

tel: 071-934 9379
fax: 071-934 9389
Mr. M. Power

<u>History</u>
The Advisory Board for the Research Councils (ABRC) was established by the Secretary of State for Education and Science in November 1972 as the successor to the Council for Scientific Policy (CSP). The Government's White Paper, <u>A Framework for Government Research and Development</u>, 1972 (Cmnd. 5046), had proposed that the C.S.P. should be replaced by a new chartered advisory body of which the Research Councils, Government Departments, and independent members (drawn from industry and the universities) would be in full membership. The C.S.P. was constituted in 1965 to advise the Secretary of State for Education and Science in his responsibility for determining the overall pattern of the resources of the Research Councils, the Science and Technology Act of 1965 having provided for the Secretary of State directly to finance the Research Councils; the C.S.P.'s task was outlined in <u>Report on Science Policy</u>, 1966 (Cmnd. 3007). The C.S.P. replaced the Advisory Council for Scientific Policy (ACSP) which had been established in 1947 to advise the Lord President of the Council in the exercise of his responsibility for the formulation and execution of government scientific policy : in effect to advise on the research effort required to increase national productivity as part of the post-War recovery programme. To help it in the discharge of its tasks the ACSP created a standing Committee on Scientific Manpower and a standing Scientific Library and Technical Information Centre. ACSP's annual reports were published as Command Papers (1963-64 report, Cmnd. 2538).

The Board's terms of reference were until the end of March 1990:-

i. To advise the Secretary of State on his responsibilities for civil science with particular reference to the Research Council system, its articulation with the universities and Departments, the support of postgraduate students and the proper balance between international and national activity;

ii. To advise the Secretary of State on the allocation of the Science Budget amongst the Research Councils and other bodies, taking into account funds paid to them by customer Departments and the purpose to which such funds are devoted;

iii. To promote close liaison between Councils and the users of their research.

From 1 April 1990 the terms of reference were amended, inter alia to include a clause requesting the Board 'to work closely with the UFC and PCFC on issues concerning the support of research in higher education institutions, and the training and support of postgraduate students.'

Until 1 April 1990 the Board consisted of a chairman and 19 other members, and the chairman or secretary of each of the five Research Councils and the chairman of the UGC (later the Chief Executive of the UFC).

ABRC advises the Secretary of State for Education and Science on his responsibilites for civil science and in particular on the allocation of the Science Budget (found from the DES Science Vote) amongst the five Research Councils (AFRC, MRC, NERC, SERC, ESRC), the Royal Society of London, and (from 1984-85) the Fellowship of Engineering. The ABRC used also to advise on the allocation of the Science Budget to the British Museum (Natural History) but since 1987 the Office of Arts and Libraries has been responsible for allocation of grant to the Museum.

The Science Budget is directed towards developing the natural and social sciences, to maintaining a fundamental capacity for research, and to supporting higher education at the postgraduate level. Annual grants to the Research Councils currently account for 97% of the total Science Budget. The Science Budget is one of the main sources of public funds for the support of basic scientific research, the other being the UGC grants. As regards the Research Councils:-

(a) the Councils support research in their own or in other research establishments. The Medical Research Council (MRC) has a few large centres, maintains many relatively small research establishments in the form of units associated with universities or hospitals, and provides block grants to certain other institutes. The Science and Engineering Research Council (SERC) has a small number of large establishments. The Agricultural and Food Research Council (AFRC) and the Natural Environment Research Council (NERC) support a considerable number of establishments and (in the case of NERC) of research vessels. Although the largest part of the Economic and Social Research Council's (ESRC) support for research is through postgraduate training awards and grants for projects in universities etc., a few units are maintained.

(b) grants are made by the Council's to research workers in universities (under the 'dual support' system) and in polytechnics. Under the 'dual support' system, universities provide, out of the grants they receive through the UGC, money for the provision and running of departments and for the salaries of those to run the departments, whilst the Research Councils make specific grants to university scientists for selected projects in response to individual applications.

(c) they support postgraduate education and research through the provision of awards to students training in the natural and social sciences and of fellowship awards to post-doctoral scientists.

(d) some of the Councils serve as contractors to Government Departments which commission work related to their policy objectives. In accordance with Cmnd.5046 funds for this purpose were transferred from the Science Budget to the Ministry of Agriculture, Fisheries and Food, the Department of Health and Social Security (and the Scottish Home and Health Department).

In 1982 ABRC for the first time published its advice. The ABRC has recently collaborated with the UGC and with ACARD in studies of the support of university scientific research and of the links between industry and higher education in research and its application respectively, and also recently received the report of a Working Party which it had appointed to study the support given by the Research Councils to in-house and university research. In June 1983 ACARD in collaboration with ABRC produced a report, Improving research links between Higher Education and Industry, H.M.S.O.

In its discussion document, A Strategy for the Science Base, 1987, the ABRC argued that science funding is too low and inter alia recommended a greater emphasis among research councils on large programme grants (rather than small project grants), the establishment of new interdisciplinary research centres (attached to one or more universities and other higher education institutions), and more concentration of research within universities, which would be classified in three tiers. The document argues for the need to concentrate substantial research activities while retaining a broader spread of undergraduate teaching. In line with this advice, SERC (which receives just over half of the Science Vote) has subsequently agreed to establish and fund a number of interdisciplinary research centres, at Cambridge, Glasgow, Liverpool, and elsewhere. In June 1989 the Secretary of State for Education and Science, in response to this discussion document, stated that the UFC would identify teaching and research funds separately for each institution and that there would be a cash transfer of c.£70M from the UFC to the research councils for research grant overheads.

In January 1990 the Government confirmed that it had rejected a suggestion (contained in the report of a review group, chaired by Mr. Dick Morris, on the distribution of responsibility for biological research between the research councils, which was submitted to ABRC in April 1989) to merge the five research councils into a single National Research Council. But from 1 April 1990 the ABRC was slimmed down from 26 to 14 members, and given the task of improving the coordination of research projects between the councils.

Bibliography

'The Advisory Board for the Research Councils', Biologist, Vol.32 No.4, 1985, pp.208-210.

Michael Shattock, 'Higher Education and the Research Councils', Minerva, Vol.27 Nos.2-3, 1989, pp.195-222.

Publications include:-

Reports
(a) 1st Report of the Board, (covers work up to Dec.1973), 1974, Cmnd.5633

2nd Report of the Board, (covers work of the two years ending in Dec.1975), 1976, Cmnd.6430

3rd Report of the Board, (covers Jan.1976-June 1978), 1979, Cmnd.7467

The 3rd Report was the last annual report as such to be published. Instead, since 1982, the ABRC has published 'in-house' its advice to the Secretary of State on the size of the Science Budget and its subsequent allocation among the Research Councils, the Royal Society, and the Fellowship of Engineering. In 1982 and 1983 the two pieces of advice were published retrospectively in one report. Since 1984 ABRC has issued two reports each year - the first being the advice on the size of the Science Budget (e.g. *Science and Public Expenditure 1987: A Report to the Secretary of State for Education & Science from the Advisory Board for the Research Councils, ABRC, 1987) and the second, the advice on the allocations of the Science Budget (e.g. * Science Budget : Allocations 1988-89 Planning Figures 1989-90 - 1990-91 : Advice to the Secretary of State for Education & Science from the Advisory Board for the Research Councils, ABRC, 1988).

(b)   *Report on Taxonomy, 1979

ACARD/ABRC/Royal Society Joint Report on Biotechnology, 1980

*Report on Energy Research, 1974 and (an update of the report) 1981

Report of the Working Party on Postgraduate Education (the Swinnerton-Dyer Report), 1982, Cmnd.8537

Report of a Joint Working Party on the Support of University Scientific Research (the Merrison Report), 1982, Cmnd.8567

*The Science Budget: A Forward Look, 1982
(recommendations to the Secretary of State for Education and Science about the distribution of the Budget for 1983-84 to 1985-86.)

First Joint Report by the Chairmen of the Advisory Council for Applied Research and Development (ACARD) and the Advisory Board for the Research Councils (ABRC), 1983, Cmnd.8957

*A Strategy for the Science Base : A discussion document prepared for the Secretary of State for Education and Science by the Advisory Board for the Research Councils May 1987, HMSO, 1987.

The support given by Research Councils for in-house and university research: the report of a working party of the Board, July 1983. Appendices include list of research establishments of the Research Councils (including grant-aided establishments) and maps indicating whereabouts of the individual Research Councils' establishments.

Review of Research Councils' Responsibilities for Biological Sciences, 1989 (report of review group chaired by Mr. J.R.S. Morris).

* Available from the Department of Education and Science.

Records
The Board's records are classed as public records. They will therefore be reviewed by the Board in due course and those of historical interest will be transferred to the Public Record Office for opening to the public when 30 years old.

ADVISORY COUNCIL FOR ADULT AND CONTINUING EDUCATION

Address and
contact of successor body
Unit for the Development of Adult Continuing Education,
94B London Road,
Leicester,
LE2 OQS

tel: 0533 542645

History
The establishment of the Advisory Council for Adult and Continuing Education (ACACE) was announced by the Secretary of State for Education and Science on 10 August 1977, following recommendations in the Russell Report on Adult Education, 1973, (which recommended the establishment of a Development Council for Adult Education in England and Wales) and in the report of the Committee on Continuing Education set up by the Open University and published in 1976. The Council, which first met in October 1977, consisted of a chairman and 22 other members, all appointed by the Secretary of State in a personal rather than a representative capacity.

Its objects were to advise generally on matters relevant to the provision of education for adults in England and Wales, and in particular:

(a)   to promote co-operation between the various bodies engaged in adult education and review current practice, organisation and priorities, with a view to the most effective deployment of the available resources; and
(b)   to promote the development of future policies and priorities, with full regard to the concept of education as a process continuing throughout life.

The Council covered a great deal of ground: it helped with new developments and responded to the effects of central and local government decisions on provision for adult and continuing education. Its publications (reports and studies) were also influential. No fewer than thirty-six reports were published; several of them provided practical advice and information on matters specially relevant to the needs of the disadvantaged.

The Council, whose sponsoring body was the Department of Education and Science, was included within the review of non Departmental public bodies. As mentioned in the report on these bodies (Cmnd. 7797, HMSO, 1980), the Council was allowed to undertake work for a further three years from 1980, with a slightly reduced grant, and at the end of this period it was not reappointed, annual savings of £82,000 (as at Jan. 1980) thereby being achieved. In 1978-79 the Council employed four persons.

In 1984 the Advisory Council was succeeded by a Unit for the Development of Adult Continuing Education, forming part of the National Institute of Adult Continuing Education.

Publications included

Annual Report, for 1978-79 (1st) and later years (HMSO).
Protecting the Future for Adult Education : A Report... (ACACE, 1981).

13

Continuing Education : From Policies to Practice : A Report... (ACACE, 1982).
Adults - Their Educational Experience and Needs : the Report of a National
     Survey (ACACE, 1982).
A Strategy for the Basic Education of Adults : Report... (ACACE, 1979).
Basic Science Education for Adults : A Report... (ACACE, [1981]).
H.A. Jones and Katherine E. Williams, Adult Students and Higher Education
     (ACACE, 1979).
Malcolm Tight, Part-time Degree Level Study in the United Kingdom (ACACE,
     1982).
Geoffrey Adkins, The Arts and Adult Education:Report of an Enquiry (jointly
     commissioned by ACACE, the Arts Council, the British Film Institute, and
     the Crafts Council) (ACACE, 1981).
Bridgid Sewell, Use of Mathematics by Adults in Daily Life (ACACE, [1981]).

Records
The records of ACACE are public records.

ADVISORY COUNCIL FOR APPLIED RESEARCH AND DEVELOPMENT
later the ADVISORY COUNCIL ON SCIENCE AND TECHNOLOGY

Address and
contact
Advisory Council on Science and Technology,
70, Whitehall,
London,
SW1A 2AS.

tel: 071-270 0105
fax: 071 270 0302
The Secretary.

History
The Advisory Council for Applied Research and Development (ACARD) was
established on 1 Dec. 1976, following an announcement by the Lord Privy Seal
in a memorandum (No. 25) submitted to the Science Sub-Committee of the House
of Commons Select Committee on Science and Technology in May 1976. Its
original terms of reference were revised and extended in 1982 and were:

'To advise the Government and publish reports as necessary on -

i.   applied research, design and development in the United Kingdom;

ii.   the application of research and technology, developed in the United
     Kingdom and elsewhere, for the benefit of both the public and private
     sectors in accordance with national economic needs;

iii.   the co-ordination, in collaboration with the Advisory Board for
     Research Councils, of these activities, with research supported through
     the Department of Education and Science.

iv.   the role of the United Kingdom in international collaboration in the
     fields of applied research, design and development related to
     technology'.

ACARD advised the Government on the exploitation of research and technology.

The members of the Council were appointed by the Prime Minister, usually for a period of three years. In addition, the Chief Scientific Adviser, Cabinet Office acted as an assessor to the Council and attended its meetings, as did the Chief Scientists of the Departments of Energy, Trade and Industry, the Environment, and the Ministry of Defence. The Council's Secretariat was provided by the Cabinet Office, Science and Technology Secretariat.

The full Council normally met six times a year, but much of its work was carried out in small Working Groups whose membership was drawn partly from the Council and partly from non-members. The subjects for Working Group investigations were generally chosen by the Council itself, although the reports on Exploiting Invention (1981) and Improving Research Links between Higher Education and Industry (1983) were requested by the Prime Minister. ACARD reports were submitted to the Government through the Prime Minister with a request for permission to publish; this permission was never refused.

In its observations (Cmnd.8591, July 1982) on the report Science and Government from the House of Lords Select Committee on Science and Technology, the Government made a number of proposals for the closer working of ACARD and the Advisory Board for the Research Councils (ABRC), including the presentation by the Chairmen of ACARD and ABRC of joint periodic reports commenting on the state of science and technology in the United Kingdom and selectively reviewing scientific opportunities and their implications. The first such joint report was published in July 1983 (Cmnd.8957).

The independent advice which ACARD submitted on the annual review of all Government funded research and development (which was also instituted in 1982) remains confidential and was not published, though the joint report of the chairmen of ACARD and ABRC includes comments on the annual review.

In its report on Exploitable Areas of Science, published in May 1986, an ACARD Working Group stated that Britain's R. and D. effort was in need of a better sense of direction and that it was necessary to set up a process to determine priorities and provide guidance to R. and D. planners in government and industry. It suggested that industry itself should set up the mechanisms for undertaking long-term research forecasting and that a small management group should steer the process of identifying exploitable scientific areas; the management group would be independent of the bodies directly concerned with the management of science budgets.

In the Conservative Party's 1987 General Election Manifesto it was proposed to extend the role of ACARD, with a view to transforming the way public money was spent on research and development, ensuring that Government spending was directed towards areas of high national priority. ACARD was reconstituted in July 1987 as the Advisory Council on Science and Technology (ACOST). ACOST's terms of reference are : 'To advise the Government on:

i   the priorities for science and technology in Great Britain;

ii   the application of science and technology, developed in the United Kingdom and elsewhere, for the benefit of both the public and private sectors in accordance with national needs;

iii   the co-ordination, in collaboration with Departmental Advisory Bodies, of science and technology activities;

iv   the nature and extent of United Kingdom participation in international collaboration in science and technology.

To publish reports as appropriate.'

ACOST is chaired by Sir Francis Tombs (Chairman, Rolls-Royce plc) and as at February 1988 fourteen of its nineteen members were previously members of ACARD. One of the first reports to be produced by ACOST was on The industrial impact of Sizewell 'B' (HMSO, 1988). An article about ACOST appeared in the THES, 21 October 1988, p.7.

ACOST is assisted by a new body, established in 1988 and based at Manchester Science Park (Enterprise House, Lloyd Street North, Manchester, M15 4EN), the Centre for Exploitable Areas of Science and Technology, later known as the Centre for the Exploitation of Science and Technology (CEST), with a chief executive and staff partly seconded from industry; it has close links with the Science and Technology Assessments Office in the Cabinet Office. ACOST reports to a Cabinet committee on research and development which is chaired by the Prime Minister.

Bibliography
Reports on the work of the Council have appeared in New Scientist. In a supplement to the 12 November 1988 issue, there is an article 'Answering to the Market' about CEST's background and work written by the Chief Executive of CEST.

Publications
ACARD's published reports date from 1978 onwards and, with the exception of the report on Exploiting Invention (1981; available from ACARD), are available from H.M.S.O. They are listed in Cmnd.8957 (July 1983; see below) and in the periodically revised Government Publications Sectional List No.32, H.M.Treasury and Allied Departments. They include reports on:

The Applications of Semiconductor Technology (1978) Industrial Innovation (1979)
Joining and Assembly: The Impact of Robots and Automation (1979)
Technological Change: Threats and Opportunities for the UK (1980)
Computer Aided Design and Manufacturer (1980)
R and D for Public Purchasing (1980)
Biotechnology (1980)
(with the Royal Society and the ABRC)
Information Technology (1980)
Facing International Competition: The Impact on Product Design of Standards, Regulation, Certification and Approvals (1982)
The Food Industry and Technology (1982)
Exploiting Invention (1981)
Improving Research Links between Higher Education and Industry (1983) (with the ABRC)
New Opportunities in Manufacturing: The Management of Technology (1983)
Exploitable Areas of Science (1986)

The Chairmen of ABRC and ACARD were requested to present periodic joint reports (though not necessarily as frequent as once a year) (see Cmnd. 8591.10). The first such report was published in 1983:-

First Joint Report by the Chairmen of the Advisory Council for Applied Research and Development (ACARD) and the Advisory Board for the Research Councils (ABRC), 1983 (Cmnd.8957).

Articles on ACARD and its work appeared from time to time in the scientific and engineering press, for instance in New Scientist and Nature.

Records
The records of ACARD are classed as public records and are subject to the provisions of the Public Records Acts. It should be noted that the results of ACARD studies were usually published through HMSO.

AERONAUTICAL RESEARCH COUNCIL

History
The Aeronautical Research Council (ARC) was established by the Government as the Advisory Committee for Aeronautics in 1909, at first reporting to the Prime Minister and subsequently to the Minister who had prime responsibility for aeronautical research. It was established to advise on problems of flight by aeroplanes and dirigibles and was composed of scientists and representatives of the Admiralty and the War Office; its president was Lord Rayleigh and its chairman Dr. R. T. Glazebrook. In 1920 it became the Aeronautical Research Committee, and in 1945 it received the title of Aeronautical Research Council.

The Council reported jointly to the Minister for Defence Procurement at the Ministry of Defence and the Minister for Aerospace at the Department of Industry.

ARC consisted of a chairman and eleven other independent members, mainly drawn from the universities and the aircraft industry, and appointed by the Ministers; and also nine official members, nominated by the Ministry of Defence, the Department of Industry, and the Civil Aviation Authority. The Council had a number of committees and working parties to assist it.

The objects of ARC were to advise the Ministers on scientific problems relating to aeronautics and astronautics; to keep under review the progress of aeronautical research and to advise the Minister on its programme and planning; to make recommendations from time to time on research which it considered desirable to initiate or terminate; subject to the needs of security, to publish the results of British research in its field; to advise on aeronautical education in the United Kingdom insofar as it was relevant to research; and to maintain contact with similar bodies or universities in the Commonwealth and foreign countries.

Unlike most of the other Research Councils, the Council was a purely advising body, reporting to the appropriate Government departments. Coming under the Ministry of Defence, the Aeronautical Research Council and its sub-committees was wound up in 1980 with estimated savings of £0.121m thereby, following a review of non-Departmental public bodies (see Report on Non-Departmental Public Bodies, Cmnd. 7797, HMSO, 1980).

The ARC was latterly based at the Ministry of Defence (Procurement Executive), The National Physical Laboratory, Teddington, Middlesex.

<u>Bibliography</u>   -

<u>Publications</u>
(a)   Reports and Memoranda series (issued through HMSO)

(b)   <u>The British Library General Catalogue of Printed Books to 1975</u>, Vol.96, 1981, pp.877-878, lists a number of publications of the Council, copies of which the Library holds. They include:-

Reports of the Aeronautical Research Committee for years 1921-22 (-1926-27), continued as Report for the year 1927-28 (-1938), continued as Review for the years 1939-1948 (—1949-54).

Report (Technical Report) of the Advisory Committee for Aeronautics (Aeronautical Research Committee - Aeronautical Research Council) for the year 1909-10 [etc.], 1919-

Combined Index to the Technical Reports of the Advisory Committee for Aeronautics, 1909-10 to 1918-19 (Reports and Memoranda No.1600; 1935).

Combined Index to the Technical Reports of the Aeronautical Research Committee, 1919-20 to 1928-29 (Reports and Memoranda No.1700; 1939).

Reports and Memoranda, no.48, etc., 1912-
(previous reports were issued as Parliamentary Papers)

Author Index to the Reports and Memoranda of the Aeronautical Research Council, 1909-1949 (Reports and Memoranda No. 2570; 1950)

Special Volumes of Technical Reports, 1955-

Current Papers, 1950-

List of Current Papers published by the Aeronautical Research Council, 1951-

[Reports], 1967-

<u>Records</u>
(a) Inasmuch as the Aeronautical Research Council was a purely advisory body, reporting to the appropriate Government departments, it records were either covered by Government security arrangements or by the marking "Personal to Members" or both.

(b)   Amongst the records of the Department of Scientific and Industrial Research in the Kew branch of the Public Record Office are the following records of the ARC:-

DSIR 22   Minutes of meetings of the ARC, its sub-committees, and panels, 1909-40:
        /1   Advisory Committee for Aeronautics, 1909-20 (Papers of the Committee in DSIR 23).
        /2-8,99   Aeronautical Research Committee, 1920-39, 1940.
        /9   ARC Panel on Airworthiness of Airships, 1924.

/10	ARC Panel on Servo-Control, 1932-35.
/11	ARC Panel on Wind Tunnel, 1935-37.
/12	ARC Panel on Free Flight, 1938.
/13	ARC Panel on Navigation, 1938-39.
/14-37	Sub-committees (wound up), 1916-35.
/38-57	Aerodynamics Sub-Committee and Panels, 1917-40.
/58-71	Engine Sub-Committee and Panels, 1920-39.
/72-77	Accidents Investigation Sub-Committee, 1920-35
/78-83	Materials and Chemistry Sub-Committee and Panel, 1920-25.
/84-85	Elasticity and Fatigue Sub-Committee, 1925-38.
/86	Seaplane Sub-Committee, 1925-38.
/87-88	Alloys Sub-Committee, 1927-39.
/89-91	Stability and Control Sub-Committee and Panel, 1928-39.
/92	Aircraft Noise Sub-Committee, 1929-37.
/93-95	Structure Sub-Committee and Panel, 1930-39.
/96	Meteorology Sub-Committee, 1935-38.
/97	Oscillation Sub-Committee, 1936-39.
/98	Fleet Air Arm Research Sub-Committee, 1939-40.

DSIR 23/1-15687   Reports and papers of the ARC, 1909-46, covering the work of the Council's Sub-committees, etc.
The papers are arranged chronologically and deal with every aspect of the work of ARC. Some of them have been published in the Reports and Memoranda ('R and M') series by HMSO.

DSIR 24/1-83   Correspondence of the ARC, 1909-45; includes
/5-12 Files dealing with designs of aircraft, airships, aeroplane carrier ships, and kite balloons, and problems of fog disposal, atmospheric discharge, and measurement of upward currents in the atmosphere; 1920-36

(c) It is understood that copies of the Council's reports were transferred to the Royal Aircraft Establishment, Farnborough, Hampshire.

AGRICULTURAL AND FOOD RESEARCH COUNCIL

Address and contact
Agricultural and Food Research Council,
Central Office,
Wiltshire Court,
Farnsby Street,
Swindon,
SN1 5AT

tel: 0793 514242
fax: 0793 514788

History
The Agricultural Research Council (ARC), as the AFRC was entitled until 1983, was established on 23 July 1931 by Royal Charter; further charters were granted in 1933, 1950 and 1967. It conducts its work under the Secretary of State for Education and Science and the Minister of Agriculture, Fisheries and

Food (MAFF). ARC was given statutory authority by the Agricultural Research Act 1956, and is a Research Council for the purposes of the Science and Technology Act 1965. In October 1983 the ARC formally adopted the title 'Agricultural and Food Research Council' in recognition of the increasing importance of food research and the expanding contribution the Council expects to make to it.

The Charter provides that the Council shall consist of a chairman and not less than 18 nor more than 21 other members; the chairman and not less than 12 nor more than 15 of the members are appointed by the Secretary of State for Education and Science; up to four members may be appointed by the Minister of Agriculture, Fisheries and Food, and up to two by the Secretary of State for Scotland.

The main objectives of the AFRC are: (i) to maintain a viable capability in basic and strategic research and to develop major new scientific initiatives; (ii) to undertake applied research to help maintain and improve the competitive position, efficiency and productivity of the UK agricultural, horticultural and food industries, and the quality of the nation's food; (iii) to provide an objective research base which can assist the framing of policy on issues such as the impact of agriculture on the environment, land use, farm safety, welfare of farm animals, and the food needs of the third world. Food research was added to the Council's remit in the late 1960s. In 1987, in response to financial stringency, each of the Research Councils identified certain areas in which they are to concentrate most of their support. In the case of the AFRC these are: cell signalling and recognition; plant gene tool-kit; plant mineral nutrient uptake and utilisation; novel vaccines and vaccination; transgenic animals; manipulation of growth regulation; controlling the functional properties of proteins and carbohydrates in foods; and human nutritive requirements.

The AFRC supervises research carried out at a number of sites throughout the UK. In October 1985 the Council published a statement of Forward Policy which stated its intention by April 1987 to aggregate the existing research stations into a smaller number of institutes, and to give each new institute a defined remit to avoid unproductive overlap, give a more efficient management structure and a more efficient use of resources. The eight new institutes established are:-

> Institute of Animal Disease Research (now the Institute for Animal Health)
> Institute of Animal Physiology and Genetics Research
> Institute for Grassland Research and Animal Production
> Institute of Arable Crops Research
> Institute of Horticultural Research
> Institute of Plant Science Research
> Institute of Food Research
> Institute of Engineering Research

Each of these institutes is the responsibility of a Director of Research. The Directors of Research, together with senior HQ staff, form a Management Board with the Secretary to the Council in the Chair.

In addition to those institutes supervised by the Council, there are seven institutes in Scotland grant-aided by the Department of Agriculture and Fisheries for Scotland (DAFS) (the Scottish Agricultural Research Institutes). The Council advises on research at the SARIs. The AFRC's institutes together with the SARIs make up the Agricultural and Food Research Service, the largest organisation funding agricultural and food research in the UK. In March 1986 the Council published its corporate plan for the next five years.

In 1987-88 the AFRC had an expenditure of around £106m and the Agricultural and Food Research Service (including institutes grant-aided by DAFS) employed about 4500 staff. It receives almost half of its total income as payment for work commissioned by government departments, under the customer-contractor arrangements adopted by the Government in 1972 (Framework for Government Research and Development, Cmnd.5046) following the Rothschild Report on Government Research and Development in 1971. The AFRC's funding in fact derives principally from two sources - grant-in-aid from the Science Budget and 'commission funds' from the MAFF. Very broadly the 'commission funds' support applied work at the AFRC's establishments and the grant-in-aid from the Science Budget supports fundamental or strategic research at the AFRC's establishments and the direct funding by the AFRC of university research. In May 1987 the Government announced that it was to sell the state's plant breeding and seed marketing organisations, including the National Seed Development Organisation (established in 1967; most of its income derives from plants bred at the PBI) and the Plant Breeding Institute (PBI; grant-aided by the AFRC), both based at Cambridge. This privatisation was effected later in 1987.

Expenditure by the AFRC on research grants to universities has been increased from 10.5% of its share of the science budget in 1983/84 to 14.3% in 1985/86. This is hoped to rise to 15.9% in 1988/89. The recently introduced university link group scheme (involving 12 universities) is proving highly successful in implementing the Council's policy of drawing complimentary work at institutes and universities more closely together.

In 1988 proposals were made for forming a new Natural Resources Research Council, based essentially on amalgamation of the AFRC and NERC, proposals which were initially put to the House of Lords' Select Committee on Science and Technology.

At the end of September 1988 the AFRC moved its offices from London to Swindon.

Bibliography
S. E. Macreavy (ed.), Guide to Science and Technology in the UK: A reference guide to science and technology in Great Britain and Northern Ireland, Francis Hodgson, Guernsey, 1971.

Articles about the Council's work appear in the scientific press including New Scientist.

Publications
Report of the Agricultural Research Council (i.e. Annual Report), 1934-, though the present series (see below) dates from May 1958 when the First Report presented to Parliament (Cmnd.432) was published.

Annual Report presented to Parliament pursuant to the Science and Technology Act, 1965. The Report for 1980-81 appears to have been the last to bear a HC number. The Reports for 1981-82 onwards bear an ISBN number and those for 1984-85 onwards bear an ISSN number also. The references for the most recent Annual Reports are:-
1977-78   HC Session   1978-79 HC7

```
1978-79    HC Session   1979-80 HC259
1979-80    HC Session   1980-81 HC3
1980-81    HC Session   1981-82 HC8
1981-82    ISBN    0 7084 254 2
1982-83    ISBN    0 7084 0273 9
1983-84    ISBN    0 7084 0308 5
1984-85    ISSN    0268-2524
1985-86    ISSN    0268-2524
1986-87    ISSN    0268-2524
1987-88    ISBN    0 7084 0480 4
1988-89    ISBN    0 7084 0492 8
```
The 1989-90 report is due to be published in November 1990.

Index of Agricultural and Food Research, 1969-

AFRC News (formerly ARC News), 1969 -

ARC Research Review, 1975-79 (discontinued).

For publications of AFRC sold but not published by HMSO see HMSO's Government Publications Sectional List No. 50: Miscellaneous List.

Records

The minutes and papers of the Council and of its various Boards and Committees (in which members of the senior academic staff of universities may participate) are preserved by the AFRC. However the Council regards the principal records of its support of research in universities as being the resulting published research papers in learned journals. Other correspondence is not necessarily preserved by the Council beyond the period during which reference to it may be required for administrative purposes. The records of the AFRC are not classified as public records.

See too the entry on the Advisory Board for the Research Councils.

ASSOCIATION OF GRADUATE CAREERS ADVISORY SERVICES

Address and contact

Association of Graduate Careers Advisory Services,
Cardiff Joint University Careers and Appointments Service,
53 Park Place,
Cardiff,
CF1 3AT

tel: 0222 874231
Mr. E.B. Marsh, Secretary

History

The Association of Graduate Careers Advisory Services (AGCAS) was established in 1967 as the Standing Conference of University Careers Services and took its present name in 1977.

AGCAS is the body through which those involved in careers advisory work with degree students (in universities, polytechnics and other institutions of higher education) in the United Kingdom and the Republic of Ireland exchange information and organise joint activity.

The Association was in fact established to:-
(i)   encourage and facilitate the exchange of views and information amongst careers advisers in higher education;

(ii)   foster and co-ordinate investigation and experiment and promote improvements in constituent services;

(iii)   encourage training in the skills and techniques appropriate to the work of its members and associates;

(iv)   express a collective viewpoint on methods relating to graduate employment.

Membership of AGCAS is both institutional and personal; it has about 450 individual members working in over 100 different Careers Services. Constituent membership is open to all institution-based careers services in universities in the U.K. and the Republic of Ireland as well as the polytechnics, colleges and Institutes of Higher Education, and the Scottish Central Institutions. Full personal membership is open to careers advisers and information officers in constituent services, whilst other senior staff are eligible for associate membership. Correspondent membership is open to anyone concerned with careers work in higher education (including overseas) but who is not employed in a constituent service.

The governing body of AGCAS is a conference of all members which normally meets biennially. It elects officers and a Standing Committee to manage the Association's business. A Plenary Committee of the heads of all constituent services is reponsible for reviewing and authorising collaborative efforts involving important matters of principle or the expenditure of time and money. AGCAS operates on a small budget: member services pay an annual subscription and support the co-operative efforts of the Association with such other resouces as circumstances permit. AGCAS has also attracted funds from other bodies to support particular projects and developments. All the work of AGCAS is done by its members who draw on the resources of their own careers services: much of its collaborative effort is organised around a system of sub-committees and working parties which are formed into five groups each of which is managed by a Group Co-ordinator who is a member of the Standing Committee. The Group Co-ordinators are responsible to the Standing Committee. AGCAS's Constitution was last revised in September 1985.

Though there is no formal link with the central AGCAS organisation, regional activities are organised by member services. Regional collaboration covers both training (non-residential one-day courses, supplementing the Training Sub-Committee's national courses) and such activities as joint visits to employers of graduates and professional organisations based in the region.

The collection of graduate employment statistics is the oldest - established AGCAS activity. A comprehensive annual series of publications, which shows what happens to university and polytechnic and college graduates immediately after graduation, this work is carried out in close co-operation with USR, the DES and the Central Services Unit (CSU: see entry for). The CSU has a very special relationship with AGCAS, providing a wide range of services, including vacancy notification, compilation of statistics, and the dissemination of information.   Since March 1980 all institutions newly admitted to membership of AGCAS also become subscribers to CSU.   CSU publishes a national series of careers information booklets, the booklets being written by AGCAS members: these booklets (70 in number) cover a wide range of graduate career fields and are made available to students, free of charge, through a member services and may be purchased by non-members from the CSU.

AGCAS is actively involved in monitoring and initiating technological developments which will aid the career guidance process. Of particular significance currently is the development of the Computer-Aided Career Guidance System (CACGS); research into computerised vacancy handling systems; and the use of video equipment in careers education.

AGCAS co-operates with and has good working relations with a large number of governmental, professional and other bodies apart from CSU and the Association of Graduate Recruiters. Officers of the Association keep in touch with senior staff of the DES, Department of Trade and Industry, Department of Employment, CVCP, Committee of Directors of Polytechnics, USR, Industrial Training Boards, and professional bodies.   Useful links have also been established with careers advisory agencies overseas.

Bibliography
No book or journal article containing an account of the work of AGCAS is known about.

Publications
AGCAS Handbook
(an invaluable source of information about systems operating in other services, including organising a "milk round", careers library organisation and equipment, latest developments in new technology, hints on writing information booklets, administering questionnaires and tests, etc.)

ROGET (Register of Graduate Employment and Training)
(AGCAS' own directory of opportunities for graduates)

AGCAS Phoenix
a quarterly journal; though written primarily as an internal publication, it is available on a subscription basis to non-members.

Newsletter
monthly; for the information of members of AGCAS.

The CSU, in close co-operation with AGCAS, publishes a series of 70 Careers Information Booklets and leaflets on individual professions and sectors (e.g. Legal Profession, Opportunities for Chemists, Careers with Music for Graduates, and Library, Information and Archive Work). Copies of these booklets may be available, free of charge, from individual careers service offices, as well as being available for sale from the CSU.

AGCAS does not produce an annual report for outside publication. It produces a general publicity leaflet about the Association and also 'Notes for new members of AGCAS'.

Records

The Secretary of AGCAS retains copies of all records believed to be of permanent value, including minutes, reports, and correspondence. An overall index is maintained for all records from 1980 onwards.

THE ASSOCIATION OF GRADUATE RECRUITERS

Address and contact

Mr. Stuart Rochester,
Secretary: Association of Graduate Recruiters,
Nevill Russell,
Chartered Accountants,
246 Bishopsgate,
London,
EC2M 4PB

tel: 071 377 1000

History

The Standing Conference of Employers of Graduates Ltd. (SCOEG) was established in February 1972 as a non-profit making company limited by guarantee. Its object was to assist in the recruitment of graduates; to act as a centre for the discussion of policy; to co-operate with university and other appointments boards and careers advisory services; and to obtain and exchange information as regards the recruitment of graduates. By 1980 SCOEG had a membership of 330 companies and corporate bodies who employed graduates.

In 1987 the name of the Standing Conference was changed to The Association of Graduate Recruiters (AGR), the status of a company limited by guarantee not being altered. The objects of AGR, which are set out in its Memorandum of Association, may be summarised as:- to facilitate the recruitment of graduates into all spheres of employment; to provide a forum for the discussion of issues relevant to graduate recruitment; to promote good relations with Graduate Careers Advisory Services and their Association (AGCAS); to promote good graduate recruitment practices; to work with institutions of higher education on matters concerning the supply of and demand for graduates entering employment; and to represent the views of employers of graduates to other organisations directly concerned in graduate recruitment, to government, to the media, and to the general public.

AGR consists of organisations which recruit and employ graduates (Full Members) or which offer services in connection with graduate recruitment (Associates). Full membership is corporate, individuals participating in AGR activities as representatives of their employing organisation and usually being managers responsible for graduate recruitment (and perhaps training and development as well). Publishers, consultants, and professional institutions are amongst those who are Associate Members. Current membership (1987) is over 400 and growing.

AGR's activities are managed by an Executive Committee which is elected by members. Committee and other members represent AGR in a wide variety of other bodies. It has extensive links with AGCAS (and its Central Services Unit) and links with the Institute of Manpower Studies, the DES, the Manpower Services Commission, the CBI, and other organisations and institutions. Through these links and through the representations it makes about the future direction of higher education and the supply of graduates the Association can exert significant influence on the graduate recruitment environment, including the way in which recruitment is conducted within universities, polytechnics, and colleges.

The Association provides a regular supply of news and information on topics relevant to graduate recruitment; conducts surveys among members; organises a three-day annual conference; arranges seminars throughout the year and at the Annual Conference; and does many other things to assist its members. AGR undertakes regular surveys of graduate starting salaries; other surveys include such subjects as forecast vacancies, attitudes to the 'milkround', and qualities sought in graduate recruits. Early each year AGR, AGCAS and the Central Services Unit for University and Polytechnic Careers and Appointments Services (CSU) publish a joint forecast of the output of graduates from universities, polytechnics, and colleges for the coming summer and an assessment of the employment opportunities available to them. This forecast is followed by a progress report on actual recruitment and shortfalls in July.

Publications
The Association of Graduate Recruiters (leaflet on objectives, activities, etc.), [1987] (the 'History' above is in part based on this leaflet).

Janus: The Newsletter of the Association of Graduate Recruiters, Nos.1-, May 1987 - to date.
(includes reports on AGR conferences and activities and on its future programme; articles on aspects of recruitment; notice board (AGCAS, etc.); recent publications, etc.).

Records
The Secretary retains the principal records of SCOEG and AGR, including the minutes, annual reports and accounts, and bona fide researchers could probably consult such records upon application and by arrangement. It should be noted that copies of the Association's annual returns and accounts are sent to the Companies Registration Office, AGR being a limited company.

ASSOCIATION OF HEADS OF PSYCHOLOGY DEPARTMENTS

Address and
contact
Dr. P.J. Barber,
Secretary,
Association of Heads of Psychology Departments,
Department of Psychology,
Birkbeck College,
Malet Street,
London,
WC1E 7HX

tel: 071 580 6622

History
Conferences of heads of university departments of psychology were held annually at least by 1955 and occupied three days a year. The agenda for the conferences was organised by the Conference's Steering Committee and, for instance, in 1956 included discussion on the questionnaire returns on the capacity and enrolments of departments of psychology which members completed.

More recently the Conference of Heads of University Departments of Psychology broadened its membership to include heads of psychology departments in Polytechnics and changed its title to the Association of Heads of Psychology Departments. Whereas attendance at the annual meeting of the Conference in the 1950s brought together twenty or so persons nowadays the Association's annual meeting is attended by a far larger number.

In fact the Association only started properly in 1988, the first meeting being held on 19 February at the University of Manchester and the second meeting being held at Plymouth Polytechnic on 27 May. According to the Association's Constitution, its aims are '(i) by meetings and other means to exchange information and to propose and initiate actions on issues of common interest, particularly those affecting teaching, training, research and administration in academic Departments of Psychology' and '(ii) to enhance the standing of the discipline of Psychology.'

Membership of the Association is open to the heads of academic Psychology Departments or their equivalents (subject to the approval of the Association on the recommendation of its Committee) in universities, polytechnics, and institutes and colleges of higher education within the United Kingdom and Eire, and the heads of such other departments as the Association on the recommendation of the Committee may consider appropriate. A minimum of two General Meetings of the Association are held each year, one of which may be the AGM. The Association's Committee is responsible for the administration of the Association and the officers comprise the Chair, Vice-Chair, Secretary, and Treasurer.

Bibliography
No history of the Association has so far been published.

Publications

Compendium of UK Postgraduate Studies in Psychology
(produced by the Department of Psychology, University of Surrey, on the initiative of the Heads of Psychology Departments Committee (sic), 1977 onwards (annual); 9th ed., Jan. 1985.

The Association is now producing various reports, one of the most recent being A Guide to the provisions made for handicapped students by Psychology Departments in the UK, [1988].

Records
The minutes of the meetings of the Association (held initially on 19 February and 27 May 1988) would be available to bona fide researchers to consult if they wished.

ASSOCIATION OF INSTITUTE AND SCHOOL OF EDUCATION IN-SERVICE TUTORS

Address and
contact
Dr. Mark T. Lofthouse,
Secretary and Treasurer,
Association of Institute and School
of Education In-Service Tutors,
School of Education,
The University Centre,
Barrack Road,
Northampton,
NN2 6AF

tel: 0604 30180

History
The Association of Institute and School of Education In-Service Tutors (AISEIT) was established in 1970. It was originally founded to highlight the role and purpose of In-Service Courses of a Non-Award Bearing nature offered by Schools of Education and Institutes of Education within the university sector. Recently it has expanded its interests to cover the whole range of INSET activities, Award Bearing and Non-Award Bearing, and is increasingly linking with other associations working in the public sector.

Membership of the Association is open to all members of staff in the university sector who have responsibilities for the provision of INSET. Two Conferences are held every year and additionally Occasional Papers are offered. Notification of Conferences is made to all members and the Annual General Meeting is held in London in December of each academic year.

Bibliography
There is no history of the Association's activities other than that provided by the Minutes of the Annual General Meeting.

Publications
Occasional Papers may be obtained from the Secretary of the Association.

Records
Minutes and correspondence together with formal Reports are held by the Secretary and Treasurer.

All further advice regarding the Association's activities should be addressed to the Secretary and Treasurer of the Association.

ASSOCIATION OF INTER-VARSITY CLUBS

Address and
contact
Mr. Martin Rooke-Matthews,
Secretary of the Association of Inter-Varsity Clubs,
26, Chesswood Road,
Worthing,
West Sussex,
BN11 2AD

tel: 0903 30175

History

The Association of Inter-Varsity Clubs (AIVC) is the national organisation to which all inter-varsity clubs and IVCs belong. The idea of inter-varsity clubs was conceived in 1946 by two undergraduates of St.John's College, Cambridge, Mr. R.N. (Reggie) Simeone and Mr. Michael Wolff who initially organised fortnightly dances in London in the Summer of 1946 under the advertised title Intervarsity Vacation Club (IVC). A committee was later assembled, with Mr. Wolff as Secretary, and a constitution was drafted, and the first bulletin was produced in July 1947. The programme of dances in London which the committee was responsible for was highly successful and in 1947 sub-clubs were born : a theatre party and a riding sub-club being amongst the first. Within several years the name of the organisation was changed to Inter-Varsity Club (still IVC) to reflect that the members were no longer students wanting vacation entertainment but graduates living in London all the year round. By the 1960s this Club had branched out into the nationwide institution it is today.

The Association provides:

1. a means of communication between Clubs through the AIVC Bulletin which is published every month.

2. a co-ordination service for special AIVC weekends and holidays organised throughout the year by many clubs, and to which members of all other clubs are invited.

3. the transfer of members between clubs.

4. help and advice on advertising, recruitment and any other subjects requested by clubs.

5. financial support to new or small clubs for publicity campaigns that they might not otherwise be able to afford.

6. insurance for clubs and their members against third party and member to member claims.

7. selective national publicity on behalf of all clubs.

8. supply of publicity and membership material to help promote a national, rather than a purely local, identity.

9. a system of mail distribution to cut down the costs of maintaining contact with the other clubs in the Association.

The affairs of the Association are overseen by a 'committee' of eight officers, who each have a specific role and as such is responsible to the Conference for his/her conduct of the task in the previous year. The Secretary carries on the official administration of the Association during the course of the year, keeps a record of each member club's constitution and ensures that they continue to comply with the objects of the Association; amongst the other duties of the Secretary is the arrangement of meetings of the officers when necessary and the compilation of minutes of these meetings.

Representatives from every club are invited to attend the Association Conference which is held annually to discuss the implementation of the Association's objectives (see details 1.-9. above) and other subjects of common interest. The Conference is the Annual General Meeting of all the Inter-Varsity clubs; in addition to the two business sessions, discussion groups on topical subjects or those of general interest to the member clubs are held.

The total number of members of clubs which form the Association rose from 3,441 in 1967 to 10,051 in 1980, falling to 7,816 in 1985. In 1986 the total was 7,584. In the AIVC Bulletin, May 1988, in which these figures are given, the totals for the clubs - forty-six in all, as at 1987 - which form the Association are given for 1967, 1970, 1975, 1980, and for each of the years 1985-87. Over the period 1967-86 the percentage of members drawn from London has fallen from 52.8 per cent to 26.4 per cent. The same statistics record 15 clubs in 1967, rising to 38 in 1975 and to 46 in 1986. The clubs are in England, Scotland, Wales, and Northern Ireland. The Association has an annual budget of c.£2,000 to publish the Bulletin, provide for publicity and administration, etc.

Each individual club publishes its own regular bulletin or programme of events and each varies slightly in its quality and in the nature of members. Most members are former students. Run entirely by the members, they organise programmes of social events (parties, pub evenings, meals out, coffee evenings), sporting events (ski-ing, walking, swimming) and cultural events (visiting theatres or attending concerts) all on a quite informal basis.

Bibliography
R. Simeone, 'How IVC Began', in AIVC Bulletin, November 1979, reprinted in AIVC Handbook, 1987, pp. 2.1-2.3.

Publications
AIVC Handbook : latest edition, January 1987.

AIVC Bulletin, a monthly bulletin, containing details of AIVC weekends, digests of member clubs' bulletins, changes of address of club secretaries, etc.

Records
Although there are records of the Association going back many years, these consist to a great extent of documents stored in cardboard boxes and passed on from Secretary to Secretary of the Association.

ASSOCIATION OF PRINCIPALS AND WARDENS
OF UNIVERSITY HALLS

Address and
contact
Mr. A.J. Parsons,
Hon.Secretary : Association of Principals and Wardens of University Halls,
Warden,
University of Wales College of Medicine,
Neuadd Meirionnydd,
Heath Park
Cardiff,
CF4 4YS

tel: 0222 755944 ext.2141

History

The Association of Principals and Wardens of University Halls (APW) was formed in 1978 at the annual conference at Dundee when the Association of Principals, Wardens and Advisers of University Women Students (APWA) joined the equivalent association of Principals and Wardens of Men's Colleges and Halls of Residence (which had been in existence since at least 1954). The Association's objects are to provide a forum for the discussion of the work and responsibilities of Principals and Wardens, including student welfare, academic progress and community life, and the management of Halls.

The Association of Principals, Wardens and Advisers of University Women Students (APWA) was established in July 1942, Miss Reynard (d.1947) of London becoming first Chairman and Miss P.E. Crump of the University of Manchester first Secretary. By July 1948 the Association had seventy-one members, comprising eleven principals, forty-nine wardens, and eleven advisers. A list of members 1947-48 reveals fifteen members in London (including Mrs. John Stocks, the future Baroness Stocks, Principal of Westfield College) and lesser numbers elsewhere (Belfast 1, Birmingham 2, Bristol 1, Cambridge 1, Dublin 1, Durham 3, Edinburgh 4, Exeter 2, Glasgow 3, Hull 1, Leeds 3, Leicester 1, Liverpool 2, Manchester 5, Nottingham 2, Oxford 5, Reading 4, Sheffield 1, Southampton 2, and Wales 5). An annual conference was being organised by at least 1947 when the subjects discussed included the feeding of university students (representations being made to the CVCP etc. regarding rations for students) and the university graduate and the nursing profession. Questionnaires were sent out to members on particular subjects (salaries and duties, vacation lets, maintenance fees, etc.), the resultant information being tabulated and distributed to members. Regional group meetings were also held from an early date. The Association regularly produced reports on matters of interest to members.

The revised Constitution of the APWA, July 1966, states that the Association's aims were to "provide a forum for the discussion of the special problems of women students and of matters affecting their well-being including, as a corollary, the work of its members in their own appointments." There were two categories of members, Full Members and Associate Members. Those eligible for Full Membership were normally women who were principals, wardens, or advisers in universities or university colleges in Great Britain and Ireland. Those eligible for Associate Membership were normally men who were principals and wardens of mixed university colleges/halls of residence in Great Britain and Ireland, and women who had retired or resigned as Full Members. Provision was also made for an Executive Committee and an annual meeting. This 1966

Constitution only modified the Association's original Constitution in small matters.

The equivalent Men's Association would seem not to have been in existence by the mid 1940s. It is believed that it had no constitution; that it was entirely made up of Wardens; that it met at the invitation of one of its members; and that it kept no records as an association.

Principals and Wardens who have administrative and pastoral responsibilities for university colleges and halls in Great Britain and Ireland are eligible for membership of APW, as are persons whose appointments are adjudged to be sufficiently comparable in scope and responsibility to the former category. A full member who retires or resigns is eligible for Associate Membership. The Association has an Annual Conference and training session during the first or second week of July. During the Annual Conference a General Meeting of the Association is held at which, inter alia, the officers and members of the Executive Committee are elected, as is noted in the Constitution adopted in 1978.

(This history is based on information and copies of records kindly made available to me by both Mr. Parsons, the Hon.Secretary of the APW, by Miss Moya Cahill, Warden of St.George's Hall, University of Reading, a former Secretary and Chairman of the APWA, and by the APW's Hon.Editor, Mr. T. Davies.)

Publications
Both the APWA and the APW have regularly produced reports on matters of interest to members.

The Association's journal, <u>Journal of the Association of Principals and Wardens of University Halls of Residence</u>, is published twice a year (in November and April); the first issue was published in November 1984.

Records
Records of the Association of Principals, Wardens and Advisers of University Women Students (comprising minute books, which incorporate accounts; notes on the annual conferences, etc.) dating from 1942 onwards, together with some records of the annual conferences of Principals and Wardens of Men's Colleges and Halls of Residence for 1954-67, are held (together with journal editorial papers) by the Hon.Editor of the <u>Journal</u> of the Association of Principals and Wardens of University Halls, Mr. T. Davies, 28, King Edward Street, Exeter, Devon, EX4 4NY.

The Hon. Secretary retains the minutes of meetings of the Executive Committee and the AGM from 1978 when the Association became one unit.

ASSOCIATION OF UNIVERSITY ACCOMMODATION OFFICERS

Address and
contact
Ms. Morag Murchie,
Honorary Secretary,
Association of University Accommodation Officers,
Accommodation Office,
University of Southampton,
Highfield,
Southampton,
S09 5NH

tel: 0703 593510

History
The Association of University Accommodation Officers (AUAO) was established in the mid 1950s, the first reported meeting being held in 1955. Its objectives are "to promote the study and discussion of problems coming within the professional activities of university accommodation officers and assistants." Full membership is open to all universities in the United Kingdom and the Republic of Ireland.

The Association is divided into six regions: Scottish/Northern Irish, Northern England, Midlands, Irish, Welsh and Southern England. The Scottish Region was the first to have regional meetings, sometimes in the middle of the academic year. The Association recognises the value of regions, particularly for training and also to involve more assistant accommodation officers. All regions meet in the autumn term, and some regions meet again in the spring term and summer term. The annual conference is held at Easter at a different university each year, and a seminar to study a particular topic in depth is normally held in July.

The first reported meeting in 1955 was in fact an unofficial small gathering of Lodgings Officers held in Exeter. Following various consultations a Lodgings Officers Conference was organised in Sheffield in 1957, invitations having been sent to English universities; 22 representatives met at this Conference and a decision was taken to meet again the following year. Conferences on this basis were held each year until 1967; Scottish Universities were represented from 1960 onwards.

In 1967 the Association of University Lodgings Wardens and Officers was formally constituted and a Constitution agreed. The host university was to provide the chairman (whereby the holder of this post would change yearly); the executive committee comprised the officers, an elected person from a university in each of the Association's 6 regions. Since 1980 a constitutional amendment has provided for a chairman as a permanent spokesman (3 year term of office, with provision for re-election), and that the Conference be organised by the host university's accommodation officer and known as conference secretary. It also provides for more involvement by assistant accommodation officers. Reflecting the increase in the variety of the work undertaken by Lodgings Officers and the general decline in the numbers of students in lodgings in individual universities, the title of the Association was changed in 1975 to its current title. Since 1979 the Association has also organised seminars, the first one being on "The use of Computers in Accommodation Work".

The Association has maintained links with and had discussions with a number of bodies, including the CVCP, DES, NUS, the Department of Environment, Institute of Housing, The United Kingdom Council for Overseas Student Affairs (UKCOSA), and the Association of Accommodation and Welfare Officers (for accommodation officers working in institutions other than universities), with whom in 1986 a joint annual conference was held.

Bibliography

J. Gray Houston, 'Association of University Accommodation Officers: A Short History' in AUAO Bulletin, November 1980, pp.37-41 (the 'History' above is based on this account).

Linda McDowell, 'University accommodation officers; welfare workers or estate agents?' in Higher Education Review, Vol. 10 No.3, Summer 1978, pp. 55-62 (based on a questionnaire survey circulated to participants at the 1975 annual conference of the AUAO).

Publications

AUAO Bulletin (published twice yearly; edited by Mr T. Flynn, AUAO's Publications Officer) University of Birmingham, Student Accommodation and Welfare Office, P.O. Box 363, Birmingham B15 2TT.
Apart from Association news, the Bulletin includes reports from individual universities' accommodation officers, articles on individual universities, information on the implication of changes in legislation affecting housing and students, and on topics of general interest.

Records

Copies of all decisions appertaining to the Association are kept with the Honorary Secretary.

It is thought that the Association would not have any objections to anybody using its data for research, provided that the Association was informed and given a copy of any research carried out.

ASSOCIATION OF UNIVERSITY PROFESSORS OF FRENCH

Address and contact

Professor M.H. Kelly,
Department of French,
University of Southampton,
Highfield,
Southampton,
S09 5NH

tel: 0703 595000

History

The Association of University Professors of French (AUPF) was really founded at an informal meeting of heads of university departments of French held at Somerville College, Oxford, on 30 and 31 March 1946. The meeting was chaired by Professor F.C.Green. There was an organising committee consisting of Professors Boase, Girdlestone, Roe, Vinaver, and Mary Williams, and sixteen other heads or their delegates were present. Though there had been previous meetings of an informal association, this meeting in 1946 established the constitution of the Association and made provision for the election of a committee and officers.

Membership of the Association is open to all holders of established or personal Chairs of French in British Universities, as well as to non-professorial heads of French departments. A conference of the Association is held each year towards the end of March at which matters of common interest (whether pedagogic or administrative) are discussed; all members receive in advance, together with the agenda for the conference, a very full record (in the form of provisional minutes) of the proceedings of the previous year's conference. There is no 'history' of the Association's activities other than the minutes of these annual meetings.

Bibliography
Christophe Campos, 'L'Enseignement du Francais dans les universités britanniques', Franco British Studies, Journal of the British Institute in Paris, No.8, Autumn 1989, pp.69-108. This paper dates the foundation of AUPF to a meeting of those responsible for departments of French studies held at Girton College, Cambridge, in 1942 at the instance of the British Institute in Paris 'in exile'.

Publications
Nothing other than the annual report of the Honorary Secretary, which is confidential to the Association.

Records
These are largely in the form of minutes and correspondence, together with formal reports from the Treasurer and the Honorary Secretary.

Apart from the Honorary Secretary's annual report, which is confidential, permission to consult the Association's records should be sought from the Honorary Secretary (who has to obtain the approval of the Association's committee before anything can be released).

ASSOCIATION OF UNIVERSITY TEACHERS

Address and
contact
Association of University Teachers,
United House,
1 Pembridge Road,
London,
W11 3JY

tel: 071 221 4370
fax: 071 727 6547
Ms. Diana Warwick, General Secretary.

History
The Association of University Teachers (AUT) was founded in June 1919, following a series of conferences, beginning in December 1917, of the

Association of University Lecturers, which itself derived from the initiative of the University of Liverpool Junior Staff Association founded in 1909. The Association was constituted as a federation of Local Associations, electing representatives to a Central Council which in turn elected an Executive Committee. Members of the Executive Committee became Conveners of the Sub-Commitees, the most important of which were the Salaries, Grading, and Superannuation Sub-Committees and the Sub-Committees on Tenure and Conditions of Service. The AUT's first President, Mr. (later Professor) R.Douglas Laurie, became Honorary General Secretary in 1920, a post he held until he died in 1953. From 1921 he was assisted by a personal secretary, Miss D.K. Davies, who until after the Second World War was the only full-time paid employee of the AUT.

In 1919-20 there were 2,277 full-time university teachers in Great Britain, excluding Oxford and Cambridge (which took no part in the AUT until the 1930s) and in June 1920 there were reported to be 1,163 members of the AUT and seventeen institutions had formed Local Associations. Between the Wars the AUT attracted into membership rather less than half of the profession. Membership was 2,470 in 1946-47 and thereafter gradually further increased, to 10,492 in 1962-63 and to 30,881 by 1978-79.

Since its foundation the AUT has extended its membership to cover academic library staff, senior administrative staff, research, computer and other related grades.

The AUT headquarters moved from Wales to London in 1955 and an Executive Secretary was appointed in 1959. In 1965 the Executive Secretary was renamed the General Secretary, with the post of Honorary General Secretary being abolished. Nowadays, in addition to its London office, the AUT has offices in Edinburgh, Birmingham, and Manchester and four regional officials (responsible for Wales and the Midlands; Scotland and Northumbria; the North West, Yorkshire/Humber, Ulster; and London).

The Scottish Association of University Teachers was formed in 1922, when the first joint Council of the four Scottish Local Associations met in Edinburgh. The Scottish AUT remained separate from the AUT until 1949 when the Scottish Association's Annual Meeting voted to affiliate to the AUT (UK) as the AUT (Scotland), a separate Section with its own constitution, officers, and Executive Committee, electing two of its members and its Secretary to sit on the Executive of the UK AUT.

The AUT is the trade union for all university academic staff and academic-related staff. Affiliation to the TUC took place in 1976. (Involvement with the TUC has also increased co-operation with other education unions.) The salary scales for academic and related staff are negotiated at national level by the AUT, the University Authorities Panel, and the Department of Education and Science. The national negotiating machinery for the teaching grades was established in 1970 and extended to cover academic-related grades in 1974. Whilst conditions of service are not determined at national level but by local negotiations between a university and the local branch of the AUT, the AUT is represented on the Joint Negotiating Committee of the University Superannuation Scheme and on the Management Committee of USS. The AUT has some 31,000 members and branches in 72 universities and university colleges.

An account of the AUT's structure, the roles of its Council and Executive, etc. appeared in several articles in AUT Bulletin in 1987, the May 1987 issue detailing the work of the seven main subcommittees of the Executive Committee.

Bibliography

Harold Perkin, Key Profession: The History of the Association of University Teachers, Routledge and Kegan Paul, London, 1969.

A.H. Halsey and Martin Trow, The British Academics, Faber and Faber, London, 1971.

T.R. Bolam, 'The Scottish Association of University Teachers', in British Universities Annual, 1964, pp. 77-82.

'Laurie Sapper, AUT general secretary 1969-1983', obituary articles, in AUT Bulletin, No.166, October 1989, p.2.

Publications

(a)   The AUT's journal, whose title has changed on several occasions:-
       The University Bulletin, 1922-28
       The University Review,   1928-62
          AUT Bulletin,Nos.1-, Oct. 1962 - (initially issued as a quarterly
                                             booklet, now published nine
                                             times a year)

(b)   AUT Woman,   1984-

(c)   Information and Services Handbook. An annual publication which provides details of AUT's services, advice, etc. (including details of USS and FSSU) and a list of firms which give price concessions or special terms to AUT members.

(d)   Conference Proceedings, Memoranda, Reports, etc.

(e)   Other publications are produced on an adhoc basis on specific topics, such as student numbers, salaries, university finance or negotiating particular improvements. Particular reference should be made to AUT's submission to the DES, The case for increased invest-ment in our universities (July 1989), a summary of which was published as a special supplement in AUT Bulletin, No.165, September 1989.

Records

(i)   The AUT has, to date, deposited the following records at the Modern Records Centre, University of Warwick Library, Coventry, CV4 7AL (tel. 0203 524219):

           MSS.27
           Printed minutes of the AUT's Council, 1919-75. 36 transfer cases of inter-war correspondence files, 1919- mid 1930s, mainly comprising correspondence between the branches and the AUT's first President Mr. (later Professor) R. Douglas Laurie, who was Honorary General Secretary 1920-53. Topics dealt with include: superannuation policy; grading and salary scales; and scope of AUT membership. There are also some subject files relating to the work of the AUT committees (e.g. the Parliamentary Committee), to AUT relations with other bodies, and the AUT professional publications. The correspondence includes isolated letters from those who were, or subsequently became, prominent academics. Most recently, a large number of subject files of AUT dating from 1920 (but mainly from 1935) to 1974 have been added to this deposit;

the principal subjects of the files are educational associations and issues, international affairs, salaries, superannuation, and university funding. Documentation on pay negotiations over a number of years has also been added to the deposit.

Some records of the Warwick University branch of the AUT are also held, ref. MSS.113:-

The Warwick branch of the AUT was founded in 1965. Some reference to the branch may be found in E.P. Thompson (ed.), Warwick University Ltd.: industry, management and the universities (Penguin Education Special, Harmondsworth, 1970).

Records include:-
AUT Central Council and committees: circulated minutes of meetings, with reports and other papers, 1965-85.
Delegates' Council papers, 1965-75 (missing Dec.1971-May 1974).
Headquarters circulars.
Warwick branch of AUT: Executive Council minutes 1977-85, and file of notices of meetings, agendas and some minutes 1968-73.
Files of reports and notes on superannuation, 1973.
Various files, including some re local issues.

For further details see:-
Richard Storey and Janet Druker, Guide to the Modern Records Centre, University of Warwick Library, University of Warwick Library Occasional Publications No.2, 1977, and the Supplement to the Guide..., compiled by Richard Storey and Susan Edwards, University of Warwick Library Occasional Publications No.9, 1981, and Richard Storey and Alistair Tough, Consolidated Guide to the Modern Records Centre, University of Warwick Library Occasional Publication No.14, 1986.

(ii)   The AUT itself retains papers for and minutes of all its meetings from 1919 onwards, also copies of published reports on salaries and gradings (periodically produced and including appendices on schemes in individual universities), etc.

It also holds the typescript history of the AUT written by Professor Douglas Laurie, 1953.

(iii)   It should be noted that, to date, the records of some branches of the AUT have been deposited with the respective University Archives or University Library, as in the case of Warwick AUT ((i) above). For instance the following records of the Liverpool branch are held by the University Archives, Liverpool, ref. A.030:-

Minutes of the Executive Committee, 1920-80
Minutes of Annual General Meetings, 1970-79
Minutes of Ordinary, Special, and
Emergency General Meetings, 1920-80
(together with a few agenda papers loose in the volumes)

The Manchester branch of the AUT has deposited records with the John Rylands University Library of Manchester (NRA Report No. 25964).

(iv)   The AUT (Scotland) has deposited records (including minute books, papers, correspondence, etc.) for the period 1922-72 with Glasgow University Library.

See too the entry for Association of University Teachers (Scotland).

ASSOCIATION OF UNIVERSITY TEACHERS (SCOTLAND)

Address and
contact
Mr. Peter Breeze,
Honorary Secretary:Association of University Teachers (Scotland),
Department of Statistics,
The University,
Glasgow,
G12 8QQ

tel: 041 330 4047

History
Local associations of university teachers were founded in 1921 in each of the four Scottish Universities then existing. Representatives of these associations met in council for the first time on 6 May 1922 in Edinburgh and the Association of University Teachers of Scotland was born. The first constitution provided, inter alia, that the Association should consist of a branch in each university, membership of which being open to all members of that university's staff, and that the objects of the Association should be (a) to advance the cause of university education, scholarship and research in Scotland and (b) to promote better acquaintance among university teachers, and to further their interests in every appropriate way.

It was not until June 1949 that the Scottish Association merged with the AUT, while retaining its separate identity as the AUT (Scotland). From the early years of the Scottish Association the AUT's attitude had been sympathetic and helpful and there was no sign of any pressure towards a closer union before the Scottish Association was ready for it. Until 1954 the number of local associations comprising the AUT (S) remained four; in 1955 the Staff Association of the Royal Technical College, Glasgow (which in 1964 became the University of Strathclyde) was given permission to form a local association of the AUT (S), in 1962 the St. Andrews AUT separated into two local associations representing the St. Andrews Colleges and Queen's College (originally University College), Dundee (which in 1967 became the independent University of Dundee), in 1964 a local association was formed at Heriot-Watt College (which in 1965 became Heriot-Watt University), and in 1967 the eighth local association in membership of the AUT (S) was inaugurated at the new University of Stirling. By far the biggest task ever undertaken by the AUT (S) was in connection with the Universities (Scotland) Bill which became an Act in 1966. Much of the AUT (S)'s work in connection with this Bill was conducted by the Association's honorary officers and the work of the AUT (S) continues to be shouldered by honorary officers.

Bibliography
T. R. Bolam, 'The Scottish Association of University Teachers', in British Universities Annual, 1964, pp.77-82.

Ronald P. Doig, 'AUT (Scotland) 1922-1972', being a Special [AUT] Supplement on the A.U.T. (Scotland) Golden Jubilee. This history is appended by lists of past and present officers of the AUTS and the AUT (S) and by a list of dates and places of AUTS and AUT (S) Council meetings since 1922.

Publications
The AUT (S) does not have anything that would qualify as "publications".

Records
(i)   Copies of minutes of the Council and Executive Committee and of all circulars are deposited in the Library of the University of Glasgow. The deposited records cover the period up to 1987. These may be consulted in the Library in accordance with the usual arrangements of the library and with the agreement of the Honorary Secretary of AUT (S), such agreement not being witheld for bona fide researchers.

(ii)   All the other papers of the Association are held by the Honorary Secretary and will eventually be handed to his successor and/or to the Association of University Teachers.

See too the entry for Association of University Teachers.

ASSOCIATION OF UNIVERSITY TEACHERS OF ECONOMICS

Address and
contact
Professor David Peel,
Secretary: Association of University Teachers of Economics,
Department of Economics,
University College of Wales,
Aberystwyth,
SY23 3DB

tel: 0970 623111 ext.3132

The Association has held an annual conference in association with the Royal Economic Society.

Publications
Proceedings of the Annual Conference (since at least the 1973 Annual Conference, whose Proceedings - the subtitle - were edited by Michael Parkin and A.R. Nobay and entitled Contemporary Issues in Economics, Manchester U.P., 1975).

ASSOCIATION OF UNIVERSITY TEACHERS
OF GENERAL PRACTICE

Address and
contact
Dr. George K. Freeman,
Secretary: Association of University Teachers of General Practice,
Aldermoor Health Centre,
Southampton,
SO1 6ST

tel: 0703 783111 ext.316

History

In the summers of 1972 and 1973 representatives of the fledgling academic departments of general practice in Britain and Ireland met for scientific informal meetings in Cardiff and Manchester respectively. At a third similar meeting at the University of Aberdeen in July 1974 it was agreed to set up the Association of University Teachers of General Practice and the chairman of the meeting, Professor Ian Richardson of the Department of General Practice at Aberdeen was elected secretary of a steering group charged with founding the Association. Because of Professor Richardson's ill health this task was delegated to Dr. (now Professor) John Howie of Aberdeen (now of Edinburgh). On 15 November 1974 most of the heads of general practice departments met and the essential decisions were taken to set up the Association. A provisional list of members (fifty persons drawn from twenty-two departments) was drawn up and formed the electorate for the elections for the first Executive Committee, which first met on 3 March 1975.

According to the Constitution of the Association (last revised in July 1987), its object is "to promote the development of General Practice as a university discipline." Membership of the Association is open, inter alia, to full-time Lecturers, Senior Lecturers, Readers and Professors (whether or not medically qualified) in university departments of General Practice or their equivalents and to part-time Lecturers or Senior Lecturers or their equivalents (including Research Fellows and Research Assistants) holding a university appointment in an academic department of General Practice or its equivalent and having a commitment equal to at least one day per week within that department. At present there are some 80 members with full-time posts and over 100 members with part-time university contracts.

The main event of the Association's calendar is the Annual Scientific Meeting. The first such annual meeting was at Southampton on 10-11 July 1975. This meeting is held at a university centre. Under the constitution sessions at the meeting may be arranged for the presentation and discussion of research work, educational or organisational problems confronting members in their university roles. Abstracts of papers to be presented at the Meeting are precirculated. The AGM is held during the Annual Scientific Meeting, the first being held at Southampton on 11 July 1975; the Chairman, Secretary, and Treasurer are elected at the AGM.

Between annual business meetings, the affairs of the Association are conducted by an Executive Committee (comprised of the officers, elected members, the head of the host department for the Annual Scientific Meeting of the next session, a representative of the Royal College of General Practitioners, and a representative of the Heads of Departments group). The Executive Committee normally meets three times a year. The current Secretary has held office since 1986 and is the third member to hold the office. The Chairmanship now normally rotates every three years; the Chairman is eligible for re-election annually for not more than three consecutive years.

More recently, in addition to the Annual Scientific Meetings, regular regional meetings have been organised for most areas of the British Isles : at present there are Northern, London, South West, and Scottish groups.

Bibliography
The Association does not have an introductory booklet, the above 'History' being based on the standard letter the Secretary sends to new members and on the information, including a copy of the Constitution, which he kindly provided.

Reports on the Association's meetings have on occasion been published in The Journal of the Royal College of General Practitioners, (e.g. Vol.25 No.155, June 1975).

Publications
AUTGP Newsletter The Newsletter (issues of which are not numbered) includes reports of regional meetings, of the annual scientific meetings, and of meetings of the Executive.
On occasion there are reports of other meetings, etc., e.g. reports on the 21st meeting of the Conference of Postgraduate Advisers in General Practice and on the 3rd European Conference on Teaching in General Practice in the November 1982 issue of the Newsletter.

Undergraduate Medical Education in General Practice (Occasional Paper No.28, Royal College of General Practitioners, London, 1984; produced by a working group of senior members of the Association.)

J.G.R. Howie, D.R. Hannay, and J.S.K. Stevenson, The Mackenzie Report : General Practice in the Medical Schools of the United Kingdom - 1986, [Association of University Teachers of General Practice, 1986]

See too History above, for reference to abstracts of papers presented at the Annual Scientific Meetings.

Records
The Secretary of the Association keeps two main groups of records : minutes of the AGMs and associated correspondence circulated to the entire membership; and minutes of meetings of the Executive Committee and associated correspondence and supporting documentation. Also retained are the successive editions of the Association's Constitution, a list of members (which is updated two or three times annually), and an explanatory note which the Secretary sends to prospective members and others enquiring about the Association. The non-current records of the Association occupy one drawer of a filing cabinet.

BRITISH ASSOCIATION OF ACADEMIC PHONETICIANS

<u>Address and</u>
<u>contact</u>
Dr. M. K. C. MacMahon,
Honorary Archivist: British Association of Academic Phoneticians,
Department of English Language,
The University of Glasgow,
Glasgow,
G12 8QQ.

tel: 041 399 8855 ext.4596

<u>History</u>
The British Association of Academic Phoneticians (BAAP) is the successor to the Colloquium of British Academic Phoneticians. The Colloquium came into being round about the mid 1950s and was originally an informal group of phoneticians based in London who met together to talk over various points relating to phonetics. Its title at one time was The Association of Phoneticians of the (British) Commonwealth.

Currently, membership of BAAP is drawn from those with a teaching or research post in phonetics in an institute of higher education in Britain or Eire. Colleagues in other countries who at one time held a post in Britain or Eire are invited to attend meetings.

<u>Records</u>
The post of Archivist was established by BAAP in 1982. What records exist are held by the Honorary Archivist in the Department of English Language, University of Glasgow; access to the records is restricted to members of BAAP.

BRITISH ASSOCIATION OF HEALTH SERVICES IN HIGHER EDUCATION

<u>Address and</u>
<u>contact</u>
Dr. C.M. Swann,
Hon. Secretary,
British Association of Health Services in Higher Education,
University Health Centre,
The University,
Southampton,
SO9 5NH

tel: 0703 557531

<u>History</u>
The British Student Health Association is the professional association of workers in student health services. In 1947, 1949 and 1951 the Nuffield Provincial Hospitals Trust sponsored national conferences of people involved in student health work and pilot surveys were organised. At the 1951 conference a British Student Health Officers Association was formed. In 1961 this Association changed its name to the British Student Health Association, and on 1 January 1989 to the British Association of Health Services in Higher Education.

The Association has Commonwealth, overseas and honorary members as well as UK members. An annual conference has been held since 1948 (before the Association was formally founded), the proceedings of the annual conference being published. Those members of the Association who are nurses have latterly organised their own three study days annually, at Easter.

The Association has a library of books and reprints, annual reports of student health services in the UK and abroad etc., the Alan Rook Library (named after the Association's first President), which is now housed at the University of London Central Institutions Health Service, 20 Gower Street, London, WC1E 6DP, where the Librarian and Archivist of the Association, Dr. Barbara Anderson, has her office. The Library has some but not all of the Annual Reports of the BSHA, and copies of the BSHA's Conference Proceedings dating from 1948, and other archive material. Members of the Association and bona fide researchers may be given access to the Library between 9.00 a.m. and 5.30 p.m. on weekdays; a telephone call (071 636 7628) in advance of a visit is appreciated although not necessary.

Bibliography

Nicolas Malleson, A Handbook on British Student Health Services (Pitman Medical Publishing Co.Ltd., 1965).

Alex Mair, Student Health Services in Great Britain and Northern Ireland (Pergamon Press, Oxford, 1967).

R.E. Boynton, 'The development of student health services', Student Medicine, vol.1 part 1, 1952, pp.4-8.

R.E. Boynton, 'Historical development of college health services', Student Medicine, vol.10 part 3, 1962, pp.294-305.

J.D. Cumming, University Health Services and University Medical Officers, 1970 (10pp.).

G. Grant, 'The organisation of university health services in Great Britain and their co-ordination with the school health service', Public Health: The Journal of the Society of Medical Officers of Health, vol. LXXX, no.2, 1966, pp.61-67.

J.P. Horder, 'The Royal College of General Practitioners and the British Student Health Association', The Journal of the Royal College of General Practitioners, vol.24, no.149, 1974, pp.863-4. A report on a symposium.

R.E. Verney, 'The history of student health services in Great Britain', Universities Quarterly, vol.9 no.1, 1954, pp.23-31. This same number also contains two other papers on Health and the Student, including one on Student Health Services, the NHS, and the University Medical Officer.

World Health Organisation, University Health Services, 1966.

P.W.W. Gifford, 'Twenty-five Years of Student Health', Modern Medicine, Vol. 19, No.8, August 1974, pp.225-226.

Agnes Wilkinson, ed., Student Health Practice (Pitman Medical Publishing Co.Ltd., 1979).

<u>Students in Need : Essays in Memory of Nicolas Malleson</u> (Society for Research into Higher Education Ltd., Guildford, 1978). Half of the chapters are devoted to aspects of student health and counselling.

<u>Publications</u>

(a)   Proceedings of the Association's Conference, 1947, 1949, 1951 and yearly thereafter.

(b)   <u>BSHA Bulletin</u>, Vols.1-, 1972- to date.

(c)   Dermot McCracken, <u>University Student Performance: the changing pattern of medical and social factors over three years and their correlations with examination results</u>, 2 vols. (BSHA, 1969). Based on a study of students at the University of Leeds.

(d.)   The BSHA has produced over twenty subject bibliographies, including one on student health services in Great Britain (covering publications up to 1979). The other subject bibliographies cover such subjects as Academic Performance and Achievement, Disabled Students, Overseas Students, Sports Medicine, Student Mental Health, Drugs, Sexual Problems, and Student Unrest.

<u>Records</u>

The Hon. Secretary retains the minutes of the Executive Committee of the Association from 1976 -to date, also copies of all the minutes of the AGMs since 1967, and a large number of other papers of the Association. All these records (together with the membership list and other current data on the Association's computer) will pass to the next Hon. Secretary in due course. It is thought that most of the Association's non-current records could be made available to bona fide researchers.

It is thought that if any records were kept prior to 1976 that then they were probably lodged in the Association's archives (see <u>History</u> above).

THE BRITISH ASSOCIATION FOR SOVIET, SLAVONIC AND EAST EUROPEAN STUDIES

<u>Address and</u>
<u>contact</u>
Mr. M.G. Basker,
Secretary: British Association for Soviet,
Slavonic and East European Studies,
Department of Russian Studies,
University of Bristol,
17 Woodland Road,
Bristol,
BS8 1TE

tel: 0272 303030 ext. 3512/3516

History

(a)   The British Association for Soviet, Slavonic and East European Studies (BASSEES) was formed in 1988 from the British Universities Association of Slavists and the National Association of Soviet and East European Studies : it was officially launched on 27 March 1988.

(b)   The British Universities Association of Slavists (BUAS) was founded in 1956.   It served as a forum for university teachers of Slavonic languages, literatures and history, and for scholars working in related disciplines.   It latterly had 260 members, and held an annual conference at which papers, representative of the range of interests of the membership, were read.   The longest established British journals in the area of Slavonic studies are the <u>Slavonic and East European Review</u>, edited from the School of Slavonic and East European Studies, University of London, and published by Cambridge University Press, and <u>Oxford Slavonic Papers</u> published by Oxford University Press.   In recent years two further journals have appeared, <u>Irish Slavonic Studies</u>, edited from the Queen's University, Belfast, and <u>Scottish Slavonic Review</u>, edited from the Universities of Edinburgh and Glasgow.

BUAS co-ordinated the participation in international conferences of British scholars working in the area of Slavonic studies, and had representatives on national bodies concerned with defending the position of modern languages in education and of area studies.   It maintained close links with the British Council, the National Association for Soviet and East European Studies, the Association of Teachers of Russian, and the Great Britain-USSR Association.

A range of study groups, each holding independent meetings and conferences and, in some cases, publishing their own journals and newsletters, came into existence;   there were groups on Slavonic and East European mediaeval studies, 18th century Russian history and literature, 19th century Russian literature, 20th century Russian literature, the Russian Revolution, Neo-Formalism, and Slavonic linguistics.

(c)   The National Association of Soviet and East European Studies (NASEES) was founded in 1961. It published a short <u>Newsletter</u> three times a year, as well as a directory of members. The occasional series <u>Soviet Studies</u> was also published under NASEES auspices. It is believed that no account of NASEES' objects and history has been published.

Bibliography

Gerald Stone, 'The history of Slavonic studies in Great Britain (until the Second World War)' <u>Osterreichische Akademie der Wissenschaften: Philosophisch-historische Klasse, Beitrage zur Geschichte der Slawistik in nichtslawischen Landern, Schriften der Balkankommission: Linguistische Abteilung</u>, vol. XXX(1985), Special Issue.

Publications

BUAS published the <u>BUAS Newsletter</u>. This appeared three times a year. There was also an annual survey of <u>BUAS Research Work in Progress</u>.

Records

(a) BUAS retained a somewhat miscellaneous archive of correspondence, mostly with members but also with various distinguished Slavists; reports from the Association's representatives on and various papers from national and international bodies; a record of the Annual Conference; and Minutes of the Annual General Meeting, Committee, and Congress Committee meetings. Current records were kept by the President, Secretary, and Treasurer.

(b) The Secretary of BASSEES has inherited the BUAS archives and it is likely that the NASEES archives are soon too to come into his possession. It has been agreed in principle that the two archives should eventually be deposited at the Leeds Russian Archive (Brotherton Library, University of Leeds; Archivist : Mr. R.D. Davies). It is envisaged that the majority of the archives will be deposited and that bona fide scholars will be able to consult them. The archives of BUAS are due to be deposited in July 1990, and the archives of NASEES sometime later.

BRITISH FEDERATION OF UNIVERSITY WOMEN

Address and
contact
British Federation of University Women,
Crosby Hall,
Cheyne Walk,
London,
SW3 5BA

Mrs. Clare Ellis, Secretary
tel: 071 352 5354

History

The British Federation of University Women (BFUW) was founded in 1907 to bring graduate women together in friendly groups all over the country. One of the earliest regional groups to be founded was that of the Liverpool Association of University Women, formed in 1908.

The Federation is made up of a number of local associations which meet regularly to hear speakers on a wide variety of subjects. In the case of the Liverpool Association, evening meetings with guest speakers and a monthly Morning Discussion Group are organised. Membership of the Federation is open to graduates of any British or foreign university (including holders of Open University, CNAA, validated and external degrees). Students in the final year of a degree course are eligible for Junior Membership, Subscription to the Federation automatically confers membership of the International Federation of University Women.

The Federation organises seminars, workshops, and an annual weekend conference. Members may also use the club facilities at Crosby Hall, Chelsea, which include accommodation, a fine medieval dining hall (removed from St.Helens, Bishopsgate, London), and the Sybil Campbell Library. Crosby Hall itself is a fully owned subsidiary company of BFUW : it is an international hall of residence for women postgraduate students (92 study bedrooms) and also acts as a club for BFUW members.

Annual Report, 1930-31 - to date

News Sheet, nos. 1-21, 1930-37; continued as The University Women's Review, nos. 22-, 1937- . This latter publication ceased production some years ago.

BFUW News. Newsletter of the Federation, produced twice yearly.

Constance E. Arregger (ed.), Graduate Women at Work: A study by a working party of the British Federation of University Women (Oriel Press, Newcastle-upon- Tyne, 1966).

M. Collins (ed.), Women Graduates and the Teaching Profession: Report of a working party of the British Federation of University Women (Manchester U.P., 1964).

Records
(a)   The Fawcett Library, City of London Polytechnic, Calcutta House, Old Castle Street, London, E1 7NT, holds some annual reports and other publications issued by BFUW (e.g. their periodical) but its holdings even of these is far from complete. The Library does not have any of the BFUW's organisational papers.

(b)   The Secretary of BFUW retains the minutes of the Federation from 1907 onwards, together with other papers.

See too the entry for the International Federation of University Women

BRITISH STUDENTS SPORTS FEDERATION

Address and
contact
British Students Sports Federation,
28 Woburn Square,
London,
WC1H 0AD

tel: 071 580 3618/9
Mr. Michael D. Lamb, Secretary

History
The British Students Sports Federation (BSSF) was established in 1971. Membership of BSSF consists of British Universities Sports Federation (BUSF), British Colleges Sports Association (BCSA), and British Polytechnics Sports Association. The Federation is responsible for the representation of British student interests in international sport (including the organisation of the British participation in Federation Internationale du Sport Universitaire activities). It acts as a consultative body for other aspects of British student sport and promotes the unification of student sport in all areas agreed by its constituent members. The Federation's affairs are conducted by a Committee.

BSSF is due to move its offices to Birmingham (address at present not known) at the end of August 1990.

Publications
Annual reports of BSSF Championships, etc. are included in the <u>Official Handbook</u> of the BCSA and in the <u>Handbook</u> of the BUSF, both of which are annual publications.

The BSSF will this academic year (1988-89) produce its first annual <u>Handbook</u>.

Every two years BSSF produces a report of the Universiade (World Student Games), the latest being on the <u>Universiade 1987 Zagreb, Yugoslavia</u> (illustrated by photographs).

The BSSF states (May 1988) that a twice-termly newsletter may also soon be produced which would be circulated to all institutions in membership of BSSF, Directors of Physical Education, etc.

<u>See too</u> entries for BUSF and FISU.

Records
Minutes for BSSF from 1972 onwards are bound and stored at its London office. Applications to view them are normally favourably received.

BRITISH UNIVERSITIES' ACCOMMODATION CONSORTIUM

<u>Address and contact</u>
Carole Formon,
General Secretary: British Universities' Accommodation Consortium Limited,
P.O. Box B87,
University Park,
Nottingham,
NG7 2RD

tel: 0602 504571
telex: 337676

<u>History</u>
The British Universities' Accommodation Consortium Limited (BUAC) has its origins in a meeting of twelve university officers who in 1970 met to consider how best to promote member institutions' accommodation facilities in vacations. Mr. Robert Watson, Steward to the Pollock Halls and later to the University Halls and Houses (both at the University of Edinburgh), became the first Secretary of BUAC and its first Chairman, serving in the latter capacity from 1975 to 1985. The first Chairman of BUAC drawn from an English university was elected in May 1988 when Mr. Willie Johnston, Conference Liaison Officer, University of Sheffield, was appointed. BUAC is a company limited by guarantee (Registration No.: England 1370080). It was incorporated as a company on 23 May 1978 and copies of its annual return and annual accounts are deposited with the Companies Registration Office.

By July 1986 BUAC's membership was fifty-two, with an annual vacation-letting income of around £40 million. By May 1988 BUAC's membership had risen to fifty-four. With 75,000 beds available in its member institutions, BUAC is the most comprehensive provider of conference, group, exhibition and holiday facilities in the country.

Bibliography
It is believed that no history of the Consortium has been published.

Publications
BUAC issues a periodically revised brochure which provides details of the facilities available at each individual university which is a member of the Consortium.

Records
General information can be provided by the Consortium's General Office.

BRITISH UNIVERSITIES FILM AND VIDEO COUNCIL

Address and contact
British Universities Film and Video Council,
55 Greek Street,
London,
W1V 5LR

tel 071 734 3687
Mr. Jim Ballantyne, Information Officer

History
The British Universities Film and Video Council (BUFVC) was founded in 1948 (as the British Universities Film Council Ltd.) by and for practising university teachers. The BUFC came into being as a representative body with membership open to all British universities and with the following objects:-

> The advancement of education in the universities and institutions of university standard in the United Kingdom by the coordination and development of the use and study of film and of related media, materials and techniques for the purpose of university teaching and research, and in particular:-
> (1)   to promote (a) the collection and dissemination of information
> (b) the distribution
> (c) the production
> of films suitable for the above purposes.
> (2)   to cooperate   with universities and similar bodies in other countries for the performance of these objects.

For the first nineteen years of its existence, the BUFC lacked a permanent secretariat and headquarters but this does not appear to have affected the momentum begun by its founding members. The British Film Institute made an annual grant to purchase films which would not otherwise be accessible and to distribute them as a special collection. A catalogue of films available for hire from various sources was compiled. Conferences were organised and the Council's journal, University Film Journal, launched in 1953. By the end of 1950s the BUFC was nationally acknowledged to be the authoritative body to speak for the universities on the use of film and related media in their work. The BUFC submitted evidence to both the Robbins Committee on Higher Education and the Hale Committee on University Teaching Methods, but it was the report of the UGC appointed Brynmor Jones Committee (to which the BUFC submitted evidence), Audio-Visual Aids in Higher Scientific Education, 1965, which had most impact on the development of audio-visual aids in universities. A main recommendation of the Brynmor Jones Report was for the creation of a national centre for the production and promotion of audio-visual materials for teaching in all sectors of education. Though the Government could not contemplate expenditure for this centre on the scale envisaged, after consultation with the DES an increase in the British Film Institute's grant to the BUFC was agreed to and in 1967 the BUFC opened a small office in London, on British Film Institute premises.

In February 1983 the BUFC moved to its present offices and shortly afterwards negotiations with the DES resulted in the BUFC being funded directly by the DES from April 1983 and in the change of its title to BUFVC. The BUFVC is also supported by the subscriptions of its members. It is a limited company with the status of an educational charity. Most British universities and polytechnics are members and a growing number of overseas members use the Council's services.

The BUFVC's premises offer various facilities to members including a Reference Library of over 2200 books and pamphlets and 100 periodicals and newsletters, 600 current catalogues of British distributors of audio-visual material, and (as part of the Slade Film History Register, which covers film material for the period 1895-1962) copies of all British newsreel issue sheets, as well as information on collections of archive film and television in the United Kingdom and overseas; an Audio-Visual Reference Centre, which provides a preview and research facility for audio-visual materials produced in universities, polytechnics and other institutions of higher education; a Higher Education Film and Video Library, which makes available films and video cassettes of interest to higher education which might not otherwise be in distribution in the United Kingdom; an Information Service; and a number of Publications (see below).

The Council has drawn attention to the need to ensure adequate training for those working in audio-visual archives, suggesting that the National Film Archive might perhaps give a lead in this. The Council was represented on a Working Party on Audio-Visual Archives, whose report to the Council of the British Records Association, March 1983, has been widely circulated to stimulate discussion of the issues it raises.

Bibliography
The British Universities Film Council 25th Anniversary Year, BUFC, 1973 (a
      short account of the origins and development of the Council).

A number of brief articles about the Council have appeared in audio-visual journals over the years. For instance, the Director of the BUFVC, Elizabeth Oliver, contributed a paper, ' The Development of a Computer Database for Education' (about the HELPIS database) to PLET Programmed Learning and Educational Technology: Journal of AETT, Vol.21 No.3, August 1984, pp.205-210.

Publications
The principal publications of the Council are:-

Annual Report (includes Accounts and Treasurer's Report, and list of representatives and their addresses)

BUFVC Newsletter (formerly BUFC Newsletter), Nos.1-61, Dec. 1967-May 1987. Appeared three times a year and included details of new audio-visual materials, members' activities, reviews, short articles, details of courses and conferences (including those run by the BUFVC). The Newsletter's function has been taken over by the Council's new Magazine, Viewfinder, Nos.1-, Nov. 1987-, which also appears three times a year.

BUFVC Catalogue: the 1983 edition was the first microfiche edition for which no print edition exists, though an accompanying booklet lists distributors' addresses; the 1983 and later editions have also brought together two catalogues, the 'Audio-Visual Materials for Higher Education' and 'HELPIS', to provide a database of over 6,000 items suitable for use in higher education. The database is now available online: under the name 'HELPIS', the database is publicly available to subscribers to the British Library's BLAISE-LINE system.

BUFVC Distributors Index: an annotated guide, organised under subject headings, to distributors of audio-visual materials. Regularly updated.

Researcher's Guide to British Film and Television Collections, BUFVC, 2nd Edition, 1985: documents the existence of film and television records that are not normally available for viewing outside the premises where they are held (i.e. basically archival collections), and covering holdings of the national archives, regional collections, television companies, newsreel, production and stock shot libraries, and specialised collections.

Researcher's Guide to British Newsreels, BUFVC, 1983: acts as a guide to the literature of the British newsreel and cinemagazine and serves as a reference document for the film researcher. The holdings of the major newsreel libraries, archives and documentation centres are indicated.

Computers for Imagemaking, published by BUFVC in association with Pergamon Press, 1981; a source book on the use of computers to produce images.

The University Film Journal, No. 1, Spring 1953 - Nos. 29-30 (double issue) October 1967.

University Vision, The Journal of the British Universities Film Council, Nos. 1- 15, Feb. 1968-Dec.1976 (the successor of The University Film Journal).

British Newsreels Issue Sheets 1913-1970: the complete collection held by the Slade Film History Register reproduced on microfiche.
The 275 microfiches in the set give summaries of over 100,000 newsreel stories. Published by Graphic Data Publishing in association with the BUFVC which administers the Slade Film History Register; October 1984.

Librarianship: A Select AV Resource List
Lists some 100 audio-visual materials for use in librarianship and information science. Produced in conjunction with the ASLIB AV Group; November 1985.

<u>Discovery and Invention: a review of films and videos on the history of science and technology</u>, BUFVC, March 1985.

Lists 265 currently available items for degree-level teaching. An appendix lists 18 items for secondary school education. Reviews are included for the majority of entries.

Copies of the Council's Newsletters, annual reports, conference leaflets, etc. have been deposited with the Holloway Collection of Contemporary Culture Records for a number of years. The Holloway Collection (at the University of East Anglia Library, The University Plain, Norwich, NR4 7TJ) was previously known as the Library of Contemporary Culture Records. (The Holloway Collection, established in 1970, is a collection of printed material relating to, resulting from, or illustrating the organisation, promotion, funding and dissemination of cultural activity, widely conceived, throughout the whole of the United Kingdom.)

<u>Records</u>

(a)   Copies of the Council's annual reports and accounts are deposited with the Companies Registration Office, Companies House, Crown Way, Maindy, Cardiff and <u>microfiche</u> copies of the same are held in the Companies Registration Office's London Search Room at 55-71 City Road, London, EC1. (It appears that the Council is not also required to deposit copies with the Charity Commission.)

(b)   The Council's records are held at its offices and include agenda and minutes of all the termly Executive Committee and Editorial Board meetings; bought and sold accounts going back a number of years; correspondence relating to particular projects; copies of all the Council's publicity leaflets; complete runs of the <u>BUFVC Newsletter</u>, <u>The University Film Journal</u> and its successor <u>University Vision</u>; copies of all BUFVC publications, etc.

(c)   The Council would have no objection to bona fide researchers having access to its records (except, of course, the most recent items.)

BRITISH UNIVERSITIES INDUSTRIAL RELATIONS ASSOCIATION

<u>Address and</u>
<u>contact</u>
Mr. C. G. Gill,
Secretary and Treasurer of the British
Universities Industrial Relations Association,
Management Studies Group,
Department of Engineering,
University of Cambridge,
Mill Lane,
Cambridge,
CB2 1RX.

tel: 0223 337733 ext. 8177

History

The British Universities Industrial Relations Association (BUIRA) was formed in 1950 in Manchester by a small group of university teachers and researchers who wished to encourage the academic study of industrial relations in Britain and to provide a forum for the discussion of research and teaching of the subject. Initially it was entitled the Inter-University Study Group in Industrial Relations; in 1951 it was renamed the University Industrial Relations Association; and in 1967 it assumed its present title.

Since its formation BUIRA has widened its membership constituency by admitting similar persons from the polytechnics and colleges of higher and further education, and since 1974 its scope has included Ireland. Eligibility for individual membership is an official academic appointment in an institution of the above types or in an approved research organisation, as well as an interest or activity in industrial relations. Members' disciplinary fields include law, economics, sociology, psychology, politics and history, as well as personnel management and industrial relations. It is not however the role of BUIRA to act as a qualifying association. Employees of companies, civil servants and trade unions' or employers' association officials are not eligible for membership. There is no provision for student, graduate or affiliate membership, although a few honorary memberships have been accorded to distinguished senior academics. The Association is the official British representative at the International Industrial Relations Association.

The membership of BUIRA was almost 400 at the end of 1986, covering most British universities and polytechnics. The Association is run by an elected President, a Secretary/Treasurer and an Executive Committee of six members. The main activity of the Association is an annual conference held over three days in early July at a university: there is a variety of formal review papers, research papers and workshop sessions. The Association also supports certain seminars on a regional basis and occasional study conferences. Publications available to members include the Research Register (on a two-yearly basis) and occasional books produced jointly with a commercial publisher, such as the Industrial Relations: an International and Comparative Bibliography (Mansell/BUIRA). An important function is the maintenance of an authoritative and representative voice for industrial relations with official bodies, government agencies, overseas industrial relations associations and other learned societies within Britain.

Bibliography

John Berridge and John Goodman, 'The British Universities Industrial Relations Association : The First 35 Years', British Journal of Industrial Relations, Vol. XXVI No.2, July 1988, pp.155-177.

Publications

Twice-yearly newsletter from Secretary - dating from 1950
Secretary's annual report and accounts - dating from 1950

Records

Annual General Meeting agenda and minutes (previously Business Meeting) from 1950.
Annual Accounts - from 1950.
Conference programmes and attendance lists from 1950.
Secretary and Treasurers' Annual Report.

Rule Book - from 1967.
Twice-yearly newsletter - from 1950.
Record of office holders and committee members.
Numerous other agenda papers, applications forms, correspondence, etc.

Non-current records are deposited at the Modern Records Centre, University of Warwick Library on a closed basis. The Secretary of the Association controls this archive and access is likely to be strictly limited to members of the Association. The following entry for this deposit (ref.MSS.52) appears in the Modern Record Centre's Guide and Consolidated Guide:

> Minutes or reports of business and other meetings, 1950-73, the earlier ones incorporated in the Association's Bulletin.
> Minutes of annual meetings, 1978-80.
> Financial statements, 1952-74, 1978-80.
> Various subject files, including re official labour statistics; submission to Heyworth Committee on Social Studies, 1963; Association's rules, mainly 1964.
> Annual conference programmes, 1952-74, 1978-80.
> Membership lists, 1953-73, 1978-80.
> BUIRA questionnaire and report re membership, role, etc., of the Association, 1971.

In 1987 the Modern Records Centre received a further deposit of administrative records of the Association, c.1978-85, including membership lists, papers re conferences, including programmes, etc.

BRITISH UNIVERSITIES SPORTS FEDERATION

Address and
contact
British Universities Sports Federation,
28 Woburn Square,
London,
WC1H 0AD

tel: 071 580 3618/9
Mr. Peter Rhodes, General Secretary

History
The British Universities Sports Federation (BUSF) was established in February 1962 to encourage the development of men's and women's sport in the universities and university colleges in the United Kingdom, and to work in consultation with its constituent bodies to arrange UK university championships, UK university fixtures and tours at home and abroad, and such other activities concerned with UK university sports as are not adequately covered by the constituent bodies.

Membership of BUSF consists of "universities" (the Athletic Unions of the sporting bodies of the universities in the UK and the university colleges of Wales) and "corporate members" (the Scottish Universities Sports Federation (SUSF), the Universities Athletic Union (UAU), and the University of Wales Athletic Union (UWAU). An annual subscription on a per capita basis is paid on behalf of each university/university college member.

The supreme governing body of BUSF is the General Council (which meets annually and to which all member universities are entitled to send two delegates). The management of the Federation is vested in the Executive Committee which, working through the officers and salaried officials, implements the policy as laid down by the General Council; the Executive Committee ordinarily meets once in each term. There are also a Steering Committee, a House Committee, and an Eligibility Committee.

BUSF currently organises forty university championships in a wide range of sports (ranging from archery and athletics to karate and table tennis) and representative matches and tours at home and abroad. BUSF also administers the sporting programme of both the British Students Sports Federation (BSSF) and the British Colleges Sports Association (BCSA) and organises, on behalf of UAU, a number of UAU championships that are held within BUSF events. BUSF also liaises with the Sports Council, the NUS, the British Universities Physical Education Association, the CVCP, the Central Council for Physical Recreation, and the national governing bodies. BUSF is a member, together with BCSA and the British Polytechnics Sports Association (BPSA), of BSSF, which is the body responsible for the representation of British student interests within the Federation Internationale du Sport Universitaire (FISU).

BUSF is due to move its offices to Birmingham (address at present not known) at the end of August 1990.

Publications

Handbook
(includes the Constitution of BUSF, the results of BUSF and BSSF championships and BUSF group tournaments for the previous season, and reports of FISU championships, and of Universiades (World Student Games, whose origins date back to 1923), and information on member universities of BUSF providing names of AU contacts, director of physical education, etc.)

The BUSF Handbook in the current format was first produced in 1970-71. Until then each domestic Championship had an individual report, all reports being bound at the end of the year in one folder. The Constitution and Representative Matches were reported in a separate booklet.

Records
Minutes for BUSF from 1962 onwards are bound and stored at its office in London. Applications to view them are normally favourably received.

See too entries for BSSF, FISU, and UAU.

CENTRAL SERVICES UNIT FOR UNIVERSITY AND POLYTECHNIC CAREERS AND APPOINTMENTS SERVICES

<u>Address and contact</u>
Central Services Unit for University and Polytechnic
Careers and Appointments Services,
Crawford House,
Precinct Centre,
Oxford Road,
Manchester,
M13 9EP

tel: 061 273 4233
telex: 666635
fax: 061 273 6657
Mr. H.B. Putt, Director.

<u>History</u>
The Unit (CSU) was created by the CVCP in August 1972 to support individual careers advisory services by undertaking centrally those tasks which are too large for the resources of any one university or which would otherwise be repeated unnecessarily in each institution, in particular to act as a central point for the exchange of information about the graduate employment market. It is funded by the universities and polytechnics of the United Kingdom, the university colleges of Eire, and one Scottish Central Institution. The Unit has expanded considerably and is a focal point of information on the supply of new graduates and the opportunities open to them for study, training, and employment: it provides a wide range of services both to careers services and to employers of graduates. It works closely with the Universities Statistical Record and the DES in order to make its predictions of graduate output, and has a very special relationship with the Association of Graduate Careers Advisory Services (AGCAS).

Since March 1980 all institutions newly admitted to membership of AGCAS also become subscribers to CSU. All new subscribers to CSU receive copies of certain publications of both AGCAS and CSU, including copies of the latest issues of Current and Forward Vacancies lists.

<u>Bibliography</u> -

<u>Publications</u>

These include:-
Annual Report of the Management Committee of CSU
<u>Current Vacancies</u> (issued fortnightly and copies supplied to each careers
centre)

<u>Postgraduate Bulletin</u> (Spring, Summer, and Autumn editions)
(provides details of postgraduate courses, research posts, and bursaries, with index, by subject and discipline, to entries)

<u>Forward Vacancies</u> (issued during the Spring and Autumn terms, each issue carries advertisements for jobs and career opportunities available to students upon completion of studies (undergraduate or postgraduate).

Records

The Unit retains the minutes of all meetings of its Management Committee, together with supporting papers, and also complete sets of statistical and other publications issued by the Director.

COMMITTEE OF VICE-CHANCELLORS AND PRINCIPALS OF THE UNIVERSITIES OF THE UNITED KINGDOM

Address and contact

Committee of Vice-Chancellors and Principals
of the Universities of the United Kingdom,
29 Tavistock Square,
London,
WC1H 9EZ

tel: 071 387 9231
fax: 071 388 8649 (Universities Information Unit fax : 071 383 5766)
Mr. Thomas U. Burgner, Secretary to the Committee

History

The Committee of Vice-Chancellors and Principals of the Universities of the United Kingdom (CVCP) grew out of the Universities Bureau of the British Empire. The CVCP began to meet informally in 1918, when regular consultative meetings of vice-chancellors and principals were instituted, but it was not placed on a formal footing until 1930. The CVCP was linked with the Association of Commonwealth Universities (as the Bureau was renamed) for many years, the ACU Secretary acting as part-time Secretary to the CVCP; the association between the two bodies ended when they separated in 1968-69. Since its inception the membership of the Committee has included the Vice-Chancellor or Principal of each of the universities in England, Scotland, and Wales which are in receipt of a grant through the University Grants Committee (now the UFC). Nowadays the Committee's membership also includes the Vice-Chancellors of the two universities in Northern Ireland, the Principal and six other persons nominated by the University of Wales, the Principal of the University of Manchester Institute of Science and Technology (UMIST), the Vice-Chancellor of the Open University (which is financed through the DES) and the Vice-Chancellor of the Cranfield Institute of Technology.

The CVCP had, and has, no executive powers, its functions being primarily consultative and advisory, but its influence has been great, and has grown with the years, particularly since the expansion of higher education in the 1960s and its contraction since the mid 1970s. One of its most influential recent reports is the <u>Report of the Steering Committee for Efficiency Studies in Universities</u> ('The Jarratt Report'), 1985. This report, inter alia, advocated the development of a range of performance indicators etc. and in consequence the CVCP and the UGC established a joint working group in October 1985 under the chairmanship of Sir Mark Richmond to report on the subject. Under proposals submitted in a report on the CVCP and on its relations with other bodies by Lord Flowers in early 1988 it is suggested that the

Committee's chairman should be on leave of absence from his university for his term of office and should be backed by an 'upgraded' secretary general. The new post of Secretary to the Committee was established later in 1988, Mr. Tom Burgner, the successful candidate, taking up the post in April 1989. At the same time the Committee was reorganised, an elected Council of twelve members replacing the General Purposes Committee, with three supporting committees (Academic Advisory, Financial Advisory, and International) assisting the Council. The new Council will appoint specialist working groups to deal with major policy issues on the Committee's behalf.

The Committee's aim is to reflect the collective view of universities and to keep all major university matters under regular review. In particular it provides an informal framework within which (a) matters of common interest to universities may be discussed, (b) a common or central arrangement for the resolution of particular problems may be reached, and (c) a university view on policy matters can be formulated and submitted to the UFC, to government and to other bodies. The concern of the Committee is with the general problems of the universities, not with the particular affairs of individual universities.

The full Committee of the CVCP was, until the reorganisation of 1988-89, supported by a general purposes committee, and standing committees which dealt with finance and development, academic affairs, staff and student matters and international university affairs. In addition there were a number of specialist sub-committees and groups covering subjects such as libraries, pensions, student awards, administrative training, and safety; special working parties were established from time to time. Recent examples were those on industry and public relations. The latter was replaced by a management committee of vice-chancellors to oversee the work of the Universities Information Unit, which is the central press office for U.K. universities and the CVCP and is based at the CVCP's offices. Another group, chaired by Professor P. A. Reynolds, on academic standards, reported in July 1986. In 1990 the CVCP established an Academic Audit Unit (AAU), to commence work in Autumn 1990. The AAU's remit is, inter alia, to consider and review the universities' mechanisms for monitoring and promoting the academic standards which are necessary for achieving their stated aims and objectives. The AAU's outline checklist for academic audit is based on the Reynolds document.

There is an Administrative Training Committee, whose aim is 'to stimulate, co-ordinate and promote the training of university administrators through the provision of a coherent training programme centred around the universities and future needs of the individual administrator and his or her university'. It publishes an Annual Report and 'Training Opportunities' (listing forthcoming CVCP and other courses and workshops, regional training activities, training materials, and publications available from the CVCP Administrative Training Officer). Introductory Courses for new recruits to university administration have been held under the Committee's auspices since 1971. In 1989 CVCP established a National Staff Development and Training Unit (NSDTU) to co-ordinate training and staff development provision across the university sector; it is based at the University of Sheffield.

The CVCP has been instrumental in the establishment of a number of other bodies dealing with specialist areas. For example, the Standing Conference on University Entrance (SCUE) has been closely involved, on behalf of the universities, in deliberations on possible changes in sixth-form curriculum and examinations. SCUE was established in 1965 by the CVCP to discuss the implications for universities of developments in the school curriculum and

examinations and to co-ordinate university policy on entrance matters generally. Membership is drawn from all UK universities. The Secretary and staff of SCUE are accommodated in the CVCP's offices at 29 Tavistock Square. SCUE's publications include <u>AS Levels and University Entrance</u> (published jointly with CVCP, last revised edition 1987; henceforth such information will be included in <u>University Entrance : The Official Guide 1989</u>, to be published in June 1988, and the successor to the <u>Compendium of University Entrance Requirements</u> which was published annually on behalf of CVCP), <u>Thinking about University?</u> (published jointly with CVCP, 1982), <u>Qualifying for University Entrance</u> (rev.ed., 1988), and <u>Current Developments in School Curriculum and Examinations</u> (published jointly by SCUE, SCDC, SEC, and CNAA, 1987). SCUE has sponsored joint conferences, e.g. on access courses (jointly with the Further Education Unit, 1987; report published) and on widening access to university education (jointly with the AUT, 1988). The CVCP administers the Overseas Research Students Awards Scheme, which was set up by the Secretary of State for Education and Science in 1979 to provide awards for partial remission of tuition fees to overseas postgraduate students of outstanding merit and research potential; the CVCP has appointed a special committee, composed of senior members of academic staff of the academic institutions in the UK at which the awards are tenable, to be responsible for the selection of award holders and the detailed management of the Scheme.

Other committees consider issues relating to the remuneration of various groups: the University Authorities Panel (UAP), for non-clinical academic and related staff; the Clinical Academic Staff Salaries Committee (CASSC), to ensure pay comparability between clinical academic staff and their counterparts in the National Health Service; and the Universities Committee for Non-Teaching Staffs (UCNS) which conducts central negotiations on pay and industrial relations issues. Following a review by the CVCP and the Committee of Chairmen of University Councils, in January 1990 both committees proposed the establishment of a new Pay and Employment Policy Committee (PEPC) and each university was asked to agree to transfer to the PEPC the mandates which it gave to the UAP in 1970, to the UCNS, and to the CASSC in 1979.

The CVCP has regular consultative arrangements with the University Grants Committee (now the UFC). It also has meetings with a variety of bodies including the Association of University Teachers, the Secondary Heads Association, the Committee of Directors of Polytechnics, the National Union of Students, representatives of local authority associations, the Confederation of British Industry, the Trades Union Congress, Members of Parliament, and the press, and has developed contacts with university heads abroad.

Bibliography

Association of Commonwealth Universities' Yearbook. Vol. 3 - Appendix   II National and Regional Inter-University Bodies. Description of the aims and structure of the Committee.

Eric Ashby, <u>Community of Universities: an informal portrait of the Association of Universities of the British Commonwealth, 1913-1963</u> (Cambridge U.P., 1963). Also describes the origins of the Committee of Vice-Chancellors and Principals.

Sir Robert Aitken, 'The Vice-Chancellors' Committee and the UGC', in <u>Universities Quarterly</u>, Vol.23 No.2, 1969, pp. 165-171.

Richard Szreter, 'The Committee of Vice-Chancellors Revisited: the pattern ten years later', <u>Educational Studies</u>, Vol.5 No.1, 1979.

Roy Butler, 'The Control and Management of Higher Education in Great Britian, with special reference to the role of the University Grants Committee and the Committee of Vice-Chancellors and Principals' in <u>Oxford Review of Education</u>, Vol.8 No. 3, 1982, pp. 265-278. This number of the <u>Oxford Review of Education</u> contains eight other papers also related to the theme of 'Higher Education and Oxford'.

<u>Publications</u> include:-
A Publications List is issued by CVCP.

Annual

<u>The Compendium of University Entrance Requirements for First Degree Courses in the United Kingdom</u>. (Published by ACU for the CVCP)
This publication has since 1987 been superceded by <u>University Entrance : The Official Guide</u>, 1987 onwards, which CVCP publishes annually.

<u>British Universities' Guide to Graduate Study</u>. (Published by ACU for the CVCP)

<u>Annual Report</u>

Regular

<u>Newsletter</u>, Nos. [1]-3, June 1977 - July 1978.

<u>Briefing</u>, Nos. 1-, 1972- to date (No. 547, November 1988) (information provided in sections 'National Press' and 'Parliamentary Briefing')

Occasional

<u>Report on the Quinquennium 1962-1967</u>. 1968. [The first quinquennium report to be issued by the CVCP]

<u>Report on the Period 1972-76</u>. 1976

<u>Research in Universities</u>. 1980

<u>Universities and Industry</u>. 1981

<u>Graduate Study in British Universities</u>. 1983

<u>Efficiency Studies in Universities: Report of the Steering Committee</u>, Chairman: Sir Alex Jarratt, April 1985

<u>Guidance on Recommended Accounting Practice in UK Universities</u>. April 1985.

<u>The Future of the Universities</u>, January 1986.
    (The CVCP's response to the Government's Green Paper on the Development of Higher Education into the 1990s).

<u>Academic Standards in Universities</u>, July 1986.
Report of the Committee on Academic Standards.
Chairman: Professor Philip Reynolds. Includes the following codes and papers:

-   Code of practice on the external examiner system for first degree and taught masters courses.

-   External involvement in the maintenance and monitoring of academic standards.

-   Code of practice on postgraduate training and research.

-   Code of practice on appeals procedures at postgraduate research degree level.

-   Universities' internal procedures for maintaining and monitoring academic standards.

Performance indicators in Universities: A First Statement of the joint CVCP/UGC working group, July 1986 (not printed).

The Universities Information Unit at the CVCP has published a series of booklets:-
(1) Universities Work for Industry (1986)
(2) Universities Work for Health (1987)
(3) Universities Work for Society n.d. [1988]
(4) Universities Work for Exports (1989)
(5) Universities Work for the Future (1989)

The Information Unit produces a brochure which lists publications available from it.

The Standing Conference on University Entrance has published the following publications, available from CVCP:

Thinking about University?, 1982 (Reprinted 1986). (Published by the CVCP for the Standing Conference on University Entrance).

A minimal core syllabus for A level mathematics, 1978.

A minimal core syllabus for A level chemistry, 1980

A minimal core syllabus for A level physics, 1980

Guidelines for written French at A level, 1986

Last four prepared jointly by SCUE and CNAA and published by CVCP. For SCUE publications see too entry on p.60.

Mature Students and Universities, 1984 (CVCP, UCCA, SCUE - available from UCCA).

University Entrance: Mature Students, 1990.

University Validation of Courses in the Polytechnics and Colleges Sector, 1990; report on the implementation of the CVCP Code of Practice of May 1987.

University Entrance: A Parent's Guide, 1990.

The CVCP Administrative Training Committee has published a number of publications, including the following, available from the Administrative Training Officer:

Information for University Adminstrators, 1982
Basic statistics and information about the British university system and related national and professional organisations.

Financial Arrangements for Universities, 1983

Handbook for University Administrators Involved in Medical Matters, n.d. [c.1983]

Records

(i)   The CVCP holds a full set of bound minutes from 1918 and, in addition, a volume of the minutes of meetings of Principals of University Colleges from 1897 to 1917. The latter meetings are known to have begun in 1884 but no earlier minutes have been located. Also held are papers dating from 1948 onwards.

        A 15 year access rule is applied, but the Committee is prepared to consider modifying this rule in individual cases.

(ii)   In view of the links between the CVCP and the ACU (see History above), earlier ACU records will include material also relating to the CVCP.

(iii)   Successive Chairmen of the Committee accumulate records which they house in their own offices or amongst their own papers, and it is their papers (held by individual universities) which, in some cases, might amplify records held centrally.

(iv)   SCUE retains extensive records and it is believed that access to them would be on the same basis as that to CVCP's own records (see (i) above).

THE COMPUTER BOARD FOR UNIVERSITIES AND RESEARCH COUNCILS

Address and
contact
The Computer Board for Universities and Research Councils,
Grove House
3rd floor,
Orange Street,
London
WC2H 7WE

tel: 071 321 0433
fax: 071 321 0528
Dr.E.J.Herbert, Secretary of the Board.

History

The Computer Board for Universities and Research Councils was set up in 1966 by the Secretary of State for Education and Science, as a result of recommendations made in the Report of the Joint Working Group on Computers for Research (commonly known as the Flowers Report). It began work in mid-1966. Its terms of reference are as follows:-

1.   To carry foward on the basis of planned development, allowing for modular growth and compatability, the proposals for providing computers for research in universities and research councils announced by the Secretary of State for Education and Science in the House of Commons on 21 December 1965 in the light of the report of the Joint Working Group on Computers for Research (the Flowers Report, Cmnd.2883).

2.   On the basis of a continuing review of needs to make recommendations to the Secretary of State in respect of the provision of computers in universities and to advise Research Councils on their computer proposals (including significant peripheral equipment, but excluding computers provided solely and essentially for the purpose of specific research projects).

3.   To satisfy itself that computers and equipment provided under the programme are effectively commissioned, adequately used, and effectively managed.

In 1970 these terms of reference were extended to cover the provision of computers for teaching purposes as well as for research as a result of the Government's acceptence of a recommendation in the report 'Teaching Computing in Universities'. The Board's terms of reference were further revised and expanded in 1986 to enable it to have the authority appropriate to its changing role and functions : they will allow it to develop its role in finding cost-effective solutions to the procurement, management and use of computing facilities in the academic community. The new terms of reference are published as Appendix VIII of the Board's Report for the period 1 April 1985 - 31 March 1988. The Board's primary concern is central computing facilities and associated software for research and teaching at universities in Great Britain; it fulfils a similar role with respect to the Department of Education in Northern Ireland in the case of Queen's University Belfast and the University of Ulster. It also advises the DES on computing expenditure for the Open University, the Royal College of Art, and Cranfield Institute of Technology. In 1989 the DES published a consultation paper on the future of the Board. The paper sets out proposals for (a) relocating the Board's Secretariat from London to Bristol, alongside the two higher education Funding Councils in 1991, and (b) establishing the Board's functions with a new executive character within the UFC.

The Board advises the DES on the purchase of computers for the computing centres in universities. While computers provided by the Board are used primarily for research, they are also increasingly used for teaching purposes. The DES allocates the funds for the Board's activities: in 1981-82 the Board's capital expenditure on computer purchase and rental for universities was £13.2m with recurrent expenditure by the Board of £14.4m in that year. In recent years the Board's programme of support for computer replacement at university sites, combined with the provision of additional facilities at national centres accessed via the Joint Academic Network (JANET), has enabled universities to share resources in a cost-effective way and, in particular, to obtain access to powerful supercomputing resources that it would be too expensive to provide at local sites. The Board operates a 7-year replacement cycle for university mainframe computers; this replaces a previous 10-year replacement cycle and 5-year mid-term enhancement programme. Nowadays all universities and a growing number of polytechnics are connected via JANET, as are the research institutes of AFRC, NERC, and SERC. In March 1987 the Board decided to establish a Combined Higher Education Software Team, initially based at the University of Bath, with responsibility for the central coordination and negotiation of software deals for most academic and research council institutions in the U.K.

In 1984 the UGC and the Computer Board for Universities and Research Councils established the Computers in Teaching Initiative (CTI) with the aims of encouraging the development of computer-asisted teaching and learning in UK universities; evaluating the educational potential of information technology at UK universities; and promoting an enhanced awareness of the potential of information technology among lecturers and students in all disciplines. In 1986 the Computers in Teaching Initiative Support Service (CTISS) was established as part of CTI; it is now based at the University of Oxford, 13, Banbury Road, Oxford, OX2 6NN. Under the auspices of CTI, 139 pilot projects on the use of computers in teaching had been established in British universities by April 1988. In April 1989 the first CTI Subject Centres, 21 in all (by February 1990), were established to provide specific and detailed support to potential users in their disciplines; the Centre for History has been established at the University of Glasgow. Each of the new Centres will be distributing its own newsletter. As part of its work in disseminating the results of CTI, CTISS publishes The CTISS File (Nos.1-, 1986-).

The Board's capital expenditure on computer purchase and rental for universities in 1978-79 amounted to some £9m (this total included building expenditure at the Board's national centres in London and Manchester). The total running costs of all central university machines and the major centres amounted to about £23m in 1978-79, the costs of the two national centres being met fully by the Board, while support for other university centres was shared between the Board and the UGC. The division of financial responsibilities for running costs between the Board and the UGC (now the UFC) has changed over the years: originally, the Board met all the additional running costs for new equipment it supplied during a quinquennium until the end of that quinquennium when responsibility was passed to the UGC. But from 1980-81 academic year onwards the Board has met the cost of maintenance, and the charges for communication links, while the UGC has assumed responsibility for staff and consumables. The Board now meets 80-85% of the cost of the two regional centres and about 40% of total running costs of university computing centres.

The Board is composed of a chairman and nine members, all of whom are academics except one who is drawn from industry or commerce. The Board is serviced by a Secretariat within the DES.

From 1 April 1991 the Computer Board will become the Information Systems Committee of the UFC; the Board will (as this Committee) continue to have largely the remit it does at present, with perhaps some extension of its activities to deal with all aspects of the electronic campus. The Board's offices are to be moved to a site at Bristol Polytechnic; at present this move is scheduled to take place in August 1991.

Bibliography
A report of a Joint Working Group on Computers for Research (Flowers Report), Cmnd.2883, 1966.

Ted Herbert, 'The Computer Board for Universities and Research Councils', The CTISS File, No.4, September 1987, p.6.

Sir Roger Elliott, 'Central Casting' in The Times Higher Education Supplement's Information Technology supplement, 18 March 1988, p.i (Sir Roger was Chairman of the Computer Board 1983-87 and his article surveys its achievements.)

Publications

(i)   Reports, published as Command Papers:

First Report, for period to 31 Oct. 1968 Cmnd.4006
Report for the period 1 Nov.1968   - 31 March 1970   Cmnd.4488
Report for the period 1 April 1970 - 31 March 1972   Cmnd.5220
Report for the period 1 April 1972 - 31 March 1974   Cmnd.5775
Report for the period 1 April 1974 - 31 March 1975   Cmnd.6221
Report for the period 1 April 1975 - 31 March 1976   Cmnd.6696
Report for the period 1 April 1976 - 31 March 1977   Cmnd.7322
Report for the period 1 April 1977 - 31 March 1979   Cmnd.7745
Report for the period 1 April 1979 - 31 March 1983   Cmnd.9215
Report for the period 1 April 1983 - 31 March 1985   Cmnd.9671
Report for the period 1 April 1985 - 31 March 1988   Cm.543

A report covering the period 1 April 1988 - 31 March 1991 will be the next report to be published in this series.

(ii)   In addition to the above reports, a small synopsis of the Board's activities for the year in question appears in each Annual Report of the DES.

Teaching Computing in Universities
(A Joint UGC/Computer Board Working Party Report), 1970.

Computers in Higher Education and Research: The Next Decade.
A discussion statement by the Computer Board, 1976.

Records

The papers of the Computer Board are public records, subject to the Public Records Acts and, like the DES, the Board endeavours to ensure that only those papers which have a need to be retained are sent to the Public Record Office.

The general guidelines in selecting papers for transfer to the PRO include the following types of record which are to be retained and transferred to the PRO:-

1. Principal policy papers, including those leading to legislation and to changes of policy.

2. Papers relating to the implementation of Board policy and to changes of policy.

3. Complete sets of minutes and papers for all Board Committees and working parties. Copies of annual and other reports.

4. Original papers relating to important scientific and technical research.

5. Papers relating to trends or developments in political, social, economic or other fields.

6. Unpublished statistical of financial data covering long periods or a wide area.

7. Papers which may be unique and have a special regional or other interest.

8. Papers with administrative value, i.e. those likely to have a direct bearing on future administrative action.

Under the terms of the '30 year rule' the first papers of the Board at the PRO will not be available for consultation until 1997.

CONFERENCE OF FINANCE OFFICERS

<u>Address and contact</u>
Mr. I. G. Thompson, I.P.F.A.,
Secretary of the Chest,
University of Oxford,
University Offices,
Wellington Square,
Oxford,
OX1 2JD.

tel: 0865 270151

<u>History</u>
The University Finance Officers Conference was established in c.1928, reference being made in its records to a Conference held on 24 March 1928, and the 1930 Conference is referred to in the minutes as the third annual conference. The earliest document in the file held by Mr. Thompson is the minutes of a meeting at Armstrong College, Newcastle upon Tyne on 23 March 1929. There were nineteen persons present from fourteen universities or colleges, including University College, Cardiff and the University College of Swansea from Wales and the Universities of Aberdeen and Glasgow from Scotland. Neither Oxford nor Cambridge was represented and no apologies for absence were recorded. At this 1929 meeting it is recorded that:-

'Discussions arose on the question of the Institutions to which invitations should be extended. It was felt that each institution - other than Medical Schools - making a Return to the University Grants Committee, should be invited to send a representative, and it was
RESOLVED - that invitations be sent to the following institutions:-

Birmingham University
Bristol University
Cambridge University
Durham University, Armstrong College
Durham University, Durham Colleges
Exeter University College
Leeds University
Liverpool University

London University
Bedford College
Birkbeck College
East London College
Imperial College
King's College
Royal Holloway College
School of Economics
School of Oriental Studies
University College
Westfield College
Manchester University
Nottingham University College
Oxford University
Reading University
Sheffield University
Southampton University College
University of Wales
Aberystwyth University College
Bangor University College
Cardiff University College
Swansea University College
Aberdeen University
Edinburgh University
Glasgow University

The objects and aims of the conferences were summarised in 1930 as:-

1. To bring the corresponding officers of the various Institutions into personal touch with each other that they may have an opportunity of discussing such matters as may be of common interest.

2. To exchange views on matters of College Accounting.

3. To discuss points arising out of the Annual Returns to the UGC with a view to obtaining uniformity under the various heads of such returns, as between Institutions.

Annual conferences were held from 1928-39, being organised by Mr. Ivor Fox, Bursar of the University of Bristol in collaboration with the host university. A conference planned for 1940 was cancelled and thereafter no conferences were held until 1952.

In 1952 the Bursar and Assistant Bursar of Leeds University offered to organise a conference, suggestions having been made that the annual conferences should be revived. A conference was held at Leeds in 1952 and one has been held annually since. It was agreed in 1952 that the organisation of the conference should be carried out by the Finance Officer of the host university. In 1959 membership of the conference was extended to include planning officers when they were not Bursars or Finance Officers. In 1960 a Conference of Finance Officers and Building Officers was held.

The conferences are held around Easter and the Finance Officer of the host university acts as convenor and as Chairman of the meetings. The Conference provides a venue for Finance Officers to discusss matters affecting the financial position of universities; to exchange information; and receive reports from members of the Conference who serve on committees whose work is of concern to the Conference (including the Senior Administrative Officers Consultative Committee and the VAT Committee of the CVCP and the Finance Group of USS). More recently the Conference has been attended by officers of the UGC and of the CVCP and the Chief Executive of USS. The 1986 Conference was held in Dublin, being hosted jointly between University and Trinity Colleges and the 1987 Conference was hosted by the University of Surrey.

Regional meetings of University Finance Officers are also held each year in the following areas: Scotland, Wales, North Eastern England, North Western England, the Midlands, and Southern England. These regional meetings submit items for the Finance Officers Conference, but items are also put forward to the Conference by individual Finance Officers.

Records

(i)   No central records are maintained, the Finance Officer of the host university being responsible for producing and circulating notes of the annual Conference.

(ii)   A continuous series of files from 1929 onwards is held at the University of Oxford, most of the files being in the University Archives. These files are consultable by arrangement with the Keeper of the Archives, University of Oxford. University records less than 30 years old are normally closed to public access. Mr. Thompson himself retains certain files relating to the Conference.
Even if anyone wanted to look at the files still held by the University Offices it would be best if they came through the Archives first. This of course only applies to UC/FF/319/1-8 and its successor files.

(iii)   The following is a list of the files of the CFO held by Oxford University Archives, Bodleian Library, Broad Street, Oxford, OX1 3BG:

UC/FF/319/1 Minutes of conferences, papers dealing with arrangements for conferences and texts of some lectures delivered at conferences, 1930-6.

UC/FF/319/2 Minutes of conferences, papers dealing with arrangements for conferences, memoranda by conferences, notebook on matters discussed at conferences, etc., 1937-40.

UC/FF/319/3 As 319/2 but minutes of more conferences, no notebook, reports by conferences on specific topics, etc., 1934-9.

UC/FF/319/4 Minutes of conferences, papers dealing with arrangements for conferences, papers and questionnaires prepared for conferences, correspondence and memoranda on further discussion of points raised at conferences, reports by conference working parties, etc., 1952-8.

UC/FF/319/5 As 319/4, 1959-62.

UC/FF/319/6 Papers and arrangements for meeting held at Oxford, 1960, 1959-60.

UC/FF/319/7 As 319/4, 1963-8.

UC/FF/319/8 As 319/4, 1969-72.

Subsequent files, and the series is still current, are held by the Filing Section, University Offices.

CONFERENCE OF TEACHERS OF REGIONAL
AND LOCAL HISTORY IN TERTIARY EDUCATION

<u>Address and</u>
<u>contact</u>
Dr. J.D. Marshall,
Chairman: CORAL,
Brynthwaite,
Charney Road,
Grange-over-Sands,
Cumbria,
LA11 6BP

<u>History</u>
The Conference of Teachers of Regional and Local History in Tertiary Education (CORAL) originated in 1978-79 as the Conference for Regional Historians. CORAL, as it quickly became, started life with about forty members from twenty-five institutions and since has grown three-fold; it has had between 110 and 140 members, nearly all teachers in tertiary education: representatives of history and other departments in colleges of higher education, universities, and polytechnics, concerned with the teaching of regional and local history to undergraduates, trainee teachers, and adult education students. About one half of CORAL members are university staff, but much of the pioneering work was done by polytechnic members.

The earliest highly organised discussion, mounted before CORAL's formal foundation, was on 'The Onset of Industrialisation in the Regions of England' and resulted in a published pamphlet. The three main objectives of CORAL, on its inception, were formulated as (a) the exploration of historical themes of common interest; (b) the dissemination and promotion of information regarding syllabus courses, research methods, and educational techniques; and (c) the promotion of common interests in a broad professional sense, and the arrangements for the representation of those interests on other and relevant bodies.

The activities of CORAL are threefold. It holds annual conferences on major themes in regional history; it regularly mounts seminars in different parts of the country on the use and scope of local sources; and it encourages the publication of academic papers in the <u>Journal of Regional and Local Studies</u> and of information and debate in its own <u>Newsletter</u> (which prior to the association with the <u>Journal</u> included full reports of CORAL conferences). CORAL's formal association with the <u>Journal</u> commenced in 1983; published twice yearly by the Humberside College of Higher Education (Inglemire Avenue, Hull, HU6 7LU), the journal has regularly published papers given at CORAL conferences, as well as reports of CORAL conferences and regular CORAL news (and a survey of the fifty or so courses in regional history run by CORAL members, 1985-86). The conferences feature a large number of papers (often pre-circulated) around the same theme; time during the conference is also devoted to classroom work and problems, and there is some field activity. Since 1979 seminars have been held in the Spring or Autumn, and have been concerned with sources commonly used by local historians and these sources' uses and limitations; some other seminars dealing with general-interest topics (including 'Local History and the Computer' and 'Publishing and the Local

Historian') have been and continue to be organised both in London and in the regions.

(This account is based on Dr. Marshall's published articles and on the detailed information he provided on the history, publications and records of CORAL.)

Bibliography

J.D. Marshall, 'The Evolution and Study of English Local History', in The Historian, No.1, Autumn 1983, pp.12-15.

J.D. Marshall, 'How Did CORAL Grow?', Local History, No.12, July/August 1986, pp.20-23.

'CORAL', The Historian (The magazine of the Historical Association), No.19, 1988, pp.30-31.

Publications

Under 'Annual Conference Papers of the Conference of Regional and Local Historians', these include:-

E.M. Sigsworth (ed.), Ports and Resorts in the Regions (Humberside College of Higher Education, 1981, pp.199, price £2.00)

A. Charlesworth (ed.), Rural Social Change and Conflicts Since 1500 (Humberside College of H.E., 1984, pp.124, price £4.00)

N. Alldridge (ed.), The Hearth Tax, Problems and Possibilities (Humberside College of H.E., 1985, price £4.00)

E. Royle (ed.), Religious Movements in the Regions of England (Humberside College of H.E., 1987, £5.00)

Patricia Hudson (ed.), Regions and Industries: A Perspective on the Industrial Revolution in Britain (Cambridge U.P., 1989).

Records

The minutes of the Conference have been kept at the Centre for N.W. Regional Studies, University of Lancaster, Bailrigg, Lancaster, which also holds a set of Newsletters, including some now scarce early newsletters issued prior to the formation of CORAL, and a number of other reports of the Conference - e.g. of a Working Party on Examinations in Local History (1981) - and Annual General Meeting reports. A.G.M. reports are also often given in the CORAL Newsletter, which has an ISSN Number 0262-7582. Further sets of newsletters are held at Wolverhampton Polytechnic. The newsletter was originally entitled the Regional History Newsletter.

Correspondence is also held by the Correspondence Secretary of CORAL and extensive files are at the Centre for N.W. Regional Studies, University of Lancaster.

Since 1986 the Newsletter has been produced by Mr. Philip Liddle, Bedford College of Higher Education, Polhill Avenue, Bedford.

CONFERENCE OF UNIVERSITY ADMINISTRATORS

Address and
contact
Mr.   Robert Ives,
Executive Secretary: CUA,
University of Manchester,
Oxford Road,
Manchester,
M13 9PL

tel: 061 275 2063

History

During the years 1961-73 Annual Conferences were organised by the Meeting of University Academic Administrative Staffs (MUAAS). At MUAAS' Conference in 1973 it was agreed to establish the Conference of University Administrators (CUA) in place of MUAAS. The first full CUA meeting took place at Southampton in April 1974.

In order to register the CUA as a charity, the 1984 AGM agreed to the dissolution of the CUA as presently constituted and to the formation of a new body with the same title and the same membership but with a revised constitution (inter alia changing the objects of the CUA slightly).   In July 1984 the CUA was officially registered as a charity.

The CUA exists for the public benefit to advance education by fostering the development of sound methods of administration of tertiary education in the University sector in the United Kingdom.

In furtherance of the above object but not otherwise CUA:

(a)   arranges an Annual Conference for the exchange of ideas in the development of the administration of tertiary education with particular reference to the University Sector;

(b)   provides a forum for discussion of current problems in tertiary education;

(c)   encourages the development of branches in individual institutions to act as a link between members and the central organisation of CUA;

(d)   issues publications from time to time in the furtherance of the objectives of the organisation;

(e)   facilitates the exchange of information on administrative activities;

(f)   establishes and maintains links with administrators in tertiary education overseas in order to further the interest of tertiary education internationally;

(g)   stimulates training activities both by provision of specific training opportunities and by the monitoring of the training programmes and policies of other organisations.

CUA's 1989 AGM confirmed various constitutional amendments, including a change in membership to reflect the decision to broaden the membership to include "members of staff of universities in the UK involved in the administration and management of tertiary education in the university sector."

The Executive Committee of the CUA carries out the policy as defined by the Annual General Meeting of the CUA; it has three sub-Committees: Conference Committee, Training Committee, and Publications Committee. The CUA's Overseas Liaison Sub-Committee, established in 1979, was in 1984 amalgamated with the International Committee of the Conference of Registrars and Secretaries (CRS) to form the International Committee of UK University Administrators. This Committee's terms of reference include the conduct of international relations on behalf of the CRS and the CUA, and the Committee reports annually to CUA and CRS. In January 1990 the Executive Committee took a step towards establishing a permanent CUA Office by appointing Mr. Robert Ives, recently retired Deputy Secretary (Services) at the University of Manchester, to the half-time post of Executive Secretary for three years from 1 March 1990. The duties of the Executive Secretary are to include responsibility for storing, selling and distributing CUA publications.

By the end of 1986-87 CUA membership had reached 1580: over 1500 CUA members in the universities, university colleges, and university - related organisations in the United Kingdom and Ireland and associate members in over 20 other countries. Membership of CUA is on a personal basis. Those eligible for full membership include members of staff of universities in the United Kingdom paid on the national salary structure for administrative staff, and members of staff who carry out administrative duties and who are paid on scales analogous to the administrative salary scales in a number of other institutions (Universities in the Irish Republic, University of Buckingham, Regional Management Service Units, UFC Secretariat, British Research Councils, ACU, CVCP, UCCA, USR, Examining Boards for the GCE, etc.). Associate membership may be extended, inter alia, to retired former members of CUA, administrative staff of universities outside the U.K. and the Irish Republic. Each institution with CUA members has a Branch Correspondent, elected by the CUA members for a period of three years. The duties of the Branch Correspondent include the circulation of the Newsletter and other publications of CUA and the recruitment of members to attend the Annual Conference (which is held at a different university each year).

CUA originated as an annual conference but nowadays CUA activities extend throughout the year. CUA has provided an aegis under which specialist groups have met to explore important topics in university administration, the resultant reports being published.

Bibliography
Geoffrey Lockwood, 'The Role of the Administrator', in The Times Higher Education Supplement, 11 April 1986, p. 17 (an account of the development of professionalism in university administration since the late 1950s with recommendations for further development in the light of the Jarratt Report.)

Stuart Bosworth, ed., Beyond the Limelight: Essays on the occasion of the silver jubilee of the Conference of University Administrators, CUA, 1986.
See particularly chapters 1 and 2 (pp.3-66) '1961-1973: A Time of Hope' by J.J.Walsh and 'To Plant Our Own Trees' by Emrys Wynn Jones.

Publications

The Publications Committee oversees the printing and publishing activities of the CUA. These include production of a <u>Newsletter</u> (Nos.1 - , August 1974- ; nowadays six issues a year); <u>Conference Proceedings</u> (for the years 1974 onwards; for years up to 1986 copies sent to those who attended the conference; copies of Conference Proceedings for 1987 and later years sent free to all CUA members); <u>Provisional Programme</u> for the Annual Conference (for the years 197? onwards); an information <u>Handbook</u> (an annual publication, issued for the years 1978 onwards until 1986 when it was replaced, for Session 1986-87 onwards, by a new booklet aimed mainly at "selling" CUA to potential new members); and <u>Membership Listing</u> (1986-87 onwards). Most recently (1986) the CUA launched a 'Good Practice' pamphlet series, those so far published being: (No.1) Frank Albrighton, <u>Can I Quote You On That?</u> (1986), (No.2) Grahame Kerr, <u>Managing People</u> (1987), (No.3) Peter Guildford and Harold Thomas, <u>The Art of Coarse Training</u> (1987), (No.4) Mike Joynson and John Wood, <u>This Committee Business</u> (1987), (No.5) Frank Albrighton, <u>Open Daze</u> [1989], (No.6) Judith Taylor and Celia Whitchurch, <u>Developing People</u>, n.d. [1989], and (No.7) Madeleine Jinkinson, <u>Interviewing People</u>, n.d. [1990]. A list of further topics which may be covered in this series is given in <u>CUA Newsletter</u>, No.63, March 1988, p.6.

In addition, the CUA has published over a dozen other reports and occasional papers, including:

<u>Forecasting and University Expansion: Interim and Final Reports of a CUA Working Group</u>, [1977 and 1978]

<u>Norms and Formulae in Resource Allocation</u>, by B.J.R. Taylor (Occasional Paper No.3), [? c.1979]

<u>Developments in Tertiary Education in Europe and the United Kingdom</u>, by R.M. Mawditt (published jointly with the AETA and the British Council), [? c.1980]

<u>Boosting University Income</u>, ed. by J.G. Kelly, 1984.

<u>Postgraduate Admissions</u>, ed. by J. Gaunt, 1984.

<u>The Modern Electronic Office</u> (Proceedings of the conference held at Aston University in September 1983) ed. by S.J. Laslett.

<u>University Administration in China</u> (Report of a study visit to China in 1982) published jointly with the Conference of Registrars and Secretaries, [?1983.]

<u>University Administration in North America</u> (A supplement to the 1979 Conference Proceedings), [?1980].

<u>Study Visit to the USA</u> (describing the visit of a CUA group in 1978) [1978.]

<u>Two European Universities</u> (A contrasting account of administrations of the Universities of Dijon and Munster) by A.J. Dale (CUA Occasional Paper No. 2), [? c.1978]

<u>Guide to the Organisation of Training Activities</u>, [? c.1983]

Administrative Staff Training: Qualifications and Training for University Administrators, 1985.

Universities and the Law, ed. Dennis Farrington and Frank Mattison, 1990. A major work from a joint CUA/CRS study group, the law is generally as stated on 1 April 1989 but the opportunity has been taken to discuss items of current interest up to 31 July 1989; it also considers the effect of the laws of Scotland and Northern Ireland where these differ from those of England and Wales.

Strategic Choice: Corporate Strategies for Change in Higher Education: Report by a CUA/APA Study Group, eds. Paul Temple and Celia Whitchurch, 1989.

Resource Allocation in British Universities, edited by Michael Shattock and Gwynneth Rigby, the report of the CUA Resource Allocation Group, was published in 1983 by the Society for Research into Higher Education, University of Surrey, Guildford, GU2 5XH. Copies may also be obtained from the CUA Publications Officer. The CUA Publications Officer also stocks copies of Professor W.A. Simpson, The 1981-84 Retrenchment of the British University System.

To celebrate the Silver Jubilee of CUA in 1986 a commemorative volume of essays, edited by Stuart Bosworth, was published by CUA and is obtainable from the CUA Publications Officer: see entry under Bibliography above.

Copies of publications still in print are available from the CUA Executive Secretary.

Records
The archive of the CUA contains papers and minutes of all CUA committees and sub-committees, its various publications (including Occasional Papers, Conference Proceedings, and Newsletter) and Conference literature (i.e. Provisional Programme and Conference Handbook). The archive is reasonably comprehensive. The archives of MUAAS, CUA's predecessor, have been deposited in the Manuscripts and Special Collections Department, the Brotherton Library, University of Leeds, and it has been proposed that CUA's own archives should also be deposited there. The CUA Archivist was the Secretary to the Executive Committee, but the archives of CUA are now the responsibility of the Executive Secretary.

CONFERENCE OF UNIVERSITY BUILDING OFFICERS

Address and
contact
Mr. Collin Ferguson,
Chairman: Conference of University Building Officers,
Estates Officer,
University of Warwick,
Coventry,
CV4 7AL

tel: 0203 523523

History

The Conference of University Building Officers was established in 1960 and provides the means whereby liaison between universities on building matters is effected; it also provides the opportunity for building officers to discuss the policies and procedures of the University Grants Committee with the UGC officers who are present.

Two conferences are held every year. The major conference is a two or three day residential conference held before Easter at a different university every year. The host university organizes this spring conference. The second conference is a half-day conference held at the University of London in September and arranged by the University's Court Department; in more recent years this conference has not been held every year but only when necessary (as when it met in 1985 to consider the Jarratt Report). This is a conference of an informal kind; it is held on the understanding that no minutes or other record will be circulated afterwards. The conferences discuss technical matters of common interest; representatives of the UGC (now the UFC) and CVCP attend to discuss the administative and financial problems of buildings administation and to assess the implications of UGC (now UFC) policies and procedures. The Conference acts as a clearing house for interpretation of new legislation affecting universities and innovations in building techniques and management measures such as energy conservation.

Bibliography

Dealing with issues of internal interest to universities, there is no published account of the Conference.

Publications

No journal is issued.

Records

As regards the spring conference, the host university organises it, issuing the agenda for it and the minutes of it. The records relating to such conferences might thus be expected to be kept by the host university; the Conference does not have a permanent Secretariat and has no central file of copies of the agenda and minutes of the spring conferences. The Steering Committee of this annual conference is composed of five persons, including the Chairman of the Conference and the Chairman of the previous year's conference.

The September conference is held on the understanding that no minutes or other record will be circulated afterwards. The only formal documents are a brief agenda listing the matters which Building Officers have suggested might be discussed, supported (in earlier years) by a short report by the officer of the CVCP in charge of their University Building Information Service (now no longer in existence), and a list of the building officers or their deputies attending the conference. The records of permanent value regarding these London conferences are held in the archives of the University of London.

CONFERENCE OF UNIVERSITY PERSONNEL ADMINISTRATORS

Address and
contact
Mr. R. F. Mackie,
Editor of CoUPA Yearbook,
Director of Personnel,
University of Edinburgh,
63, South Bridge,
Edinburgh,
EH1 1LS

tel: 031 667 1011 exts. 4510 - 4513

History

The Conference of University Personnel Administrators (CoUPA) meets over several days each year during September, and has done so since 1973. The main purpose of the Conference is to provide an opportunity for personnel administrators in universities to meet together to discuss current developments and other matters of mutual interest. Papers on all aspects of university and personnel management are presented for discussion by speakers from within and outwith the university system, representing national agencies, industry and commerce, trades unions, academic staff and, not least, the members of CoUPA itself.

The Conference is organised by rotation through the seven UCNS (Universities' Committee for Non-Teaching Staffs) regions, with one university carrying the burden for most aspects of organisation for that time, including accommodation, programme and entertainment. The first Conference was held at the University of Lancaster (23-25 September 1973). Subsequent Conferences have been held at universities and at a university college in England, Scotland, and Wales, with the 1986 Conference being held in Ireland, at Trinity College, Dublin (10-13 September). CoUPA is almost certainly unique within the university system in that it has neither committee nor office-bearers. Its only claim to corporate identity is a Yearbook listing all known practitioners within the university system in the British Isles. This is currently produced by Dick Mackie, Director of Personnel at Edinburgh University, who by default, thereby falls to act as the normal contact point!

Bibliography

It is believed that there is no published history of CoUPA.

Publications

Yearbook Currently issued at about two yearly intervals, the latest edition is that for 1988. In addition to listing all those university administrators and members of staff of the CVCP, UAP, UCNS, CCNTS, etc., who spend a substantial proportion of their time in personnel management, the Yearbook provides a 'Personal' section, recording retirements, appointments, etc. and a list of members of the UCNS Regional Groups and a chart indicating the relationship between the CVCP and the UAP etc., and their composition.

Records

There are no records of the meetings of CoUPA, at least not in the form of proceedings. One former member produced a brief report on one or two of the early conferences but their present location is not known.

The current Editor of the <u>Yearbook</u> has a copy of back issues and hopes at some stage to produce some additional copies of earlier issues to aid future historians.

CONFERENCE ON UNIVERSITY PURCHASING

<u>Address and</u>
<u>contact</u>
(for the 1991 Conference)
Mr. Martin Lightbown,
Purchasing Co-ordinator,
University of Nottingham,
University Park,
Nottingham,
NG7 2RE

tel: 0602 484848 ext.3310

<u>History</u>
The first Conference on University Purchasing (COUP) was held in 1976 at the University of Stirling and was organised by the Scottish Universities. Since 1977 university purchasing conferences have been held biennially and the venues have included Durham, Cardiff, London, and Edinburgh. COUP 87 (the seventh Conference) was held over three days at the University of Liverpool in September 1987 and attracted 250 delegates and over fifty exhibitors. COUP 91 will be held at the University of Nottingham and will be organised by the University's Purchasing Co-ordinator.

In its formative years COUP offered a meeting place for the exchange of information between delegate buyers and exhibition suppliers. There was soon a consensus amongst university supplies officers that more effective purchasing would be facilitated by concerted and continuing action to persuade the supply side to focus on the global universities' business for their sales and marketing strategies. University buyers were to develop joint initiatives via regional and subsequently national commodity purchasing groups to secure cost reductions. Each COUP event has promoted this activity, with an increasing range and number of companies participating in the conferences by their presence on the exhibition stands (a feature of COUP arrangements), and presenting papers at the plenary sessions and taking part in discussions. The last few conferences have been dominated by consideration of the further efforts required to respond to the financial retrenchment of universities and the efficiency studies carried out by the Jarratt Committee re-emphasised the need for universities increasingly to organise their buying power to secure maximum reductions in purchasing and supply costs. The flow of contract details and buyers guides throughout universities and associated colleges is being improved and extended, assisted by the biennial conferences. At the Conference held at the University of Liverpool in 1987 the exhibition included demonstrations of a computerised classification system for the detailed analysis of purchasing patterns developed by the N.E. Universities Management Services Unit and of the N.W. Universities' computerised buyers' guide.

Bibliography
[K.J. Fitzgerald], 'COUP 87 : Conference History and Exhibition Layout',
    University of Liverpool, 1987.

Records
Records of individual conferences might be expected to be kept by the host
university for each conference. COUP does not have a permanent secretariat.

See too pp.126 and 185

CONFERENCE OF UNIVERSITY REGISTRARS AND SECRETARIES

Address and
contact
Mr. Derek A. Schofield,
Business Secretary: Conference of University Registrars and
Secretaries,
Secretary and Registrar,
University of Southampton,
Highfield,
Southampton,
SO9 5NH

tel: 0703 595000
fax: 0703 593939

History
The Conference of University Registrars and Secretaries (CRS) was established
certainly by April 1954, when it met in Belfast. It acts as the co-ordinating
body for the Registrars and Secretaries of the universities of the United
Kingdom and as the formal channel of communication between Registrars and
Secretaries and the CVCP, the UAP, the UCNS, etc.

The full Conference meets annually at a different constituent university on
each occasion. Throughout the year much of the work of the Conference is
undertaken by five regional groups of Registrars - the North (which includes
Northern Ireland), the Midlands, the South, Scotland, and Wales - which
normally meet once a term. The Conference appoints annually a Steering
Committee, which is representative of the Regional Groups. Specialist Sub-
committees are appointed by the Conference, on the recommendation of the
Steering Committee, for specific purposes. A member of the Conference acts as
Business Secretary, normally for a period of two years.

In 1983 a joint CRS-CUA (Conference of University Administrators)
International Committee of U.K. university administrators was created, in
place of the CRS International Committee and the CUA Overseas Liaison
Committee; this joint committee presents an annual report to both the CUA and
the CRS.

Records
The Conference has not agreed any policy relating to the retention of its
papers, but so far as copies (to be found in individual universities) of the
Agenda papers for the Conference and the Minutes arising on the Annual Meeting
are concerned the Conference feels that they might by retained for a period of
ten years.

It is likely that in the next year or so the Conference will endeavour to establish a full record of its activities over the years, and centralise the keeping of Conference agenda, minutes, etc.

CONFERENCE OF UNIVERSITY TEACHERS OF GERMAN IN GREAT BRITAIN AND IRELAND

Address and
contact
Dr. John L. Flood,
Joint Honorary Secretary: Conference of University
Teachers of German in Great Britain and Ireland,
Institute of Germanic Studies,
University of London,
29, Russell Square,
London,
WC1B 5DP

tel: 071 580 2711 & 071 580 3480

History
The Conference of University Teachers of German in Great Britain and Ireland was founded in 1932 and has convened annually ever since. Membership is available automatically to all full-time teachers of German in British and Irish universities. In addition, university teachers of related subjects (such as Dutch, Scandinavian Studies, Linguistics, and Educational Studies) and full-time teachers of German in polytechnics and other institutions of higher education are admitted to associate membership on application.

Bibliography
A history of German Studies in the British Isles, sponsored by the Conference, is in preparation.

The University Archives, Liverpool, holds the manuscripts of several unpublished essays by Professor W.E. Collinson (Professor of German, University of Liverpool, 1914-54), including one on German Studies at University College London and another on the Department of German in Liverpool, ref. D.5/2 and 4 respectively.

Publications
Regular newsletters (issued to members only)

Research in Germanic Studies (annually; issued free to members and also available for purchase to non-members)

Bulletin of Work in Progress (biennially; issued to members only)

German Language from School to University (2nd ed., 1980)

Records
(a)   Many of the papers of the Conference are held by the officers.

(b)   Other papers of the Conference are deposited at the Institute of Germanic Studies (address as above) as part of a collection relating to the history of German Studies in the United Kingdom. Access to the archive is restricted and persons desiring access should apply in writing to Dr. Flood (address as above).

(c)   It should be noted that, apart from the Conference's papers, the Institute of Germanic Studies' collections of archives (mainly correspondence) include the Majut, Bithell, and Breul correspondence, of interest to those working on the history of Germanic studies in the Universities of Leicester, London, and Cambridge respectively. Access is restricted to these collections and persons desiring access should apply in writing to Dr. Flood in his capacity as Deputy Director of the Institute.

CONGRESS OF UNIVERSITY CONVOCATIONS
AND GRADUATE ASSOCIATIONS

Address and
contact
Dr. H.M.Longbottom,
Secretary: Congress of University Convocations and Graduate Associations,
5, Lindsay Avenue,
West Point,
Manchester,
M19 2AR
tel: 061 224 9960

History
The Joint Steering Committee of Convocation (as the Conference of University Convocations was entitled until 1950) was established in July 1918 at a meeting at Manchester of representatives of the 'Combined English Universities Constituency', that is the Universities of Birmingham, Bristol, Durham, Leeds, Liverpool, Manchester, and Sheffield which were provided with two Members of Parliament under the Representation of the People Act, 1918 (7 & 8 Geo. 5 c.64) (the other University Constituencies provided by this Act were: the Universities of Oxford and Cambridge, with two M.P.s each, the Universities of London and Wales with one M.P. each, and the Universities of Aberdeen, St. Andrews, Edinburgh, and Glasgow with three M.P.s between them.) The Committee was intended to be strictly non-political and non-partisan. Its principal business was the selection of candidates for the combined universities constituency, but it also discussed such subjects as the training of graduates; the value of degrees; the employment of graduates; the participation of graduates in university affairs, in industry, in education, and in the Civil Service; student problems, the welfare and accommodation of students; university entrance requirements, etc.

In 1948 the university parliamentary franchise was abolished upon the repeal of most of the Representation of the People Act, 1918, under the Representation of the People Act, 1948. In 1950 the Joint Standing Committee became the Conference of University Convocations (CUC) "to sustain the position of Convocations as continuing independent but constituent parts of their universities and to foster the development and use of the graduate body as a source of informed opinion, reference and advice for the support and enhancement of universities,their graduates and the community at large." In July 1989 the CUC was reconstituted with effect from 1 September 1989, the Conference becoming the Congress of University Convocations and Graduate

Associations in name and function. It is non-party-political and encourages and facilitates communication and collaboration between its members and with other organisations with similar interests.

The Conference (now the Congress) assembles in plenary session normally once a year during the Easter Vacation, for two or three days, at one of the member universities. The main theme and arrangements for the Annual Conference (now entitled the Annual Assembly) are the responsibility of the host university, aided and advised by the CUC's officers. Recent subjects for consideration at the Annual Conference have included Adult and Continuing Education; Universities, Industry, and Commerce; Overseas Students; University Finance; and Universities within Society. A particular concern and achievement of CUC over recent years has been to advise and support the emerging Convocations of some of the newer universities. In 1981 CUC made a well organised protest at the Government's financial cuts as they effected universities and, as an independent body acting in support of the universities, CUC has made a number of representations including a submission to the UGC in 1983 in response to a UGC questionnaire (which resulted in the UGC's advisory report, A Strategy for Higher Education into the 1990s, H.M.S.O., 1984.) In 1987 CUC published an influential report, In Support of Higher Education, which was produced by a working party which consulted the AUT, NATFHE, NUS, CVCP, SCOEG (now AGR), CUA, and SCUI0. In common with these other organizations, this report stresses the need for higher education to respond both to student demand and to the demand for graduates from employers and also the need for urgent attention to be given to the funding of higher education institutions and to students. It endorses the target of 600,000 full-time and sandwich students in higher education by 1990. In adapting the report the CUC invited all the bodies concerned with higher education to join it in a conference to agree a basic statement of common cause free from sectional interest which would be presented to the Government, all the political parties, and the educational press. CUC has set up two special committees: an Internal Affairs Committee and a Standing Committee on Education (which is approaching the task of organising nationally the defence of higher education). The theme of CUC's meeting in April 1988 was 'Uncertainty in Higher Education'.

Membership of the CUC was originally open to the convocations (or any duly incorporated similar body) of every university in the United Kingdom. However, not all universities had incorporated a graduate body (e.g. the University of Sussex) and so in 1980 the constitution of CUC was revised to admit a recognised graduate body where there is not strictly a convocation. In the past some graduate organisations have been associated with the CUC less formally than by full membership. At present (1987) there are twenty five members of CUC, including Cranfield Institute of Technology and the University of Dundee (which is acting to represent the Scottish universities). The Universities of Oxford and Cambridge have never yet been members.

(This account is largely based on K.W.Allen's account: see Publications below)

Publications
K.W.Allen, Conference of University Convocations, n.d. [1986]. This account of the objectives, functions and history of the CUC, includes a list of U.K. universities (with an indication which are members of CUC) and a list of the venues of each Annual Conference, together with the names of the President, the Secretary, and the Treasurer of the CUC, for 1952-86.

Records

(i) As regards records of the Combined English Universities Constituency:

   (a) Sheffield University Archives hold some papers comprising correspondence, including election addresses and official papers for elections and by-elections 1918-46.

   (b) Liverpool University Archives hold lists of electors for the University 1918-45 and a Parliamentary Registration Receipt Book 1928-47; Liverpool University : Special Collections Department of Sydney Jones Library holds correspondence etc. of Miss Eleanor Rathbone (M.P. for the Combined English Universities, 1929-46).

(ii) As regards records of CUC, Mr. K.W. Allen (Clerk to Convocation, The City University Convocation, Northampton Square, London, EC1V 0HB and, over the period 1972-81, Treasurer of the CUC) states that they are very scanty. Over the past few years in a personal capacity he has been trying to gather together what records he can find, depositing them in the University of Reading's Library, Whiteknights, Reading, RG6 2AE. These deposited records include the Minute Book of the Joint Standing Committee of Convocations 1918-56, Minute Book of JSCC Executive Committee 1929-68, Conference papers 1971-80, Reports and papers relating to conference themes 1970-81, Hon. Treasurer's Bank Account Book 1952-70 and Cash Book 1952-68, Balance sheets 1945-66, and miscellaneous papers 1960s-80s (including further Hon. Treasurer's records).

Dr. Longbottom states that all the records of CUC prior to his becoming Secretary in 1983 were deposited with the University of Reading.

Mr. Allen has personal copies of minutes and some other papers of CUC going back to c.1955 when he personally first became involved in CUC.

It is possible that there may be records throwing light on CUC's history amongst the records of the original members. In the case of the University of Liverpool's Convocation, the Convocation records in the custody of the University Archives (Standing Committee: Minutes 1906-27, Agendas and Reports 1907 - to date; Register of Members [c.1905-c.1919]; Receipt Book 1918-48) make the occasional reference to CUC.

CO-ORDINATING COMMITTEE FOR THE TRAINING OF UNIVERSITY TEACHERS

Address and
contact
Dr. Christopher C. Matheson,
Dean of Students,
University of East Anglia,
Norwich,
NR4 7TJ.

tel: 0603 56161 ext.2492.

History

The Co-ordinating Committee for the Training of University Teachers (CCTUT) was established by the CVCP in February 1972 to keep the training needs of university teachers under continuous review. The formal terms of reference of the Committee were:

1. to keep the training needs of university teachers under continuous review;

2. to keep itself informed about current provision for the training of university teachers;

3. to assess the need for additional courses to be provided on a regional or national basis;

4. to encourage the development of such courses at suitable centres;

5. to disseminate information about the availability of courses; and

6. to offer advice to universities on the principles on which their own internal training arrangements might be drawn up.

These terms of reference enabled the Committee to engage in a variety of activities at local, regional, national, and international level. A fundamental element of CCTUT's work was reviewing training needs and collecting and disseminating information about training provisions. CCTUT also devoted much of its effort to advising universities on their own training, by visits of the Committee's successive Co-ordinating Officers to universities and by means of publications, conferences and workshops.

The Committee's membership was drawn from nominees of the CVCP, the AUT, the NUS, and the UGC. Until August 1973 the Committee was serviced by the Secretariat of CVCP, thereafter by the two successive Co-ordinating Officers (Mr. A. Main of the University of Strathclyde 1973-76, Dr. C. C. Matheson of the University of East Anglia 1976-81, both on temporary secondment from their university posts). The Committee's office was located at the university of its Co-ordinating Officer.

In the context of the development by individual universities of their own training arrangements and in the light of the report of a Review Group chaired by Sir Harry Pitt and reactions to the same, the CVCP decided in 1980 to phase out CCTUT, withdrawing financial support as from 1 August 1981. CCTUT itself ceased to exist on 31 July 1981. CVCP felt that the organisation of training activities could more effectively be carried out by universities on a local or regional basis but, to encourage liaison arrangements, CVCP established, as from the beginning of the 1981-82 session, a new Committee on the Training of University Teachers (CTUT) 'to meet from time to time to review the current provision for the training of university teachers and to ensure that universities were made aware of this provision'.

Membership of CTUT is drawn from nominees of CVCP, AUT, and NUS; CTUT is serviced by the Secretariat of CVCP.

Bibliography
Christopher C. Matheson, Staff Development Matters: Academic Staff Training and Development in Universities of the United Kingdom, A Review: 1961-1981, CCTUT, 1981. (See particularly Chapters 5 and 6 for an account of CCTUT's work).

Publications (see too above).
Impetus (journal) Nos. 1-11, Feb. 1975-March 1979.

Nexus (disseminator of information about conferences, etc. and CCTUT activities) Nos. 1-10, June 1977-July 1981.

A. N. Main, The Training of University Teachers in the United Kingdom: Problems and Prospects, June 1975.

CCTUT Occasional Publication: No.1 D. Mack, The Workshop Way, 1979. (Report on CCTUT's national conference, Stirling, 1978).
[No later numbers were published]

Records
The archives and copies of CCTUT publications have not been deposited with any library or university archives.

The CVCP should have a full set of publications, whilst Dr. Matheson retains his own full set. CVCP also have a full set of Committee minutes. Dr. Matheson retains all the Committee's working files.

COUNCIL OF MILITARY EDUCATION COMMITTEES OF THE UNIVERSITIES OF THE UNITED KINGDOM

Address and
contact
Commander J.F.W.Exworthy, R.N. (Retired),
Secretary: Council of Military Education Committees,
Careers Advisory Service,
University of Southampton,
Highfield,
Southampton,
SO9 5NH

tel: 0703 592824

History
The Central Organisation of Military Education Committees of the Universities and University Colleges was set up in September 1919 following a conference of representatives of Military Education Committees of universities. (Military Education Committees (MECs) owe their origin to the requirement of the then War Office when the Officers Training Corps (OTC) was founded in 1908, it being stipulated that any university wishing to furnish a contingent of the OTC must have a Committee of Military Education appointed by the university.) Apart from minor changes in name, to take account of the granting of charters to former university colleges, and in its terms of reference, the Central Organisation remained substantially as founded until 1970 when the name was changed to Council of Military Education Committees of the Universities of the United Kingdom in order clearly to express the fact that it was not an organisation with an executive role but rather an advisory and co-ordinating body. Provision was also made in 1970 for the representation of universities and other institutions of higher education not furnishing Service Units.

The terms of reference of COMEC are:-

a.   to consider matters of policy covering the units of the Armed Services within the universities and to advise the Ministry of Defence and the universities thereon.

b.   to assist in the co-ordination of the work of the universities and such other institutions of higher education as may be nominated for membership, in defence studies.

c.   to facilitate such systematic instruction and training of candidates for commissions in the Armed Services as may be required by the Ministry of Defence.

d.   to promote for these purposes the co-operation of the universities and other institutions of higher education with the Ministry of Defence.

COMEC also seeks to maintain a close liaison with other appropriate bodies.

The membership of COMEC includes not only the constituent MECs (represented at meetings by the chairman or his deputy and two non-Service members) but also the senior officers of the three Services responsible for the university service units and the appropriate officials in the Ministry of Defence. The Council normally meets once a year. The Executive Committee of COMEC, consisting of the officers and eight elected members, normally meets three times a year. The working expenses of COMEC are defrayed by an annual subscription payable by each constituent university within a MEC.

Bibliography
M.N. Naylor, <u>Council of Military Education Committees of the Universities of the United Kingdom : Notes for Guidance</u>, April 1985 (includes historical background, on which the above history is based, recommended terms of reference for MECs and suggested rules of University Royal Naval Units, University OTCs, and University Air Squadrons.)

Records
The Secretary of the CMEC retains records going back to 1919, including the minutes of the annual meeting of the Council.

COUNCIL FOR NATIONAL ACADEMIC AWARDS

Address and
contact
Council for National Academic Awards,
344-354, Gray's Inn Road,
London,
WC1X 8BP

tel: 071 278 4411/2/3/4/5
fax: 071 833 1012
Mrs. Rosemary Mayes, Head of Documentation and Membership
Christine Jamieson, Publications Officer

History

The Council for National Academic Awards (CNAA), is the largest single degree-awarding body in the United Kingdom. An autonomous body, unique in British higher education, the CNAA was established by Royal Charter in September 1964 to replace the former National Council for Technological Awards, itself set up by the Minister of Education in 1955. It is empowered to award degrees, diplomas, certificates, and other academic awards to students who have successfully completed approved courses of study or research at institutions in the United Kingdom, other than universities, which have been approved by the Council.It is financially self-supporting. Council members are appointed by the Secretaries of State for Education and Science and for Scotland. In 1978-79 it employed 121 persons.

In September 1974 the CNAA merged with the former National Council for Diplomas in Art and Design (set up by the Ministry of Education in 1961), and in September 1976 it accepted responsibility for the postgraduate award of the Diploma in Management Studies from the Committee for the Diploma in Management Studies in England, Wales, and Northern Ireland and the Scottish Joint Committee for Diplomas in Management Studies. In 1986 the Secretaries of State for Education and Science and for Scotland decided to reject the central recommendation of a committee which had been established under the chairmanship of Sir Norman Lindop, to investigate public sector degree standards and validation, and to leave all polytechnic and degree validation under the control of the CNAA.

In the last few years, the Council has been revising its role to enable it to delegate more responsibility for course validation, review and approval to some polytechnics and colleges. In 1987, after extensive consultation, the Council's charter and statutes were changed to enable the Council to introduce a system of 'accreditation', and the first 21 institutions were accredited by CNAA from April 1988. By 1989, it is expected that the institutions educating some 80 per cent of all students on CNAA-approved courses will be accredited by the Council.

Accredited institutions have authority to validate, monitor, review and approve new taught degree, certificate and diploma courses on the Council's behalf, and to modify existing courses. In other institutions associated with the CNAA, the Council retains responsibility for the final approval of all courses. All awards, in both accredited and associated institutions, are made by CNAA under the provisions of its royal charter, and the academic standards required are the same under both forms of relationship.

The Council works through a system of 'peer review', whereby academics, industrialists and professional and other independent experts scrutinise course proposals submitted to the Council by polytechnics, institutes and colleges and decide whether they can be approved by the CNAA.

Bibliography

Michael Lane, Design for Degrees: New Degree Courses under the CNAA - 1964-1974, Macmillan Press, 1975; describes the establishment and development of CNAA 1964-74.

The Council: Its place in British Higher Education, CNAA, London, 1979.

Alan Matterson, <u>Polytechnics and Colleges</u>, Longman, 1981; includes a chapter on higher education in England and Wales and otherwise places public sector higher education in a broad national context.

<u>Work of the Council</u>, CNAA, London, 1982; a booklet for members of the Council's Committees, Boards and Panels.

Martin Davis, 'Prelude to partnership: the CNAA and the polytechnics 1964-74', in <u>Higher Education Review</u>, Vol.13 No.2, Spring 1981, pp.22-37. (A more extensive assessment of the CNAA's development may be found in Martin Davis' unpublished Loughborough University doctoral thesis, 'The development of the CNAA 1964-1974: a study of a validating agency'.

<u>Academic Validation in Public Sector Higher Education: The Report of the Committee of Enquiry into the Academic Validation of Degree Courses in Public Section (sic) Higher Education</u> (Chairman: Sir Norman Lindop), Cmnd. 9501, HMSO, 1985.

Robert Strand, <u>A Good Deal of Freedom: Art and Design in the Public Sector of Higher Education, 1960-82</u>, CNAA, London, 1987.

<u>The work of the Council</u> [for National Academic Awards], CNAA, London, 1988 (descriptive leaflet)

<u>The Times Higher Education Supplement</u> includes the occasional article about the CNAA, e.g. that on management education and the CNAA, 'On-site training', by CNAA's Chief Executive, in the 10 March 1989 issue.

Publications
A list of current CNAA publications is available on request from the CNAA Publications Unit. A full list of all documents issued, including regulations, statements, circulars, conference reports and responses to government consultations, is also produced.

CNAA's regular and other publications include:-

<u>Annual Reports</u>, 1964/65 - to date (those for 1964/65 - 1974/75 inclusive are now out of print; those for 1976 onwards are still available).

<u>Handbook of CNAA's policy and regulations</u>, 1983 (1st edition) (copies from 1984 are available)

<u>CNAA Higher Education News</u> (published three times a year), 1987-to date; serves as a public relations medium for CNAA.

<u>CNAA Information Services Digest</u> (published three times a year), 1988-to date; concerned with higher education in general.

<u>Compendium of Degree Courses</u> 1970-74 (annual)

<u>Directory of First Degree Courses in Art and Design</u>, 1974

<u>Directory of First Degree Courses</u>,1975-78 (annual), and 1978/79

Directory of First Degree and Diploma of Higher Education Courses, now entitled Directory of first degree and undergraduate courses, 1979/80 - to date (annual) (1983/84 being published in October 1983) (copies from 1983-84 available)

Directory of Postgraduate Courses, 1976, and 1977/78

Directory of Postgraduate and Post-Experience Courses, 1978/79 - to date (annual) (1983/84 being published in October 1983) (copies from 1983-84 available)

Records
(i)   The Council maintains a central filing area in which are kept complete records, either on paper or on microfiche, of all course submissions from Institutions including approval documents and associated reports and correspondence; and complete sets of committee papers and institutional review documents and reports.

Access to the Council's files is granted for bona fide research subject to agreement on the purposes of the research and confidentiality. The Council's statement on 'Principles for Access to the Council's Files' provides details; the agreement of institutions is required before their files can be accessed.

(ii)   The Kew branch of the Public Record Office holds the following records of CNAA:-

DB1 National Council for Technological Awards: minutes of the Council, the Governing Body, Executive Committee, Joint Standing Committee of the Boards of Studies, Boards of Studies, Higher Awards Committee, and other Boards and panels; also NCTA's reports, 1955-64.

DB2 CNAA: Annual Reports for 1964-65 to 1987-88.

DB3 CNAA: minutes of Council, committees, boards, working parties, panels, and sub-committees, 1964-80.

DB4 National Council for Diplomas in Art and Design : minutes of Council, committees, panels, and consultative meetings, 1961-74.

DB1,2 and 4 are open without restriction.

See the PRO's lists for fuller details of the above.

Papers about CNAA's establishment are to be found in UGC 7/934.

DATA PROCESSING OFFICERS' CONFERENCE

Address and
contact
Mrs. R.S. Gilmore,
Hon. Secretary: Data Processing Officers' Conference,
Director of Management Information Services,
University of Warwick,
Coventry,
CV4 7AL

tel: 0203 523523

History

In the early 1960s only a few United Kingdom universities used computers for administrative purposes. Nowadays practically all have data processing sections within their administrations. Since 1971 the senior staff responsible for the data processing function in each institution, the Data Processing Officers (DPO), together with representatives from UCCA, USR, UGC (now UFC), and CVCP, have met annually at the DPO Conference. The first conference, in 1971, was at Brunel University, under the chairmanship of Mr. (now Professor) R.W. Ewart, of The Queen's University of Belfast.

The annual conference is normally held in early January and provides a forum for the study of developments in data processing systems for student and financial administration, personnel and buildings records, etc., and their related computer hardware and software. In addition, there are two working groups which meet to discuss common technical matters. Recent co-operative work has been in on-line systems, use of microcomputers, and the whole field of office automation. Technical seminars are also occasionally organized.
Until the Lancaster conference in April 1975, secretarial duties were performed by the host university member. Mr. J.C. Fox (Data Processing Officer, University of Lancaster) was elected Secretary and held the post since this 1975 conference until the late 1980s. The current Chairman is Mr. Alan Todd of the Management Information Services Division, University of Birmingham; his predecessors include Mr. R.W.Prince of the University of Edinburgh (July 1976 - September 1977), Mr. A.F.Angus of the University of London (September 1977 - January 1979), and Mr. J.J. McCloy of The Queen's University of Belfast (January 1979-late 1980s).

Bibliography
None known

Publications
None known

Records
The Hon. Secretary retains copies of the minutes from 1975 onwards. They may be consulted, if of interest, at any time.

THE ECONOMIC AND SOCIAL RESEARCH COUNCIL

Address and
contact
The Economic and Social Research Council,
Cherry Orchard East,
Kembrey Park,
Swindon,
SN2 6UQ

tel: 0793 513838
fax: 0793 487916
Mr. Christopher Caswill, Second Secretary (Research)

History
The Economic and Social Research Council (ESRC) was established in 1965 as the Social Science Research Council (SSRC) by Royal Charter, upon the recommendation of the Heyworth Committee on Social Studies which reported in 1965 (Cmnd.2660). The Clapham Committee had, in 1946, considered the establishment of a Social Science Research Council (Report of the Committee on the Provision for Social and Economic Research: Cmd.6868). The Royal Charter, granted on 29 October 1965, was amended on 20 June 1973. In November 1983 the Privy Council agreed to the Council's request to change its title to the Economic and Social Research Council (ESRC) as from 3 January 1984.

The objectives of the Council remain as defined in the Royal Charter:
"(a) to encourage and support by any means research in the social sciences by any other person or body;

(b) without prejudice to the foregoing paragraph, to provide and operate services for common use in carrying on such research;

(c) to carry out research in the social sciences;

(d) to make grants to students for postgraduate instruction in the social sciences;

(e) to provide advice and to disseminate knowledge concerning the social sciences."

The ESRC is one of the largest sources of funds in the UK for research and training in the social sciences. The social sciences are concerned with the study of human behaviour and of man in society in many different aspects: psychological, sociological, economic, and political.

The Council itself consists of the Chairman and not more than nineteen and not less than thirteen members. It meets three times a year. The ESRC as at 1st January 1982 had some seventy committees, steering committees, sub-committees, panels, boards, and working groups; there are seven Standing Committees, also committees on International Affairs, Postgraduate Training (jointly with the Science and Engineering Research Council), Information, Finance and General Purposes, and Research Resources and Methods. More recently, its subject committees were replaced by six multi-disciplinary committees dealing with support for research and training within policy-related areas: Social Affairs, Education and Human Development, Economic

Affairs, Industry and Employment, Government and Law, and Environment and Planning. The structure and procedures of the Council were again changed with effect from September 1987 whereby the Council's committee structure was replaced by a Training Board, a Research Grants Board, and three new Research Development Groups (as the Subjects Committees are now entitled): Human Behaviour and Development RDG; Society and Politics RDG; and Industry, the Economy and the Environment RDG. In addition, a small Advisory Group on Research Resources was established. The Council derives its funds mainly by a grant-in-aid from the DES, although it also receives funds for the support of social science research from other government departments and from foundations. In 1978-79 ESRC employed 208 staff and was responsible for £16m expenditure. The ESRC's 1988/89 budget is £27.7m, of which £16.17m supports a wide programme of research and £7.47m is committed to the support of postgraduate training in the social sciences.

In 1982-83 nearly half the ESRC's annual grant-in-aid was devoted to postgraduate training in the social sciences. The remainder was largely used for research initiatives (usually in areas of public policy), research grants to universities, polytechnics, and recognised research institutes, including the financing of four university-based Research Units (set up for ten year periods) and seven Designated Research Centres (funded for eight year periods and located at universities and other academic institutions). These Units and Designated Research Centres were concerned with areas of social science research such as industrial relations, urban and regional development, and ethnic relations.

In 1983 these Research Units comprised the Cambridge Group for the History of Population and Social Structure (University of Cambridge), the Centre for Socio-Legal Studies (Wolfson College, University of Oxford), the Industrial Relations Research Unit (University of Warwick), and the Research Unit on Ethnic Relations (University of Aston in Birmingham). ESRC and the MRC jointly financed the Social and Applied Psychology Unit at the University of Sheffield. In 1983 the Designated Research Centres comprised the Centre for Labour Economics (London School of Economics), the Centre for Population Studies (London School of Hygiene and Tropical Medicine), Centre for Urban and Regional Development Studies (University of Newcastle upon Tyne), Centre in Comparative Industrial Structure and Efficiency (National Institute of Economic and Social Research), Survey Methods Centre (a division of Social and Community Planning Research), Thomas Coram Research Unit (University of London Institute of Education), and Centre in Health Economics (at the Institute of Research in the Social Sciences, University of York). Almost all of these Units and Centres are still (1988-89) in existence, funded by ESRC; ESRC's Annual Report for 1988-89 lists the 19 'research centres' which the Council was then supporting. As centres' Council funding comes to an end they will henceforth be invited to participate with other applicants in an annual competition for funding, the first competition taking place in autumn 1989; each new centre is to receive financial support from ESRC for ten years, subject to a satisfactory mid-term review.

Mention should also be made of the ESRC Data Archive, a ESRC Research Centre. Established in 1967 at the University of Essex, Colchester, the primary objectives of the Data Archive (which is very largely funded by the ESRC) are the acquisition, storage, and dissemination of computer-readable copies of social science data sets for further analysis by researchers. The Data Archive is Britain's largest repository of machine-readable survey data (holding as it does some 2500 data files) and in particular contains a large number of holdings in the fields of political science, sociology, education, social administration and planning. The majority of surveys available relate to post-war Britain, or to Britain in a comparative context; they include the 'classical' academic studies as well as more recent major academic surveys, and commercial surveys of interest to social scientists (e.g. the regular opinion polls). The Archive contains large holdings of Government-sponsored surveys, including the Family Expenditure Surveys, the General Household Surveys and the 1981, 1971, and 1966 Census ward library data. The Data Archive's publications include a <u>Data Catalogue</u> (2 vols., hardback and paperback, 1986; available for purchase from Chadwyck Healey, Cambridge or for reference in most research-oriented libraries) and the <u>Data Archive Bulletin</u> (published three times a year and available free of charge to interested individuals or institutions). The Bulletin includes details of new acquisitions to the Archive. Data-sets are listed in category order, using the classification system employed in the Data Catalogue: this system includes the following categories:-

VI B. Higher Education (with subsections 1. General 2.Satisfaction and Choice, 3. Student Life and Values, and 4. Career Aspirations and Achievement); VI C. Further and Adult Education; VI D. The Teaching Profession (1. General; 2. Recruitment, Training and Career Aspirations); X. Health, Health Services and Medical Care; XXV. Science and Technology.

In response to a recommendation from the ABRC, etc., the ESRC in early 1988 decided to move its offices from London to Swindon, to share an office block with the SERC. It moved to temporary buildings in Swindon later in 1988, pending the completion of permanent premises in 1990-91.

Bibliography
<u>Advisory Board for the Research Councils: Report of the Working Party on Postgraduate Education</u> (the Swinnerton-Dyer Report), Cmnd.8537, H.M.S.O., April 1982.

<u>An Enquiry into the Social Science Research Council by Lord Rothschild</u>,Cmnd.8554, H.M.S.O., May 1982.

<u>Advisory Board for the Research Councils/University Grants Committee: Report of a Joint Working Party on the Support of University Scientific Research</u> (the Merrison Report), Cmnd.8567, H.M.S.O., June 1982.

<u>The Structure of the Economic and Social Research Council 1988</u>, ESRC, [1987] (details the responsibilities, remits and memberships of the Council's Boards and Groups.)

Cyril S. Smith and Otto N. Larsen, 'The Criterion of "Relevance" in the Support of Research in the Social Sciences: 1965-1985', <u>Minerva: A Review of Science, Learning and Policy</u>, Vol.27 No.4, 1989, pp.461-482. (Mr. Smith was Secretary of the SSRC/ESRC 1975-85.)

It should be noted that most books and journal articles describing or assessing the social sciences in the United Kingdom during the last 20 or so years have some reference to the Council and its work. A recent and important example is Martin Bulmer (ed.), <u>Social Science Research and Government: comparative essays on Britain and the United States</u> (Cambridge U.P., 1987) which includes a chapter on the ESRC. Likewise <u>The Times Higher Education Supplement</u> reports upon developments involving the Council, for example reporting an interview with the Council chairman in the 27 October 1989 issue, and publishing an article on the Council-backed Ethnic Relations Unit in the 18 May 1990 issue.

Publications

The ESRC issues a Publications List which lists both its own publications and also books sponsored by the ESRC, and its Research Units, etc.; the list includes a list of books now out of print and is provided with an index of titles.

The principal on-going publications of the Council are:-

ESRC Annual Report, first published in August 1966 (House of Commons Session 1965-66 Paper 199).
    The Annual Report of the ESRC to the Secretary of State for Education and Science is published in October: the Annual Report was published as a House of Commons Paper up to the Annual Report for 1979-1980 inclusive, the Annual Reports for 1980-1981 onwards being published by the Council itself. It gives an account of ESRC's activities during one financial year (1 April-31 March); the work of its Research Units and Designated Research Centres is also described. The ISBN for the 1980-1 and later annual reports commences 0 86226; the ISSN for the 1981-82 and 1982-3 annual reports is 0262-5482 and for later annual reports is 0226-2043.

ESRC Newsletter, first published in Nov. 1967, and subsequently published three or four times a year.
    It contains articles on research projects, a full list of recent research awards and end-of-grant reports lodged in the British Library Lending Division, in addition to news items from the Council and its committees, details of new publications, etc.

Research Supported by the ESRC, first published as a separate volume in 1968, then bound in with the Annual Report until 1972, when once again it became an independent volume published by ESRC.
    This annual publication contains details and abstracts of all research projects receiving support during one financial year (1 April- 31 March). The work of the ESRC Research Units amd Designated Research Centres is also described.

ESRC Student Handbook, first published in 1966.
    Published annually, this gives information to students and social science departments of universities and polytechnics about the Council's schemes for allocating postgraduate training awards. It contains the terms and conditions of awards and gives details of the courses and research training programmes eligible for ESRC support.

Records

The ESRC is not subject to the provisions of the Public Records Acts, but has come to an arrangement with the Public Record Office whereby files relating to research grants are deposited in the P.R.O., usually some eighteen months or two years after the date of conclusion of the grant; these deposited files become subject to the normal arrangements appertaining to public records. The P.R.O. has allocated the group code EY for ESRC records.

Applications to consult ESRC files would be judged by the ESRC case by case on the individual merits of the request. The Council's files often contain confidential comments by referees, which it is not customary to release.

See too the entry on the Advisory Board for the Research Councils.

EDUCATIONAL TELEVISION ASSOCIATION

Addresses and
contacts
Educational Television Association,
King's Manor,
Exhibition Square,
York,
YO1 2EP

tel: 0904 433929

Administrator: Josie Key

Company Secretary of the Educational Television Association: Mr. Roy Stares, Head of Communication Services, Luton College of Higher Education, Park Square, Luton, Bedfordshire, LU1 3JU; tel: 0582 34111

Editor of the Journal of Educational Television: Mr. Paul Kelley, Television Literacy Project Director, Hereford School, Westward Ho, Grimsby; tel: 0472 79241

History

The Educational Television Association brings together institutions and individuals using television and other media for education and training. Member institutions include universities, polytechnics, colleges, local education authorities, schools, training boards, broadcasting organisations, the armed services, as well as commercial and industrial organisations, in the United Kingdom and elsewhere. The Association is a registered Charity (No.325081-R) and also a Company limited by guarantee registered in England (No. 1167427).

The activities and services now offered to members include the Journal of Educational Television, the Association's Newsletter (published quarterly), the Annual Conference, and regional meetings throughout the year, and access, through the Executive Committee, to related organisations, and to the Association's own Technical Liaison Committee, Design Liaison Committee, Research Group, and other expert sub-committees.

Publications

(a) Journal of Educational Television and its predecessors

NECCTA Bulletin (Bulletin of the National Educational Closed Circuit Television Association, as the Association was then entitled):
[No.1] Autumn 1968 (duplicated)
2 [Spring 1969]
3-11 [undated but appear to have been published twice a year (Spring or Summer, and Autumn or Winter - rather irregularly) between Autumn 1969 and January 1975]

Journal of Educational Television (a continuation of the Bulletin, renamed) Nos.1-3, March, August, and November 1975.

Journal of Educational Television and Other Related Media
Vol.II No.1 Spring 1976 (first issue of restyled Journal)

Vol. II nos.2-4, Summer, Autumn and Winter 1976
Vol. III Nos.1-4, Spring, Summer, Autumn and Winter 1977
Vol IV Nos.1-3, Spring, Summer and Autumn 1978
(no Winter issue; the cover of No.2 bore the new name of the Association, the Educational Television Association)
Vols. V and VI: three issues each, 1979 and 1980
Vol. VII: three issues (Spring, Summer, and Winter), 1981.

Journal of Educational Television (reverting to the earlier, simpler title)
Vol.8: three issues, March, June, and October 1982
Vol.9: Nos.1-3, March, July, and October 1983
(Henceforward three issues a year are published, in March, July, and October).
The Journal of Educational Television, the official journal of the Association, is an international forum for discussion and reports on developments in the increasingly important and rapidly expanding field of the use of television and related media in teaching, learning and training.

(b) ETA News and its predecessors

NECCTA News (members - only publication): started in about February 1976 and published four times a year (February, May, August and September) until issue No. 9.

Newsletter (of the ETA): issues 10-26, 1978-Nov. 1982
(a continuation of NECCTA News, renamed)

ETA News: issues 27 onwards, May 1983 onwards.
(a continuation of the Newsletter, renamed)

(c) Apart from the above ((a) and (b)) regular publications of the Association, there have been other occasional publications. For example, in the earlier days of the Association its Technical Committee wrote and published in the Journal a series of Technical Papers which were available as reprinted 'Green Papers', and there have been occasional publications of this type since, as for instance a current document on 'Safety in Studios'.

A 'Directory of Members' has been a regular feature of the Association's services to its members, originally as an updated loose-leaf publication but currently a stitched booklet. The Directory lists all the member institutions, organisations and individuals, with details of the television studio and other equipment owned by members, of the types of work carried out by their central service units, and the main interests of their staff.

FEDERATED SUPERANNUATION SCHEME FOR UNIVERSITIES

Address and
contact
Federated Superannuation Scheme for Universities Secretariat,
University of London,
Hut 2 - Room A,
Senate House,
Malet Street,
London,
WC1E 7HU

tel: 071 323 4525
Mr. E.W.H. Clark, Secretary (from 1 July 1990)

History

The Federated Superannuation Scheme for Universities (FSSU) was established in 1913. Under the Scheme insurance policies, paid for by both the employer and the employee, vested entirely in the employee if he left one university for another. The Scheme allowed the beneficiary to choose whether to buy an endowment lump sum or a deferred annuity policy. As Professor Leslie Hannah has written, the FSSU 'was widely admired, not only because of its entrenched rights for leavers, but also for its money-purchase formula in which the individual could choose between many different insurance policies and gain the benefits appropriate to his circumstances, while maximizing his return on lifetime pension savings' (Inventing Retirement..., p.108).

In 1980 modifications had to be made to the FSSU Scheme to enable it to qualify as an exempt approved scheme under the new tax code introduced in the Finance Acts of 1970 and 1971. The effect of the changes was to move FSSU away from its current basis, where the entire proceeds of policies could be taken as a wholly tax-free cash payment on retirement towards a basis where the retirement benefits relating to post-1980 service are normally paid principally in the form of taxable pension. However, counter-balancing improvements to FSSU operated from 1980, in the form of a reduction in members' net contributions to the Scheme and the higher benefits FSSU policies provided through freedom from tax. Members were given the option to transfer to USS. The Scheme is divided into the 1946 Scheme and the 1980 Scheme.

Bibliography

C.R. Macdonald, Fifty Years of the F.S.S.U. (London, 1965).

Leslie Hannah, Inventing Retirement : The development of occupational pensions in Britain (Cambridge U.P., 1986)

Publications

FSSU Grey Books
Provide full details of the FSSU and Modified FSSU schemes.

Records

The FSSU office retains Minutes of the Central Council and of the Executive since the formation of the FSSU. It also holds copies of rules of the schemes and also correspondence files.

No records of individual members are held centrally, being held only in the individual universities and other institutions concerned.

JOINT MATRICULATION BOARD

Address and
contact
Universities of Manchester, Liverpool, Leeds, Sheffield and
Birmingham Joint Matriculation Board,
Manchester,
M15 6EU.

tel: 061 273 2565
Secretary to the Board: Mr. Colin Vickerman.

History
The Joint Matriculation Board (JMB) was originally constituted in 1903 on the dissolution of the federal Victoria University.   In the Charters then granted to each of the three independent Universities of Leeds, Liverpool and Manchester, they were to co-operate by means of a Joint Board "for the regulation and conduct of matriculation examinations (including the conditions of exemption)", the Statutes of these universities prescribing the constitution and duties of the Joint Board, the appointment of its members, etc.   The University of Sheffield joined the Board in 1905, and the University of Birmingham in 1916.

Until 1917 the JMB conducted various certificate examinations for pupils in secondary schools, in addition to its Matriculation Examination.   In 1918 the JMB was "approved" by the Board of Education as one of the examining bodies to which the conduct of the School Certificate and Higher School Certificate examinations (instituted in 1918) was entrusted.   The Board came to be widely regarded as a model for the conduct of pre-Second World War school examinations.   In the years immediately after the War there were very large increases in examination activities.   The General Certificate of Education was introduced by the Ministry of Education in 1951, in place of the School Certificate and Higher School Certificate examinations.   The Matriculation Examination proper was last held in 1937 but the JMB continues to determine and administer the General Requirement which students must satisfy before entering upon a course leading to a first degree in any one of the five constituent Universities.   The replacement nationally of GCE 'O'Level , the Certificate of Secondary Education (CSE), and the joint 'O' Level/CSE, by the new General Certificate of Secondary Education (GCSE), the first certificates for which were awarded in 1988, has also entailed the reorganisation of the 22 GCE and CSE examining boards into five Examining Groups (six groups including Northern Ireland) and the JMB comes into the Northern Examining Association for this purpose. The Northern Examining Association is the largest (both in terms of geographical size and of population) of the Examining Groups; it is made up of the JMB and the four Regional Examining Boards in the North of England. The NEA'S Council has two major committees, Finance and Examinations; there are also 52 Subject Committees. Proposals are now being considered to establish a new fully-integrated organisation responsible for A-level and AS-level examinations as well as the GCSE and Records of Achievement, in place of the present association of five separate boards. The work of the Examining Group is monitored by the Secondary Examinations

Council (SEC), now the School Examinations and Assessment Council. The Board occupied new premises from the end of 1962. More recently it obtained a computer installation.

The JMB consists of 32 members (of whom four are appointed annually by each of the five constituent Universities, and twelve are appointed annually on the nomination of teachers' associations and Education Officers). An additional eleven members of the Board's Examinations Council also attend meetings of the Board, but without having the voting rights of full members. To assist it in its work the JMB has an Examinations Council (responsible, within financial limits determined by the JMB, for all matters relating to the conduct and improvement of the GCE examination). The Examinations Council appoints Subject Committees and Preparatory Sub-Committees as well as ad hoc committees; the Awarding Committee, the Appeals Committee, and the Research Advisory Committee are all also responsible to the Examinations Council. There is also a Standing Joint Committee of the teachers' associations, with its own extensive arrangements for the collection of comments on each year's examinations submitted by teachers through their associations. The Board's Matriculation Committee advises the JMB on all matters relating to the application of the Board's university entrance requirements.

(The above account is mainly drawn form the 'General description of the Joint Matriculation Board' which is published as an appendix in the Board's Annual Report).

Bibliography
James A. Petch, Fifty Years of Examining: The Joint Matriculation Board 1903-1953 (George G. Harrap & Co. Ltd., London, 1953)

Publications
Annual Report - the latest published being the 86th Annual Report to the Universities constituting the Board for the year ended 30 Sept. 1989, 1990.
(ISBN 0 901628 88 3)

The JMB's other publications comprise those relating to:-
   (a)   the G.C.E.
   (b)   University Entrance Requirements
   (c)   Occasional Publications
   (d)   Research Reports

Those publications which are still available, for sale or for issue free of charge, are listed in an appendix of the JMB's Annual Report.

Records
The Board has retained a complete set of the minutes of meetings of the Board and its Standing Committees. It has also retained important correspondence with officers of the Board.

LIBRARIANS OF INSTITUTES AND SCHOOLS OF EDUCATION

Address and
contact
Mr. Roy Kirk, Honorary Secretary,
Librarians of Institutes and Schools of Education,
University of Leicester School of Education Library,
21, University Road,
Leicester,
LE1 7RF

tel: 0533 523735

History
This professional group was formed in 1954 at an inaugural meeting held in Manchester on 9 April 1954. Initially it was entitled 'The Librarians of Institutes of Education'. It is clear that some concept of co-operation was already in hand before the official formation of the group and that the Manchester meeting regularised activities that had already begun; conferences of Institute of Education librarians had been held at least from 1951. Reference to this can be found in the two cited articles by W.L.Saunders and C.B.Freeman. The librarians of Institutes and Schools of Education (LISE) group in fact developed out of the formal and informal co-operation between librarians of Institutes of Education and colleges of education since the establishment of Institutes of Education (each with their own library) which had been advocated by the Committee to consider the supply, recruitment and training of teachers and youth leaders, whose report, 'Teachers and youth leaders' (McNair Report), was published in 1944.

The current revised Constitution, drafted in 1978, states:-

'The objects of the group shall be to advance public education and for this purpose (but not otherwise) to provide books and services in support of study and research in education and to serve the information needs of educational institutions established for the public benefit. To these ends the group shall foster co-operative enterprises, assist and advise on individual projects and to support a publishing programme planned and co-ordinated by a Publications Sub-Committee'.

The Officers of the group consist of Chairman, two Vice-Chairmen, Secretary and a Treasurer. The group has a membership of 26 University Institute and School of Education libraries in England, Wales and Northern Ireland.

The co-operative projects organised by LISE include:-
Union catalogue of holdings of member libraries kept at Birmingham University Faculty of Education Library.
Union list of periodicals held by member libraries (see publications list).
Co-operative storage of obsolete textbooks.
Co-operative storage of Examination Board syllabuses, regulations and examination papers (CSE and GCE).
Co-operative storage of yearbooks in the subject area of education.
Co-operative storage of books on educational systems in major countries.

LISE itself meets regularly to exchange ideas and information and continues to be an important and expert voice, helping to foster the idea of a national education library service. LISE's Publications Sub-Committee has itself undertaken a publishing programme over the years.

The Library Association itself has sought to assist LISE Libraries: the Colleges, Institutes, and Schools of Education Section of the Association was founded in 1961, and the Association in 1963 published a definitive statement of the work and aims of LISE libraries.

As a result, however, of the report of the Committee of Inquiry into Teacher Education and Training, 'Teacher education and training' (James Report), 1972, the links between universities and colleges of education were weakened, the university based Area Training Organisations (ATOs) abolished, and Institutes of Education left with a diminished responsibility for teacher education, whereby their specialist libraries developed a new relationship with the libraries of their parent universities.

Bibliography

M. Argles, 'Thirty years on - an age of SNAFU: Problems of co-ordinating education libraries for the 1980s' in Education Libraries Bulletin, Vol.21, Part 3, Autumn 1978, pp.1-13.

A.K.D. Campbell, [Correspondence] 'The future of library services for teacher education',in Education Libraries Bulletin, Vol.19, Part 3, Autumn 1976, pp.25-26.

C.B. Freeman, 'Education libraries' in P.H.Sewell,ed., Five years work in librarianship 1956-1960, Library Association, 1963, pp.37-41.

C.W.J. Higson, 'Libraries of the University Institutes of Education' in Education Libraries Bulletin (amalgamation of the University of London Institute of Education Library Bulletin and the International Society of Training College Librarians Newsletter), No.1, Spring 1958, pp.2-9.

R. James, (with a comment by J.E.Vaughan), 'The future of library services for teacher education', in Education Libraries Bulletin, Vol.19, Part 2, Summer 1976, pp.1-8.

Library Association, 'Libraries in institutes and schools of education: recommendations approved by the Council 1963', in Library Association Record, Vol.65(9), 1963, pp.331-332.

J.V. Marder, 'Educational research: national resources for local users', Paper given to the annual conference of the British Educational Research Association, Westfield College, 1976, p.4.

J.V. Marder, 'Institutes and School of Education libraries', in H.A.Wheatley, ed., British librarianship and information science 1966-1970, Library Association, 1972, p.397.

P. Platt, 'The future of the Libraries of Institutes and Schools of Education', in British Journal of Teacher Education, Vol.1, No.2, April 1975, pp.221- 226.

W.L. Saunders and C.B.Freeman, 'The libraries of institutes of education' in Library Association Record, Vol.55(7), 1953, pp.207-212.

W.L. Saunders and C.B.Freeman, 'A nation-wide library service for educational studies: an aspect of the work of Institutes of Education', in Educational Review, Vol.6(1), 1953, pp.49-54.

W.H. Shercliffe, 'Education libraries', in P.H.Sewell, Five years work in librarianship 1961-1965, Library Association, 1968, pp.53-59.

J.E. Vaughan, 'National resources for the study of education: comments on the statement from the Librarians of Institutes and Schools of Education' in Education Libraries Bulletin, Vol.20, Part 1, Spring 1977, pp.1-9. (reviews the historical development of the libraries of the institutes and schools of education, and selects the major proposals for the constitution of the Librarians of the Institutes and Schools of Education group and notes possible developments from these in the light of the current situation in higher education).

J.E. Vaughan, 'Waiting for Godot again and again', in British Journal of Teacher Education, Vol.1(3), 1975, pp.417-420.

Publications
(a) by LISE

Acronyms and initialisms in education: a handlist. Edited by Joan V. Marder, 1981.

Acronyms and initialisms in education: a handlist. 2nd and 3rd editions. Ed. Edited by Joan V. Marder, 1984, 1986.

British education theses index 1950-1980. Edited by J.R.V.Johnson, 1984. [A microfiche publication that has been up-dated twice since 1980].

Co-operative projects: a descriptive pamphlet, 1969.

Education in France: a union list of stock in Institute of Education Libraries. Edited by Joan V.Marder, 1964.

Education in France: a union list of stock in Institutes and Schools of Education Libraries. Edited by Joan V.Marder, 2nd ed., 1971.

Education in Germany: a union list of stock in Institute of Education Libraries, 1960.

Education in Germany: a union list of stock in Institute of Education Libraries. Rev. ed., 1963.

Education in Germany: a union list of stock in Institute of Education Libraries. Edited by John S.Andrews, 3rd ed., 1979.

Library provision for teachers: three discussion papers, 1968.

List of educational pamphlets of the Board of Education 1904-1943 with locations in Institute of Education Libraries, 1969.

Novels with a background of school: a union list of books in the stock of Institute and School of Education Libraries, 1970.

Novels and plays with a background of school. A union list of books in the stock of education libraries in British universities. Complied by A.K.D.Campbell, 2nd ed., 1979.

PERDAS 1950-1980. A list of theses, dissertations and projects on physical education, recreation, dance, athletics and sport presented at United Kingdom Universities. Compiled by J.S.Keighley, 1981.

Union list of periodicals held in Institute of Education Libraries as at 31 May 1966, 1966.

Union list of periodicals held in Institute of Education Libraries. Edited by J.M.Smethurst, 2nd ed., 1970.

Union list of periodicals held in Institute of Education Libraries. Edited by Sylvia Stevenson, 3rd ed., 1975.

Union list of periodicals held in Institute of Education Libraries. Edited by Joan V.Marder, 4th ed., 1977.

Union list of periodicals held in Institute of Education Libraries. Edited by Joan V.Marder, 5th ed., 1980.

(b) initiated by LISE members

Board of Education circulars [in the Libraries of Institutes and Schools of Education]: a finding list and index by John E.Vaughan. History of Education Society, 1972.

Sources for the history of education: a list of material (including school books) contained in the Libraries of the Institutes and Schools of Education, together with works from the Libraries of the Universities of Nottingham and Reading. Edited by C.Winifred J.Higson, Library Association, 1967.

Supplement to the Sources for the history of education: a list of material added to the Libraries of the Institutes and Schools of Education 1965-1974 together with works from certain University libraries. Edited by C.Winifred J.Higson, Library Association, 1976.

A finding list of histories of girls' schools and related biographical sources. Edited by I.Barbara Barr. 1984.

Second supplement to the Sources for the history of education. Edited by Gwen F.Smith and Roy W.Kirk. 1985.

British Education Index was originally initiated by LISE in 1954 and was edited and published by LISE members until the British National Bibliography, and subsequently the British Library Bibliographic Services Division, assumed publication and editing in 1970 (see p.296).

(c) LISE also publishes a leaflet guide for probationary teachers:

Study and library facilities for teachers: Universities, Institutes and
    Schools of Education etc.

A Directory of addresses, telephone numbers, staff and opening hours for
    Institute and School of Education Libraries within the LISE group is
    available for group use.

Records
(a)   Copies of minutes for the period 1951-1975 from main LISE meetings (two
        or three a year) and Publications Sub-Committee meetings (two or three a
        year) are deposited with the Modern Records Centre, University of
        Warwick Library together with circulars, correspondence, and subject
        files of LISE for 1952-82 and publications 1957-77. More recently, files
        of LISE's Publications Sub-Committee, 1970s-1980s, have been added to
        the deposit. These archives are available to all bona fide researchers
        on application to the Modern Records Centre, (their ref. MSS.235).

(b)   Subsequent minutes are held by the Secretary. Correspondence is held
        by the individuals involved in particular activities of the group.
        These papers are confidential and are not available for consultation,
        but the aim is to deposit papers regularly every five years with the
        Modern Records Centre where they will be available for consultation in
        the usual way.

        It should be noted that the Modern Records Centre, University of Warwick
        Library also hold minutes (1968-1986), annual reports (1961-1985),
        newsletters (1962-1986), and some other records of the Library
        Association Education Librarians' Group (ref. MSS.274).

MEDICAL RESEARCH COUNCIL

Address and
contact
Medical Research Council,
20, Park Crescent,
London,
W1N 4AL

tel: 071 636 5422 ext.247
Miss Mary Nicholas, Archivist.

History
The Medical Research Council (MRC) originated in the Medical Research
Committee established in 1913 to implement a provision of the National
Insurance Act of 1911 whereby a penny per annum per head of the insured
population was allocated, from parliamentary funds, to purposes of research.
The Council itself was established in 1920 under a provision of the Ministry
of Health Act 1919 and was incorporated by Royal Charter in 1920. During the
period (1914-33) that Dr. Walter M. Fletcher was Secretary, the Council was
dominated by basic medical scientists, in particular by Fletcher himself.
Until 1965 the MRC was responsible to a ministerial Committee of the Privy

Council; thereafter, by virtue of the Science and Technology Act 1965 (1965 c.4), the functions of this Privy Council Committee were absorbed by the Secretary of State for Education and Science. In 1966 the Council was granted a new Charter.

The Council's principal objective is to advance knowledge that will improve physical and mental health and to develop the biomedical sciences as such, to maintain a fundamental capacity for research and to support higher education. The Council runs its own research establishments - two large institutes (the National Institute for Medical Research, Mill Hill, and the Clinical Research Centre, Harrow), and 56 (since reduced in number) units and establishments which are mainly located in university departments, medical schools, and hospitals (38 of these units and establishments being closely associated with universities); it awards long- and short-term grants for research in universities and elsewhere, including a large cancer research laboratory; and, to develop the biomedical sciences, it awards fellowships and studentships to graduates. As at 1 January 1989 the number of MRC research establishments was 52.

The National Institute for Medical Research at Mill Hill, London is one of MRC's largest research establishments. In July 1987 it had 525 staff, over 100 visiting workers, and a total budget of £11m, and 21 research teams organised into four main Groups: Genes and Cellular Controls, Infections and Immunity, Physiological and Neural Mechanisms, and Technology. It has close working links with the adjacent MRC Collaborative Centre which was set up to engage with industrial partners in projects of direct commercial application arising from the work of MRC establishments.

The MRC has always believed that the work it supports should complement research undertaken in universities and in NHS establishments, and therefore maintains close links with those bodies. In its support for research in universities the MRC mainly provides grants as long as the work is scientifically acceptable and funds are available - either a project grant (maximum 3 years) or a programme grant (which can provide support for at least 5 years and is extendable for a second or third 5-year period). In fact some 40% of the Council's grant is devoted to the support of research and training in the universities. The Council pays the annual UK subscription to the European Molecular Biology Laboratory and the International Agency for Research on Cancer. In 1978-79 the MRC employed 3,730 staff and was responsible for expenditure of £62M. The Council's grant-in-aid for the financial year 1988-89 totalled £149.7M, and as at 1 January 1989 it employed 3,425 full-time staff and 446 part-time staff. It has received a substantial proportion of its income as payment for work commissioned by Government Departments, under the customer-contractor arrangements adopted by the Government in 1972 following the Rothschild Report on Government Research and Development in 1971; in 1978-79 about one fifth of its total income came from commissioned research but since the transfer-back of funds from the Health Departments, commissioned research has accounted for less than 1% of the MRC budget.

The MRC is assisted by research boards: the Neurobiology and Mental Health Board; Cell Biology and Disorders Board; Physiological Systems and Disorders Board; Tropical Medicine Research Board; and the Clinical Research Board. In 1988-89 the MRC established a Subcommittee of the Council, the Strategy Committee, to advise Council on the development and definition of corporate strategy, etc., and to ensure that the research activities supported by the Boards are consistent with the Council's overall strategy, and to allocate resources accordingly.

Bibliography

A. Lansborough Thomson, Half a Century of Medical Research. Vol.I: Origins and Policy of the Medical Research Council (U.K.), HMSO, 1973; Vol.2: The Programme of the Medical Research Council (U.K.), HMSO, 1975. Vol.2's appendices include a list of MRC Research Establishments, past and present, with the names of their successive directors and senior members of the external scientific staff. (nowadays sold but not published by HMSO)

Neil Morgan, 'A note on the proposed amalgamation of the Lister Institute of Preventive Medicine and the Medical Research Committee: philanthropy and state support of medical research, 1914' in Annals of Science: An International Review of the History of Science and Technology from the Thirteenth Century, Vol.43 No.3, May 1986, pp.287-289.

Joan L. Austoker and Linda Bryder (eds.), Historical Perspectives on the Role of the MRC: Essays in the History of the Medical Research Council of the United Kingdom and its Predecessor, the Medical Research Committee, 1913-1953 (Oxford U.P., 1989).

Felicity Jones, 'The slow and painful death of progress' (on the MRC's shrinking budget, the closure of MRC units, and the future funding of medical research) in The Times Higher Education Supplement, 13 Feb 1987,p.10.

New Scientist reports and comments upon developments in the Council's work, e.g. Max Perutz's article reviewing the ABRC proposal to establish a National Research Council in the 15 July 1989 issue, and the proposals to replace the Clinical Research Centre at Harrow (probably by the end of 1994) by a new national centre at Hammersmith Hospital referred to in the issues of 16 September 1989 and 28 April 1990.

Publications

Annual Reports to Parliament of the Committee and Council from 1914 onwards, initially published by H.M.S.O., nowadays sold but not published by H.M.S.O. The latest, covering the period April 1988 - March 1989, was published in December 1989.

Medical Research Council Handbook for 1970-71 onwards (annual publication)

Special Report Series, published by H.M.S.O.

National Institute for Medical Research: Scientific Report for 1968-69 onwards (annual publication)

Clinical Research Centre: Scientific Report for 1970-71 onwards (published every two years)

For publications of MRC sold or published by HMSO see HMSO's Government Publications Sectional List No.50 (periodically revised).

Records

The MRC's non-current records are held at the MRC's offices, principally in the Registry, the Secretariat, and the Archives. Whilst the MRC's records are not subject to the provisions of the Public Records Acts, a reviewing schedule is in operation making provision for the disposal (to Archives, for destruction or review, after a certain number of years) of the non-current records of the Council; this schedule is currently under review. It has been agreed that no surviving records for the period 1913-54 shall be destroyed; apparently a number of records for the pre 1954 period were destroyed some years ago.

The Registry's files mainly date from the mid 1970s onwards, provision being made for the transfer of non-current records to the Archives (whose office is situated in an adjacent room). The Registry has custody of approximately 60,000 files. The Registry does not have a register of files as such but there exists for every file or group of related files a card providing a description, covering dates, and reference of each file; there are two sets of subject card indices to these files, for 1954-72 and for 1973 to date. Each file includes a card which records the names of the successive MRC officers who have borrowed the file and the dates of borrowing: this card is removed from the file and kept in a separate drawer for issued files whilst the file is on issue.

The Secretariat, on another floor of the MRC's offices, has retained what is believed to be a complete set of file copies of the Minutes and Agendas papers of the Council and its Boards; a separate sequence of signed Minutes is also kept by the Secretariat. There are several sequences of subject and person card indices, compiled on the basis of the Minutes: (a) 1920-69: Council, (b) 1920-69: separate sequences per Council Board, and (c) 1970-to date: Council and Boards: a single card index.

The Archives has basement storage for two sequences of files, for the period pre 1954 (some 7,500 files) and for 1954-75, the files being held in metal boxes; including agenda papers, these files apparently number about 60,000 in all. Finding aids comprise (i) a list of subjects with corresponding numbers which relate to a separate card index which gives the separate file reference, and (ii) a number of separate lists of files providing a description, covering dates (not always provided), and reference, the files generally not being listed in any particular order. The Archives staff have prepared lists of the pre 1954 records preparatory to their transfer (in 1991) to the Public Record Office; a subject index is being compiled to these lists. Bona fide researchers are able, by appointment, to consult the records in the custody of the Archives. The PRO has allocated the group code FD for the MRC's records it receives.

The MRC's Library includes copies of (a) the Annual Reports of the MRC 1914 onwards, (b) the MRC Handbook 1970 onwards, and (c) the MRC's Special Report Series 1915 onwards.

See too the entry for the Advisory Board for the Research Councils.

NATIONAL ASSOCIATION OF TEACHERS IN FURTHER AND HIGHER EDUCATION

Address and
contact
National Association of Teachers in Further
and Higher Education,
27 Britannia Street,
London,
WC1X 9JP

tel: 071 837 3636
The Librarian

History
The National Association of Teachers in Further and Higher Education (NATFHE) was formed in 1975 by the amalgamation of the Association of Teachers in Technical Institutions (ATTI) (founded in 1904 as the Association of Teachers in Technical Institutes) and the Association of Teachers in Colleges and Departments of Education (ATCDE) (formed in 1943 by the amalgamation of the Training College Association (TCA), founded in 1891, and the Council of Principals (CP), founded in 1913).

The ATTI was established originally by teachers of technical subjects in the London area but support soon spread to the provinces. It changed its name in 1907 to its final form. Its aims were broadly to advance technical education, to assist the interchange of ideas on teaching, to express teachers' views on educational matters and to safeguard their professional interests on conditions of service matters. It affiliated to the National Union of Teachers in 1941.

The NATFHE is the only organisation representing lecturers in all sectors of public service further and higher education. Its 76,000 members work in Colleges of Further Education, Colleges of Technology, Colleges of Education, Polytechnics, Institutes of Higher Education, Tertiary Colleges, and in institutions of agricultural, penal, art, and adult education. It is both a trade union and a professional association representing its members in negotiations on salaries, pensions, and conditions of service at national and local levels and being involved in educational policy making and the promotion of public sector further and higher education. (Some members of staff of universities, as for instance, in departments of adult education/extra-mural studies, were members of NATFHE prior to joining their university's staff.)

The Association is represented on many official educational bodies, including the Further Education Curriculum Review and Development Unit, the Business and Technician Education Council, the City and Guilds of London Institute, and the National Advisory Body for Public Sector Higher Education. NATFHE has joint membership agreements with a number of other teacher unions and is affiliated to several other organisations including the Trades Union Congress. It has worked closely with the AUT, and AUT and NATFHE issued joint statements on research in higher education and on student maintenance in 1989 (reproduced in AUT Bulletin, No. 165, 1989, pp.8-9).

The overall policy making body of NATFHE is its Annual Conference, which consists of members of the National Council, together with over 300 delegates from the Regions. Between Annual Conferences policy is decided by the National Council which meets three times a year. Assisting the National Council is the National Executive and its three policy Sub-committees (Educational Policy; Finance and General Purposes; and Salaries, Superannuation and Conditions of Service). At NATFHE's Head Office, the Information Department handles publicity and press relations, produces the NATFHE Journal and the Journal of Further and Higher Education, a diary, recruitment material, newsletters, and a variety of general information for members and lay officers. The library houses a comprehensive stock of further education publications and also handles enquiries and provides general information.

At the local level the NATFHE membership is grouped into Branches (of which there are over 550); in each local authority area there is a NATFHE Liaison Committee representative of all the Branches in the area. NATFHE Branches are grouped into fourteen Regions within England, Wales, and Northern Ireland, the Regional Councils having Standing Committees to assist them in their consideration of issues and problems raised by Branches and referred from national level. Subject Sections have been established for a number of subjects (e.g Art Education, Health Education, History, and Modern Languages) to provide an opportunity for lecturers, members of the Association, working in a particular area of the curriculum to come together to share experiences and discuss developments in their field of teaching. Section activities include the organisation of conferences and courses, the publication of journals and occasional papers, and research. There is also a NATFHE Lesbian and Gay Studies Section.

Bibliography (see too section on Records below)
(a) ATTI
John Wilson, W.Ing, and A.E.Evans, The Association of Teachers in Technical Institutions: The First Half-Century 1904-1954, ATTI, n.d.[c.1955]. For the period 1914-54 a year by year summary of the Association's activities and of events in the sphere of technical education is provided.
(loan copy available on application to the Librarian of NATFHE)

David Farnham, 'The Association of Teachers in Technical Institutions (1904-14) : A Case-Study on the Origins, Formation and Growth of a White-Collar Organization' in International Review of Social History,Vol.19 Part 3, 1974, pp.377-395.

C.A. and P.L.Horn, 'Aspects of the development of teacher trade unionism in Britain 1860-1919' in Journal of Further and Higher Education, Vol.3 No.2, 1979, pp.3-10.

David Farnham, 'The Association of Teachers in Technical Institutions, its formation, growth and collective activities 1904-1914'; M.Sc. long essay, London University (LSE), 1969.

Gary Morton, 'Communications in the Assocation of Teachers in Technical Institutions'; submitted as part of M.A. degree in industrial relations, Warwick University, Summer 1972. Manuscript.

D.S. Pearsall, 'The Association of Teachers in Technical Institutions, a study of its development and organisation'; dissertation for M.A. degree, University of Warwick, 1969.

A.I.R. Swabe, 'The Association of Teachers in Technical Institutions: structure and trade union activities, 1918-1931'; submitted as a long essay as part of the degree of M.Sc., London University, 1971.

A.I. Swabe, 'The Association of Teachers in Technical Institutions, 1904-45: white collar unionism among professional people'; M.Phil. thesis, London School of Economics, 1977.

D. Bright, 'Union character and membership heterogenity: a study of the representation of polytechnic teachers with the ATTI'; Ph.D. thesis, Newcastle Polytechnic, 1979.

Tricia Leman, 'The Campaign for Women's Rights in Three Trade Unions'; M.A. thesis, Warwick University, 1980.

Sandra Turner, 'The ATTI: a case study of teacher unionism'; Ph.D. thesis, Bristol University, 1979.

J.R. Wall, 'Attitudes towards teacher unionism, further and higher education'; M.A. thesis, Thames Polytechnic, 1978/79.

(b) ATCDE
Joan D. Browne, Teachers of Teachers: a history of the ATCDE, Hodder and Stoughton in association with NATFHE, 1979.

(c) General
Albert A. Blum (ed.), Teachers unions and associations; a comparative study, Chicago: University of Illinois Press, 1969.

P.H.J.H. Gosden, The Evolution of a profession: a study of the contribution of teachers' associations to the development of school teaching as a professional occupation, Oxford: Basil Blackwell & Mott Ltd., 1972.

R.D. Coates, Teachers unions are interest group politics: a study of the behaviour of organised teachers in England and Wales, Cambridge University Press, 1972.

Ronald A. Manzer, Teachers and politics: the role of the National Union of Teachers in the making of national education policy in England and Wales since 1944, Manchester University Press, 1970.

Maurice Kogan, Educational policy making: a study of interest groups and Parliament, Allen and Unwin, 1975.

Publications (of NATFHE)
(see too section on Records below)

(a) Journals
NATFHE Journal
Journal of Further and Higher Education

(b) Newsletters
Polytechnic News
Council News
NEC Bulletin
Health and Safety Bulletin
NATFHE Campaigner
NAB Briefing
Sister

(c) Conference
Annual Reports
Statements of Accounts
Minutes of Annual Conferences
Resolutions adopted by Annual Conferences

In addition, NATFHE has published a number of policy statements/briefing material, discussion papers, etc., a list of most of which is available from the Publications Officer. They include <u>Future Trends in Further and Higher Education</u> (1983). It has also published <u>College Administration: A Handbook</u>, ed. Ian Waitt, 1980, a book of almost 900 pp. which includes a useful summary of the development of further and higher education from 1944 onwards.

<u>Records</u>
(a) At present, NATFHE Council Minutes, Executive Committee papers, Conference Reports, publications, and some correspondence are kept on a long term basis at Head Office. Applications to consult these documents should be made to the General Secretary or the Librarian. Most of these Council Minutes, Executive Committee papers and also circulars have been microfilmed, one copy of the microfilm being used as a working copy and another copy of the microfilm to be stored elsewhere than the Head Office.

(b) The Modern Records Centre, University of Warwick Library, Coventry, CV4 7AL, holds the following records of the NATFHE, its constituents and predecessors, ref.MSS.176:-
Association of Teachers in Technical Institutes, later entitled
Association of Teachers in Technical Institutions

Council minutes, 1904-69.
Executive Committee minutes, 1904-05, 1908-11, 1913-75.
General Purposes Committee minutes, 1905-06.
Finance Committee minutes, 1905-68.
Delegate Meetings minutes, 1909-14.
Annual Meetings minutes, 1915-16, 1918-57.
Special Conference Committee minutes, 1908, 1912, 1922-31.
Legal Committee minutes, 1905-12.
Press & Printing Committee minutes, 1905-11.
Burnham Committee circulated minutes, 1944-57.
Burnham Technical Committee minutes, 1920-7, 1929, 1931-7, 1940-70.
Salaries Committee minutes, 1955-72.
Higher Education Advisory Panel minutes, 1964-8, 1971-2.
CAT Committee minutes, 1962-5.
Universities Committee minutes, 1965-7.
Education Committee minutes, 1962-72.
Regional Colleges Committee minutes, 1964-8.
Various Joint Committees' minutes, between 1923 and 1959.
East Anglian Division minutes, 1946-75.
Kent Divison minutes, 1960-7
London Branch/Division minutes, reports, etc., 1922-7, 1936-60.
 Accounts, 1914-25; relief of Belgian technical teachers fund accounts, 1914-16.
 Subject files, 1926-60, particularly re salaries, superannuation, and National Certificates.
Branch subscription accounts, 1909-14.
Press-cuttings, 1923-36, 1955-63.

Training College Association
Many of the TCA's records were destroyed by bombing in 1942 and little appears to survive before 1918.

94 folders of papers, including some minutes, 1918-44. Subjects include: salaries; tenure and other cases, 1930s; proposals to reduce training college places, 1932; Joint Standing Committee with Council of Principals; Joint Agency for Women Teachers; Central Council for School Broadcasting.

Midland Branch minutes, 1928-54.
North East Branch minutes, 1933-55.
History section minutes, 1931-9.
Domestic Science section minutes, 1936-9.
Journal of Experimental Pedagogy (including 'Training College record'), 1911-22.
Training College Bulletin, 1923-43 (incomplete)

Council of Principals
Minutes, 1929-38. See also Principals' Panel below
Men Principals' group minutes, 1929-35.

Association of Teachers in Colleges and Departments of Education
Executive Committee minutes, 1943-75.
Council minutes, 1958-75.
Finance & General Purposes Committee minutes, 1943-75.
Conditions of Service Committee minutes, 1945-74.
Principals' Panel minutes, 1943-75.
Lecturers' Panel minutes, 1958-75.
Salaries Committee and Pelham Panel minutes, 1945-74.
Education Policy Committee minutes, 1960-75.
Research Committee papers, 1964-74.
Joint Standing Committee with NUT, 1950-63.
Extensive series of subject files, covering such topics as relations with other bodies, TUC affiliation, 1971, strikes, 1969-70, a proposed European training college, 1951-3, and in-course wastage, 1970-1.
Year Books, 1944-64; Conference Reports, 1964-75.
Bulletin of Education, 1943-53 (incomplete).
News Sheet, 1953-71; ATCDE News, Communique, 1971-5.
Papers relating to National Advisory Council, 1949-59.
West Midlands Branch Secretary's files, 1972-5.
For Midland and North East branches, see TCA branches above.
Coventry College of Education branch: files of ATCDE and other material held for members' information.

National Association of Teachers in Further and Higher Education
9 transfer cases of records relating to Burnham committees, superannuation, National Certificates, and other topics.

The Modern Records Centre also holds ATTI/NATFHE circulars 1961-79 and ATTI/NATFHE Solihull Branch minutes and correspondence, 1963-79, amongst the records of Cyril Collard/NATFHE Solihull Branch (ref. MSS.155).

NATIONAL INSTITUTE OF ADULT CONTINUING EDUCATION
(ENGLAND AND WALES)

Address and
contact
National Institute of Adult Continuing Education
(England and Wales),
19B De Montfort Street,
Leicester,
LE1 7GE

tel: 0533 551451

History
The National Institute of Adult Continuing Education (England and Wales) (NIACE) was established as the National Institute of Adult Education (England and Wales) in 1949 essentially through the merger of two different bodies, the British Institute of Adult Education and the National Foundation for Adult Education.

The British Institute of Adult Education was founded in 1921 as a group of interested individuals, largely due to the efforts of Lord Haldane and of Albert Mansbridge who hoped that the foundation of the Institute would 'create a widespread public opinion which shall ultimately win for adult education its rightful place in the national system... Essentially it will be an instrument of research and propaganda.'

The British Institute of Adult Education directed attention to the possibilities open to local and other authorities and brought together all those interested in adult education through its annual conferences and meetings and through its influential publications (including a Handbook and Directory of Adult Education and its journal Adult Education), and its 'Art for the People' experiment in the 1930s (about which a report was published by the Institute in 1935, Art for the People...). The British Institute had a Scottish branch, on whose behalf was published C. Cochrane... and D.M. Stewart, Survey of Adult Education in Scotland, 1938-1939 (T. and A. Constable, Edinburgh, 1944).

The National Foundation of Adult Education was founded in July 1946 as a grouping of local authorities. On 1 April 1949 the British Institute of Adult Education merged with the National Foundation to become the National Institute of Adult Education (England and Wales). This merger was based mainly on local education authorities, but also made provision for individual members. The National Institute's administration, like that of the British Institute, was by a representative Council and Executive Committee.

The National Institute has since 1949 been a major non-governmental force in the development of the adult education service. It has undertaken a number of major as well as smaller enquiries and published a number of books and pamphlets. The circulation of the journal Adult Education has been greatly increased and a Year Book published since 1961. In 1966 it founded the journal Teaching Adults. Understanding, nationally and internationally, between bodies engaged in adult education has also been fostered by the Institute's conferences and meetings. It enjoys the status of an independent consultative and advisory body, whose objects are not competitive with the day-to-day work of any of its members. For the support of its work the Institute has had to rely heavily on the contributions of its corporate members (who include local education authorities) and on grants made by the Department of Education and

Science and private foundations.

In 1983 the name of the National Institute was changed to its current name. In 1984 it became responsible for a Unit for the Development of Adult Continuing Education (UDACE) (which succeeded the Advisory Council for Adult and Continuing Education which had been established in 1977); the Unit is based at 94B London Road, Leicester. Since 1980 the Institute has had an Adult Literacy and Basic Skills Unit (ALBSU) which, inter alia, has undertaken projects and produced a number of publications; the Unit is based at 229/231 High Holborn, London. ALBSU's brief has since been extended.

The constitutional object of NIACE is 'the promotion of the study and the general advancement of adult continuing education'. It provides information and advice; conducts research and enquiries; organises conferences and seminars; publishes journals, books and directories; and possesses a reference library and operates a computerised database of bibliographical information. The Institute is active in further developments through the Unit for the Development of Adult Continuing Education, through the management of a major element of the DES Adult Unemployed Programme (REPLAN), through ALBSU, and through its Wales Committee (which is based at Cardiff). REPLAN (which is not an acronym) was started by the DES in 1984. Funded by the DES, the Welsh Office's Education Department, and supported by the Manpower Services Commission/the Training Agency of the Department of Employment, REPLAN is a programme to promote the development of learning opportunities for unemployed adults by encouraging and supporting changes in education and training in England and Wales. The NIACE's contribution is made through the staff of its eight REPLAN Regional Offices and a central unit at its headquarters. The Further Education Unit, an independent body, funded by the DES and based at the DES' Elizabeth House offices, is also a major contributor to REPLAN, developing projects, etc., and cooperating with NIACE. NIACE has links with the International Council for Adult Education, the European Bureau of Adult Education, the Commonwealth Association for Education and Training of Adults, the Council of Europe, and the British Council.

Under the new director of NIACE, Mr. Alan Tuckett, there were proposals to reorient some of the Institute's priorities, giving more emphasis to communications (for instance through improved press coverage, and the change of the journal Adult Education from quarterly to monthly publication), developing networking arrangements with different organisations, and proposals for direct involvement by adult students.

Membership of the Institute is composed of eight categories of members: organisations, institutions, and individuals.

NIACE is a registered charity, No. A319262.

Bibliography
E.M. Hutchinson (ed.), Aims and Action in Adult Education 1921-1971: A Memoir to mark fifty years of service by the British and National Institutes of Adult Education (NIAE, London, 1971).
(Dr. Hutchinson served as Secretary of the National Foundation for Adult Education 1946-49 and of the National Institute of Adult Education (England and Wales) from 1949-71).

Adult Education : A Plan for Development (the Russell Report), HMSO, 1973.
Includes a section on the NIAE, pp.141-143.

Report of the Open University Committee on Continuing Education (the Venables Report), 1976.

Publications include:-
The Journal of Adult Education..., from Sept. 1934 entitled Adult Education, Vols. 1-, 1926-

Teaching Adults, Vols.1-, 1966-

The Handbook & Directory of Adult Education..., 1926-

The Tutor in Adult Education... A report of a joint committee appointed by the British Institute of Adult Education and the Tutors' Association (Carnegie U.K. Trust, Dunfermline, 1928)

Adult Education after the War: A report of an enquiry made for the British Institute of Adult Education... (Oxford U.P., 1945).

Year Book of Adult Continuing Education (formerly Year Book of Adult Education), 1969-

The Challenge of Change: Developing Educational Guidance for Adults, 1986 (the first major report by the Unit for the Development of Adult Continuing Education).

Adult Education in the United Kingdom. A directory of organisations, 1950-60; superseded by Adult Education in 1961 [etc.]

Adult Education in 1961 [etc.], 1961 and annually to 1968, the 1968 edition being subtitled A Directory of Organisations; continued as A Directory of Organisations, 1969 and annually thereafter.

Brian Groombridge (reporter), Education and Retirement : An enquiry [by NIAE] into the relevance of education to the enjoyment of leisure in later life (1960).

Museums and Adult Education : The report of a working party appointed by the National Institute of Adult Education (1956).

Studies in the Education of Adults (formerly Studies in Adult Education), Vols.1-, 1969-; issues since 1974 published by NIAE, later NIACE, with previous issues being published by David and Charles, Newton Abbot, for UCAE.

Residential Short Courses, 1950- (issued twice yearly).

The University of Nottingham Department of Adult Education in association with NIAE commenced publication of Nottingham Studies in the Theory and Practice of the Education of Adults in 1975.

A.K. Stock and D. Howell (ed.), Education for Adult Immigrants [1976].

Thomas Kelly (ed.), A Select Bibliography of Adult Education in Great Britain (NIAE for NIAE and UCAE, 3rd ed., 1974). Continued as J.E. Thomas and J.H. Davies (eds.), A Select Bibliography of Adult Continuing Education in Great Britain including works published to the end of the year 1981 (1984). Continued as J.H. Davies and J.E. Thomas (eds.), A Select Bibliography of Adult Continuing Education (5th ed., revised and updated, 1988; containing references to material published up to the end of 1987).

Joy Groombridge (ed.), Learning for a Change (1987). A booklet of short summaries of the work of some of the NIACE's REPLAN projects. NIACE REPLAN has also published a series of summary reports (REPLAN Briefing), etc. The DES itself has published REPLAN Review (Nos.1-, August 1986-).

Alan Rogers (ed.), Group Projects in Local History (Dawson, Folkestone, for NIAE, 1977).

NATIONAL UNION OF STUDENTS

Address and
contact
National Union of Students,
461, Holloway Road,
London,
N7 6LJ

tel: 071 272 8900

History

The origins of the National Union of Students (NUS) may be traced back to the Inter-Varsity Association which was set up in 1921 by those from England who had attended the first congress of the Confédération internationale des étudiants (CIE), which had been established in 1919 in Prague. At a conference in London in September 1921 called by the Association and attended by students from universities and university colleges in England and Wales it was decided to dissolve the Association and establish a National Union of Students and in February 1922 a 'National Union of Students of the Universities and University Colleges of England and Wales' was formally established. The original objects of the NUS were 'to represent past and present students from a National and International point of view, and to render possible the co-operation of the body of students in England, Wales, Scotland, and Ireland with the students of other lands' and 'to promote the educational and social interests of students in entire independence of all political or religious propaganda.' Membership was open to the student organisations of universities and university colleges (and, from 1937, of institutions of further education). The NUS was initially administered by a council and an executive.

In the early years the NUS was particularly successful in co-operating with the AUT (through a joint committee, formed in 1927) in investigating the present methods of university education which culminated in two important reports, The Future of University and Higher Education (NUS, 1944) and 'Report on University Developments' (AUT) published in The Universities Review 1944-45; the NUS also in this period drew attention to the problems posed by unemployment among graduates and proposed solutions; and finally in this period the NUS established a travel bureau.

By 1942-43 the NUS' membership was in the region of 50,000, with representation from all universities; the NUS also now admitted teacher training and technical colleges to full membership. Attendance at its annual congresses in 1941-43 was a thousand or more. In addition to the AUT, NUS had established contacts with the UGC, CVCP, government departments, etc. In 1947 the NUS was affiliated to the International Union of Students (founded in 1946), though in 1955 it withdrew completely, the IUS being considered to have become a communist body. In the period c.1955-68 the NUS developed its contacts with the UGC and the CVCP and the Department of Education, etc. and submitted important evidence to several government committees, including that on Higher Education (Robbins Committee).

In 1969 NUS claimed a membership of over 407,000, of which only about 169,000 were in universities. During the period 1968-70 universities were to witness student disturbances but were also (to some extent in response to the joint statement of the NUS and CVCP of October 1968) making or improving existing arrangements for participation by students in the government of universities.

NUS Marketing was set up in 1977 by the NUS to provide products and services for young people. It was incorporated into NUS Services Ltd. in 1985. The four major areas covered by the company (which is based at 2nd Floor, Rigby House, 34 The Parade, Watford, Hertfordshire) are International Student Identity Card, National Student Promotions, National Student Discount Scheme, and Great Staff Merchandising. As part of an expansion of its commercial interests, NUS in April 1990 decided to launch NUS Services Ltd. in August 1991; this company is an amalgam of two, formerly separate, activities National Student Services Organisation (a purchasing co-operative) and NUS Services Ltd., the new company taking over the latter's name. There are other companies which have been set up by the NUS, and which are mainly in the insurance sector : Endsleigh Insurance Services Ltd. (incorporated 13 August 1965, no. 856706), which was founded by the NUS to look after the special insurance needs of students and young people, graduates and academics and which is now owned by two major insurance groups and has main centres in almost fifty cities; Endsleigh (Underwriting Agents) Ltd. (incorporated 2 May 1978, no. 1365923); Endsleigh Insurances (Brokers) Ltd. (incorporated 21 July 1978, no. 1379864); Endsleigh Trustee Services Ltd. (incorporated 4 March 1982, no. 1619914); and Endsleigh Financial Services Ltd. (incorporated 24 November 1987, no. 2197894), all these companies having registered offices at Endsleigh House, Ambrose Street, Cheltenham, Gloucestershire, GL50 3NR; and also Endsleigh Life and Pensions Ltd. (incorporated 24 September 1987, no. 2168755) with its registered office at 2 Oriel Terrace, Oriel Road, Cheltenham, Gloucestershire, GL50 1XP; and The National Union of Students International Centre Ltd. (incorporated 10 July 1958, no. 607785) with its registered office at 461 Holloway Road, London, NUS' offices.

Informal meetings of senior staff in Students' Unions have taken place for many years but in 1979 those arrangements were formalised through the establishment of the Student Union Senior Officers Conference (SUSOC). SUSOC is the established base for the collection and dissemination of information of value to permanent staff and also organises and co-ordinates training for Students' Unions' staff. SUSOC has a Standing Committee.

According to a recent NUS 'guide', the NUS has 1.25 million members in affiliated institutions (in universities, polytechnics, and colleges). It stands for 'the right of students to be treated as independent adults..; the right of young people to real training, educational and employment opportunities when they leave school; the right of students to appeal against academic decisions that affect their future, and a fair system of academic justice; the right of students to comment on the content and structure of their courses, and to press for changes where necessary; the right of students to a broadly-based education system that goes beyond lectures and classrooms, and presents new ideas, intellectual challenging and cultural experience', and 'the right of students and young people, as full members of society, to discuss and comment on the issues that affect them.' NUS provides local student unions with information, research and training and supports student Area Organisations. Representatives of student unions are kept in touch with developments through NUS information newsletters and conferences (the two conferences a year, at Easter and at Christmas, deciding NUS policy). A free magazine, National Student, is made available to students in individual student unions. NUS has an annual income of about £2 million.

In April 1988 the Secretary of State for Education and Science announced a government inquiry into the status and organisation of student unions in universities, polytechnics, and colleges, and the links between them and the NUS. The inquiry results were published in September 1989 and the Government decided to defer legislation (or consideration of legislation) on the subject.

Bibliography

Eric Ashby and Mary Anderson, The Rise of the Student Estate in Britain (Macmillan, London, 1970).

Brian Simon, 'The student movement in England and Wales during the 1930s', History of Education, Vol.16 No.3, 1987, pp.189-203.

Alexander Cockburn and Robin Blackburn (eds.), Student Power: Problems, Diagnosis, Action (Penguin Books in association with New Left Review, 1969).

Report from the Select Committee on Education and Science Session 1968-69 : Student Relations Vol. I Report, Vols. II - VII Evidence and Appendices and Documents; Session 1968-69 449-i to vii, HMSO, 1969.

David Caute, Sixty-Eight : The Year of the Barricades (Hamish Hamilton, London, 1988).

Ronald Fraser (et al.), 1968 : A Student Generation in Revolt (Chatto and Windus, London, 1988).

Publications include:-

Annual Report of the Council (for 1925-1926), 1926-?

NUS News Bulletin, [pre 1930]-?

NUS News, [pre 1957]-1958; continued as Student News, nos. 40-,1958-?

The National Union News : Bulletin of the National Union of Students..., ? (relates to date) 1922- 24.

NSM : The monthly journal of the National Union of Students, Issues 1-, 1987-

Graduate Employment : A report of the 1937 Congress of the National Union of Students of England and Wales [1937]

The Students Travel Guide, 1958-?

Year Book, later entitled Endsleigh Diary 1931-
     Endsleigh Diary replaces the NUS Yearbook which listed all the colleges etc. in membership of NUS and the addresses of other organisations which might be useful to Student Unions' officers. The diary, which is published by Endsleigh Insurance Services Ltd. on behalf of the NUS, combines directory information with a desk diary (based on the academic year). The directory information in the Diary includes a list of past Presidents of NUS, membership of NUS National Executive, NUS Wales/UCMC Executive, NUS Scotland Executive, NUS Staff List, NUS Areas and affiliated colleges, Endsleigh Insurance Services Ltd. Company Directory (head office at Cheltenham Spa, Gloucestershire), list of constituent organisations (including numbers of full- and part-time students in each who are affiliated to NUS), and "useful addresses".

National Student Magazine (covers popular culture, the arts, and current affairs), 1985-

Grants Handbook Vol.1 : Survey of local education authorities awards (1977)

Educational Charities : a guide to educational trust funds (1979)

Report of the Commission on Teaching in Higher Education presented to Liverpool Conference of National Union of Students, April 1969 (1969)

FE Can Really Change Your Life : the experience of Afro-Caribbean and Asian students in further education (1987) (report of a seminar organised by NUS)

Hugh Lanning, Victimisation Handbook (1975)

also Nurseries in Colleges and Universities : A Report by the EOC based on a survey carried out by the NUS (Equal Opportunities Commission, Manchester, 1980)

Records
It is believed that some records may have been disposed of upon the move of the NUS' offices to their current address in the mid 1980s.

The NUS has recently deposited a substantial number of its non-current records with the Modern Records Centre, University of Warwick Library (ref.MSS.280). The deposit mainly covers the 1960s-1980s and deals with a wide range of NUS activities and concerns, including, for example, its structure and functions in the 1970s, NUS services, Field Officers' work, art college closures and international affairs (especially South Africa, also Chile).

The papers of D. Gilles, a former Executive Committee member, have been deposited in the M.R.C. (ref. MSS.280), and a file of the NUS General Secretary related to the 'King and Country' debate, 1933-34, has been deposited in the M.R.C. by Mr. R. Blatchford of Blackheath (ref. MSS.280).

THE NATURAL ENVIRONMENT RESEARCH COUNCIL

Address and
contact
Natural Environment Research Council,
Polaris House,
North Star Avenue,
Swindon,
Wiltshire,
SN2 1EU.

tel: 0793 411500
fax: 0793 641652
Mrs. Ellie Skehan

History
The Natural Environment Research Council (NERC) is one of the five British research councils financed largely by a grant-in-aid from Parliament through the Department of Education and Science. The balance of its income is from commissioned research carried out for customers in the public and private sectors in this country and overseas.

Established by Royal Charter in 1965, NERC has responsibility for planning, encouraging and carrying out research in the physical and biological sciences which explain the natural processes of the environment. Only through such studies can an understanding of man's impact on his surroundings and their influence on his activities be achieved and sensible policies for the exploitation of natural resources be formed. NERC's subject coverage may be broadly defined as the Solid Earth (geology, geophysics, geochemistry, mineralogy, petrology, and glaciology) the Seas and Inland Waters (physical oceanography, marine life sciences, hydrology, etc.), the Terrestrial Environment (terrestrial ecology and soil science), and the Atmosphere (atmospheric, earth and life sciences). The NERC's annual report includes a section of Science Reports, describing the main features of the research carried out at the Council's institutes and at universities and polytechnics receiving financial support, under the following headings prior to the 1988-9 Report: The Solid Earth, The Seas-Physical, The Seas -Biological, Inland Waters-Physical, Inland Water-Biological, The Terrestrial Environment, the Atmosphere, and Co-ordinated Services (Computing Service, Technology Division, Research Vessel Services).

The Council carries out this research and training through its own institutes and grant-aided associations, and by grants, fellowships and other post-graduate awards to universities, polytechnics and other higher education establishments.

NERC comprised (as at the beginning of 1987) the following institutes: (a) nine component research institutes: British Geological Survey (formerly Institute of Geological Sciences, which was formerly the Geological Survey of Great Britain, founded in 1835), Institute of Oceanographic Sciences (formerly the National Institute of Oceanography, founded in 1949), Institute for Marine Environmental Research, Institute of Terrestrial Ecology (formerly part of the Nature Conservancy), Institute of Hydrology, Institute of Virology, the British Antarctic Survey, Sea Mammal Research Unit, Unit of Comparative Plant Ecology, and (b) three grant-aided research associations: The Marine Biological Association of the United Kingdom, the Scottish Marine Biological Association, and the Freshwater Biological Association. By the Science and Technology Act 1965, NERC took over the activities of the Nature Conservancy, a body which was set up on 23 March 1949 by Royal Charter as a Committee of the Privy Council with the functions of providing scientific advice on the conservation and control of the natural flora and fauna of Great Britain, establishing, maintaining, and managing nature reserves, and the organisation and development of research and scientific services related thereto. By the Nature Conservancy Act, 1973, a new Nature Conservancy Council was established as an independent body to carry out the functions relating to conservation then being performed by the Nature Conservancy as a committee of NERC.

It should be noted that the names of some of the components of NERC's Institutes have recently (1987-9) been changed: for instance the Institute of Oceanographic Sciences' Wormley Laboratory and Bidston Observatory have now (from 1 April 1987) become the Institute of Oceanographic Sciences, Deacon Laboratory, Wormley and the Proudman Oceanographic Laboratory, Bidston Observatory, Birkenhead respectively. NERC's annual report includes an appendix listing the various institutes, units, etc. of the Council.

NERC maintains a fleet of four ocean research vessels which are also used by universities. In addition, two research ships are maintained by the British Antarctic Survey to supply their five stations in Antarctica.
Under its Research Grants scheme, NERC provides financial help to universities

to enable investigators to pursue their own research projects which NERC has selected as having outstanding scientific merit, timeliness, or promise. NERC also supports universities through its training awards scheme, basically comprising Advanced Course Studentships, Research Studentships, and Research Fellowships. The percentage of the Council's Science Budget which has been made available to universities has increased from 9.8 in 1984 to 21.6 in 1988-89, as part of a long-standing commitment to increase its support for university based research.

In 1978-79 NERC employed 3,136 staff and was responsible for expenditure of £49.8m. In 1988-89 NERC was responsible for expenditure of £128.14M and as at October 1989 employed in the region of 2,970 staff in all. It receives approximately 30 per cent of its income as payment for work commissioned by Government Departments, under the customer - contractor arrangements adopted by the Government in 1972 following the Rothschild Report on Government Research and Development in 1971. Commissioned research income fell by a third between 1979 and 1983 and in 1985 stood at £27 millions of the Council's £90 millions annual budget. In February 1985 NERC published its first five year corporate plan (as nowadays required of all research councils) projecting a cut in the number of scientists and support staff employed from 3,130 to 2,230 in 1990, a closure of some laboratories, and a reorganisation of NERC's administration (including the appointment of three new 'directors of science' to control divisions looking after Earth Sciences, Terrestrial and Freshwater Sciences, and Marine Sciences), with the general objective of 'maintaining scientific efficiency, value for money and productivity'. Unlike the other major NERC establishments, the British Antarctic Survey (BAS) has had its budget considerably increased, following the Falklands War.

NERC and SERC share a library (P.O.Box 18, Swindon, Wiltshire, SN2 1ET: tel. 0793 26222 ext. 2292) which holds copies of the two Councils' Annual Reports, NERC Newsjournal, etc.

In 1988 proposals were made for forming a new Natural Resources Research Council, based essentially on an amalgamation of the AFRC and NERC, proposals which were initially put to the House of Lords' Select Committee on Science and Technology.

Bibliography
Jon Turney, 'Scientists defend their own habitat', in The Times Higher Education Supplement, 5 April 1985, p.11.

Articles about NERC appear in the scientific press, including New Scientist (e.g. issue of 18 November 1989 which includes a review of reports on the future of the earth sciences published by the Royal Society and NERC in October 1989.)

Publications
Annual Report (Report of the Council for...published by HMSO; covers period 1 April - 31 March.)

NERC Newsjournal (quarterly). Published from the early 1970s onwards; the issue for March 1986 is Vol.3 No.9. Apart from Council and general news, short papers on their research contributed by staff of NERC research institutes, etc., and news on research funded by NERC, this journal lists recent NERC research grant awards.

Policy Reviews

Scientific Reports

University Support

Occasional Publications

List of Publications

It should be noted that each of NERC's research institutes publishes various reports, and that NERC's own annual report publishes a list of reports and reviews which the headquarters has published during the year under review. Taking the case of the Institute of Oceanographic Sciences (IOS), its publications comprise: Annual Report, Collected Reprints (a yearly volume of reprints from periodicals and conference proceedings of papers by IOS staff), Discovery Reports (an irregular series of monographs devoted mainly to marine biology), MIAS [Marine Information and Advisory Service, IOS, Wormley, Godalming, Surrey] News Bulletin, IOS Report, and IOS Cruise Report.

Records
(a)   NERC's signed minutes and committee papers are retained permanently. Research grant papers for all research projects are kept permanently (unless the research is abandoned when the papers are destroyed after five years) as are papers relating to finance. Student files are kept for ten years and then destroyed. Destruction schedules make provision for periods of retention ranging from one to twenty years, as well as for permanent preservation.

(b)   The minutes and reports of the Geological Survey of Great Britain, founded in 1835, are stated to be held in the British Geological Survey's library which was recently moved from Exhibition Road, London to the BGS's headquarters in Keyworth, Nottinghamshire, (please contact Mr. McKenna at Keyworth for further information).

(c)   The majority of the archives of the British Antarctic Survey (prior to 1962 entitled the Falklands Islands Dependencies Survey (FIDS)) and of FIDS are held by the British Antarctic Survey Archives, BAS, High Cross, Madingley Road, Cambridge, CB3 0ET. The records of FIDS/BAS while part of the Colonial Office, 1945-67, are classified as public records and are subject to the thirty year rule. See G.J. Smith and J. Rae, B.A.S. Archives : Guide to Holdings (British Antarctic Survey, NERC, Cambridge; 1st edition, 1987).

(d)   Once they are thirty years old non-current records held by NERC are open to public inspection at NERC's offices on the same basis as records in the Public Record Office.

See too the entry on the Advisory Board for the Research Councils.

NORTH EASTERN UNIVERSITIES PURCHASING GROUP

Address and
contact
North Eastern Universities Purchasing Group,
NEUPG Office,
c/o University of Hull,
Hull,
HU6 7RX

tel: 0482 465354 and 466403
fax: 0482 465936
Secretary: Mr. L.F. Hodge

History
Conferences on university purchasing (COUP) are held regularly, usually once every eighteen months or two years. Most universities are members of regional purchasing groups which have been established to improve purchasing arrangements within and among universities. The North Eastern Universities Purchasing Group was formed in 1975.

Records
The Secretary holds the records of preliminary meetings, and of meetings of the Co-ordinating Committee and of the various specialist commodity groups, with the exception of the stationery and office supplies commodity group which has been serviced from the University of Sheffield since 1981.

The Secretary also holds the annual reports of the main committee and of the various commodity groups.

NORTH EASTERN UNIVERSITIES REGIONAL MANAGEMENT SERVICES UNIT

History
The Yorkshire and North Eastern Universities O & M Unit started its life on 1 April 1967, the day its Director began work. One of the first two such regional units to be established (the other being the Universities of Scotland O & M Unit), the Unit initially worked for a consortium of seven universities - Bradford, Durham, Hull, Leeds, Newcastle upon Tyne, Sheffield and York. The Universities of Leicester, Loughborough, and Nottingham joined the North Eastern Universities O & M Unit (as it was renamed) in August 1969. In 1986 the name of the Unit was changed to the North Eastern Universities Regional Management Services Unit. The Unit was financed by equal contributions from each member university.

The Unit's purpose was set out in its terms of reference: to study and advise on matters of university management or administration referred to it by member universities, and in association with the member universities to encourage the best possible management practices. The Management Committee of the Unit met twice a year and consisted of one representative of each member university; a Vice-Chancellor was the Chairman (usually for three years at a time), the Finance Officer of the University of York acted as the Treasurer, and the Director of the Unit was Secretary.

The Unit latterly had a staff of five: a Director (Mr. D. Edwards), three members, and a secretary. Its office was at the University of Leeds (Room 11/80, Physics/Admin. Building, Leeds, LS2 9JT; tel. 0532 465712).

The Management Committee for the ten member universities decided to disband the Unit, based in the University of Leeds, at the end of July 1988. It is believed that the universities now, if necessary, employ consultants for any future work/study exercises.

Bibliography (see too Publications below)
John Fielden and Geoffrey Lockwood, Planning and Management in Universities, Chatto and Windus for Sussex U.P., 1973, pp.330-331.

Publications
North Eastern Universities O & M Unit : Report by the Management Committee
Reports issued by the Unit for member universities: the titles of and the names of the universities commissioning the reports since the Unit's inception in 1967 are listed in Appendix C of the Report by the Management Committee, July 1981. Some of these reports are still confidential.

Records
The Director of the Unit held the minutes of the Management Committee from its inception in 1967, together with minutes of earlier, preliminary meetings. He also held a complete set of the Unit's reports. Requests to consult the Unit's records and reports were to be addressed to the Unit's Management Committee through the Director. Copies of all reports published by the Unit have been placed in the archive section of the University of York.

NORTH WESTERN UNIVERSITIES' MANAGEMENT SERVICES UNIT
(and NORTH WESTERN UNIVERSITIES' JOINT CONSULTATIVE COMMITTEE ON PURCHASING SERVICES AND SUPPLIES)

Address and
contact
North Western Universities' Management Services Unit,
2B Cambridge Street,
P.O. Box 147,
Liverpool,
L69 3BX

tel: 051 794 3132
Mr. J.L. Ross, Director, North Western Universities' Management
Services Unit
Mr. D.C. Cowan, Regional Purchasing Coordinator, NW Universities'
JCC on Purchasing Services and Supplies

History
Following a pattern by which a number of universities joined together to provide an Organization and Methods service, a Unit was created late in 1967

to serve the Universities of Lancaster, Liverpool, Manchester, and Salford, and the University of Manchester Institute of Science and Technology. Nowadays the member institutions of the Unit are the universities of Birmingham, Liverpool, Manchester, and Salford, the University College of North Wales (Bangor) (UCNW), and the University of Manchester Institute of Science and Technology (UMIST). The Unit consists of a Director, a Senior Management Services Officer, two Management Services Officers, a Regional Purchasing Coordinator, a Secretary, and a Clerk/Typist. It has been and continues to be accommodated at the University of Liverpool. The Unit is financed by contributions from member institutions apportioned on the basis of student numbers. The Universities of Aston, Keele, and Lancaster contribute towards the Unit's costs in proportion to their student numbers but at a fifth of the rate per student contributed by the six member institutions, this lower contribution being in respect of the three universities' sharing of the joint purchasing arrangements of the Unit. The Management Committee consists of three (previously two) representatives of each of the six member institutions.

In addition to its O. and M. and management services activities, the Unit has provided the secretariat for the North Western Universities' Joint Consultative Committee on Purchasing Services and Supplies. Group purchasing in the North West comprises nine institutions, including Liverpool, and members of the Unit service five specialist commodity groups covering computer consumables, furniture and soft furnishings, laboratory supplies, maintenance materials, and stationery and office equipment. The title of the Joint Consultative Committee may soon be changed to North Western Universities' Purchasing Group. The North Western region is represented at the Conference on University Purchasing (COUP) and liaises closely with other regional purchasing groups, exchanging minutes of meetings, annual reports, and details of negotiated prices among the regions.

Reflecting the change in the role of the Unit and in recognition of the development within the Unit of expertise in the capability and application of new office technology, the O. and M. Unit was formally redesignated in April 1986 as the North Western Universities' Management Services Unit.

The severe financial constraints imposed upon universities in recent years have brought increasing pressure to make even more effective use of resources and to make fundamental changes in respect of both organisations and methods of work. In particular, the recommendations of the Jarratt Report on Efficiency in Universities identified specific areas for improvement. Over the past decade, the combining of the purchasing power of the universities has produced substantial savings through joint tendering, joint negotiation and preferential terms. The Unit itself provides a considerable source of expertise and experience for effecting economies and increasing levels of effectiveness and efficiency in the individual institutions in the projects which they commission it to undertake.

Publications
Both the Unit's Management Committee and the Joint Consultative Committee on Purchasing Services and Supplies produce annual reports, copies of which are submitted to the member institutions. A version of the Management Committee's annual report has been incorporated in the annual reports of the member institutions. For instance, a report appears in the University of Liverpool's annual Report to the Court for 1968-69 onwards to 1984-5 inclusive, (no reports being published in the Report to the Court for 1975-6 to 1977-78 inclusive).

Records

(a)   The University Archives, Liverpool (P.O. Box 147, Liverpool, L69 3BX) hold the signed copies of the Committee's Minutes, 9 Nov. 1967-18 April 1986 (ref. A.095/1-5).

(b)   The Secretary of the Management Committee (currently Mrs. E.A. Finch, Administrative Assistant, Administrative Services, Senate House, Abercromby Square, University of Liverpool, P.O. Box 147, Liverpool, L69 3BX) holds the signed copies of the Committee's Minutes, 3 Oct. 1986-to date (2 vols.), correspondence, etc. These Minute Books incorporate copies of the minutes of the Joint Consultative Committee on Purchasing Services and Supplies for 30 May 1986-to date.

(c)   The Minute Books incorporate annual and other reports (including copies of the minutes of the Joint Consultative Committee on Purchasing Services and Supplies) submitted to the Committee for the period August 1971- to date.

(d)   The Unit itself holds (i) copies of its annual reports and of the Minutes of the Management Committee and of the Joint Consultative Committee on Purchasing Services and Supplies, (ii) copies of the project reports which its members have produced (both in a separate, bound, sequence, and also in the relevant file of correspondence etc. re the particular project).

SCHOOLS COUNCIL FOR THE CURRICULUM AND EXAMINATIONS

Address and
contact (of successor bodies)

School Examinations and Assessment Council,
Newcombe House,
45, Notting Hill Gate,
London,
W11 3JB.

tel: 071 229 1234

National Curriculum Council,
15-17 New Street,
York,
YO1 2RA

tel: 0904 622533

History

The Schools Council for the Curriculum and Examinations, commonly known as the Schools Council, was established in 1964. On the examinations side it took over work which had previously been carried out, since 1917, by the Secondary Schools Examination Council.

An independent body, the Schools Council was funded half by the Department of Education and Science and half by local education authorities. Its functions were mainly to promote education by carrying out research into, and keeping under review, the curricula, teaching methods, and examinations in schools, and to advise the Secretary of State on examination policy. It funded a large number of research projects, many of them in close co-operation with the staff of individual universities. It also performed a co-ordinating function in relation to the GCE and CSE boards.

The constitution of the Council reflected the statutory and traditional distribution of responsibility for the work of the schools in that central Government, the local authorities, and teachers effectively directed its activities, while user interests (employers, parents, further and higher education) were also represented. The Council was administered by a Governing Council (whose chairman was appointed by the Secretary of State for Education and Science), a majority of whose members were teachers. The Governing Council, which was ultimately reponsible for the Council's policy, was assisted by a number of inter-related committees (including a Finance and Priorities Committee, introduced under the new constitution adopted in 1978) and sub-committees. In response to some criticism of its work, especially on the curriculum side, the Council adopted a new constitution giving greater representation to central and local government and the "users" of the school system in September 1978.

In 1978-79 the Council employed 143 members of staff and spent £2.748m gross.

In March 1981 the Secretary of State for Education and Science appointed Mrs. Nancy Trenaman to review the functions, constitution and methods of work of the Council, and to make recommendations. Mrs. Trenaman recommended that the Council should continue and with its present functions, though she suggested that the Council should review its constitution and committee structure. On 22 April 1982 the Secretary of State announced in the House of Commons that the Schools Council was to be disbanded and in its place was to be set up a school curriculum development committee and a Secondary Examinations Council (SEC).

The SEC was established as a company limited by guarantee on 23 May 1983, wholly funded by the DES. It was responsible for promoting improvements in school-based examinations and other systems of assessment in England and Wales and for advising the Secretaries of State for Education and Science and for Wales on national examinations policies and their implementation. Sir Wilfred Cockcroft was appointed full-time Chairman and Chief Executive of the SEC for five years on 23 November 1982; the membership of the SEC was announced on 2 March 1983. The SEC was established in the same building as the Schools Council, Newcombe House. Under the Education Reform Act 1988, the School Examinations and Assessment Council (SEAC) was established as an independent Government Agency to advise the Secretaries of State on all school examinations and assessment matters; it replaces SEC and is responsible for developing the assessment system at ages 7,11,14 and 16 for the national curriculum.

Details of the School Curriculum Development Committee's form and functions were finalised in discussion between the DES and the local authority associations. In August 1983 Professor Roger Blin-Stoyle, F.R.S., was appointed Chairman of the Committee. Mr. Keith McWilliams was appointed Chief Executive. Half the membership of the Committee was appointed on the nomination of the local authority associations and the Welsh Joint Education Committee; the Secretaries of State appointed the remainder in a personal capacity. Members of the Committee were appointed and the Committee established later in 1983. The Schools Council was dissolved later in 1983 after the School Curriculum Development Committee had been established. The School Curriculum Development Committee (SCDC) was also based at Newcombe House and an Information Centre served both the Committee and the SEC. Under the Education Reform Act 1988, the SCDC was replaced by the National Curriculum Council (NCC), which exists to keep all aspects of the curriculum for maintained schools under review, etc.

Bibliography

Report of the Working Party on School Curricula and Examinations (The Lockwood Report), H.M.S.O., 1964.

Derek H. Morrell, Education and Change, the Joseph Payne Memorial Lectures of the College of Preceptors, May 1966.

Ronald Manzer, 'The Technical Power of Organised Teachers' in Teachers and Politics, University of Manchester Press, 1970.

Jack Wrigley, 'The Schools Council' in Educational Research in Britain 2, J. Butcher and H. B. Pont (eds.), U.L.P. 1970.

Geoffrey Caston, 'The Schools Council in Context', Journal of Curriculum Studies, May 1971.

John Nisbet, 'The Schools Council' in Case Studies of Educational Innovation: 1 At Central Level, CERI/OECD, 1973.

Schools Council, Pattern and variation in Curriculum Development Projects, Macmillan Education, 1973.

Schools Council, Evaluation in Curriculum Development: Twelve Case Studies, Macmillan Education, 1973.

Anne Corbett, 'The secret garden of the curriculum - who should hold the key to the door?', Times Educational Supplement, 13 July, 1973.

Schools Council, Dissemination and In-Service Training. (Pamphlet 14), 1974.

Secondary Education, March 1974. The whole issue.

Colin Richards, 'The Schools Council - a critical examination', Universities Quarterly, Summer 1974.

Ian Parry, 'The Schools Council and Primary Education', Ideas, June 1974.

A. J. Light, 'Schools Council and the development of the secondary curriculum' in Ideas, October 1974.

Robert Bell and William Prescott (eds), The Schools Council: a second look, Ward Lock Educational, 1975.

Dennis Lawton, The politics of the school curriculum, Routledge and Kegan Paul, 1980 (Chapter 5 is devoted to the Schools Council.)

Elizabeth Adams, 'And never the twain shall meet: The Schools Council', in Higher Education Review, Vol. 15, No.3, Summer 1983, pp.38-53. (An assessment of the past 18 years of the work of the Council, now to be disbanded, and the implications for the future of the curriculum and examinations.)

Schools Council, Issues and Achievements: a response to the proposals of the Secretary of State for Education and Science for disbanding the Council, June 1982.

Maurice Plaskow (ed.), Life and Death of the Schools Council, Falmer Press, London, 1985.

Publications
The Schools Council published a large number of publications, publishing a checklist of titles in print. They basically comprise the following, those marked with an asterisk * being recurring publications put out by the Council itself.

H.M.S.O. published the Schools Council's Working Papers, Examination Bulletins, Curriculum Bulletins etc. until 1969 and a list of publications in these series which are still available from HMSO are listed in their Government Publications Sectional List No.2. From July 1969 until March 1980 new publications in the series of Working Papers and Bulletins were published for the Schools Council by Evans/Methuen Educational and subsequently by Methuen Educational.

*Schools Council Reports:
covers the first three years (1964-67) in one volume and thereafter each year covered in a separate volume.

*Working Papers Nos. 1-, 1965-

*Examination Bulletins Nos.1-, 1963-
(the first four titles were published for the Secondary Schools Examination Council whose work was taken over by the Schools Council).

*Curriculum Bulletins Nos.1-, 1965-

Non-series Publications, 1966-

Committee for Wales Publicatons, 1967-
(originating from the Schools Council's Committee for Wales).

Research Reports, 1968-

Research Studies, 1972-

Teaching Materials from Curriculum Development Projects, 1970-

Tests, 1968-

Films (included within the catagory of project publications)

Curriculum Discussion Kits, 1970-

*Schools Council Pamphlets, Nos.1-, 1969-

Field Reports, Nos.1-, 19

*Information Leaflets

*Schools Council Project Profiles and Index
(a set of information sheets on the Schools Council and Nuffield Foundation curriculum research and development projects, updated annually), 1972-

* Link, 1979- (formerly Project News a 6-monthly news sheet, 1972 onwards)

*<u>Occasional Bulletins</u> from the Subject Committees

*<u>Schools Council News</u> 1979- (formerly <u>Dialogue</u> from 1968, then <u>Newsletter</u> from 1977)

<u>Records</u>
(i)   Record copies of all the publications of the Schools Council and project materials were kept in the Council's Information Centre. The Information Centre serving the SEC and the SCDC held these publications and papers together with the records of the major committees of the Schools Council.

(ii)   The Kew branch of the Public Record Office now holds the following records of the Schools Council:-

   EJ1 Agenda and minutes of the Council and the majority of its subsidiary committees, working parties and groups, for the period 1964-84.

   EJ2 Numbered Papers issued by the Council's committees etc., 1964-83, and a few papers of the Secondary Schools Examination Council etc., 1961-3.

   The papers of the Secondary Schools Examination Council may be found in ED 147/212-326 and other documents re the Schools Council in ED 147/833-907, at the Kew branch of the PRO.

(iii)   The Institute of Education, University of London, also holds copies of Schools Council publications.

SCIENCE AND ENGINEERING RESEARCH COUNCIL

<u>Address and</u>
<u>contact</u>
Science and Engineering Research Council,
Polaris House,
North Star Avenue,
P.O.Box 18,
Swindon,
Wiltshire,
SN2 1ET.

tel: 0793 411000 ext.1438
     0793 411438
fax: 0793 411400
Mr. John Merchant, Secretary of the Council

<u>History</u>
The Science and Engineering Research Council (SERC) was founded, as the Science Research Council, by Royal Charter in 1965, taking over six national research establishments and the basic research functions of the former Department of Scientific and Industrial Research. The Council's title was changed to its current title in 1981, reflecting the Council's increased emphasis on engineering.

The SERC supports fundamental research in astronomy, the biological sciences, chemistry, engineering, mathematics, and physics. The Council devotes most of its resources to:

1. helping university and polytechnic staff to carry out basic research at the forefront of their subjects, either in their own institution or in one of the Council's own research establishments or, if necessary, elsewhere;

and
2. enabling suitable graduates to receive further training or to carry out independent research.

The SERC awards grants to help pay for equipment, materials or travel which are required for a research project and to enable a university or polytechnic to employ additional staff to work full-time on a project, or to invite to the United Kingdom leading scientists from other countries. More recently SERC has instituted and funded Interdisciplinary Research Centres (each generally drawing upon staff within individual departments in several universities), the first four to be announced (by February 1988) being at the Universities of Cambridge (on superconductivity), Glasgow (on engineering design), Liverpool (on surface science), and Oxford (on molecular sciences).

The SERC has four research establishments: the Royal Greenwich Observatory at Cambridge (founded in 1675 at Greenwich), the Royal Observatory at Edinburgh, the Rutherford Appleton Laboratory, Didcot, and the Daresbury Laboratory, Warrington, Cheshire (founded in 1958), which all publish annual reports. SERC also has four Directorates: for Application of Computers to Manufacturing, Information Technology, the Teaching Company Scheme, and Biotechnology. The Royal Greenwich Observatory moved in 1990 from Hurstmonceux to a new building next to the Institute of Astronomy, University of Cambridge.

The SERC also arranges for British university scientists and its own scientific staff to have access to several major international scientific facilities. In particular, SERC participates in CERN (the European Centre for Nuclear Research), the European Space Agency (ESA), the Institute Laue-Langevin, the La Palma Observatory, the UK infra-red telescope in Hawaii, the Anglo-Australian Telescope, and the European Incoherent Scatter Facility. These facilities are available to university researchers.

Together with the Department of Trade and Industry, the Ministry of Defence, and industry, SERC sponsored a five year programme (the Alvey Programme) of pre-competitive collaborative research in the enabling technologies of information technology. The programme commenced in 1983 and in 1987 HMSO published Evaluation of the Alvey Programme : Interim Report. The European equivalent of this programme is ESPRIT (see p.210). Together with the Department of Trade and Industry, SERC supports another programme which has proved a very successful system of collaboration between industry and higher educational institutions, the Teaching Company Scheme (TCS). Under TCS, academic staff are seconded part-time to work with a company.

Most of the Council's business is carried out through its four Boards: the Astronomy and Planetary Science Board; the Engineering Board; the Nuclear Physics Board; and the Science Board.

In 1978-79 SERC employed 2,785 staff and was responsible for £157m expenditure. On 31 March 1989 SERC's staff numbered 2,705 and in 1988-89 SERC was responsible for £365.5M expenditure.

Bibliography

A Review of the Framework for Government Research and Development: a review of the changes announced in Cmnd.5046, Cmnd.7499, HMSO, 1979.

Articles on the work of the Council appear in the educational and scientific press, including New Scientist (which reported at length on the proposal to move the Royal Greenwich Observatory) and The Times Higher Education Supplement (which reported on SERC under its chairman since 1985, Professor Bill Mitchell, in its edition of 13 May 1988).

Publications

Annual Report (covers period 1 April-31 March), sold by HMSO; the Reports bear an ISSN: 0261-7005.

SERC Bulletin (formerly SRC Bulletin) Feb. 1977- to date. Includes details of new publications from SERC, as well as summaries of the Council's policies, programmes, and reports; nowadays normally three issues a year of the Bulletin are published.

For publications of the Royal Greenwich Observatory (including tercentenary Historical Review by W.H.Mc.Crea published in 1975) published or sold by HMSO see HMSO's Government Publications Sectional List No.50 (periodically revised).

Records

The Central Office of SERC, whilst not subject per se to the Public Records Acts of 1958 and 1967, adheres to that legislation, including the "First Review" five years after the date of the last paper on the file and the "Second Review" twenty-five years after the file was opened. Only a very small proportion of records will be of a kind to require permanent preservation. The Public Record Office has allocated the group code EV for the records of SERC, although at present no records of SERC have been transferred to the PRO.

Most SERC policy files will be the subject of the Second Review, but the bulk of the Council's routine work is of the short-term variety, the resultant records seldom being kept for more than seven years.

Research grant records in respect of investigators in universities are normally kept for seven years after the termination of the grant or for three years if the application was unsuccessful. Files in respect of SERC supported postgraduate students are normally retained for five years after the end of period of support. Included in the SERC's records are, of course, copies of all letters, reports, etc. that originate in SERC, including those to universities.

The general aim in this field of activity is to preserve records that have or are likely to have some importance in the wider historical sense, as well as those that are deemed necessary for adequate chronicling of the activities of a particular institution. Thus each institution must be responsible for the documents it originates although, where there is joint responsibility for a particular paper or set of papers, there should be consultation.

In the case of the Royal Greenwich Observatory, the archives were deposited on permanent loan in Cambridge University Library in 1989-90; they are administered by the Library's Department of Manuscripts and are held as part of the Department's collections. All of the RGO's records have the classmark 'RGO', there being 175 classes within the classmark. To date (July 1990) there are full handlists to approximately 50 of these classes, with brief identifying lists to perhaps 20 classes more. There are card indexes to some 40,000 names in the correspondence of the seventh Astronomer Royal, Sir George B. Airy (Astronomer Royal 1835-81) (class RGO 6), to the papers of the Board of Longitude (RGO 14), and to the papers of the Royal Observatory, Cape of Good Hope (RGO 15). There is no published guide to the collection. All the finding aids may be consulted at the Department of Manuscripts' Reading Room, Written application to view the RGO archives must precede any visit to Cambridge University Library and all enquiries should be addressed to Mr. Adam Perkins, RGO Archivist, Department of Manuscripts, Cambridge University Library, West Road, Cambridge, CB3 9DR (tel. 0223 333000).

The RGO's archival collections of glass plate negatives of celestial objects and other subjects have been transferred to the Royal Greenwich Observatory, Madingley Road, Cambridge, CB3 OEZ (tel. 0223 374000).

The Kew branch of the Public Record Office holds the following records of the Royal Greenwich Observatory:- Observations, Computations, Mathematical papers, etc., of Astronomers Royal, 1630-1774. These records bore the class reference PRO 28/50-81 but they have now been reclassified as RGO classes.

See too the entry on the Advisory Board for the Research Councils.

SCOTTISH TERTIARY EDUCATION ADVISORY COUNCIL

Address and
contact
Scottish Education Department,
43 Jeffrey Street,
Edinburgh,
EH1 1DN
Scotland

tel: 031 556 8400
telex: 000000
Mr. Simon Hook

History
The Scottish Tertiary Education Advisory Council (STEAC) was appointed in July 1984 by the Secretary of State for Scotland, as a temporary body for an initial period of two years, with the following terms of reference, agreed by the Secretary of State for Education and Science : 'To consider and report on the future strategy for higher education in Scotland, including the arrangements for providing institutions with financial support and the general principles which should govern relationships between universities and other institutions; to advise the Secretary of State on such other matters as he may remit to the Council; and to collaborate as necessary with the University Grants Committee, the National Advisory Bodies for local authority higher education in England and Wales, the Manpower Services Commission and other appropriate bodies.' STEAC's term was later entended for a further year.

The origins of STEAC are to be found in the former Council for Tertiary Education in Scotland (CTES), which was established by the Government in 1979 to advise the Secretary of State on such questions relating to tertiary education in Scotland as he remitted to the Council and on such other matters as the Council considered relevant to the development of non-university tertiary education and its relationship with university education in Scotland. CTES reported in 1981 in favour of a national authority to oversee Scottish non-university tertiary education, answerable to the Secretary of State (Review of Structure and Management, CTES, 1981) but the Government rejected this proposal in favour of a new body with an advisory role only.

In a report in 1985 (Cmnd. 9676), STEAC proposed an overarching body to be responsible for academic planning across the universities, Central Institutions, and colleges of education in Scotland and for allocation of resources within a system of funding unified under the Secretary of State, but a majority of the Standing Committee of the Scottish Universities opposed such a proposal, as did the UGC.

Following consideration of this recommendation of STEAC and in the light of the Croham Committee's report on the future of the UGC, the Secretary of State for Scotland announced on 1 April 1987 the Government's decision that the new Universities Funding Council would have a Scottish Committee. In consultation with the SED, this Scottish Committee will consider demand for and the balance of provision between the parts of the higher education system in Scotland. The new procedures for planning and co-ordination for higher education are intended to enable the Scottish universities to maintain their role as part of the UK university system, but also to plan their provision in conjunction with the Central Institutions and the rest of the Scottish higher education system.

As regards STEAC's other recommendation in its 1985 report, that provision of teacher training in Scotland should be rationalised, the Secretary of State for Scotland in July 1986 decided that as from 1 April 1987 the training of physical education teachers, both men and women, should be centralised on the site of the former Dunfermline College of Physical Education; that Dunfermline College be merged with Moray House College of Education; and that Aberdeen and Dundee Colleges of Education be merged under the new title of the Northern College of Education.

STEAC's fixed term of office expired in July 1987 and the Secretary of State for Scotland, having in mind no further tasks for it, decided to dissolve the Council, commending in particular the breadth and clarity of its strategy report.

Bibliography
Walter M. Humes, The Leadership Class in Scottish Education (John Donald Publishers Ltd., Edinburgh, 1986) includes a section on the structure and management of tertiary education, with references to STEAC.

'STEAC Completes its Term of Office', Scottish Office News Release, 0992/87, 28 July 1987.

Tom Bone, 'The Scottish Dimension', in Higher Education Quarterly, Vol.41 No.1, 1987, pp.43-56. (Dr. Thomas Bone was Vice-Chairman of STEAC)

Publications

Future Strategy for Higher Education in Scotland : Report of the Scottish
    Tertiary Education Advisory Council on its Review of Higher Education in
    Scotland (Chairman : Mr. Donald M. McCallum), Cmnd. 9676, HMSO, 1985.
    Chapter 2 provides an outline of the main features of current higher
    education provision in Scotland.

Business and Management Education in Scotland, HMSO, 1987.
    In January 1986 STEAC had been asked to undertake a review of the
    Scottish Business School and this report was the product of the review.

Records

The Scottish Education Department holds records for STEAC and the former CTES.
These records will be available to the public after thirty years have elapsed.

SCOTTISH UNIVERSITIES CAMPUS HOTELS

Address and
contact
Scottish Universities Campus Hotels,
P.O. Box 808,
Edinburgh,
EH14 4AS
Scotland

tel: 031 449 4034
telex: 727918
Mr. Sinclair G. Leask

History

The Scottish Universities Campus Hotels (which adopted its current title in
1987) originated as the Scottish Universities Accommodation Consortium (SUAC)
in 1986. A unified marketing body, Campus Hotels is composed of the
accommodation and other facilities which the Universities of Aberdeen, Dundee,
Edinburgh, Glasgow, St.Andrews, Stirling, and Strathclyde, and Heriot-Watt
University make available to the public, generally during the Easter and
Summer holidays, although some of the universities make their facilities
available at other times of the year also. Campus Hotels offers the most
comprehensive conference, exhibition and accommodation packages available in
Scotland, attracting over forty per cent of all conferences held north of the
Border. It is not a registered company.

Bibliography

No book or journal article has been published about Campus Hotels.

Publications

Brochure : 'Accommodation Campus Hotels Scotland' [1986]

Brochure : 'Conference Scotland' [1988]

Records
The principal records of Campus Hotels and of SUAC are retained by the Campus Hotels' office and certain of the non-current records might be consulted by bona fide researchers by appointment.

SCOTTISH UNIVERSITIES MANAGEMENT SERVICES AND EFFICIENCY UNIT

Address and
contact
Mr. Brian P. Clapp,
34, Buccleuch Place,
Edinburgh,
EH8 9JT
Scotland

tel: 031 667 1011 ext. 6531/6835

History
The Unit was founded on 1st May 1967 as the Universities of Scotland Organisation and Methods Unit and was retitled the Scottish Universities Management Services and Efficiency Unit on 1st February 1987. The new name reflected more accurately the remit of the Unit as it developed over the years.

The Unit and the North Eastern Universities O & M Unit were both established in 1967. They were the pioneer members of a group that has expanded to include Units for the North-Western and Southern Universities, for the London University colleges, and for the Open University, and individual O & M presences in East Anglia, Exeter, Newcastle, Sheffield, Oxford and Keele.

The Units originated as a consequence of questions in Parliament on efficiency in universities which were then followed by contacts between the DES and the CVCP to discuss possible action. These contacts resulted in the CVCP setting up a sub-committee under Sir Charles Wilson, Principal of the University of Glasgow, to devise a scheme for the organisation of regional O & M groups. The sub-committee subsequently selected Scotland and the North-East as the areas in which to start the scheme. The minutes of the opening meeting on the matter between the sub-committee and the Scottish and North-Eastern Secretaries and Registrars record Sir Charles as explaining that the "background to the present meeting was the considerable amount of public pressure on the subject of organisation and method studies, to which the Vice-Chancellors' Committee had felt bound to respond".

The parliamentary initiative did not seek to distinguish between "central" administration and administration in academic departments. From their inception, however, the Units have mainly been steered towards work in non-academic areas. In recent years this has changed with the Scottish Unit in particular deploying up to 25% of its resources in academic departments.

The Unit was supported by all eight Scottish Universities - Aberdeen, Dundee, Edinburgh, Glasgow, Heriot-Watt, St.Andrews, Stirling and Strathclyde. Its Committee of Management was made up of senior academic and administrative staff from these institutions. There was a staff of five: a Director, three consultants, and a secretary. The operating costs of the Unit are allocated between the supporting universities by means of a formula taking into account both usage and institutional size.

The early retirement of staff, coupled with problems of attracting staff to posts on university salary scales and the increasing use of outside consultants, led to the closure of the Unit officially on 30 September 1989, but Mr. Brian Clapp, the Unit's Director, is not due fully to retire until the end of September 1990. The Management Committee of the Unit is still in existence but it is probable that it will be finally wound up at the end of September 1990. It should be noted that the work undertaken by the Unit is one of the matters with which the Secretaries' Committee of the Scottish Universities, 'The Scottish Secretariat', will be concerned; the current (June 1990) Secretary of the 'Secretariat' is Mr. R.L. Crawford, Academic Registrar, University of Strathclyde, Glasgow, G1 1XQ, Scotland.

In addition to the projects undertaken for the individual Scottish universities and the joint projects undertaken for some or all of the Scottish universities, the Unit periodically undertook, on a fee basis, work for external bodies and institutions (for instance, more recently, the Queen's University, Belfast).

Bibliography
There is no published history of the Unit.

Records
(a)   The Minutes of the Management Committee are held by Mr. Clapp and copies are also held by the Secretaries of the eight supporting universities.

(b)   Mr. Clapp holds two full sets of its commissioned reports. The projects completed and/or reports submitted by the Unit are listed in the annual Report of the Committee of Management of the Unit (year to 31 July).

(c)   It is likely that the minutes, reports, and other Unit records which Mr. Clapp holds will be deposited with a Scottish university record repository.

SCOTTISH UNIVERSITIES SPORTS FEDERATION

Address and
contact
Mr. D.G. Mieras,
Hon. Secretary,
Scottish Universities Sports Federation,
Sports Centre,
Heriot-Watt University,
Riccarton,
Currie,
Edinburgh,
EH14 4AS
Scotland

tel: 031 449 5111 ext. 4050

History

The Scottish Universities Sports Federation (SUSF) - originally the Scottish Universities Sports Board - was inaugurated on 29 April 1955 at a meeting held in Edinburgh attended by representatives of the athletic clubs of the universities of Aberdeen, Edinburgh, Glasgow and St.Andrews. The Sports Board was accepted as a corporate body of the British Universities Sports Board; both Boards later changed their titles to Federation - the British in 1962, and the Scottish in January 1974. The number of universities in Scotland meanwhile increased from four to eight, Strathclyde, Dundee, Heriot-Watt and Stirling universities being added to the Board/Federation.

The Federation is the governing body for inter and international university sport for Scotland. It is run by an Executive Committee, the Presidents of the Athletic/Sports Unions of the member universities, and three honorary officers, Chairman, Secretary, and Treasurer.

Bibliography

Nothing published.

Publications

A Handbook is issued for information to each university; it is basically loose leaf, and is annually updated.

Records

The minutes, reports, correspondence and accounts are held by the Honorary Secretary and may be studied in situ.

SOCIETY FOR THE PROTECTION OF SCIENCE AND LEARNING

Address and contact

Miss E. Fraser,
Secretary,
Society for the Protection of Science and Learning Ltd.,
20/21 Compton Terrace,
London,
N1 2UN

tel: 071 226 6747 : Tuesdays and Thursdays only

History

The Society for the Protection of Science and Learning was founded in May 1933 as the Academic Assistance Council, changing its title to the Society for the Protection of Science and Learning in 1936. It was formed to assist scholars and scientists who, on grounds of religion, race or opinion, were unable to continue their work in their own country. By March 1936 it could be stated that the Council's services had been needed chiefly to help the 1300 university teachers displaced in Germany (after Hitler came to power) and that it had also assisted refugee scholars from Russia, Portugal and other countries. Assistance in the form of short-term financial help with money raised by appeals to the academic and business communities allowed the Society to assist several thousand emigré scholars by the outbreak of the Second World War. After the outbreak of war, many academic refugees who came to Britain from Allied countries occupied by the Germans sought help from the Society. In more recent years, after the War, the Society has continued its work on a smaller scale, assisting refugees from Poland, Hungary, South Africa, and many other parts of the world. By 1958, as Lord Beveridge wrote, the Society had assisted 2,600 men and women : "individually they are of outstanding importance", including world-famous scientists and scholars. Of the refugee scholars registered with the Society, 16 have received knighthoods, 16 have become Nobel Laureates, 71 Fellows or Foreign Members of the Royal Society of London, and 50 Fellows or Corresponding Fellows of the British Academy.

Since the War, the Society has helped displaced and persecuted scholars from many countries, including Hungary (particularly in 1956 in response to the uprising and subsequent expulsion of many university teachers), South Africa, and the USSR, and, more recently, academics who have suffered as the result of political changes in Czechoslovakia, Greece, Poland, Brazil, Biafra, Bangladesh, Chile, Argentina, Zambia, the former Rhodesia, Uruguay, Ethiopia, Iran, Iraq, and Turkey.

Nowadays the Society tries to assist people dismissed from university teaching or research positions in overseas countries for reasons of racial origin, political or religious belief. It co-operates with other concerned bodies, including Amnesty International, and World University Service. The Society holds an annual meeting but does not nowadays issue any publications (apart from its appeal document, 1987). It is both a company limited by guarantee and also (since 1959) a registered charity (no.207471).

(For further details see the bibliography below, in particular Lord Beveridge's account, and also the introduction to Nicholas Baldwin's guide to the Society's archive, 1988, for which see Records (a) below.)

Bibliography
Lord Beveridge, A Defence of Free Learning (Oxford U.P., London, 1959)
    Lord Beveridge was a founder and Hon. Secretary of the Academic Assistance Council 1933-38, Vice-President of the Society for the Protection of Science and Learning 1938-44 and the Society's President from 1944.

A.[Ari] J. Sherman, Island Refuge : Britain and Refugees from the Third Reich, 1933-1939 (Elek, London, 1973).

Bernard Wasserstein, Britain and the Jews of Europe, 1935-1945 (Institute of Jewish Affairs, London, 1979).

Herbert A. Strauss and Werner Röder (eds.), International Biographical Dictionary of Central European Emigrés 1933-1945 (3 vols; K.G. Saur, Munich, London, New York, Paris, 1983).
    The title of this work as quoted is the alternative English title of Werner Röder and Herbert A. Strauss, Biographisches Handbuch der deutschsprachigen Emigration nach 1933, 3 vols. in 4, 1980-83.

J.C. Jackman and C.M. Borden, The Muses Flee Hitler : Cultural Transfer and Adaptation, 1930-1945 (Smithsonian Institution Press, Washington, 1983).

Miriam Kochan, Britain's Internees in the Second World War, (Macmillan, London, 1983).

Peter Kroner (ed.), Vor fünfzig Jahren : Die Emigration deutschsprachiger Wissenschaftler 1933-39 (Gesellschaft für Wissenschaftgeschichte, Munster, 1983).

Robin E. Rider, 'Alarm and Opportunity - Emigration of Mathematicians and Physicists to Britain and the United States, 1933-45', Historical Studies in the Physical Sciences, Vol.15 Part 1, 1984, pp.107-176.

P.K. Hoch, 'The Reception of Central European Refugee Physicists of the 1930s : USSR, UK, USA', Annals of Science, Vol.40 No.3, 1983, pp.217-246.

Michael R. Marrus, The Unwanted : European Refugees in the Twentieth Century (Oxford U.P., New York, 1985).

'Appeal : The Society for the Protection of Science and Learning Limited', 1987. (provides an account of the Society's origins and aims, and its present needs, and also lists the members of the Council of the Society.)

Since 1988 Oxford University Press has published a new quarterly journal covering the interests of the Society, etc., the Journal of Refugee Studies.

Publications

Annual Reports, 1934, 1935, 1937, 1938, 1946.
Newsletter, nos. 1, 2 and Interim Report no.3 etc., 1947-50.
A Crisis in the University World (pamphlet), 1935.

Records

(a) The archives of the Society principally for the period up to 1958 are held by the Department of Western Manuscripts, Bodleian Library, Broad Street, Oxford, OX1 3BG. The archives comprise more than 5,000 files. The bulk of the archive consists of series of case files concerning individual refugees, in many academic fields. There are also series of administrative records and correspondence with other refugee groups and with national and international organizations. Whilst the majority of the archives deposited cover the period up to 1958, there are also Committee/AGM papers up to 1986, and some files of correspondence with other organisations and case files of some individual refugees for the post-1958 period. Included in the deposited archives are also copies of the Society's publications.

Records more than thirty years old are available for research. For access to personal files which relate to people still living and for permission to see material less than thirty years old, application should be made to the Society's Secretary; both the Bodleian Library and the Society must be satisfied that any person wishing to work on the archive is a bona fide scholar. Written permission should also be sought for the use of any of the archive in published work and for photocopying.

Copies of the Catalogue of the archive (list and index; 207pp.) may be consulted at the Bodleian Library, the other copyright libraries, the National Register of Archives (NRA 31126), the Royal Society, the

Wellcome Institute for the History of Medicine, the Wiener Library, the German Historical Institute, and the Hebrew University of Jerusalem. In addition the Bodleian Library has published a useful guide (24pp.) to the archive by Nicholas Baldwin, <u>The Society for the Protection of Science and Learning Archive</u> (1988), which is available from the Bodleian Library and from the Society (£1.50 incl. postage and packing).

It is envisaged that in due course records of a more recent date will gradually also be deposited by the Society at the Bodleian Library.

(b)   The Society retains at its office its original minute books, card indexes of refugees, and the bulk of the case files relating to individual refugees assisted since 1960. The Society's Honorary Secretary, Mr. Iain R. Wright, also has special responsibility for the Society's archives.

SOUTHERN UNIVERSITIES' MANAGEMENT SERVICES

<u>Address and
contact</u>
Southern Universities' Management Services,
The University of Reading,
Building L11,
London Road,
Reading,
RG6 2AH

tel: 0734 874711
Mr. R.I. Hunter, Director

<u>History</u>
The Southern Universities' Organisation and Methods Unit (which in 1987 changed its title to Southern Universities Management Services) was formed in 1968 at the instigation of a group of universities. Nowadays it has eight constituent members, the Universities of Bristol, Essex, Exeter, Reading, Southampton, and Surrey, and Brunel University and the City University. The Management Committee (which meets twice a year) consists of one representative of each member university together with a Vice-Chancellor as chairman. The Chairman of the Southern Universities' Purchasing Consortium is invited to attend Committee meetings. The staff of the Unit comprises a Director, two Management Services Officers, and a part-time Secretary.

The terms of reference of the Unit are to provide assistance and advice in all aspects of administration, at the request of member universities. The Unit provides a management consultancy service for its members covering most aspects of administration. It would not normally undertake detailed work measurement or computer programming. The majority of the Unit's time is devoted to projects in a formal programme of work approved by the Management Committee. Between fifteen and twenty major projects are completed each year. Informal advice and information is an important, but less time-consuming, task.

<u>Bibliography</u>   -

Publications

Annual Report
(supplied to the university representatives on the Management Committee, who circulate it at their discretion)

Reports
(all, or nearly all, reports are commissioned and are confidential to commissioning universities unless they agree to circulation to specific or all universities.)

Records

Management Committee minutes, Annual Reports, and all commissioned reports are preserved in the Unit's Offices. If space was at a premium the older material would be deposited with the University of Reading's Archivist.

Access for research would be considered at the time of request.

SOUTHERN UNIVERSITIES' PURCHASING CONSORTIUM

Address and
contact
Southern Universities' Purchasing Consortium,
The University of Reading,
Building L11,
London Road,
Reading,
RG6 2AH

tel: 0734 874711
Mr. M.J. Barnes, Secretary

History

The Southern Universities' Purchasing Consortium (SUPC) was formed in 1974. It was preceded by a Working Party which considered the joint purchase of stationery amongst a number of universities. Membership of the Consortium comprises the Universities of Bath, Bristol, Cambridge, East Anglia, Essex, Exeter, Kent, Reading, Southampton, Surrey, Sussex, and Warwick, Brunel University, City University, and Cranfield Institute of Technology. The secretariat is provided by the Southern Universities' Management Services unit on a part-time basis.

The Consortium is required to provide a reliable and cost-effective purchasing service to its member universities, co-ordinating purchasing activities to the mutual benefit of all its members; every effort is made to keep administrative overheads to a minimum and to avoid any unnecessary bureaucracy. At a national level, co-operation takes place with other regional university purchasing consortia. Collaboration with government departments has proved fruitful and regular use is made of the contractual arrangements afforded by the Property Services Agency and HMSO. The 'For Sale and Wanted' Bulletin is circulated nationally by purchasing consortia and is welcomed by member institutions of SUPC.

Bibliography   -

Publications

Annual Report [of the Chairman]   (Produced at the end of each financial year. Copies are distributed to all member universities, CVCP, UGC, and Southern Universities' Management Services Management Committee, and other regional purchasing consortia.)

Buyer's Guide   (The major means of disseminating information regarding purchasing arrangements and the contracts available.)

Records

Minutes are taken, and formally accepted and approved, of all Consortium meetings.
Notes are taken and circulated of specialist commodity group meetings (each of which is chaired by a convener) and of meetings of conveners.

All minutes and notes since SUPC was formed are available.

A central file is also kept by the Secretary of all correspondence. Conveners (who must be members of the SUPC Committee) and the Chairman are required to send copies of the letters they produce to the Secretary. General correspondence since 1974 is available; contractual correspondence and price lists are only retained for two years.

Catalogues are available for some suppliers.

STANDING CONFERENCE OF ARTS AND SOCIAL SCIENCES

Address and
contact
Professor J.H. Westergaard,
Convenor of SCASS,
Faculty of Social Sciences,
The University,
Sheffield,
S10 2TN

tel: 0742 768555 ext. 6328

History
The Standing Conference of Arts and Social Sciences in Universities (SCASSU) was formed on 16 April 1984 at the University of Leeds, by resolution of the first conference of Deans of Faculty in the United Kingdom. The aims of SCASSU, as defined in its Constitution, were "to interpret, explain and safeguard the role of university teaching and research in the Arts and Social Sciences, with particular but not exclusive reference to the organisation,

144

funding, uses and public standing of academic work in these disciplines in the United Kingdom."

The affairs of SCASSU between General Meetings are managed by a Steering Committee which is empowered to make its own arrangements for appointment of any officers or of any sub-committees or working groups, one or more of its members being designated to have special responsibility for finance. The Steering Committee convenes an AGM to consider the activities of SCASSU, its financial accounts, elections to the Steering Committee, etc; provision is also made for extraordinary General Meetings to be convened. Until recently, membership of SCASSU was confined to institutional affiliation by or on behalf of university faculties of arts or social sciences in the UK and by the CNAA in respect of its concerns with higher education in the arts and social sciences. The 1987 AGM amended the Constitution to allow affiliation by departments and small departmental groups in universities which do not have formal faculty structures and such bodies are now admitted to associate membership. SCASSU's membership already extended to three-quarters of Britain's universities and consideration was now given to extending membership to relevant faculties or schools in the non-university sector of higher education. The Steering Committee proposed a major set of amendments to the AGM in September 1988, designed to extend the Conference's remit to these 'public sector' institutions and also to modify the Conference's name: SCASSU henceforth included Polytechnics and Colleges Funding Council sector faculties and the Conference was renamed the Standing Conference of Arts and Social Sciences (SCASS).

From the outset, SCASSU (now SCASS) has led a vigorous campaign to promote the interests of the academic area it represents, particularly by encouraging dialogue between delegations of its Steering Committee and those responsible for planning and resource allocation in higher education. It has regular contact with leading members of the UGC and has visited the DES on several occasions (meeting successive Secretaries of State) and it has also had meetings with education spokesmen and Members of Parliament across a wide political spectrum.

In the first five years of its existence SCASSU/SCASS has already organised four major conferences : on 'The Arts Graduate in Society' at the University of Dundee in September 1985; on 'Lost Opportunities' at the Institute of Historical Research, University of London in September 1986; on 'The Future of the Arts and the Social Sciences' at the University of London in February 1988; and on censorship in academic work, 'Who sets the Agenda?', in May 1989. These conferences have featured major speakers such as the Chairman of the UGC, the Chairman of the NAB, and the Under-Secretary of State at the DES. Each conference focuses on a theme of particular topical relevance.

Bibliography
SCASSU Information Leaflet and Enrolment Form.

SCASSU Constitution, 1985, revised 1987.

Jennifer Birkett, 'The state of the arts and the arts of the state', AUT Bulletin, March 1990, pp.4-5.

Publications
(a)   Reports of the founding meeting in 1984 and of subsequent AGMs (1985, 1986, 1987).

(b)   Reports of public conferences (Dundee 1985, London 1986, and London 1988).

(c)   <u>Newsletter</u>, circulated to member faculties and schools at irregular intervals since a year or two ago (as at March 1988).

(d)   Statements or responses on matters of current policy (e.g. 'contract funding', the Education Reform Bill, and 'performance indicators' to take recent instances) which are now usually reproduced in the <u>Newsletter</u> as well as being sent directly to interested parties and sometimes to the press.

(e)   Occasional letters to, or articles in, the press either directly from SCASSU or by Steering Committee members writing in their own names but arguing a case agreed or endorsed by SCASSU.

Records

Hitherto, the officers of the Steering Committee (Convener, Deputy Convener, and Treasurer) have, on their individual responsibility, generally retained copies of the principal records of SCASSU (including Steering Committee minutes and the publications referred to above).

The Steering Committee recognises the need to ensure that a complete set of its main records is assembled and maintained centrally and its current review will also consider how far arrangements should be made for copies of such principal publications as conference and annual meeting reports to be lodged with the copyright libraries.

<u>Bona fide</u> researchers would be allowed access to the published material in the records of SCASSU (subject perhaps to a small charge if there were any costs involved for SCASSU). SCASSU would be willing to consider requests for access to unpublished material (e.g. minutes).

STANDING CONFERENCE OF NATIONAL AND UNIVERSITY LIBRARIES

Address and contact

Standing Conference of National and University Libraries,
102 Euston Street,
London,
NW1 2HA

tel: 071 387 0317
Miss Gillian M. Pentelow, Secretary

History

The Standing Conference of National and University Libraries (SCONUL) was founded in 1950 to represent the interests of the libraries of member institutions by providing a forum for the exchange of information and the marshalling of collaborative effort. It also represents the interests of its members to government, official and semi-official bodies. SCONUL was incorporated in England as a company limited by guarantee (Regd. No. 1436951) and registered as a charity in 1980.

SCONUL holds plenary meetings twice yearly at which each member institution is represented by its chief library officer. In place of its Groups, SCONUL now has a number of Advisory Committees concerned with more general issues as well as with area specialisms. The current Advisory Committees are those on American Studies; Automation Policy; Buildings; Copyright; Education, Training and Staffing Matters; Information Services; Inter-Library Loans and Access to Materials; Investigatory Projects; Latin American Materials; Manuscripts; Medical Materials; National Co-ordination; Orientalist Materials; Recurring Expenditure; Relations with the Book Trade; and on Slavonic and East European Materials.

Membership of SCONUL is by invitation and with few exceptions the universities in the UK and the Republic of Ireland are members, together with all the major national libraries; the PRO and all the Divisions of the British Library are represented in the membership.

SCONUL is entirely self-financed and an elected Council of ten Representatives of member institutions undertakes the responsibility of a board of management. SCONUL has had a full-time Secretariat since 1970.

SCONUL operates a clearing centre for applicants for the SCONUL Trainee Scheme, which places aspiring post-graduate entrants to the profession in a university or national library for a year's practical experience prior to attending a full-time course at a school of library and information studies.

SCONUL is represented on a number of bodies, including the International Federation of Library Associations and Institutions, the Committee on Libraries of the CVCP, and the Joint Consultative Committee of ASLIB, the Institute of Information Scientists, the Library Association, and the Society of Archivists. It has observer status on certain Library Association committees and on the Council of Polytechnic Librarians. In 1989 the Society of Archivists published the report of a joint working party of the Society and SCONUL, The Role and Resources of University Repositories : Report and Discussion Document, which, inter alia, recommended the establishment by the UFC of a procedure for the recognition of centres of archival excellence and that the Society and SCONUL should promote a survey similar in type and objective to this report to be conducted on the collecting policies of polytechnics and colleges of higher and further education.

Bibliography
While a 'total' history of SCONUL has not been published, a good account of the events leading up to its establishment is T.H. Bowyer, 'The founding of the Standing Conference of National and University Libraries' in James Thompson (ed.), University Library History: An International Review (Clive Bingley Ltd., 1980), pp.208-228; this includes a short list of references (which include W.A. Munford's A History of the Library Association, 1877-1977, L.A., London, 1976).

There are also articles/chapters on SCONUL by K.W. Humphreys in Libri, Vol.7, 1956 (pp.41-44) and Libri, Vol.12, 1962 (pp.56-60), by H.J. Heaney in H.A. Whatley (ed.), British Librarianship and Information Science 1966-1970 (The Library Association, London, 1972), pp. 676-9, and by Anthony J. Loveday in H.A. Whatley (ed.), British Librarianship and Information Science 1971-1975 (The Library Association, London, 1977), pp.354-360.

There has also been an input by SCONUL from time to time in the Library Association's publication Year's Work in Librarianship.

Publications include:

Standing Conference of National and University Libraries (1985). A broadsheet
    providing details of SCONUL and listing examples of submissions made by
    SCONUL on matters affecting university and national libraries 1954-84.

Annual Reports (includes a Review of the Year: terms of reference, membership,
    and report on the work of the Advisory Committees; and the text of
    submissions made by SCONUL to Government, etc.), 1969 - to date.

SCONULOG, 1969 - to date.

Solanus : Bulletin of the Sub-Committee on Slavonic and East European
    Materials of the Standing Committee on [sic] National and University
    Libraries, 1966- to date (the sub-title being changed).

Gregory Walker et al. (eds.), Directory of Libraries and Special Collections
    on Eastern Europe and the USSR (Crosby Lockwood and Son, London, 1971;
    for Sconul's Slavonic and East European Group).

Robert Collison and Brenda E. Moon (compilers), Directory of Libraries and
    Special Collections on Asia and North Africa (Lockwood, London, 1970;
    for Sconul's Sub-Committee of Orientalist Libraries).

ISG News: Newsletter of the Sconul Information Services Group/Advisory
    Committee, Nos. 1-, 1975- ; ISG News will shortly be suspended (March
    1988).

Rosemary Webber (compiler), World List of National Newspapers: A union list of
    national newspapers in libraries in the British Isles (Butterworth,
    London, 1980; compiled under the auspices of Sconul in contract with the
    SSRC).

Some of SCONUL's official documents, which are in a numbered sequence, are
    occasionally released for general use.

Records

(a)   The closed files of SCONUL, dating mainly from 1950-79, have been
       deposited at University College London and are administered by the
       Manuscripts Department of the Library there. These records (of which a
       four page list is available) include correspondence of the Chairman and
       the Secretary of SCONUL, SCONUL accounts, SCONUL sub-committee and
       working party files (including some minutes), and SCONUL trainee scheme
       files. They do not include the minutes of SCONUL's Council, etc.
       Access to these records will be freely given to those requiring access
       and who have obtained prior written clearance from the Chairman or
       Secretary of SCONUL.

(b)   Recent dead files are retained by SCONUL's Secretariat prior to transfer
       to University College London. Such files might be consulted by bona fide
       researchers but each application would have to be considered by SCONUL's
       Council after addressing the Secretary in the first instance.

(c)   All the minutes of SCONUL, both of the Conference itself, the Council
       and the various Sub-Committees and Advisory Committees are all retained
       at SCONUL's Secretariat. Similarly, these minutes are also subject to
       control over access: SCONUL would not automatically make them available

to any enquirer but would require individuals to apply and state their case in writing in advance.

STANDING CONFERENCE OF UNIVERSITY INFORMATION OFFICERS

Address and
contact
Mr. Euan Beattie,
Secretary: SCUIO,
Public Relations Officer,
University of Salford,
Salford,
M5 4WT
tel: 061 745 5325
fax: 061 745 5999

History
The origins of the Standing Conference of University Information Officers (SCUIO) date back to c.1969. It is an association of staff in universities who have specialist responsibilities for press and public relations and other aspects of internal and external communications. Its membership covers virtually all the universities in the British Isles. Its Annual Conference, held in September, aims to brief members on national developments affecting universities and to develop professional public relations expertise in universities, with particular reference to the needs of new entrants to university information work. SCUIO maintains liaison with a number of national agencies of relevance to higher education.

Publications
Newsletter
Public directory of University Information Offices (annual publication)

Periodic reports, the most recent being Higher Education in the Federal Republic of Germany: Study Tour April 1979.

Records
(a)   At its 1979 conference SCUIO decided that henceforth a record of its business meetings, which are normally held twice a year, should officially be kept; the conference did not consider any other documentation worthy of retention.

(b)   On his own initiative Mr. R. D. Nimmo, Bursar of Brunel University, Uxbridge, Middlesex, UB8 3PH, during his period of office as Chairman of SCUIO in the late 1970s, commenced the compilation of an official record of all documents that might be considered relevant for retention.

STANDING CONFERENCE ON UNIVERSITY TEACHING AND RESEARCH IN THE EDUCATION OF ADULTS

Address and
contact
Mr. Alan Wellings,
Secretary: SCUTREA,
Division of Continuing Education,
Tapton Hall,
The University of Sheffield,
Sheffield,
S10 2GJ

tel: 0742 768555

History
The Standing Conference on University Teaching and Research in the Education of Adults (SCUTREA) was founded in 1971.

The object of SCUTREA is to further the study of and research in the education of adults. Membership is open to UK university departments and institutions which provide a regular teaching programme for educators of adults leading to university degrees or diplomas, or undertake regular and substantial research on the education of adults. Membership is also open to individuals from the UK and overseas who satisfy these criteria.

Publications
Publications Catalogue (lists the publications of participating institutions of SCUTREA).

SCUTREA Papers Papers read at the inaugural (1970) and later (1971 onwards) annual conferences, published as Papers Read At/From The...Inaugural/ Annual Conference...

STUDENT CHRISTIAN MOVEMENT

Address and
contact
Student Christian Movement,
186 St.Paul's Road,
Balsall Heath,
Birmingham,
B12 8LZ

tel: 021 440 3000
General Secretary: Revd. T.E. McClure

History
The origins of the SCM may be traced back to the Students' Foreign Missionary Union which was initiated at a Missionary Convention for Young Men in London on 15 October 1889, the Revd. C.H. Spurgeon being one of the speakers, and 1500 students attending. Though this organization soon began to decline as its members left college, the seed of the Student Volunteer Movement had been

planted in Britain. At a conference in Edinburgh in April 1892, at which the SFMU in London was represented, the Student Volunteer Missionary Union of Great Britain and Ireland (SVMU) was inaugurated (the SFMU being merged in the new body). The membership of SVMU was to consist of "all students who shall sign" a declaration stating that they were "willing and desirous God permitting to become a foriegn missionary", and an Executive Committee was shortly afterwards constituted. By 1893 SVMU had 491 members.

It was men from the older universities of England and Scotland who led SVMU in the early years but the increase in the number of university colleges, etc. in the latter half of the 19th century led to a focus of attention on their needs. An inter-university conference was held in Glasgow in January 1893 and in the Summer of 1893 the Inter-University Christian Union was founded "to unite in work and interest the various universities, colleges, medical schools, etc. of the United Kingdom, by means of conferences, deputations, correspondence, and such other means as may be thought effective". In 1894 the Union's name was changed to the British College Christian Union (BCCU).

As Canon Tatlow chronicles in his monumental history of the SCM, for the first three years of the Movement no one took any interest in its basis and religious position. This situation was rectified in 1901 when it was decided that those wishing to join the BCCU would be understood to accept a declaration of their faith in Christ as their Saviour, Lord, and God. At the same time a Constitution was adopted which specified the objects that the B.C.C. Union's three departments (created in 1897) should have - the Student Volunteer Missionary Union's object was to be to unite those students whose purpose it was to become foreign missionaries; the General College Department's object was to be to organize affiliated Christian Unions in universities and colleges, other than theological colleges, and to aid such Unions; and the Theological College Department's object was to be the same as those of the two other Departments in so far as they were applicable to theological colleges.

The growth of the Movement was remarkable. The SVMU was responsible for an international missionary conference for students in Liverpool in January 1896 (over 700 students attending, with 20 nationalities being represented, 74 universities and colleges in Great Britain and Ireland alone being represented). In 1895 at a meeting in Sweden the World's Student Christian Federation was formed to rally students under the slogan 'The Evangelization of the World in this Generation' with the active support of the SVMU. The Federation's organ was <u>The Student World</u>. The British Movement in fact owed much to contacts with similar movements in America and in Europe in particular. The Liverpool 1896 conference was the first of a series of international missionary conferences which were to be held every four years (apart from the period of the First World War); the 1912 Conference, held also in Liverpool, was the first such conference to combine the missionary incentive with a deep concern with poverty and social evil at home. In 1917, during the War, the Student Movement House was founded in London (moving from 32 Russell Square to Gower Street in the late 1930s) as a memorial to the students killed in the War and as a permanent centre of social life for British and overseas students.

The Quadrennial Conference of 1921 generated an impetus which led to great increases in staff, to provide more travelling secretaries and more help, though Eric Fenn in his history believed that the record of the SCM showed a growing uncertainty and confusion of thought and will in the post-War period up to 1929, springs of new life thereafter appearing. The SCM in 1922-24 had a special secretary for technical colleges and again from 1932 the interest of the Movement again began to centre in the student destined for an industrial career. From 1924 meetings (the 'Modern Universities Conference') bringing together the leaders of SCM and leaders in the general life of the universities, both ancient and modern, were held. The developing interest in social thinking and action was to lead to the rise of what was known as the 'Industrial Department', with an initial conference held in 1932 centring on the preparation of men for leadership in industry and the role of Christianity in industry, and resulting in local initiatives and Christian associations bringing together employers, trades unionists, university staff and students.

The SCM began, as Eric Fenn notes in his history, in an 'undenominational' temper of mind but developed an 'inter-denominational' position. It owed its origin to the evangelical movement but by concentrating on the basic truths of the Gospel it sought to undercut ecclesiastical differences. The missionary impulse led it into the international arena and the World's Student Christian Federation, which began as a purely Protestant movement, slowly developed a wider basis with similar and allied movements in Orthodox countries.

The SCM soon became the focus of Christian discipleship and mission among university and college students throughout Britain. According to its constitution, the principal object of the SCM was, and is, to advance the Christian religion among students. For over half a century SCM was a major influence on the life of the churches, not least by communicating a wider vision of one church in one world. As Martin Conway wrote in 1971, 'in the 1950s the coherence of the Christian enterprise in higher education depended above all on the SCM, strongly aware that it had embodied a continuous and indigenous Christian tradition in the universities for the best part of 100 years' (The Christian Enterprise in Higher Education: an attempt to see straight in England in 1970, Church of England Board of Education, London, 1971). He added 'it had branches in all the universities and virtually all the Teacher Training Colleges... nationally it employed a sizeable staff... but it is clear that [now] the SCM is no longer the major organ of Christian community... within higher education.'

Nowadays SCM is steadily growing again. In a space of a few years, new branches have appeared in polytechnics, universities, and colleges, and more ecumenical chaplaincy groups are recognizing the benefits of associating with the SCM. The process of SCM re-establishing contact with the student world in earnest has been traced back by the present General Secretary to the first National Congress, held in Manchester over the New Year 1976-77. Currently there are about 70 ecumenical groups meeting regularly in colleges, polytechnics and universities throughout Britain; SCM is now represented in about half the institutions of higher education in Britain. This growth owes much to the policy of having most of SCM's staff "in the field". Britain is divided into the nations of Scotland and Wales and three English regions, each being served by at least one full-time staff member. The SCM has a Scottish Council. The SCM's work is co-ordinated and administered by a small central staff, based in Birmingham, who also provide support and resources for the regional/national secretaries.

Local groups of students bring together students for study, discussion and worship. Not all groups do the same thing : some have large speaker or debating meetings, others meet less formally; some confine their programmes to a weekly meeting, while others look for more active ways of involvement in the life of the community and the churches. Regular regional conferences are held and also an annual National Congress (which extends over several days) which is open to members of chaplaincy groups, denominational societies and anyone else who wishes to participate. SCM's programme at all levels of the movement involves considering issues of a political and social nature.

SCM is represented by staff and students on various boards and committees of the British, Scottish, and Welsh Councils of Churches, the British Youth Council, and other bodies with related concerns. SCM is a member of the World Student Christian Federation (WSCF), which brings together nearly 100 SCMs throughout the world and which allows students to take part in conferences, leadership training courses, and study visits, mainly in other parts of Europe.

SCM is a movement of students with many points of view; a belief that the Christian faith is bigger than any one expression of it and a commitment to relate that faith to the whole of human life brings together members. SCM is proud of its unique place in the history of the modern ecumenical movement and hopes that the churches will be challenged by its witness and encouraged to seek new initiatives in Christian unity and renewal.

SCM is a registered charity (no. 241896).

Bibliography
Tissington Tatlow, The Story of the Student Christian Movement of Great Britain and Ireland (SCM Press, London, 1933).
(Includes accounts of the origins and development of the World's Student Christian Federation, Art Students' Christian Union, etc. Canon Tatlow was Travelling Secretary of SVMU 1897-8 and General Secretary 1898-1900 and 1903-29.)

Eric [A.H.] Fenn, Learning Wisdom : Fifty Years of the Student Christian Movement (SCM Press, London, 1939).

Ruth Rouse, etc., The World's Student Christian Federation : a history of the first thirty years (SCM Press, London, 1948).

J. Davis McCaughey, Christian Obedience in the University : studies in the life of the Student Christian Movement of Great Britain and Ireland, 1930-1950 (SCM Press, London, 1958).

David L. Edwards, Movements into Tomorrow : a sketch of the British SCM (SCM Press, London, 1960).

Peter Gee, 'Fifty Issues : Ten Years of Movement', in Movement, no.50, Spring 1982. This is mainly a history of the magazine, Movement, but there are also general references to the SCM itself.

T.E. McClure, 'The Student Christian Movement Today', in The Modern Churchman, N.S., Vol. XXVI No.4, 1984, pp.13-18.

A Wider Vision : The Student Christian Movement looks to the future, n.d. [c.1986] (leaflet about the SCM, incorporating deed of covenant, banker's order, and donation forms).

By way of further background there is W.R. Niblett, ed., The Expanding University : a report (of a conference held by the University Teachers' Group at St.Anne's College, Oxford, in 1961), Faber and Faber, London, 1962.

S.J.K. Baker, 'Christian Students : The Early History of the Student Christian Movement in the University of Liverpool', The University of Liverpool Recorder, No.104, February 1989, pp.27-29. As with many universities, published details of the SCM in a university may often be found in successive editions of the students' handbooks, diaries, and gazettes (or equivalent publications in the case of other universities), even when no records of the SCM appear to survive or no history has been written.

Publications include:-

(a) The Student Volunteer, 1893-8; title changed to The Student Movement in 1898, 1898- (no longer published).

Movement (magazine), first published as Bilbo in late 1971, the change in title taking place in Summer 1972 (issue no.3); Movement is now published three times a year.

From early 1973 until September 1979 every issue of Movement included a pamphlet insert, commencing with Theology and Sexual Politics (April 1973) and ending with Abortion: the tragic dilemma (February 1979) and Estranged Relations (September 1979; a brief guide to Anglo/Irish history).

(b) SCM Paperbacks, series commenced in 1961 but now no longer published. Includes Charles E. Raven, St.Paul and the Gospel of Jesus : A Study of the Basis of Christian Ethics, 1961, and David L. Edwards, ed., The Honest to God Debate : Some reactions to the book 'Honest to God'..., 1963.

(c) SCM Greenbacks, series commenced in 1963 but now no longer published. Includes Herbert Waddams, A New Introduction to Moral Theology, 1964.

(d) A Book of Prayers for Students (1st ed., 1915).

Will Reason, Drink and the Community (1920).

Students and the Church : The report of a Commission appointed by the General Council of the Student Christian Movement (1923).

Ronald H. Preston, ed., University Pamphlets (1946).

W.E. Beveridge, Managing the Church (1971) and Trevor Beeson, An Eye for an Ear (1972), both in the SCM Centrebooks : Christian Casebooks series.

Religion and Theology : A Book Guide, 1st ed., 1976, 7th ed., 1982.

Naming the Beast : The Changing Face of Apartheid (1980).

Neil McIlwraith, ed., Ghost Town : Poverty and Prophecy in the Inner City (1982).

Margaret Halsey, The Ivory Tower? (1983).

Robert Anderson, ed., Baptism, Eucharist and Ministry (1983).

Richard Woods, Surviving as a Student (1986).

Alison Webster, <u>Labour Pains</u> (1987); a SCM resource pack on 'work'.

SCM publishes a list of its more recent publications.

Records

(a)   The SCM's archives are housed in the Central Library, Selly Oak Colleges, Bristol Road, Birmingham, B29 6LQ (Librarian : Mr. Michael Walpole). They include minute books from the 1880s onwards; headquarters correspondence 1874 onwards; SVMU papers 1874-1908; Art Students' Christian Union papers 1897-1920; annual reports 1897-1976; and World('s) Student Christian Federation (WSCF) annual reports 1899-1949. The Art Students' Christian Union was established in 1897 and the WSCF in 1895.

The archives have been listed on 5" x 3" card index cards.

Bona fide researchers may consult the archives, preferably by prior appointment.

(b)   A certain amount of material, mostly dating from the 1970s, is awaiting sorting and cataloguing and is still held at SCM's Birmingham office. Eventually these records will also be deposited in the Library of the Selly Oak Colleges.

(c)   The records of SCM held at SCM's office may be consulted by bona fide students by appointment. As regards recent unpublished material, SCM would simply wish to reserve the right to veto publication of items of a sensitive nature.

THE UNITED KINGDOM COUNCIL FOR OVERSEAS STUDENT AFFAIRS

<u>Address and</u>
<u>contact</u>
The UK Council for Overseas Student Affairs,
60, Westbourne Grove,
London,
W2 5SH

tel: 071 229 9268/9
Mr. Andrew P. Masheter, Secretary

<u>History</u>
The UK Council for Overseas Student Affairs (UKCOSA) was established with government funding in 1968 to look after the needs and promote the interests of overseas students in the UK and of those working with them. The Council was established following the decision to introduce differential fees between overseas and "home" students. UKCOSA's membership consists of public and private academic institutions and professional, academic, voluntary and student organisations. The main forum for the exchange of information and ideas on overseas student affairs, UKCOSA liaises with the Government, the British Council and organisations overseas. It provides an information and training service to members (including a management consultancy service). It is funded by membership subscriptions and by grants from the Government, industry, and charitable sources. In August 1987 the staff of UKCOSA was

reorganised into four units, reflecting its priorities : Advice and Training; Institutional Policy and Development; Policy and Profile; and Finance and Administration. Details are provided in the Christmas 1987 issue of UKCOSA News.

UKCOSA has further developed its work in the area of staff training and development, consultancy visits to institutions, production of training packages, etc. in the last few years with the assistance of funds from the British Council and the Leverhulme Trust.

The Council's annual conference provides an opportunity for institutional staff to mix informally with those working on overseas student questions at a national level, providing an opportunity for cross-fertilisation of concerns and ideas. The 1987 annual conference, 'A national policy on international education', focussed on current policies in those areas of educational planning, aid and foreign affairs which relate to international education in general and overseas students in particular. The 1989 annual conference took as its theme 'Student mobility into the 1990s'.

Bibliography
There is no published history of UKCOSA, although there are occasional handouts detailing aspects of its work.

Higher Education Quarterly, Vol.41 No.2, Spring 1987, includes a number of papers on overseas students in the UK, most of the papers being originally commissioned by The Overseas Students Trust (177 Vauxhall Bridge Road, London, SW1V 1ER).

John O'Leary, 'An invisible export', The Times Higher Education Supplement, 16 June 1989, p.7
(An account of policies towards overseas students and their numbers since 1978/9.)
(THES, 25 May 1990, p.10, reports on UKCOSA's recent troubled finances.)

Publications
Michael Kendall and Anne Hawker (compilers), Overseas Students in Britain : An annotated bibliography (Research Unit for Student Problems in association with UKCOSA, 1968).

Standards and Responsibilities in the Education of Overseas Students in Britain : a Conference Report (UKCOSA, 1981).

Valerie Shawcross and Jane Goldsmith, It Ain't Half Sexist Mum (UKCOSA and World University Service, 1985).
(A study of the situation of women overseas students in Britain.)

Stephen Shotnes (ed.), The Teaching and Tutoring of Overseas Students (UKCOSA, 1985). Report of a workshop organised by UKCOSA under the auspices of the Extension Programme for Overseas Student Advisers funded by the British Council.

UKCOSA News. In Vol.19 No.4, Christmas 1987, there is a list of UKCOSA publications in stock. In addition to two of the above publications, they include:-

International Comparisons in Overseas Student Affairs (essays)

Towards a Policy on International Education (UKCOSA position papers)

Continuing Crisis: The Response to Overseas Student Groups in Hardship (report)

Overseas Students - Who Learns What? (essays)

Developing a Policy for Recruiting Overseas Students (Parts 1 & 11)   (report of conference organised by UKCOSA in conjunction with the Further Education Staff College)

Orientation : A Practical Guide for Those Working with Overseas Students

Overseas Students - At Home in Britain? (essays)

Records
UKCOSA retains Executive Committee minutes and annual reports dating back to its establishment.
Requests by bona fide researchers to consult these documents should be made, in writing, to the Director of UKCOSA, and will be considered on merit.

UNIVERSITIES' ATHLETIC UNION

Address and
contact
Universities Athletic Union,
Suite 36,
London Fruit Exchange,
Brushfield Street,
London,
E1 6EU

tel: 071 247 3066
fax: 071 247 4174
Mr. Gregory Gregory-Jones, Chief Executive

History
(a) Universities' Athletic Union

The Universities' Athletic Union (UAU) grew from and continues the work of the Inter- 'Varsity Athletic Board which was constituted in 1921. At the Presidents' Inter- Guild Conference held at Manchester in 1918 resolutions were passed in favour of a close association in the various branches of athletics between the universities. At the next conference, at Liverpool in 1919, the delegates decided to set up an organisation whereby the only existing Inter-'Varsity Competition (the Christie) could be extended to cover all universities wishing to co-operate. In 1921 a constitution of the Inter- 'Varsity Athletic Board had been formed and ratified by ten universities and university colleges. In 1929 the Board revised its constitution and renamed itself the Universities'

157

Athletic Union, the affairs of the Union being managed by a General Committee and an Executive Committee. For the purpose of the Union Championships, the universities were divided into three, later four, groups.

The first Championship meeting was in Track and Field events in 1919, and in 1921 Championships were also organised in Association and Rugby Football and Hockey. The Union in the years up to 1939 extended its scope until not only all the universities and university colleges of England and Wales were participating regularly in one or more of its activities, but also certain of the clubs of the Scottish and Irish universities were also competing in its annual Championships. Participation in the International University Games has continued since Great Britain first sent a team to Paris in 1928.

With the incorporation in 1979-80 of the Women's Inter-University Athletic Board, the Constitution of the UAU was revised. The 'Universities Athletic Union incorporating The Women's Inter-Universities (sic) Athletic Board' has as its objects the promotion and development of sporting activities in the universities and colleges of universities; and the organisation of championships between universities and of representative matches. Membership of the UAU is confined to the universities or constituent colleges of a university of England and Wales. The management of the UAU is vested in the officers and General Committee, an Executive Committee, a House Committee, and Divisional Committees.

(b) Women's Inter- University Athletic Board

The Women's Inter- University Athletic Board (WIUAB) was founded in 1923 to encourage and co-ordinate women's athletic activities in the universities and university colleges of England and Wales. Its work was similar to that of the UAU and it was from the original title of the men's organisation, the Inter-'Varsity Athletic Board, that it derived its name. The origins of the WIUAB may be traced back to an Inter-'Varsity sports contest in Manchester in 1921 which the Manchester University Women's Athletic Club organised.

Athletics, Swimming, and Hockey were the first events to be organised by the Board. By 1925 membership had increased to thirteen universities and a netball event had been instituted. In 1933 women were included for the first time in the British Universities team which competed at the International University Games in Turin, and the Board afterwards inaugurated annual Representative matches. During the Second World War only a limited number of regional championships were held. By the 1960s the Board had twenty affiliated universities and was organising events in eleven different sports.

The Board was affiliated to the majority of the governing bodies of sport.

In 1979-80 the WIUAB became part of the Universities' Athletic Union.

The UAU is affiliated to the British Olympic Association, the Amateur Athletic Association, the Amateur Boxing Association, the Amateur Fencing Association, and other leading governing bodies of sport in this country.

Bibliography
'Universities Athletic Union', <u>The University of Liverpool Students' Handbook</u>
     <u>1937-78</u> pp.95-96. (pp.97-106 comprise championship tables.)

<u>50 Years of University Sport</u> [? London, 1969]

Publications
<u>Official Handbook</u> This annual publication inter alia provides lists of
     affiliated universities (with year of affiliation, etc.), the UAU's
     Constitution and regulations, results for the past Session, a short
     annual report, lists of past officers of the UAU and of the WIUAB, and
     lists of previous winners (arranged per sport).

Records
The UAU holds minutes, accounts, and results, etc. of more recent date.
Access is restricted and it is necessary to apply in advance to consult the
records, etc.

The University of Liverpool Archives hold on deposit the archives of the UAU
itself for 1919-c.1987 (ref. D.528) and also the records of the Western
Division of the UAU for 1963-1987 (ref. D.473).

THE UNIVERSITIES CENTRAL COUNCIL ON ADMISSIONS

Address and
contact
The Universities Central Council on Admissions,
P. O. Box 28,
Cheltenham,
Gloucestershire,
GL50 1HY

tel: 0242 222444
Mr. Philip Oakley, General Secretary and Chief Executive

History
The Universities Central Council on Admissions (UCCA) was established by the
Universities of the United Kingdom, on the initiative of the CVCP, in 1961, to
act as a central clearing-house for applications for entry to full-time first
degree and first diploma courses in the universities. UCCA was incorporated
as a registered company on 26 November 1981 (company number 1600362) and,
accordingly, copies of its annual report and accounts are transmitted to the
Department of Trade and Industry's Companies Registration Office, Cardiff. At
the same time as being registered as a Company limited by guarantee, UCCA was
granted the status of an educational charity.

UCCA is managed by a Council of Management on which all the universities in
the United Kingdom except the Open University and the University of Buckingham
are represented, together with separate representation on behalf of the
Committee of Vice-Chancellors and Principals of the Universities of the United
Kingdom and co-opted members who include Heads of Schools and Colleges of
Further Education. The Council of Management meets twice yearly. Detailed
control of its operations is exercised by an Executive Committee elected from

the Council of Management. This is supported by three sub-committees: a Finance and General Purposes Committee, a Technical Committee and a Statistics Committee.

UCCA is a relatively small company employing about 120 permanent staff of whom about 40 are directly concerned in data processing; from August to January the permanent staff is assisted by a further 40-50 temporary employees. In 1968 UCCA agreed also to manage the Universities Statistical Record (USR: see separate entry.) UCCA's work is financed in respect of the universities admissions scheme by contributions from member institutions and fees paid by applicants. The University Grants Committee meets the cost of the Universities Statistical Record by a direct grant.

The Polytechnics Central Admissions System (PCAS) was established in 1984 for which UCCA acts as an agent, processing the necessary computer and other services. In Autumn 1989 UCCA and PCAS opened talks on the possible introduction of a single application form for both sectors.

The admissions scheme operated by UCCA provides for:
(a)   the receipt in the UCCA office of the application forms of candidates for admission to full-time first degree and first diploma courses in the universities;

(b)   the simultaneous transmission by the office of a copy of each application form to every university named on it by the candidate;

(c)   the communication to the candidate by the office of the decision made by each university on his application;

(d)   the communication by the office to each university of periodical information about the decisions made by other universities with respect to that university's own candidates;

(e)   a Continuing Application Procedure (CAP), enabling a candidate who has received no offer to make an additional application as soon as he receives his last rejection slip;

(f)   a 'Clearing operation' each September which enables candidates whose original applications were unsuccessful to be reconsidered by other universities still prepared to consider them.

The Admissions Officers' Conference, which is organised by UCCA, has been held annually since 1966. The Conference provides for regular consultation with university representatives about the operation of the UCCA scheme and is designed to enable questions of admissions procedure which cannot appropriately be raised at meetings of the Council of Management to be discussed in detail and on a working level with UCCA officers. It also provides a means for UCCA committees to test university reaction to proposed changes. Although many substantial modifications to the UCCA scheme have been initiated by the Conference, it is not a policy-making body and decisions cannot be made on questions of general policy within the Council's jurisdiction. Recommendations arising from discussion at the Conference which could involve a change of policy must be referred through the appropriate UCCA Committees to the Council of Management.

The Conference spreads over two days and specific aspects of admissions procedure are discussed by small groups which report to the plenary session held on the second day. Each institution which admits students under the UCCA scheme is invited to send not more than two representatives at its own expense.

The Universities' Statistical Record (USR) is managed by UCCA : see separate entry for USR.

Bibliography

Ronald Kay, UCCA: Its Origins and Development 1950-85, UCCA, 1985.

Carolyn Dempster, 'The Gospel According to UCCA' (on UCCA's silver jubilee) in The Times Higher Education Supplement, 4 July 1986, p.12.

Publications

These include:-

Annual Report, for 1961-3 (published in 1964) onwards.

Statistical Supplement (to the Annual Report) for 1964-5 (published in 1966) onwards.

UCCA handbook 'How to apply for admission to a university' (produced annually).

This UCCA business: Introducing UCCA: What it does, how and why, 1984.

Examinations and grants: Notes for university selectors 1985-6

Records

There is a strong demarcation between the administrative records of UCCA on the one hand and their operational records on the other.

(a) Administrative records -
Minutes and agenda papers (including reports) of the Council and its Executive Committee: all retained from 1961, in volumes and ring binders. The destruction of the papers of minor sub-committees after 20 years has been proposed, but this is not yet agreed.
Correspondence: policy files retained.
Financial records: disposed of under audit procedure, the main accounts being retained.
Publications: published reports, statistical supplements, and handbooks are retained with an issuing stock, copyright copies being lodged with the British Library. Procedural handbooks are not systematically kept.

(b) Operational records -
Applications from candidates for admission to university are, subsequent to their copying for distribution to the universities concerned, kept on reel microfilm in numerical code order: there is no alphabetical index of names on this microfilm, individual cases only being retrievable by quoting the candidate's number.

Applications are also processed to produce a machine-readable tape, a basic edition of which is retained as back-up to statistical productions.   There are probably facilities for transferring the information on these tapes to standard format if necessary.

Case correspondence is destroyed after closure of the case.

Xerox copies of each application form of a candidate are supplied to every university named on the form by the candidate, but in most cases it is believed universities do not retain these copies once they have completed their admissions.

(c) Copies of the agenda and minutes of all the Admission Officers' Conferences held since 1966 are retained in the UCCA office but these are not available for researchers to consult.

UNIVERSITIES AND COLLEGES CHRISTIAN FELLOWSHIP

Address and
contact
Universities and Colleges Christian Fellowship,
38 De Montfort Street,
Leicester,
LE1 7GP
tel: 0533 551700
General Secretary: Dr. Robin J. Wells

History
The Universities and Colleges Christian Fellowship (UCCF) originated as the Inter-Varsity Fellowship (to which the Evangelical Christian Union was affiliated). It is the co-ordinating body for the inter-denominational evangelical student 'Christian Unions' in Britain. Founded in 1928 by fourteen University Christian Unions, there are now affiliated groups in almost all the British universities, 86 colleges and polytechnics and contacts in over half the other colleges.

The Tyndale Fellowship for Biblical Researches, 36 Selwyn Gardens, Cambridge, is affiliated to UCCF.

UCCF Associates is a section of UCCF whose aims are to spread the knowledge of Christ throughout the world by every means available and in particular to further the student work of UCCF by prayer, encouragement, counsel, and finance; to play a major part in the overseas student work of UCCF, especially through hospitality and prayer; to foster constructive Christian thought and to help in the production of evangelical literature; etc. UCCF Associates publishes a journal, Christian Graduate which changed its name to Christian ARENA in September 1983. (Christian ARENA, Vol.39 No.2, was published in June 1986).

UCCF Associates published Science and Christian Belief (some papers presented to various conferences of the Research Scientists' Christian Fellowship) for the Fellowship in 1985. The Fellowship itself was started in the 1940s.

Bibliography
F.D. Coggan (ed.), Christ and the Colleges: A History of the Inter-Varsity Fellowship of Evangelical Unions (London, 1934).

Geraint D. Fielder, 'Excuse me Mr. Davies-Hallelujah!' Evangelical Student Witness in Wales, 1923-1983 (Evangelical Press of Wales, Bridgend, 1983).

Geraint Fielder, Lord of the Years (UCCF, Leicester, 1988) (this book, due out in April 1988, the 60th anniversary, will trace the history of UCCF and will supersede Contending for the Faith)

UCCF is also to publish [in 1988] a booklet (title yet to be decided) to replace For the Faith of the Gospel.

For the Faith of the Gospel, 1928-78 : the IVF/UCCF Story (UCCF, Leicester, [1978])

Douglas Johnson, Contending for the Faith : a History of the Evangelical Movement in the Universities and Colleges (Inter-Varsity Press, Leicester, 1979).

Publications include:
CU News, Nos.1-, 1975-; has been superseded by Cubit, which is published termly.

RS Today, Vol.1 No.1-, [? 1975] - (still published)

ICCF Broadsheet Inter- College Christian Friendship, continued by Broadsheet/UCCF Colleges' Department 1976- (no longer published).

Witnessing for Christ in the Universities : A terminal magazine and prayer report, [1928]; continued as New series vols.1 and 2, 1929-30; continued as The Terminal Magazine of the Inter-Varsity Fellowship of Evangelical Unions, Vols.3 and 4, 1930-32; continued as The Inter-Varsity Magazine, Vols.5-17, 1932-51; continued as Inter-Varsity, 1951-.

The Christian Graduate, 1948-; renamed Christian ARENA in September 1983. (The Christian Graduate united under one cover all the bulletins and letters which had previously been issued only to members of the various sections of UCCF; Vol.41 No.1 of Christian ARENA was published in March 1988.)

IVF Prayer Circular, 1945-; now entitled UCCF Focus: Prayer Diary.

F. Houghton (ed.), Effective Witness in Strategic Centres: A Symposium by University Men (London, 1933; 2nd ed., 1935).

D.F. Ellison Nash... and Douglas Johnson, The Discipline of Leadership : Suggestions for the organization of University Christian Unions (London, 1949).

Richard Buckham and David Bebbington, History and Christianity: A Bibliography (1977) (prepared for the Historians Study Group of the UCCF Associates).

Records
The UCCF retains at its office (a) minute books for the Universities' and Colleges' General and Executive Committees, (b) minute books for the Theological Students' Fellowship (about to be renamed the Religious and Theological Students' Fellowship), and (c) a number (about a dozen) of Christian Union minute books dating from the 20th century (though generally

such minute books are held in the university or college to which they pertain).

THE UNIVERSITIES COMMITTEE FOR NON-TEACHING STAFFS
(and CENTRAL COUNCIL FOR NON-TEACHING STAFFS
IN UNIVERSITIES)

Address and
contact
The Universities Committee for Non-Teaching Staffs,
29, Tavistock Square,
London,
WC1H 9EZ

tel: 071 387 9231
Secretary and Industrial Relations Officer: Mr. S.P. Rouse

History
The Universities' Committee for Non-Teaching Staffs (UCNS) was established in 1970, with the support of universities, by the Committee of Vice-Chancellors and Principals. It is an autonomous body and all the universities in the United Kingdom, except Cambridge, are members. It represents these universities as employers in a national collective bargaining system of dealing with salaries, wages and working conditions of over 60,000 members of the non-teaching staff of universities, and a variety of other matters of mutual interest to universities as employers and to those employed in universities. Before 1970 national machinery in respect of non-teaching staff was confined to the Universities' Committee on Technical Staffs (established in 1952) which conducted central negotiations on pay for technical staff.

The Committee's total membership in 1982 comprised 73, comprising representatives of all universities (except Cambridge) on the basis of one member per 5,000 students, together with the chairman (currently, 1988, Professor B.E.F. Fender, C.M.G., Vice-Chancellor of the University of Keele) and two vice-chairmen (currently, 1988, one vice-chairman, Dr. B.C.L. Weedon, Vice-Chancellor of the University of Nottingham). The University of Cambridge sends observers to the Committee's meetings. The Committee meets in full session about twice a year and is primarily concerned with the determination of policy issues.

The Committee is supplemented by seven regional groups which meet regularly (at least once a term or more frequently) to exchange views and formulate a regional consensus on policy matters. These regional groups are: Scotland (covering the following universities: Aberdeen, Edinburgh, Dundee, Glasgow, Heriot-Watt, St.Andrews, Stirling, and Strathclyde); North-East (Bradford, Durham, Hull, Leeds, Newcastle, Sheffield, and York); North-West (Belfast, Lancaster, Liverpool, Manchester, Salford, Ulster, and UMIST); Midlands (Aston, Birmingham, Keele, Leicester, Loughborough, Nottingham, and Open University, with an observer from Cranfield); Wales and West (Aberystwyth, Bangor, Bath, Bristol, Cardiff, Exeter, Lampeter, Swansea, UCCA, Welsh National School of Medicine, UWIST, and Welsh Registry); South (Brunel, East Anglia, Essex, Kent, Oxford, Reading, Southampton, Sussex, and Surrey, with observers from Cambridge); and London (City University, and London University). In addition, an Executive Committee, comprising representatives nominated partly by UCNS and partly by the regional groups, is concerned with the day-to-day work of the UCNS. The permanent Secretariat of the UCNS services the various Committees and is responsible for day-to-day advice and guidance to individual universities on a wide range of topics in the industrial relations field.

A major part of the activities of UCNS is conducted through joint committees with the trade unions. The Central Council for Non-Teaching Staffs in Universities (also established in 1970) is the umbrella body, a joint central body made up of university and trade union representatives, which provides a forum for discussion and consultation whose aim is to promote and preserve good industrial relations. Representation on the Central Council is drawn equally from the university representatives on the Executive Committee of UCNS and from officials drawn from the seven participating trade unions (ASTMS (which later amalgamated with TASS to become the Union for Manufacturing, Science and Finance, MSF), AUEW, GMWU, NALGO, NUPE, TGWU, UCATT) which have negotiating rights in universities. There is no formal written constitution for the Central Council. The Central Council has established recommended guidelines for disputes and dismissal procedures and has also circulated a guide "Recommended basis for Superannuation Schemes for non-FSSU Staffs", etc. (see under Publications below).

Detailed consultation and negotiations with the trade unions for each of the main groups of staff takes place through the UCNS' three subsidiary joint Committees: Technical Staffs, Clerical and Certain Related Administrative Staffs, and Manual and Ancillary Staffs. Management, staff, and the trade unions are all represented on these three joint Committees.

When UCNS came into existence in 1970 there existed only one agreement for technical staff which applied to all universities. Since then the various joint committees of UCNS have negotiated agreements covering pay and conditions of service which, in the main, have been adopted by many, though not all, universities. At the individual university level the development of joint procedures has been fostered by the UCNS, one of the first tasks of the Central Council having been to prepare recommended guidelines on representation and negotiations with non-teaching staffs.

Following a review by the CVCP and the Committee of Chairmen of University Councils, in January 1990 both committees proposed the establishment of a new Pay and Employment Policy Committee (PEPC) and each university was asked to agree to transfer to the PEPC the mandates which it gave to the UAP, UCNS, and CASSC. To preserve the valuable contribution of UCNS and its associated regional groups, it was proposed that the PEPC would delegate appropriate responsibilities to a UCNS composed of sixteen members (to include the chairmen elected by each of the seven UCNS regional groups).

Bibliography
'A national collective bargaining system in the United Kingdom dealing with salaries, wages and working conditions of non-teaching staffs' in Association of Commonwealth Universities Bulletin of Current Documentation, No.35, Oct. 1978, pp.2-4.

Ron Hayward, 'Universities and the Trade Unions' in Stuart Bosworth (ed.), Beyond the Limelight : Essays on the Occasion of the Silver Jubilee of the Conference of University Administrators, CUA, 1986, pp.115-125.

Publications

The UCNS does not publish annual reports or a newsletter. Its publications are limited to:-

(a) A Manual of Implementation (the Blue Book) for Technical Staffs, which sets out the job evaluation scheme and grading structure.

(b) A Scheme of Salaries and Conditions of Service for Clerical and Certain Related Administrative Staffs.

(c) A Handbook of Agreements and Wage Rates and Terms and Conditions of Service for Manual and Ancillary Staff.

The two publications (b) and (c) are up-dated regularly. Copies of all three publications are normally held in the personnel departments of individual universities, though it should be noted that some universities have their own schemes and do not recognise the UCNS schemes.

The Manual of Implementation (the Blue Book) for Technical Staffs will be revised by the Joint Committee for Technical Staff in Universities (JCTS). In fulfilment of the commitment given as part of the technicians in universities pay settlement negotiated in 1986, the JCTS appointed a Joint Working Party which agreed that the Advisory Conciliation and Arbitration Service (ACAS) should carry out a review of the technical staffs' job evaluated grading scheme and the consequential report on the pilot survey produced by ACAS in July 1987 is now subject to negotiations.

The Central Council for Non-Teaching Staffs has produced joint documents on pensions, maternity leave, time-off arrangements, and disclosure of information, but no collection of agreements in handbook form has been produced.

Records

All minute books, agenda papers and circulars are preserved in the UCNS offices. Most date from 1970 apart from technical staff matters which go back to the mid-1950s.

All Management documents are confidential but any bona fide researcher's application to examine items which are no longer the subject of current debate would be judged on its merits. This policy applies to Joint Minutes too.

UNIVERSITIES COUNCIL FOR ADULT AND CONTINUING EDUCATION

Address and
contact
Professor Christopher Duke,
Honorary Secretary,
Universities Council for Adult and Continuing Education,
Department of Adult and Continuing Education,
University of Warwick,
Coventry,
CV4 7AL

tel: 0203 523523

History

The Universities Council for Adult Education (UCAE) was constituted in May 1947, when it succeeded the former Universities Extra-Mural Consultative Committee (which had been established in 1926). The Council was constituted for the interchange of ideas and formulation of common policy on university adult education. UCAE was concerned with the whole range of extra-mural teaching. Membership of the Council was open to any university or university college in the United Kingdom and associate membership to any university or university college in the Commonwealth and to such other universities and colleges as the Council might invite. Each university or college was normally represented on the Council by the head of the department of adult education and by a representative of its Senate; this representation of universities and colleges on the Council was the distinguishing feature of UCAE, the former Universities Extra-Mural Consultative Committee having consisted of extra-mural heads only. By 1970 thirty-nine universities and university colleges in the UK were members of the Council, and there were seven associate members. Under the chairmanship of successive vice-chancellors, UCAE became increasingly influential. From 1950-51 it included representatives from Scotland and Northern Ireland, and a number of Commonwealth universities were welcomed to associate membership from time to time.

By 1956 the proportion of extra-mural work carried out by universities in collaboration with the WEA had fallen to 40% and, reflecting the changes in provision for adult education, the Central Joint Advisory Committee on Tutorial Classes was in 1958 replaced by a joint consultative committee of the WEA and the UCAE.

The UCAE changed its title to the Universities Council for Adult and Continuing Education (UCACE) in August 1981. Membership is open to any university or university college in the UK; Associate Membership is available, subject to the Council's approval, to any university or university college outside the UK.

Bibliography

Thomas Kelly, <u>A History of Adult Education in Great Britain</u>, 2nd ed., Liverpool U.P., 1970 (the above 'History' is, by kind permission, mainly drawn from Professor Kelly's <u>History</u>)

Publications include:

Annual Reports (including statistical tables of courses, enrolments, subjects, and staffing.)

Summer Schools for Overseas Students (annual).

<u>University Adult Education in the Later Twentieth Century</u> (UCAE, 1970; a Statement submitted by UCAE to the Committee on Adult Education chaired by Sir Lionel Russell.)

<u>Studies in Adult Education</u>, later entitled <u>Studies in the Education of Adults</u>, Vols.1-, 1969- (nowadays a joint publication of NIACE jointly with UCACE and SCUTREA.)

Thomas Kelly (ed.), <u>A Select Bibliography of Adult Education in Great Britain</u> (NIAE for NIAE and UCAE, 3rd ed., 1974.)

Records
It is understood that the Hon. Secretary holds some of the UCACE's records and that it is intended to deposit them at the Manuscripts and Special Collections Department, Brotherton Library, University of Leeds.

UNIVERSITIES COUNCIL FOR THE EDUCATION OF TEACHERS

Address and
contact
Universities Council for the Education of Teachers,
58, Gordon Square,
London,
WC1H 0NT

tel: 071 580 8000
Miss Mary Russell, Secretary

History
The Universities Council for the Education of Teachers (UCET) was formally constituted in the summer of 1967 by the amalgamation of the Conference of Institute Directors and the Conference of Heads of University Departments of Education. It began work in September 1967. Because of the considerable expansion of teacher education in the 1960s and the greater involvement of the universities through the institution of B.Ed. degree courses, the work of these two associations had increased to such an extent that the need for a permanent secretariat and central office facilities became imperative. It was also felt that the activities of the two associations should be more closely related, reflecting at the national level the movement towards Schools of Education at the local level.

The objects of UCET as set out in its Constitution are:-

1. To provide a forum, at the national level, for the discussion of all matters relating to the education of teachers which are the proper concern of the universities.

2. To make a contribution to the formulation of policy in this field of work, and to this end to seek appropriate liaison with other bodies and associations which are concerned with matters of policy.

3. To act as a clearing house for the collection and exchange of information about the work of Institutes, Schools and Departments of Education in their approving and providing of courses for the initial, advanced and in-service education of teachers.

UCET is financed by subscriptions from the universities, all British universities which are concerned with the education of teachers contributing to its upkeep. All directors of University Schools, Institutes, and Departments of Education are members of the Council of UCET, ex officio, attending the AGM of Council and the termly meetings of its Standing Committees.

The conduct of UCET's business between the AGMs is carried out through an Executive Committee, which in turn delegates various aspects of the Council's work to four Standing Committees and a Research Committee. The formulation of Council policy on research and development in teacher education is the direct responsibility of the Executive Committee, aided by the Research Committee (which provides, through its own membership, for liaison with the DES, ESRC, the Schools Council, and the National Foundation for Educational Research). The Standing Committees all have sub-committees and have arrangements for liaison with the DES, the CVCP, the NATFHE (formerly ATCDE), the NFER, and other bodies concerned with teacher education.

Bibliography
UCET Bulletin No. 1, Autumn 1969, provides an account of the origins and functions of the Council, and how the Council works.

Publications
(a) UCET Bulletin Nos. 1- to date, Autumn 1969-; prepared annually, the Bulletin gives an account of the work of UCET throughout the year.

(b) Qualifications in Education: nomenclature and relationships of initial and advanced awards and higher degrees in England and Wales, 1969, revised 1977.

Higher Degrees in Education, 1968.

Advanced Courses in Education, 1970.

The Inservice Education of Teachers: in the light of the White Paper, 1970.

The Education of Teachers: Looking to the Future (evidence submitted to the James Committee), 1971.

Alternative to James, 1972.

UCET on James, 1972

PGCE Working Papers, 1975.

The PGCE Course and the Training of Specialist Teachers for Secondary Schools: A Consultative Report, 1979.

University Courses in Education open to students from Overseas, 1981, new edition 1983. (annual publication)

Postgraduate Certificate in Education Courses for Teachers in Primary and Middle Schools: A further consultative report, 1982.

Norman Haycocks - a tribute, 1982.

(c) Apart from the above printed publications, UCET has from time to time circulated widely duplicated copies of reports. In particular, the results of its annual survey of posts taken up by students successfully completing PGCE or concurrent courses in universities are made available to anyone requesting a copy, as well as the press and interested parties.

Records
(a) Minute books, as well as copies of the annual Bulletins, are kept in the UCET office, as are all agenda papers, on file. Bona fide researchers may, on approval by the Executive Committee, consult them.

It is hoped to arrange the deposit of the records of UCET itself (and including copies of the annual Bulletins) for the period up to the early 1980s with the Library of the Institute of Education, University of London, 20 Bedford Way, London, WC1H OAL.

(b) The Modern Records Centre, University of Warwick Library at present holds the following records of UCET's predecessors (ref. MSS. 264), but it is understood that later in 1990 they will be transferred to the Library of the Institute of Education, University of London:-

Conference of Institute Directors

Conference and other minutes, 1957-67.

Minutes of meetings with the Ministry of Education/Department of Education and Science, 1960-66.

National Advisory Committee on the Training and Supply of Teachers, circulated papers, 1960-67.

Subject files and correspondence, 1957-67.

Conference of Heads of University Departments of Education

Conference and other minutes, 1959-67.

Subject files and correspondence, 1958-66.

UNIVERSITIES FEDERATION FOR ANIMAL WELFARE

Address and
contact
Universities Federation for Animal Welfare,
8, Hamilton Close,
South Mimms,
Potters Bar,
Hertfordshire,
EN6 3QD

tel: 0707 58202
Lt.-Col. T.J. Reynolds, Secretary

History
The University of London Animal Welfare Society was founded in 1926 by Major Charles W. Hume (1886-1981). It expanded to other universities and in 1938 was formed into a federation, the Universities Federation for Animal Welfare (UFAW). The UFAW is a company limited by guarantee (registered in England: no. 579991) and is also a registered charity (no. 207996). As a company, it was incorporated on 14 March 1957.

The UFAW is concerned with the promotion of humane behaviour towards wild, domestic or laboratory animals, in the UK or abroad. The objects of the Federation are set out in its Memorandum of Association. Those relevant to animal welfare and which control the Federation's methods of achieving its aims are:-

To promote humane behaviour towards wild and domestic animals in the United Kingdom and abroad so as to reduce the sum total of pain and fear inflicted on animals by man, and in the pursuance of this aim to enlist the energies of members of universities and professional men and women; obtain and disseminate relevant knowledge; help teachers to provide humane education; co-operate with Government Departments, Parliament, the Churches, the learned societies and other bodies in action favourable to such humane behaviour; pursue any other charitable activities conducive to the end in view and appropriate to the character of a university organisation.

To seek the aid of biological research workers and others in fostering in laboratories in the United Kingdom and abroad consideration for the physical and mental comfort of experimental animals, avoidance of procedures which involve serious suffering, and the development of techniques calculated to reduce discomfort to a minimum, but so that the Federation shall not engage on either side in public controversies relating to the legitimacy of making scientific experiments on animals.

To collect, index and disseminate by publication or otherwise such information as may be necessary or desirable for the promotion of the objects of the Federation or any of them.

UFAW encourages, sponsors and commissions research to improve the welfare of animals. It makes representations and submits comments to government departments. In the education field it organises a seminar and a workshop each year; it offers Vacation Scholarships; and its staff deliver lectures and talks at various courses, universities, etc. In memory of its founder, a Hume Memorial Lecture is delivered annually, the first being given in 1982. UFAW publications include handbooks, proceedings of UFAW symposia and UFAW workshops, reports of surveys (Dogs in London; etc.), the Hume Memorial Lectures, etc. Some of its research projects are financed by outside grants.

Any person may be accepted as an Associate Member; a voting Member has to be a graduate or undergraduate or member of a University or College of University status, or a member of the teaching or administrative staff of any such University or College or a person with such professional qualifications as the Federation's Council shall accept. The membership of UFAW (which is drawn from those in the UK and overseas) has remained steady, although its presence in the universities had declined, the Report 1984-85 stated.

On 1 January 1987 the Council of UFAW assumed responsibility for the management of the Society for Animal Welfare in Israel (SAWI), which was founded in 1958 by Miss Marguerite Silverman and which raises funds in the UK. SAWI remains an independent registered charity (No. 206494) but is now located at the UFAW's offices in South Mimms.

On 6 April 1987 the Council of UFAW assumed responsibility for the trusteeship and management of the Council of Justice to Animals and Humane Slaughter Association (CJA and HSA), now usually known as the Humane Slaughter Association (HSA), which was founded in 1911 and whose staff moved from London to share offices with UFAW in South Mimms in 1978. The HSA remains an independent registered charity (No. 209563).

UFAW sold its field centre, Holy Island (off the West Coast of Scotland), in 1983-84 after operating it as a nature reserve (with Eriskay ponies, Soay sheep, etc.) and letting self-catering accommodation on the Island for a number of years. The decision to sell the Island was taken in the light of the steadily increasing excess of expenditure over income and the general decline in more recent years in its use by school groups and by individuals for scientific research projects.

Bibliography

'Major C.W. Hume, OBE, MC, BSc' (obituary) in UFAW Report and Accounts 1981-1982, p.1

C.W. Hume, The Status of Animals in the Christian Religion (1957).

C.W. Hume, Man and Beast (1962).

Publications, include:-

(a)   UFAW Report and Accounts (annual, submitted to the AGM; 61st Annual Report is for the year ended 31 July 1987).

Information Leaflets (e.g. on Guinea-Pigs and on Hamsters and Gerbils, both [1980]).

The UFAW Courier (last issued in 1965; it is proposed to revive this publication).

UFAW News-Sheet (annual; no.23: April 1987).

(b)   Trevor Poole (ed.), The UFAW Handbook on the Care and Management of Laboratory Animals (Longman Group UK Ltd., Harlow; 6th ed., 1987). This Handbook first appeared in 1947.

UFAW (ed.), The UFAW Handbook on the Care and Management of Farm Animals (Churchill Livingstone, Edinburgh and London, 1971).

(c)   Hume Memorial Lectures.

(d)   UFAW Research Publications.

Records

The Secretary states that comprehensive records are kept in the UFAW's office.

UNIVERSITIES FUNDING COUNCIL

Address and
contact
Universities Funding Council,
14, Park Crescent,
London,
W1N 4DH.

tel: 071 636 7799 ext. 205
fax: 071 631 4227
Ms. Jo Wilkinson

History

Though the University Grants Committee (UGC), the predecessor of the Universities Funding Council (UFC), dates from 1919 - being appointed by the Chancellor of the Exchequer as a Standing Committee of the Treasury under a Treasury Minute of 14 July 1919 - a Vote for University Colleges in Great Britain was first introduced in 1889 with an ad hoc Committee being appointed by a Treasury Minute to advise on its allocation.

Between 1889 and 1911 the majority of the grants for universities and university colleges were administered by the Treasury, assisted from time to time by special ad hoc Advisory Committees (in 1906 a standing Advisory Committee) appointed by successive Chancellors of the Exchequer. In 1911 the administration of the main grants to the English university institutions was transferred to the Board of Education, assisted by a new Standing Committee appointed in July 1911 by the President of the Board Of Education and known as the Advisory Committee on University Grants. The latter Committee was dissolved in 1919 and in its place the UGC appointed "to enquire into the financial needs of university education in the United Kingdom and to advise the Government as to the application of any grants that may be made by Parliament towards meeting them." The UGC was originally intended only to be an advisory body but in practice the allocation of money between university institutions has been almost entirely entrusted to the UGC by the Government.

Ministerial responsibility for the UGC was moved from the Treasury to the Lord President of the Council in December 1963 and later, from 1 April 1964 onwards, to the new Secretary of State for Education and Science. The UGC was to retain its traditional position in relation to the universities and to Whitehall, on the 'buffer' principle.

The developments in the work and nature of the Committee from 1919-46 were steady, but not dramatic. In the post-1946 period the UGC's functions and activity changed in a marked way. A network of sub-committees concerned with particular topics and areas was now established and increasingly the influence of the Committee's views on almost every topic of importance to universities grew. Even when the quinquennial system went into abeyance in the later 1970's the UGC continued to send detailed guidance to the universities and to encourage or discourage, to finance or not to finance particular developments and academic studies in particular universities.

The UGC's terms of reference, (revised in July 1946 and modified in 1952), were:

"To enquire into the financial needs of university education in Great Britain; to advise the Government as to the application of any grants made by

Parliament towards meeting them; to collect, examine and make available information on matters relating to university education throughout the United Kingdom; and to assist, in consultation with the universities and other bodies concerned, the preparation and execution of such plans for the development of the universities as may from time to time be required in order to ensure that they are fully adequate to national needs."

The UGC's latest terms of reference dated from 19 September 1983 and were almost identical to those which date from 1952 (quoted above) with "Great Britain" being amended to "United Kingdom" in the first clause, the UGC formally resuming the advisory role for the universities in Northern Ireland it had long exercised in practice, and the words "on matters" being deleted in the third clause.

In 1948, grants-in-aid to university departments of agriculture in England and Wales were transferred from the Ministry of Agriculture and Fisheries, and in 1949 responsibilites for grant-aiding the Glasgow Veterinary College and in 1950 for the Royal Veterinary College were taken from the Secretary of State for Scotland.

The main task of the UGC was to distribute between university institutions the grants (£1273.9m in 1983-84) which the Government funds for their activities as a whole.

The financial assistance provided by the Government to universities through the UGC covered four broad categories of expenditure: recurrent, non-medical capital, medical capital, and furniture and equipment. In the past the over-all sum determined by the Government emerged from discussions related to an agreed target for student numbers, but more recently it was determined in accordance with what it was believed the nation could afford. In accordance with the Government's expenditure plans for 1981-82 to 1983-84, published in March 1981 (Cmnd.8175), universities suffered substantial reductions in grant up to 1983-84 on a scale not previously experienced: the overall loss of recurrent resources between 1979-80 and 1983-84 was forecast as likely to be in the range 11% to 15%. In 1983-84 the Exchequer grants allocated by the UGC amounted to £1,192m for recurrent grant and an additional £81.9m for equipment and furniture grant. The UGC (UFC) grant list latterly covers 43 universities (34 in England, one in Wales, and eight in Scotland) but there are 51 institutions in all on the grant list including seven within the University of Wales and two Business Schools. The grant list includes the universities of Oxford and Cambridge but their individual colleges are not supported by UGC (UFC) grant. The UGC (UFC) also acts as confidential adviser to the Government on the needs, interests, and views of universities; interprets to universities the national interests and Government purposes, for instance, in making its allocations of resources, commenting upon the development plans of individual institutions; and collects and publishes statistical and other data concerning the university system and its costs. Liaison, consultation and dialogue is maintained by the UGC (UFC) not only with the Government, but also with the Vice-Chancellors and Principals of universities, severally and collectively; with governing bodies, administrations, staff, and students of universities in the course of its quinquennial visitations, etc; with the Research Councils; with professional bodies concerned with the output of universities as a source of potential employees and of service or research; and with other bodies. The UGC was appointed to perform what was strictly speaking an advisory role. However, though the Government determines the total amount of grant, as a matter of policy it always accepted the UGC's recommendations on its distribution, so that in practice it was the UGC who were the arbiters in this effect; the arrangements thus achieved the effect of an arm's length relationship.

In addition and more recently since the mid 1980s, the UGC also assisted the universities through funding the INSET (In-service Education of Teachers) programme, and the UGC PICKUP (Professional, Industrial and Commercial Updating Programme) programme. The DES also funds its own PICKUP in Universities programme. (The third national PICKUP in Universities Conference was held in 1989.) The PICKUP funding is to encourage universities, polytechnics and colleges to increase and improve their provision for the vocational updating of those in employment. PICKUP in Progress, published by the DES three times a year, includes reports on schemes. INSET funding provides for the retraining and continuing education of teachers. In 1983 the UGC began its "new blood" lectureship scheme, the aim being to create permanent posts for young academics in British universities; in the first year the scheme provided 792 lectureships, mostly in science and engineering.

The Committee, when at full strength, consisted of a full-time chairman and 20 part-time members, 14 of whom held senior academic posts in universities. The Committee as a whole was appointed by the Secretary of State for Education and Science. The Main Committee was supported by 14 (latterly 12) standing advisory sub-committees and by working parties or panels set up to undertake particular enquiries. The Secretary of the Committee and the Committee's office staff were full-time civil servants, on the strength of the DES. The Chairman, who was appointed full-time from academic life for a limited period, was also on the DES strength. The UGC was not therefore in form an executive body with a budget of its own or employing its own staff.

The contraction in the overall funding of the University system from the last of the expansion in 1978 resulted in a number of reports being published, amongst them A Strategy for Higher Education into the 1990s: The University Grants Committee's Advice (HMSO, 1984) which recommended that more government funds should be channelled into higher education to meet new demands. The Government's Green Paper, The Development of Higher Education into the 1990s (Cmnd. 9524, HMSO, 1985) did not, however, follow the UGC's advice. Sir Edward Parkes, Chairman of the UGC, 1978-83, delivered an address to a meeting of the CVCP in September 1983 in which he chronicled the funding of universities 1978-83 and considered the roles of the DES, UGC, the Research Councils, etc., and the influences most likely to affect the shape of the university system over the next decade; this address was made available to universities and, for instance, was published in the University of Liverpool's Staff Newsletter, No.137, Nov. 1983, pp.1-15.

Much of 1985-86 was taken up with the UGC's analysis of the universities' responses to the UGC's planning letter and, in particular, with an assessment of the research strengths of each department in each university. Following upon the UGC's Circular letter 18/85 on rationalisation, in the same year, 1985-86, the UGC completed reviews of Italian and Scandinavian studies and made proposals for rationalisation in those subject areas; it also considered reports on Asian and African Studies, on Town and Country Planning, and Librarianship and Information Studies; and announced its intention to undertake reviews of further subject areas, commencing with the Earth Sciences and the History and Philosophy of Science. In response to the requests in the UGC's Circular (issued in December 1985), universities provided the UGC with their detailed institutional plans covering the period up to 1990. These plans were submitted to the UGC in support of bids for restructuring funds for the costs of (a) premature retirement of staff, (b) of new staff appointments, (c) of staff transfers to and from other institutions, and (d) of physical restructuring projects, etc. In 1986 the UGC carried out a "research selectivity" exercise, universities being informed into which category (outstanding, better than average, about average, or below average within the UK) their individual cost centres or departments/subject areas were considered to fall. A further research selectivity exercise was carried out in 1989. (Details of these ratings were published in the THES, 30 May 1986 and 1 September 1989.)

In 1985-86 the UGC had twelve Sub-Committees, whose main activity was resource allocation : Agriculture and Veterinary Studies, Arts, Biological Sciences, Business and Management Studies, Dental Studies, Education, Equipment, Mathematical Sciences, Medical, Physical Sciences, Social Sciences, and Technology; it also had a Panel on Studies allied to Medicine.

The role and functions of the UGC were reviewed by a committee (Chairman: Lord Croham) appointed by the Secretary of State for Education and Science. The Croham Committee asked management consultants, Coopers and Lybrand Associates, to analyse and report on the procedures adopted by the UGC for the allocation of resources to universities, and their operation in practice; the functions and methods of operation of the sub-committees; and the staff of the UGC; and all of these with particular regard to the efficiency, economy and effectiveness of the UGC, the fulfilment of the UGC's terms of reference and the adequacy of the means for doing this.

The Committee's report (Review of the University Grants Committee) was published by HMSO in January 1987 (Cm 81). Inter alia, it recommended that the UGC should be renamed the University Grants Council and should have a new structure. A part-time chairman from outside the academic world would be appointed, and also a director general (an academic), and a secretary. The current eleven subject sub-committees should be throughly reviewed or be replaced by three boards. The report also recommended that the Council should be smaller than the present UGC, with half the members drawn from outside academic life. It also recommended that, provided inflation remained below five per cent, the Government should announce cash sums for the funding of universities every three years. The report advocated a UGC with more independence but more accountability to Parliament, industry, and government. AUT Bulletin No.145, April 1987, included extracts from the Report.

The Government's initial response to the Croham Report was given in the White Paper, Higher Education : Meeting the Challenge, Cm 114, HMSO, 1987.

In its Education Reform Bill, which was introduced in the House of Commons in November 1987, the newly re-elected Conservative Government proposed that the UGC should be replaced by a Universities Funding Council (UFC), covering the whole of England, Scotland, and Wales. The UFC would have fifteen members, to be appointed by the Secretary of State for Education and Science, six to nine of whom would be drawn from higher education and the remainder from other backgrounds. The UFC would administer the funds provided by the Secretary of State for supporting the provision of education, research and other activities at universities in Great Britain. The UFC would be independent of Government, with power, among other things, to appoint its own staff. The Bill provided that the Secretary of State may attach terms and conditions to the funds he provides, as may the UFC in distributing them to individual universities. (The allocation of funds to universities under the proposed new contractual arrangements may be compared with the "customer-contractor" principle established in the 1972 White Paper, Framework for Government Research and Development, Cmnd. 5046.) The Bill, as amended, received the Royal Assent (as the Education Reform Act 1988) on 29 July 1988. There was extensive comment etc. on the Bill in the correspondence and other columns of the 'quality' national press. The universities in Northern Ireland continue to be funded directly by the Northern Ireland Department of Education (on the advice of the UFC).

The section of the Act providing for the establishment of the UFC came into force on 1 November 1988. The UGC ceased to operate on 31 March 1989.

The UFC has stated its general aim to be 'the maintenance and development of universities as high-quality and cost-effective institutions, providing for the advancement of knowledge, the pursuit of scholarship and the education of students, thereby playing their parts in meeting national needs.' Amongst the UFC's particular aims are a growing range of choices to be provided, with individual institutions identifying their particular strengths and opportunities and developing them accordingly. Without prejudice to the level of Government support, the UFC desires to see an increase in the level of universities' general income derived from non-Government sources.

It appears that the UFC will operate differently from the UGC, meeting perhaps only six times a year and considering mainly policy matters. The UFC's Chief Executive (Sir Peter Swinnerton-Dyer, lately the UGC's Chairman) has executive responsibility and groups similar to the UGC's subject Sub-Committees will be retained as advisory bodies to the Secretariat. It seemed likely that, at least in its early years, the UFC would basically follow the UGC's funding practices, more detailed contractual arrangements possibly not being introduced until after Session 1990-91. The UFC has a Scottish Committee.

In its Circular Letter 39/89, December 1989, the UFC set out in detail its plans for the future funding of the university system, based on the numbers of students each institution is prepared to teach. This marks a radical shift away from the traditional method of formula funding. In respect of the planning period 1991-92 to 1994-95, (a) for funding on teaching-based criteria universities are invited to submit offers of student places; (b) funding on research-based criteria will be determined in the light of information available to the UFC, including the outcome of the recent research assessment exercise; and (c) for continuing education, universities are invited to submit offers for a portfolio of provision. Universities are also invited to submit planning statements, including financial forecasts for the period 1991-92 to 1994-95. The Government has decided to shift the balance of public funding for higher education towards fees (which rise for home-based undergraduate students from £607 in 1988-89 to £1,675 for 1990-91), to signify a move towards a more market-orientated system, and the UFC invites universities to attach offer prices per student in each subject group according to the numbers of undergraduates and postgraduates they are prepared to teach during the planning period. The offer price may match the guide price provided by the UFC or be set at a lower level (to improve an institution's chance of having its offer accepted in full by quoting a price below the guide price). Universities' bids have to be submitted to the UFC by 22 June 1990; the UFC hopes to inform universities of its decisions by early 1991, each institution being told the grant it can expect to receive from the UFC for the academic year 1991-92 together with the number of funded student places and the prices for teaching that have been accepted. UFC's plans reflect the Government's expectations that the numbers of full-time and sandwich course students will grow by just under 10% between 1988-89 and 1992-93.

The UFC occupies the UGC's (old) offices at 14 Park Crescent, but in August 1991 is due to move to Bristol.

177

Bibliography

Eric Hutchinson, 'The Origins of the University Grants Committee', in <u>Minerva, A Review of Science, Learning and Policy</u>, Vol.XIII No.4, Winter 1975, pp.583- 620.

Christine H. Shinn, 'The Beginnings of the University Grants Committee', in <u>History of Education</u>, Vol.9 No.3, 1980, pp.233-243.

Tom Owen, 'The University Grants Committee', in <u>Oxford Review of Education</u>, Vol.6 No.3, 1980, pp.255-278. (An account of the origins and development of the work of the UGC).

John Pratt, 'The UGC Department', in <u>Higher Education Review</u>, Vol.7 No.2, Spring 1975, pp.19-31.

Sir Robert Aitken,' The Vice-Chancellors' Committee and the UGC', in <u>Universities Quarterly</u>, Vol.23 No.2, 1969, pp.165-171. This same number of <u>Universities Quarterly</u> also contains three other papers about the UGC and about the universities and the State.

'Composition and Procedures of the University Grants Committee' a Memorandum by the University Grants Committee published as Appendix 5 of the <u>Appendices to the Minutes of Evidence taken before the Committee of Public Accounts</u>, Session 1966-67, HC, pp.245-252, Appendices 6 and 7, being memoranda by the UGC on the assessment of recurrent grants and non-recurrent grants, appear on pp.252-258 of the same volume.

Sir John Wolfenden, 'The Work of the University Grants Committee in Great Britain' in <u>Overdruk uit Universiteit en Hogeschool</u>,jaargang 15 nr.3, Nov.1968, pp.167-178.

University Grants Committee, <u>The University Grants Committee: Terms of Reference, Brief History, and Membership</u>, n.d. [1982] (a 12pp. booklet; includes statistics of qualifications obtained, full-time teaching and research staff, and student numbers for Great Britain in 1970-71, 1975,1979, and 1980.)

Roy Butler, 'The Control and Management of Higher Education in Great Britain, with special reference to the role of the University Grants Committee and the Committee of Vice-Chancellors and Principals' in <u>Oxford Review of Education</u>, Vol.8 No.3, 1982, pp.265-278. This number of the <u>Oxford Review of Education</u> contains eight other papers also related to the theme of 'Higher Education and Oxford'.

'A crucial new phase for the UGC' in <u>The Times Higher Education Supplement</u>, 22 July 1983, pp. 8-9. (examines the complex workings of the UGC, providing an outline of its organisation and committee system and the way it works, with a list of members of the main Committee and of the individual sub- committees.)

Graeme C. Moodie, 'Buffer, Coupling, and Broker : Reflections on 60 years of the UGC' in <u>Higher Education</u>, Vol.12 No.3, 1983, pp.331-347.

Michael Shattock and Robert Berdahl, 'The British University Grants Committee 1919-83 : Changing relationships with government and the universities' in <u>Higher Education</u>, Vol.13 No.5, 1984, pp.471-499.

178

Ngaio Crequer, 'UGC under scrutiny: The guardians of knowledge' in The THES, 14 March 1986, p.10 (on the work of the UGC's sub-committees). See too Ngaio Crequer's article on the Croham Committee's enquiry in The THES, 7 March 1986, pp.12-13.

Alan Jones, 'The University Grants Committee: Reflections on a Year's Secondment' in Stuart Bosworth (ed.), Beyond the Limelight: Essays on the Occasion of the Silver Jubilee of the Conference of University Administrators, CUA, 1986, pp.177-190.

Graeme C. Moodie, 'Le Roi est Mort; Vive le Quoi? Croham and the Death of the UGC' in Higher Education Quarterly, Vol.41 No.4, Autumn 1987, pp.329-343.

Christine H. Shinn, Paying the Piper : The Development of the University Grants Committee 1919-1946, The Falmer Press, London, 1986.

Coopers & Lybrand Associates, National Data Study (Committee of Vice-Chancellors and Principals' Steering Committee for Efficiency Studies in Universities, 1985)
(includes a chapter on the UGC and its information requirements)

'Changing of the old guards in an executive fashion' in The THES, 31 March 1989, pp.6-7 (includes diagrams illustrating the essential differences between the old and new systems).

Publications
UGC Reports have been published for the following quinquennial and other periods of years:
        [1920], dated 3 February 1921 (Cmd.1163)
        (states that UGC's previous report was submitted,
        to the Treasury, in March 1920)
        1920/21 - 1923/24, published in 1925
        1924/25 - 1928/29, published in 1930
        1929/30 - 1934/35, published in 1936
        1935 -47, published in 1948
        1947-52, published in 1953 (Cmd.8875)
        1952-57, published in 1958 (Cmnd.534)
        1957-62, published in 1963 (Cmnd.2267)
        1962-67, published in 1968 (Cmnd.3820)
        1967-72, published in 1974 (Cmnd.5728)

The quinquennial system was abandoned in 1975-76.

The UGC produced Returns from Universities and University Colleges in receipt of Treasury later Exchequer Grant for each academic year (annual statistical returns) from 1919-1920 (Cmd.1263) to 1965-66 (Cmnd.3586), the Returns for the inter-War period not, however, being published as Command Papers though they were published by H.M.S.O: from 1958-59 these Returns incorporated an Annual Survey. After 1965-66 the annual Returns were replaced by a special volume (Vol.6) in the Department of Education and Science's annual series, Statistics in Education, but the Annual Survey was continued as a separate UGC publication. Prior to 1919-20 Reports from Universities and University Colleges in Great Britain participating in the Grant-in-Aid were published as Command Papers, up to 1914-16 (Cd.8138).

The UGC also published <u>Departmental Expenditure Schedules</u> (arranged per University or University College) for each Academic Year, for the Years 1920-21 - 1937-38.

The UGC's separate <u>Annual Survey</u> for each academic year has been published since 1965, in the Command Papers series:-

Academic Year	Year of Publication	Command No.
1963-64	1965	Cmnd. 2571
1964-65	1965	Cmnd. 2846
1965-66*	1967	Cmnd. 3192
1966-67	1968	Cmnd. 3510
1967-68	1969	Cmnd. 3914
1968-69	1970	Cmnd. 4261
1969-70	1971	Cmnd. 4593
1970-71	1972	Cmnd. 4893
1971-72	1973	Cmnd. 5836
1972-73	1974	Cmnd. 5766
1973-74	1975	Cmnd. 6034
1974-75	1976	Cmnd. 6435
1975-76	1977	Cmnd. 6750
1976-77	1978	Cmnd. 7119
1977-78	1979	Cmnd. 7646
1978-79	1980	Cmnd. 8031
1979-80	1981	Cmnd. 8359
1980-81	1982	Cmnd. 8663
1981-82	1983	Cmnd. 8965
1982-83	1984	Cmnd. 9234
1983-84	1985	Cmnd. 9489
1984-85	1986	Cmnd. 9815
1985-86	1987	Cm. 262
1986-87	1989	Cm. 789

*includes a Review of University Development, 1962-63 to 1965-66.

<u>Statistics of Education Vol.6 - Universities</u> has, since 1982, been replaced by two volumes in a new annual three-volume series, which also incorporates the UGC's <u>First Destination of University Graduates</u>. The first edition of this new series, <u>University Statistics</u>, (covering the academic year 1980-81) was published for the UGC by the USR in 1982 as follows:-
Vol. 1 - Students and Staff
Vol. 2 - First Destinations of University Graduates
Vol. 3 - Finance

<u>First Employment of University Graduates</u>, 1961-62 to 1970-71 (1963-72), continued as <u>First Destination of University Graduates</u>, 1971-72 (1973), - 1979-80 (1981).
In more recent years this volume was published separately for the UGC by the USR. For later volumes in the series see the entry for <u>University Statistics</u> on p.187.

The UGC has also periodically issued a report on a particular subject, for instance the <u>Report of a Working Party (of ABRC/UGC) on the Support of University Scientific Research</u> (Cmnd.8567), 1982, and <u>Report of the Continuing Education Working Party</u> (UGC, 1984). The UGC has also published several reports of its recent subject reviews, including <u>University Chemistry - The</u>

Way Forward : The Report of the Chemistry Review (HMSO, 1988) and The Future of University Physics : The Report of the Physics Review (HMSO, 1988), the Review Committees which prepared these two reports being chaired by Professor F.G.A. Stone and Professor Sir Sam Edwards respectively, and Building for Success in the Earth Sciences: The Second Report of the Earth Sciences Review (HMSO, 1989), which followed the consultative 'Oxburgh' report, Strengthening University Earth Sciences (1987).

In 1989 the UGC published Veterinary Education into the 21st Century: Report of the Working Party on Veterinary Education (the'Riley Report'), which recommended the reduction in the numbers of veterinary schools from six to four; in the light of the reaction to this report the Secretary of State for Education and Science and the Minister of Agriculture, Fisheries and Food appointed a committee chaired by Dr. E.S. Page, whose report, Review of Veterinary Manpower and Education (1989) recommended that the intake of the veterinary schools be increased.

The UGC also issued a booklet of guidance on the correct procedure under which building grants are approved, entitled 'University Buildings Projects - Notes on Control and Guidance', 1982.

Records

(i)   The UGC (UFC) is subject to the provisions of the Public Records Acts 1958 and 1967 and any documents concerning its national policy are kept and eventually made available for public inspection in the Public Record Office after 30 years have elasped from the closing of the records. Normally such papers are contained on files dealing with specific subject matters but there are occasions when major policy is involved in connection with an individual university, whereby a file relating to that institution can be regarded as being of historical interest. Apart from matters of a purely ephemeral nature, other papers are retained for a minimum period of five years.

(ii)   The following records of the UGC are held at the Public Record Office, Ruskin Avenue, Kew, Richmond, Surrey, TW9 4DU, and (except where noted below) are subject to a closure period of 30 years from the date of last entry:-

UGC 1   Minutes of meetings of the Committee, 1919-76. 96 vols. and files (Vols. 1&2 cover 1919-33 and 1934-39 respectively)
From 1972 onwards, the minutes, agenda and papers were incorporated into one file series.

UGC 2   Agenda for Committee meetings, together with supporting papers, 1919-71. 189 files.
(records for 1929 and for meetings on 30 January 1945 and 6 December 1950 are wanting; no meetings were held in 1932)

UGC 3   Returns from Universities and University Colleges in receipt of grants, 1919-69. 50 vols. Open without restriction.
(returns for 1923-24 are wanting; the 1919-20 and 1920-21 returns are printed)

For the years 1967-69 the returns take the form of copies of Vol.6 (Universities) of <u>Statistics of Education</u>.

UGC 4   Departmental Expenditure Schedules, 1921-38.17 vols.
(Schedules of the Committee's expenditure on grants, showing amounts allocated to each institution, arranged under the different purposes for which the grants were made.)

UGC 5   Miscellanea, 1911-42. 17 vols. and files.
(Reports, minutes, memoranda, etc., of Board of Education Departmental Committees on the University of London and on the Medical School at Cardiff, and of the Board's Advisory Committee on University Grants 1911-19; correspondence and papers concerning the deputation to the President of the Board of Education and the Chancellor of the Exchequer from University institutions, 23 November 1918; papers and accounts relating to Irish universities and colleges, 1918-42; a specimen file of interviews with representatives from provincial institutions (Birmingham, Bristol, Cambridge, Exeter, Leeds, Liverpool, Manchester (2), Nottingham, Oxford, Reading, Sheffield, and Southampton), 1936; and files (1938-42) relating to University organisation and finance during the War.)

UGC 6   Reports and Annual Surveys 1935-85. 29 vols. (all printed)
(Reports of the UGC, 1935-57 (Reports for 1935-47, 1947-52, and 1952-57, and Interim Reports for 1947-51 and 1952-56); and three special reports on technology in universities (1950), methods used by universities of contracting, recording, and controlling expenditure (1956), and the superannuation of university teachers (1960); and annual surveys 1964-65 to 1984-85 inclusive.

UGC 7   Registered files. These files include:-

8-126	Quinquennial Estimates, 1945-66, principally file per named university or college.
127-139	Annual Grants, (a few files per university), 1944-69.
140-146	Agricultural Education, 1945-67.
163-168	Chairs and proposed chairs, 1953-64.
169-198, 218-236	Proposed new universities, 1944-71.
372-381	Expansion of universities, 1955-64.
569-577	Halls of residence, 1944-67.
578-588	Capital investment programme, 1949-70.
589-600	Libraries, 1945-69.
654-681	Medical Education, 1944-68.
840-862	Salaries, 1944-72.
863-967	Technological Education (etc.), 1945-69.
968-986	Committee of Vice-Chancellors and Principals, 1944-67.

987-1056	University building works programme, 1946-70.
1058-1061	Correspondence with the Treasury, 1910-36.
1062-1063	Constitution, statutory powers and administration of the UGC, 1919-43.
1064	Correspondence concerning education in medical and surgical units in hospitals, 1920-29.
1067	Postgraduate medical studies, 1920-29.
1068	Correspondence with the Board of Education, 1917-23.

UGC 8 Minutes of meetings of the UGC's Sub-Committees, 1946-72. 105 files.

UGC 9 Agenda for meetings of the UGC's Sub-Committees, together with supporting papers, 1946-72. 590 files.

(iii) Past members of the UGC or of one of its Sub-Committees have been known to deposit Committee papers with a university. The UGC advised that such papers are subject to the Official Secrets Act and should be destroyed when the individual's membership ceases; the UGC retained copies of these papers and they will eventually become available to the public in the Public Record Office.

UNIVERSITIES' SAFETY ASSOCIATION

Address and
contact
Mr. B. Mallows,
Acting Honorary Secretary: Universities' Safety Association,
Safety Officer,
University College,
51 Park Place,
Cardiff,
CF1 5AT

tel: 0222 874000

History
The Universities' Safety Association (USA) was established in 1971. At the time there were very few full-time University Safety Officers and so it was provided that the constituent members of the USA should be the universities themselves. In all but name the USA soon became a forum for University Safety Officers since virtually all member universities were represented at USA functions by the University Safety Officer where one had been appointed.

One of the aims in the formation of the Association was the exchange of information between the safety organisations in different universities, and the Association's newsletter, Safety News, was launched for this purpose in 1972. Nationally, shortly afterwards, in July 1972 the report of the Committee on Safety and Health at Work (Chairman: Lord Robens) was presented to Parliament (Cmnd. 5034) and emphasised that more legislation does not necessarily give more safety and that collaboration is better than compulsion;

it, inter alia, recommended that there should be a new 'Authority for Safety and Health at Work' and a new unified Act to replace the current variety of legislation. The end result was the Health and Safety at Work etc. Act 1974.

In c.1978 the subject of qualifications of safety professionals, of interest to both the TUC and the Health and Safety Executive, led to the formation of the Institute of University Safety Officers (IUSO) the aims of which are "...the furtherence of the interests of Safety...the advancement of Safety knowledge of its members, the maintenance of the professional standards of the members and the preservation and enhancement of their status including representation on bodies of influence considered beneficial to the Institution". The IUSO may be contacted per its Secretary, Ms. L.J. Shaw, Robens Institute, University of Surrey, Guildford, Surrey, GU2 5XH. The USA has continued to conduct seminars and conferences and to keep members informed by publishing a newsletter, and continues to represent its members on other agencies' committees, etc.

The USA has an annual general meeting and holds an annual conference, and one-day conferences, seminars and symposia. Its day-to-day work is organised by an Executive Committee, of which the Chairman, Deputy Chairman, Secretary, Treasurer, (and, in the earlier years, Editor, and the current Conference Secretaries) are members. It holds joint meetings with other bodies and is represented on other bodies (e.g. the Liaison Committee for Professional Occupational Health and Safety Organisations). More recent issues of the USA's Safety Digest have included minutes/reports of meetings of the Scottish Universities Safety/Security Officers. The full membership of the USA now approaches 90 and includes both Universities and Polytechnics; there are also a number of Associate Members.

Bibliography
Margaret R. Hastings (ed. and chief compiler), The Health and Safety Directory 1989/90 (Kluwer Publishing Ltd., Brentford, 1989)

Publications

Universities' Safety Association : Safety News, Nos.1-17, Jan. 1972 - May 1983.

Universities' Safety Association : Safety Newsletter, 1983-84.

Universities' Safety Association : Safety Digest, [Nos.1] May 1984- to date.
(No.24, Dec. 1987)

UNIVERSITIES OF SCOTLAND JOINT CONSULTATIVE AND ADVISORY COMMITTEE ON PURCHASING

Address and
contact
Universities of Scotland Joint Consultative
and Advisory Committee on Purchasing,
34, Buccleuch Place,
Edinburgh,
EH8 9JT

tel: 031 667 1011 ext.6531
Mr. J. Douglas Bell, Secretary

History

Most universities are members of regional purchasing groups which have been established to improve purchasing arrangements within and among universities.

The Universities of Scotland Joint Consultative and Advisory Committee on Purchasing was established in 1975. Its remit is:-

'To promote co-operation between Scottish universities in the purchase of materials, equipment, furnishings and services in order to obtain the maximum benefits available to the Universities and to this end:-

(i)   to arrange for the exchange of information between member universities on the use of suppliers, their prices and terms generally;

(ii)   to encourage purchase on a group basis whenever possible;

(iii)   to establish links with other university purchasing groups and also non-university purchasing authorities having similar interests;

(iv)   to establish and co-ordinate the activities of appropriate sub-committees and specialist commodity groups;

(v)   to prepare a report once a year for the Courts of the individual Scottish universities.'

The Joint Committee comprises senior academic, senior administrative and specialist purchasing personnel. The detailed investigative work and discussion with contractors is carried out by the specialist Commodity Groups (referred to above) composed of specialist and/or technical representatives of the universities.

Within Scotland the Joint Committee constitutes a forum for information exchange, collaboration and negotiation. Beyond this the Committee freely exchanges information, in the form of Group minutes, buyers' guides, and contract notes, with the regional university purchasing consortia in England and Wales which operate along lines akin to those of the Committee. This inter-regional co-operation is often taken further and the various purchasing consortia/groups have combined to reach national supply agreements which are of general benefit.

The Universities of Scotland are represented at the Conferences on University Purchasing. The Conference is the national conference for university officers engaged in purchasing and is usually held once every eighteen months or two years at a different university: for instance in 1981 the Conference was hosted by the University of Wales in Cardiff and in 1983 it was hosted by the University of London.

Publications

Report of the Joint Committee (annual report submitted to the Courts of the individual Scottish Universities; the 6th Annual Report covers the period 1 August 1981 - 31 July 1982.)

THE UNIVERSITIES' STATISTICAL RECORD

Address and
contact
The Universities' Statistical Record,
P.O. Box 130,
Cheltenham,
Gloucestershire,
GL50 1HY

tel: 0242 222444
Mr. Philip Oakley, Secretary
Dr. A.W. Nichol, Executive Secretary

History
The Robbins Report drew attention to the lack of adequate statistical information about higher education, and stressed the importance of devising arrangements to provide comprehensive statistics for the future, particularly regarding the movement of staff and students into, within, and out of higher education. After various consultations UCCA (which already had much of the information required of students) joined the CVCP, UGC, DES, and the SED in a feasibility study whose report, produced in 1968, was accepted, subject to the incorporation of safeguards to protect individual confidentiality, by the CVCP in October 1968, it being recommended to universities that they should co-operate in the establishment of the scheme.

The Universities' Statistical Record (USR) was established under the joint auspices of the UGC and the CVCP in late 1968, within the organisation of UCCA, UCCA providing managerial, technical and publishing services in return for funding by the UGC. The information gathered in the 'pilot' year of 1968/69 became the start of the undergraduate record, which came into full operation with the undergraduate entry of October 1969. The postgraduate and staff records were started from 1970/71.

USR is managed by UCCA under the supervision of a Policy Group and a Management Committee acting on behalf of the UGC (UFC) and the CVCP. The Record (a computer-based information system) is compiled by means of annual returns from each university in five main areas: undergraduate, postgraduate, first destination of graduates, staff, and continuing education. The supply of information from the Record is confined to aggregate statistics which are widely used for government and other publications, and for resource allocation, manpower planning, etc. No information about any individual may be released from the Record except to the person concerned or to his or her university.

The Croham Report (Cm 81, HMSO, 1987) recommended that the UGC should reappraise its management information requirements which, it foresaw, would require a re-examination of the relationship between the UGC and the USR, including the scope for the integration of all or part of the USR's work within the UGC's Management Information Service. The Government's initial response to the Report, Higher Education : Meeting the Challenge (Cm 114, HMSO, 1987) did not include reference to this recommendation.

Bibliography

Universities' Statistical Record: An Explanatory Note prepared by the University Grants Committee and the Committee of Vice-Chancellors and Principals for the information of members of universities, December 1970.
(includes specimen print-out from the Undergraduate Record with an interpretation of the headings used for coding purposes.)

Ronald Kay, UCCA: Its Origins and Development 1950-85, UCCA, 1985.

Coopers & Lybrand Associates, National Data Study (CVCP, 1985)
(Commissioned by the Steering Committee for Efficiency Studies in Universities, this study covers the USR, UGC, DHSS, etc.)

Publications

University Statistics : a three-part series which consists of the following volumes: Vol.1 Students and Staff, Vol.2 First Destinations of University Graduates (previously published separately for the UGC by the USR : see p.180), Vol.3 Finance. Covers the years 1980-81 (University Statistics 1980, USR on behalf of UGC, 1982) to date. This series replaces Vol.6 (Universities) of the DES' Statistics of Education series which itself ended with the 1979 edition.

Records

Returns made by the universities to USR are in various formats: documentary, punched card, and magnetic tape. These data bases are used to compile (a) annual statistical reports associated with UCCA's annual report, (b) further standard statistical reports, and (c) statistical statements in response to enquiries from interested bodies (including employing firms). The enquiry results are retained in a series which starts on microform and is now a COM fiche; there are no on-line search facilities or index. Appraisal of machine-readable records is practised, an estimated 60% of tapes being retained.

Access to statistical information relating to individual universities which is not subsequently available in published form is within the determination of each university concerned.

UNIVERSITIES SUPERANNUATION SCHEME LIMITED

Address and
contact
Universities Superannuation Scheme Limited,
Richmond House,
Rumford Place,
Liverpool,
L3 9FD

tel: 051 227 4711
Mr. P. Stirrup, Chief Executive Officer.

History

The Universities Superannuation Scheme Limited (USS) was incorporated as a registered company on 18 April 1974 (Registration No.1167 127). The more immediate background to the setting up of USS was the inadequate pension provision for university staff in the postwar period and the poor benefits deriving from insurance policy based money purchase schemes which had led to the setting up of an interim supplementation scheme in 1953 and the Supplementation Scheme for FSSU members in 1960. Under USS the current contribution to USS from employers is 18.55% of the salaries (less £100 in each case) of all contributing members of USS; the employees' contributions are 6.35% of salary (less £100). USS is a final salary scheme and guarantees an annual pension of 1/80th of pensionable salary for each year of pensionable service and a tax free lump sum equal to three times the member's annual pension subject to Inland Revenue limits; all pensions are increased annually in line with increases in the cost of living. Widow's, dependent widower's and children's benefits are payable. A lump sum benefit is also payable on death in service and may be payable on death after retirement.

USS is responsible for administering the principal pension scheme for the academic and senior administrative staff of all United Kingdom universities. USS is amongst the largest occupational pension schemes in the UK and, at 1 April 1988, had approximately 62,000 contributing members; 13,000 pensioners, including widows and children; and 9,000 members entitled to deferred benefits. The value of the Fund's investments was estimated at £4,000 million.

Bibliography

Sir Douglas Logan, The Birth of a Pension Scheme: A History of the Universities Superannuation Scheme, Liverpool U.P., 1985.

'USS Annual Report' (for 1985-86), in AUT Bulletin, No.141, November 1986; extracts from and comments on the annual report.

Publications

Copies of the following publications are available both from USS and from the employers of USS members.

Universities Superannuation Scheme and Universities Supplementary Dependants (and Ill-health Retirement) Pension Scheme: A guide for members, USS, June 1985.
(originally issued in 1975).

Universities Superannuation Scheme : A Guide for Members, USS, October 1988.

Trust Deeds and Rules and Amending Deeds for USS and USDPS.

Annual Reports and Accounts.

Actuarial Valuation Reports (valuations are carried out at least once every three years, the most recent being at 31 March 1990, which will be published in early 1991.)

Records

Minutes of Board of Directors and of Management Committee are retained permanently.

Correspondence is generated mainly in two ways:

1. Queries about the membership details of individuals, especially relating to previous employment, war service, etc. This will probably be kept permanently.

2. Changes in the rules, e.g. as between the relative entitlement through war service of lecturers and other university members of staff. A total of over 300 photocopies of any significant documentation are sent out regularly, the originals being retained permanently.

USS maintains a computerised data base containing salary, superannuation history, and personal details, including career history, of members of USS. Data on each member is supplied by his/her university on manually completed forms and up-dated in the same way as relevant events take place (e.g. on retirement). Salary data is frequently supplied to USS on magnetic tape. Data processing is carried out by USS.

UNIVERSITY ASSOCIATION FOR CONTEMPORARY EUROPEAN STUDIES

Address and
contact
Eva Evans,
The Executive Secretary,
University Association for Contemporary European Studies,
King's College,
Strand,
London,
WC2R 2LS

tel: 071 240 0206

History
The University Association for Contemporary European Studies (UACES) was formed in 1968 by a group of British university teachers and some members of the research staff of the Royal Institute of International Affairs. The main objective of the Association is to provide resources and facilities to bring together academic staff, research workers, and postgraduate students actively engaged in teaching and research in contemporary European studies in the UK. It aims to provide a channel of communication for its members and to develop links with institutions of the European Community, other European organisations, government departments and academic organisations in the UK and overseas, particularly in continental Europe and the USA. Active links are maintained with other bodies including the UK Association for European Law, the Royal Institute of International Affairs, the Association for the Study of German Politics, the Association for the Study of Modern Italy, and the Association for the Study of Modern and Contemporary France, and with the Brussels and London offices of the European Communities and the European Parliament.

UACES has a wide membership in British universities and polytechnics: by 1985 there were 300 individual and 70 corporate members. The Association has an Executive Secretary and a permanent Secretariat in London.

The Association's activities are principally the organisation of conferences and meetings and publication and the provision of information. It organises and sponsors residential and one-day conferences. An Annual Conference is held each January. Both current events as well as more long-term and research-orientated fields are covered by its conferences and by the study groups it supports. The teaching of European studies is the subject of occasional workshops and conferences.

UACES is now an active publishing house with its own imprint and ISBN (0 906 384). The main thrust of its publishing is in four directions - the dissemination of information about European studies through registers of research and courses for staff; teaching aids; proceedings series, in which conference reports and an Annual Review of the Activities of the European Communities are published; and occasional papers, in which one-off conferences etc. are published. For further details see below.

Bibliography
'University Association for Contemporary European Studies' (A history of the Association, details of its activities, and membership application form; the above <u>History</u> is drawn from this pamphlet.)

Publications
(i)   <u>Newsletter</u> (published, three times a year, for UACES' membership and a few related bodies; it does not have an ISSN number).

UACES published the very early editions of the European Documentation Centres Newsletters (Nos.1-, 1975-) but this is now being handled by the Association of EDC Librarians.

(ii)   UACES other publications include:-

Eva Evans (ed.), <u>Register of Courses in European Studies in British Universities and Polytechnics 1986/87</u> (1986) (and earlier editions dating back at least to 1973; published in alternate years, the next edition will be that for 1988/89.)

Eva Evans (ed.), <u>Register of Current Research into European Integration 1987/88</u> (1987) (First published in 1973; published in alternate years, the next edition will be that for 1989/90.)

John E. Pemberton (compiler and editor), <u>European Materials in British University Libraries : A bibliography and union catalogue</u> (1973).

C. Bettinson, <u>European Studies and Related Degree Courses in UK Universities, Polytechnics and other Colleges; a students' guide</u> (1986).

*   G. Denton (ed.), <u>Reform of the CAP and Restructuring of the EEC Budget</u> (1983).

C. Brewin and R. McAllister, <u>Annual Review of the Activities of the European Communities 1984</u> (1985).

A. Butt Philip, <u>Pressure Groups in the European Community</u> (1985).

* M. Smith (ed.), <u>The US and the EC : New Administrations and Continuing Problems</u> (1981).

* M. Smith (ed.), <u>The US and the EC : National Economic Strategies and International Coordination</u> (1982).

* M. Smith (ed.), <u>Trade Relations between the EC and the US: Common Cause or Divergent Paths?</u> (1983).

* M. Smith (ed.), <u>Technological Change and US/EC Relations : Challenges and Responses</u> (1985).

* papers presented at UACES conferences

(iii)　　<u>UACES/Allen and Unwin</u>
Series of 'Studies on Contemporary Europe', which include:-

John S. Marsh and Pamela J. Swanney, <u>Agriculture and the European Community</u> (1980).

Sidney Pollard, <u>The Integration of the European economy since 1815</u> (1981).

Michael Smith, <u>Western Europe and the United States : the Uncertain Alliance</u> (1984)

(iv)　　UACES is responsible for the <u>Journal of Common Market Studies</u>, (Vols.1-, 1962-). The journal is published, four times a year, by Basil Blackwell for UACES.

<u>Records</u>
The UACES Secretariat retains its minutes since 1968, but it is felt that they are private in nature. A full account of the activities of the Association is found in its Newsletters of which office copies are kept and could be made available to researchers in the office.

UNIVERSITY AUTHORITIES PANEL

<u>Address and</u>
<u>contact</u>
University Authorities Panel,
29, Tavistock Square,
London,
WC1H 9EZ

tel: 071 387 9231
fax: 071 388 8649
Mr. D.D.A. Leslie, Senior Administrative Officer.

<u>History</u>
The University Authorities Panel (UAP), representing all the universities in the United Kingdom, was established in 1970 by the Committee of Vice-

Chancellors and Principals as part of the national machinery for negotiating the salaries of university non-clinical academic and related staff. The UAP was established following discussions between the DES, the UGC, the CVCP, and the AUT, and consultation with individual universities.

In the post-Second World War period up to 1962 and in the period 1964-66 increases in salaries of non-clinical academic and related staff were awarded directly by the Government after consultation with the UGC (which consulted the CVCP and the AUT). In 1963/64 a review of the remuneration of academic staff was undertaken by the National Incomes Commission. Between 1967 and 1970 academic salaries were the subject of a standing reference to the National Board for Prices and Incomes.

The UAP's membership (which is appointed by the CVCP) consists of five Vice-Chancellors and five lay members of University Councils, under the chairmanship of a sixth Vice-Chancellor. Its main work is the negotiation of salary agreements; it has also been involved in discussions on the procedures and criteria for probation, and on national salary structures for academic-related staff.

As regards the salaries negotiating machinery, the UAP is represented at both stages. The first stage, Committee 'A', consists of the UAP, acting for the universities as employers, and the AUT, meeting under an independent chairman; UGC officers attend as advisers and assessors. Once Committee 'A' has reached agreement its proposals are considered and decided upon in Committee 'B'. In Committee 'B' DES officials (advised by the UGC, now the UFC) represent the Government, and the chairman of Committee 'A' and a joint UAP/AUT team represent Committee 'A'; a DES official acts as chairman. If agreement cannot be reached in Committee 'B', arbitration may be resorted to if the two sides so agree.

Following a review by the CVCP and the Committee of Chairmen of University Councils of the arrangements for the representation of universities in their role as employers in national collective bargaining with staff and for the conduct of negotiations, in January 1990 the CVCP and the Committee proposed the establishment of a new Pay and Employment Policy Committee (PEPC). Each university was asked to agree to transfer to the PEPC the mandates which it gave to the UAP in 1970, to the UCNS, and to the CASSC in 1979.

In May 1990, Committee 'A' submitted a report in which it argued the case for new salary negotiating arrangements and urged the Government to review the negotiating machinery.

Bibliography
Ron Hayward, 'Universities and the Trade Unions', in Stuart Bosworth (ed.), Beyond the Limelight : Essays on the Occasion of the Silver Jubilee of the Conference of University Administrators (CUA, 1986), pp.115-125.

Publications
The Panel has not issued any publications.

Records
The Panel's records are kept in the offices of the Committee of Vice-Chancellors and Principals. The agenda papers, supporting documents and

minutes - which are all classified as confidential to members of the Panel - have been selected for long-term preservation and date from the Panel's establishment. Copies of circular letters to universities on all aspects of the Panel's work are also preserved. All other correspondence and papers are being kept for the present, and no decision has yet been taken on how long these should be retained.

The CVCP has adopted conditions which provide for the Committee's minutes to be available for study by bona fide scholars and researchers, subject to a fifteen-year period of restriction on access. It had been recognised that after referring to the minutes a researcher would often wish to consult other material in the Committee's archive, and in such cases requests for access to specific papers would need to be made separately and would then be considered, on an individual basis. Any approach to the UAP for access to its records would be considered sympathetically using the same procedures as for the CVCP.

UNIVERSITY CATERING OFFICERS CONFERENCE

Address and
contact
Mr. George Donaldson,
Hon. Secretary: University Catering Officers Conference,
Residential Officer (Catering),
University of Dundee,
3 Cross Row,
Dundee,
DD1 4HN

tel: 0382 23181 ext. 4039

History
The first official meeting of University Catering Officers was held at Hotelympia on 24 January 1964 and was convened by Mr. Russell E. Taylor of the University of Edinburgh who acted as Honorary Secretary. Fifteen persons were present at this meeting, including the Catering Adviser to the Treasury and representatives of twelve universities (including Cambridge, London, and Liverpool), and it was agreed to hold a two-day conference at the University of Keele in July 1964, with three principal sessions (devoted to costing, staffing, and bulk buying) and that one representative (the senior Catering person) from each university should be invited to attend.

The 27th Annual Conference is due to be held at the University of Sheffield in 1990.

Records
Minutes of meetings, 24 January 1964 - to date, and other records of the Conference are held by the Hon. Secretary.

WORKERS' EDUCATIONAL ASSOCIATION

Address and
contact
Mr. Robert Lochrie,
General Secretary,
Workers' Educational Association,
Temple House,
9, Upper Berkeley Street,
London,
W1H 8BY

tel: 071 402 5608
fax: 071 402 5600

History

The Workers' Educational Association (WEA) originated in 1903 as the Association to Promote the Higher Education of Working Men, largely through the endeavours of Albert Mansbridge, supported by Dr. J. Holland Rose (editor of the University Extension Journal) and the Revd. (later Bishop) Charles Gore. In 1905 the name of the Association was changed to the Workers' Educational Association. The WEA's objective was 'to stimulate and to satisfy the demands of adults, in particular members of workers movements, for education by the promotion of courses and other facilities and generally to further the advancement of education to the end that all children, adolescents and adults may have full opportunities for the education needed for their complete individual and social development.' The WEA has been most active in the field of adult education. Its early active supporters included a number of prominent university staff, including A.L. Smith, Sir Oliver Lodge, and Sir Alfred Dale and by the end of its first year (1903-04) the Association had 135 members and eleven affiliated co-operative societies. The first branch was established shortly afterwards, in 1904, at Reading and the first national conference was held in 1905, in which year Albert Mansbridge became the WEA's first full-time General Secretary.

Co-operation with the universities was established in individual cases, commencing at Oxford in 1907-08 (pioneering tutorial classes under Oxford auspices starting work in January 1908), and soon extending to other parts of the country including Cambridge, London, Manchester, Liverpool, Leeds, and Sheffield, whose universities established joint committees with WEA representatives/branches. In 1910 representatives of the various universities formed a Central Joint Advisory Committee for the discussion of common problems and the tutorial class system further developed and spread. From 1923 this Committee's work was supplemented by periodical meetings of extra-mural officers which in 1926 were formalised through the establishment of the Universities Extra-Mural Consultative Committee. In 1958 the Central Joint Advisory Committee was replaced by a joint consultative committee of the WEA and the UCAE.

By early 1914 the WEA had 179 branches and 11,430 individual members; it also had 2,555 affiliated organisations of which 953 were trade unions, trades councils, or trade union branches. By May 1945 the number of branches was 876 and the branch membership 37,159; district membership was 5,424 and there were 2,660 affiliated societies. By session 1948-49 tutorial classes totalled 889, constituting almost fourteen per cent of all classes.

In the period 1947/48 to 1968/69, the number of courses arranged jointly between universities and the WEA remained relatively static, but the number of courses provided by the universities independently increased nearly six-fold over this period. The extent of joint provision has varied over this period : by 1968/69 four universities were arranging over 80 per cent of their programme jointly with the WEA while seven universities and colleges arranged under 20 per cent jointly.

Nowadays the WEA is organised in approximately 900 branches, 20 districts and a national organisation. It employs nearly 250 full-time staff : tutor organisers, development officers, administrative and secretarial staff, in addition to the very many part-time tutors. WEA districts each employ a professional secretary and a field and office staff. The WEA provides for over 180,000 students in over 10,000 courses.

The WEA remains a federation of educational and workers organisations; it is a national, non-party political, non-sectarian, independent and voluntary movement. It receives financial assistance from both central and local government as well as from voluntary sources. Its districts have been recognised as responsible bodies receiving direct grants from central government since 1924. In 1988-89 the DES reviewed the current formula for grant-aiding the WEA and enquired into the WEA's financial management and procedures, both in the WEA nationally and at district level. The Government rejected the report of the DES' internal auditor and decided that the grant to the WEA should be paid through local authorities. The WEA's governing body is still the Central Council, its decisions being implemented by an Executive Committee. The twenty Districts of WEA are governed by Councils which are representative of branches, affiliated bodies and individual subscribers; each District is served by a full-time Secretary and a full-time field staff. The Districts work closely with university extra-mural departments in the provision of three year tutorial classes, through joint committees and other means.

The aims of the WEA are to provide men and women with opportunities for a liberal education directed to personal development by the provision of social education to improve the effectiveness of those participating in community affairs, whether in trade union, political, or social service. It encourages cultural pursuits and seeks to secure improvement in the public educational system and the removal of inequalities of educational opportunity.

The WEA holds a residential conference biennially, at which representatives of branches, districts and nationally affiliated organisations meet to shape the Association's policy. At a special Conference held in June 1988, the WEA adopted a new Constitution, the WEA remaining an unincorporated association, registered as a charity, but clarifying the relationships between Branch, Districts and the National Executive Committee, preserving the independence of Districts and Branches within a national structure.

Bibliography
Albert Mansbridge, An Adventure in Working-Class Education: being the story of the Workers' Educational Association 1903-1915 (Longmans, Green and Co., London, 1920).

T.W. Price, The Story of the Workers' Educational Association from 1903 to 1924 (The Labour Publishing Co.Ltd., London, 1924). With an introduction by R.H. Tawney.

H.P. Smith, <u>Labour and Learning : Albert Mansbridge, Oxford and the W.E.A.</u> (Basil Blackwell, Oxford, 1956).

Mary Stocks, <u>The Workers' Educational Association : the first fifty years</u> (George Allen & Unwin Ltd., London, 1953).

Bernard Jennings, <u>New lamps for old? : University adult education in retrospect and prospect</u> (University of Hull, 1976).

A.J. Corfield, <u>Epoch in Workers' Education : A History of the Workers' Educational Trade Union Committee</u> (WEA, London, 1969).
(the Committee, which had links with WEA, was formed in 1919; in 1964 it was absorbed into the TUC's centralised scheme of trade union education.)

Bernard Jennings, <u>Knowledge is Power : A Short History of the W.E.A. 1903-78</u> (Department of Adult Education, University of Hull, 1979; Newland Papers No.1).

Roger Fieldhouse, <u>The Workers' Educational Association : Aims and Achievements 1903-1977</u> (Publications in Continuing Education, Syracuse University, New York, 1977).

<u>Adult Education : A Plan for Development : Report by a Committee of Inquiry appointed by the Secretary of State for Education and Science under the Chairmanship of Sir Lionel Russell C.B.E.</u> (HMSO, 1973).

Ted Mooney, <u>J.M. Mactavish : General Secretary of the WEA, 1916-1927 : the man and his ideas</u> (Liverpool Branch of WEA, 1979).

Brian Simon (ed.), <u>The Search for Enlightenment:The Working Class and Adult Education in the Twentieth Century</u> (Lawrence and Wishart, London, 1990). Focuses in particular on the history of independent working-class education but also covers developments within trade union education, the universities and the WEA in the period since the Second World War.

Some Districts of the WEA have celebrated their Jubilees etc. with published histories, e.g. A. John Allaway, <u>Challenge and Response : WEA East Midland District 1919-1969</u> (WEA East Midland District, 1969); W.J. Souch, <u>The History of the Reading Branch of the Workers' Educational Association, 1904-1954</u> (Reading, 1954); H.G. Crudge, <u>1911-1961 : Fifty years in the life of a voluntary movement</u> (Bristol, 1961; about the Western District of WEA); and V. Williams and G.J. White, <u>Adult Education and Social Purpose : A History of the WEA Eastern District 1913 to 1988</u> (WEA Eastern District, 1988).

Publications include:-

<u>Bibliography on Adult Education</u>

<u>Publications Lists</u> : General; Social Studies; Trade Union Studies and Industrial Relations.
<u>Annual Report</u> (the British Library holds an incomplete set from the 9th Annual Report, for 1912, onwards).

The Students' Bulletin vol.1 (1924-25); after April 1925 incorporated with The Highway; The Highway : a monthly journal of education for the people(1908- ?1950).
(the Annual Reports of the WEA for 1920-23 were published in this journal); succeeded by The Summer Highway (June-Sept. 1950).

Topic (1951-?). Discontinued a number of years ago.

Topics for Discussion (1943-?). Discontinued a number of years ago.

WEA News, Vol.1 No.1-, 1969-; succeeded by WEA News New Series Nos.1-, 1971- to date (twice a year).

S.G. Raybould, University Standards in WEA Work (London, 1948).

Studies for Trade Unionists, 1975- to date.

Trade Union Studies Journal, 1-, 1980- to date.

WEA Arts Newsletter, Nos.1-[2], 1981-? On its discontinuation, a page in WEA News was allocated to the subject for a short time.

Women's Studies Newsletter, Nos.1-, 1977- to date.
(twice-yearly journal for supporters of and participants in women's education).

Copies of a number of WEA publications may be found in university libraries, e.g. in the Adult Education section of the Education Library, University of Liverpool, which holds incomplete copies of the annual report, journals, etc. of the WEA, together with published histories of districts, etc.

Records
(a)   It is understood that the minutes of the WEA's Executive Committee together with a set of the annual and biennial reports of the WEA and a set of the annual reports of WEA Districts are held at the WEA's London offices. At present (March 1989) the WEA's library is being reclassified and its contents in some cases rehoused; a new acquisition policy is being introduced.

(b)   The records of some WEA Districts and Branches have been deposited in record repositories, e.g. the records of the North Wales district, 1925-73, are in the Department of Manuscripts, The Library, University College of North Wales, Bangor. The National Register of Archives (Royal Commission on Historical Manuscrips, Quality House, Quality Court, Chancery Lane, London, WC2A 1HP) has entries (copies of lists of records or brief details of records) for the records of over 40 WEA Districts and Branches in England and Wales which have been deposited in local authority and university record repositories. These records comprise minutes and, in a number of cases, also such records as annual reports, correspondence, accounts, log books, and copies of (WEA branch etc.) publications.

ASSOCIATION OF COMMONWEALTH UNIVERSITIES

Address and
contact
Mr. Peter Hetherington,
Deputy Secretary General,
The Association of Commonwealth Universities,
John Foster House,
36, Gordon Square,
London,
WC1H OPF

tel: 071 387 8572
fax: 071 387 2655

History
The Association of Commonwealth Universities (ACU) is a voluntary organisation which was founded in 1913 as the Universities Bureau of the British Empire; in 1948 the Bureau was renamed the Association of Universities of the British Commonwealth, this name being changed to The Association of Commonwealth Universities in 1963 upon the Association's incorporation by Royal Charter. In 1963 the ACU had 133 members.

The oldest international inter-university association in the world, by 1986 the ACU had 297 institutions in membership in 29 Commonwealth countries (in Asia, Europe, Canada, the Caribbean, Africa, and Australasia and the Pacific); by 1988 ACU's membership had risen to 319.

The purpose of the ACU is to promote contact and co-operation between the universities of the Commonwealth. In particular the ACU:

1.   Organises conferences in different parts of the world. Commonwealth Universities Congresses are held every five years (their Proceedings being published), and Conferences of the Executive Heads of Commonwealth Universities every two or three years. Between Congresses the annual meetings of the ACU's Council become, in effect, inter-university conferences when joint sessions are held with executive heads in the country visited. The Council is assisted by an Executive Committee, a Budget Review Committee and (for each Congress) a Conference Organising Committee.

2.   Promotes the movement of staff between Commonwealth universities by helping member institutions to fill vacant academic posts; by two schemes of travel grants for senior university administrators; and by programmes of academic exchanges between member institutions in developing countries.

3.   Assists the mobility of students between countries through its administration of several scholarship schemes, including (a) the British part (900 graduate awards) of the Commonwealth Scholarship and Fellowship Plan, (b) the Marshall Scholarship Programme, and (c) the Commonwealth Foundation Medical Electives Bursaries Scheme.

4. Provides information about the universities of the Commonwealth, and about fellowships and scholarships for travel between them, through some 20 publications (see below), an awards information service, a documentation service, and a personal information service.

5. In 1987 launched an appeal (to coincide with the 75th anniversary of ACU in 1988) to raise £3 million to finance a new fellowship programme. Fellows will be chosen from inside or outside universities and will concentrate on subject areas in which the needs of developing countries are particularly great.

Bibliography

Eric Ashby, Community of Universities: an informal portrait of the Association of Universities of the British Commonwealth, 1913-1963, Cambridge U.P., 1963.

The Association of Commonwealth Universities: what it is and what it does. Annual publication of the A.C.U.

T. Craig, 'The Commonwealth community of universities', in The Round Table, No. 287, July 1983, pp. 331-338.

J. Pickford, 'We are all human face' in Commonwealth, Vol. 25 No.6, June 1983, pp. 187-189.

A. Christodoulou, 'Something to celebrate', in The Times Higher Education Supplement, 11 March 1983, p.13. (1983 was the A.C.U.'s 70th anniversary year.)

Renate Simpson, How the PhD came to Britain: a century of struggle for postgraduate education, Society for Research into Higher Education, Guildford, 1983. The flyer for this book described it as bringing out 'the vital role played by the Universities Bureau of the British Empire (predecessor of the Association of Commonwealth Universities)... to persuade the universities to co-operate with each other in providing postgraduate courses and degrees, not only for British students but also for those from America and the Empire.'

'Commonwealth : a special report to mark the 14th Commonwealth Universities Congress', The Times Higher Education Supplement, 29 January 1988, pp.i-xi.
This report looks at recent developments in the ACU and in all twenty-nine Commonwealth countries or groups of countries with universities.

Publications

The ACU produces some 20 publications (which are listed in a ACU leaflet), principal amongst which are the following. Copies are sent free to member institutions.

A.C.U. Bulletin of Current Documentation, nos.1-, June 1971- (nos. 1-3 entitled A bulletin of current documentation.)

Awards for Commonwealth university academic staff, 1972/74- (1971-) (1972/74-78/80 (1971-77) entitled Awards for Commonwealth university staff.)

Commonwealth universities yearbook, 1914-
      (Earlier titles: The yearbook of the universities of the Empire,
      1914-47; The yearbook of the universities of the Commonwealth, 1948-57.)
      The yearbook includes a detailed entry for each university institution,
      including lists of academic and senior administrative staff.

The Compendium of University Entrance Requirements for First Degree Courses in
      the United Kingdom, 1963-86.
      (1963-1975/76 (1963-74) entitled A Compendium ...)
      The compendium was published by the ACU for the CVCP. Since 1987 it has
      been superseded by University Entrance:The Official Guide, which CVCP
      publishes annually.

Congress of the Universities of the Commonwealth. Report of proceedings, 1912-
      (1912-)
      (1912-36 - Congress of the Universities of the Empire...)
      The ACU Secretary General's Quinquennial Reports were published
      until 1979 as appendices in these Reports.

Higher education in the United Kingdom, 1936- (a handbook for overseas
      students, published until 1984 in conjunction with the British
      Council, thereafter by ACU alone; the 1987-89 edition, published in
      1987, was published by Longman for the ACU.)

Scholarships guide for Commonwealth postgraduate students, 1973/75- (1972-).

Amongst other, recently published ACU publications are:
List of University Institutions in the Commonwealth (32nd,1990)
      (An annual publication which gives full postal addresses and personal
      names of executive heads of Commonwealth universities and of the officer
      at each of them to whom general enquiries should be addressed.)

British Universities' Guide to Graduate Study, 1985-Annual; published for the
      CVCP.

Research opportunities in Commonwealth Developing Countries

The ACU Reference Library, which includes the calendars and prospectuses of
most universities in the United Kingdom and other Commonwealth countries, as
well as copies of the ACU's own publications, is open (by appointment) to the
public without charge during office hours. It comprises some 13,000 volumes.

Records
The ACU holds minute books from October 1919 to date and printed Annual
Reports from 1932 to date. Apart from these records the ACU holds very few
records for the pre-1945 period; it is understood that most of their
correspondence files were destroyed when their office was bombed during the
Second World War. Post-war records, other than minutes and Annual Reports,
have retention periods determined by individual departments, in one case
involving the systematic weeding of files so as to retain only those items
considered most likely to be of permanent value. It should be noted that the
ACU's files have, of course, in general, never contained internal university
documents relating to the Bureau/AUBC/ACU.

The ACU also holds a complete set of the minutes of the Commonwealth
Scholarship Commission in the United Kingdom (CSC) (established by statute in
1959 as the UK agency for the Commonwealth Scholarships and Fellowships Plan).

The secretariat of the CSC is based at the ACU.

At present the ACU is not able to open its old minutes or correspondence files to researchers, unpublished material not being available for consultation.

ASSOCIATION DES UNIVERSITÉS PARTIELLEMENT OU ENTIÈREMENT DE LANGUE FRANÇAISE

Address and
contact
Association des Universités partiellement ou entièrement de langue Française,
Universite de Montreal,
Case postale 6128,
Montreal,
H3C 3J7,
Canada

tel: (514) 343-6630
telex: 055-60955

Secretaire General: M. Maurice-Etienne Beutler
Directeur des Communications: M. Jean-Claude Castelain

History
The Association des universités partiellement ou entièrement de Langue Française (AUPELF) was founded in 1961 at Montreal as the Association des universités entièrement ou partiellement de Langue Française, changing its title to the current one in 1967. Its aims are in the fields of documentation, co-ordination, co-operation, and exchange.

A community of university institutions, the Association has as its essential objective the development of 'une conscience internationale et d'un esprit de coopération au service de la pluralité culturelle et du progrès scientifique'. Towards this end it devotes itself particularly to the following tasks:-

'(a) une réflexion permanente sur l'évolution de l'université, sur son rôle et sa place dans la société nationale et internationale, ainsi que sur les structures et les moyens de l'université;

(b) la mise en oeuvre de formules propres à promouvoir la rencontre des cultures et le rôle de l'université comme élément vital de développement socio-culturel;

(c) l'amélioration constante de la circulation de l'information scientifique entre les institutions membres;

(d) la mise à la disposition des membres de services ainsi que de formules d'échanges et de relations internationales;

(e) l'aménagement de l'espace culturel, scientifique et technique d'expression française, dans la perspective du co-développement.'

The organs of the Association are the General Assembly (which meets every three years), the Council of Administration (which meets at least once a year and executes the decisions of the General Assembly), the Scientific Council (which is charged by the Council of Administration with the evaluation and orientation of the activities of the Association's programme), and the General Secretariat. The permanent executive organ of the Council of Administration, the Secretariat General has its offices at the University of Montreal and regional bureaux for Europe at Paris, for Africa at the University Cheikh Anta Diop at Dakar, Senegal, for North America at its offices at Montreal, and for the Caribbean at the State University of Haiti, Port-au-Prince.

AUPELF is an international non-governmental association, recognised by UNESCO which brings together universities which use French. Its network is worldwide and comprises some 200 Francophone university institutions and associations and 400 departments of French studies of non Francophone universities. It is a member of the Consultative Council of the Agence de Coopération Culturelle et Technique (ACCT) and an associate member of the International Association of Universities.

The Association has a Fonds International de Coopération Universitaire (FICU) and a Université des Réseaux d'Expression Française (UREF). FICU was created by the Association in 1968 and has as its objective the 'renforcement de la coopération internationale au sein du monde francophone dans les domaines de l'enseignement supérieur et de la recherche.' FICU is administered by a committee composed of representatives of AUPELF's Council of Administration and of the group of government or private contributors; the committee meets once a year. UREF was established by the decision of AUPELF's General Assembly at Marrakesh in November 1987, to be a major element of the structure and action of AUPELF, of which it is an integral part. UREF is charged with the task 'd'animer et d'organiser l'activité des réseaux institutionnels, des réseaux thematiques d'échanges et de recherche partagée et des réseaux de didacticiels ainsi que de mettre en oeuvre les moyens et les instruments de soutien au fonctionnement des réseaux.' The Council and the Scientific Council of UREF are respectively the Council of Administration and the Scientific Council of AUPELF.

The AUPELF contributes an annual grant towards the Observatory on University Management, Louvain-la-Neuve, Belgium (which was founded in 1982 and aims to observe university management in a group of countries and which publishes a twice-yearly Bulletin, Synobs).

Bibliography

Richard Jones, L'AUPELF, une idée en marche. Une jeune histoire, un grand dessein (AUPELF, 1987). Published on the occasion of the Association's 25th anniversary, this history includes, in an appendix, a complete list of AUPELF's publications from its foundation up until December 1987. Other appendices list past and present members of the successive Councils of Administration; provide a chronology of principal events in the life and work of AUPELF; list institutional members as at 1 August 1987; and publish the text of the Statutes of AUPELF approved by the General Assembly in 1984.

L'AUPELF en bref, AUPELF, 1988.

Statuts of AUPELF; latest edition, after the modification made by the General Assembly, 24 November 1987.

Publications include:-
(a)   Richard Jones, op cit. (see, in particular, appendix III listing AUPELF publications)

(b)   Monographs
Almost one hundred titles in all (by October 1987) including thematic papers published in the Association's journal and other series amongst which are:

L'audiovisuel dans l'université (Colloque de Liège, 24-28 Septembre 1973), 1974.

Les bibliothèques universitaires : automatisation, gestion et coopération, 1978.

Catalogue de publications périodiques, 1964.

La recherche scientifique et technique et le développement du Tiers Monde : (Actes du colloque, Lyons, France, 1981), 1982.

L'Université, l'éducation permanente et la société. Compte rendu du colloque tenu à Abidjan sous la présidence de M. Jean Garagnon, 20-28 Mars 1970, 1970.

(c)   Journal and other serial publictions
Twenty-one such series are listed in Richard Jones, op.cit. appendix III, including:

Les Cahiers de l'AUPELF, Vols. 1-[9], 1965-73; annual.

Les colloques de l'AUPELF, Vols. 1-[7], 1965-71; annual.

Idées : innovations, démarches, expériences dans l'enseignement supérieur, 1975-; an irregular publication.

La Lettre de l'AUPELF, Nos.1-, May 1986-; published every two months.

Perspectives universitaires : la nouvelle revue de l'AUPELF, Vols.1-, 1982-; successor of La Revue de l'AUPELF.

La Revue de l'AUPELF, 1962-80.

Universités : Journal de l'Association des universités partiellement ou entièrement de langue française, Vols.1-, 1980-; quarterly; Vol.9 No.1 was published in March 1988 and contains a report on the decisions of the General Assembly meeting at Marrakesh.

(d)   Compte rendu... (Proceedings) of General Assemblies and Conferences, 1961-.

(e)   Joint editions
Publications published jointly with another body and publications of joint studies etc. published by AUPELF or another body. These include:

Bulletin of the Association d'études linguistiques interculturelles africaines (AELIA), published by AUPELF, nos. 1-, 1979- (twice annually).

AUPELF and CNRS (Centre d'êtude du française moderne et contemporain): Archives de la linguistique française: collection de documents relatifs à la langue française publiés entre 1500 et 1900, micro-réédités sous la dir. de Bernard Quemada (France-Expansion, Paris, n.d.)

(f)   Liste des Institutions Membres de l'AUPELF; latest edition, 8 June 1988.

(Apart from the regional committees and institutional associations, the members listed are drawn from 31 countries, which are principally in West Europe, Africa, Canada, and the Caribbean.)

(g)   It should be noted that AUPELF sends copies of its publications to the Documentation Centre of the ACU in London, and notably the Acts of its General Assemblies.

Records
The archives of AUPELF are accessible to bona fide researchers after agreement with AUPELF and with the Archives Service of the University of Montreal (CP 6128, Succursale A, Montreal, Quebec, H3C 3J7, Canada) which has them in its care.

COMMONWEALTH SECRETARIAT

Address and
contact
Commonwealth Secretariat,
Marlborough House,
Pall Mall,
London,
SW1Y 5HX

tel: 071 839 3411

Director, Education Programme

History
The Commonwealth Secretariat was established in 1965 by Commonwealth Heads of Government who saw it as 'a visible symbol of co-operation which animates the Commonwealth'. Through its Education Programme, the Secretariat encourages and supports educational consultation and co-operation among Commonwealth countries through conferences, seminars, workshops, meetings of experts, and training courses for educational personnel (usually funded by CFTC); contributes to educational development through studies of particular problems, handbooks, directories, etc. and by providing information; and organises triennial conferences of Ministers of Education. The tenth of these conferences, held in Nairobi in 1987, set the following priorities: multilateral co-operation in distance education, student mobility and higher education co-operation, vocationally-oriented education, science and mathematics education, and education in small states.

Technical assistance for economic and social development is available to Commonwealth developing countries through the multilateral Commonwealth Fund for Technical Co-operation (CFTC) which was set up in 1971. The CFTC provides assistance through five programmes: General Technical Assistance Division, Fellowships and Training Programme, Technical Assistance Group, Industrial Development Unit, and the Export Market Development Division.

Bibliography

A Year Book of the Commonwealth ('The Commonwealth Yearbook') (HMSO for the Foreign and Commonwealth Office; latest edition, 1990).

Publications

Commonwealth Secretariat : Publications, 1989, Commonwealth Secretariat, London, 1989.
(The latest list of titles published by the Secretariat)

The Commonwealth Secretariat's other publications include:-

Reports of the Secretary-General (biennial; the 11th Report covers the period July 1985-June 1987).

Report of the Tenth Conference of Commonwealth Education Ministers, Commonwealth Secretariat, 1988.

Annual Report of the Commonwealth Secretariat's Education Programme, 1985-86, 1986-87, and 1987-88.

Commonwealth Student Mobility : Commitment and Resources, 1987.

Institutional Links in Higher Education in Commonwealth Asia, 1987.

Institutional Links in Higher Education in Commonwealth Africa, 1986.

Towards a Policy for Women Overseas Students in the UK, 1986.

Commonwealth Scholarship and Fellowship Plan : annual reports, (26th annual report, for the year ending 30 September 1985, was published in 1986).

Commonwealth Scholarship and Fellowship Plan : Report of second ten-year review committee, 1982.

Towards a Commonwealth of Learning : A proposal to create the University of the Commonwealth for co-operation in distance education, 1987.

Handbook for Students: A guide for students in receipt of CFTC awards, 3rd ed., 1987.

Michael Collins (ed.), Guide to Education and Training Resources in the Developing Countries of the Commonwealth : a selection of post-secondary courses and institutions (CFTC, Commonwealth Secretariat, London, 3rd ed., 1983).

CFTC's Education and Training Programme in the Caribbean : Report of a regional seminar, 1981.

Records
The records of the Commonwealth Secretariat's work in education are not [at present] available to the public, but all publications of the Secretariat may be referred to if prior arrangement is made with the Secretariat's Librarian.

See too entry for ACU.

(The ACU holds a complete set of the minutes of the Commonwealth Scholarship Commission in the United Kingdom (CSC), established by statute in 1959 as the UK agency for the Commonwealth Scholarship and Fellowship Plan. The secretariat of the CSC is based at the ACU.)

COUNCIL OF EUROPE

Address and
contact
Council of Europe,
Maison de l'Europe,
BP 431,
R6-67006 Strasbourg Cedex,
France

tel: 88 61-49-61
telex: 870943

History
The Council of Europe was created by the Statute which was signed in London on 5 May 1949 on behalf of the Governments of Belgium, Denmark, Eire, France, Italy, Luxembourg, the Netherlands, Norway, Sweden, and the United Kingdom. Over ten further countries have since joined and remained members (including the Federal Republic of Germany). The aim of the Council is 'to achieve a greater unity between its members for the purpose of safeguarding and realising the ideals and principles which are their common heritage and facilitating their economic and social progress'. The aim is to be pursued, according to the Statute, by the 'discussion of questions of common concern and by agreements and common action in economic, social, cultural, scientific, legal and administrative matters and in the maintenance and further realisation of human rights and fundamental freedoms.'

The principal organs of the Council are the Committee of Ministers (of Foreign Affairs) and the Parliamentary (formerly Consultative) Assembly, assisted by the Secretariat and a number of committees of experts including the Council for Cultural Co-operation (CCC). The CCC implements the Council's educational and cultural programme which gives priority, inter alia, to the reform and development of tertiary education, adult education and community development. It administers the Cultural Fund and the Council of Europe Higher Education scholarships, and its activities include co-operation in research and the management of the European Documentation and Information System in Education (EUDISED). EUDISED is a database containing abstracts in English, French and German and is available online and in printed form as EUDISED R and D Bulletin : a multilingual thesaurus in nine language versions for indexing educational information. The Council's Documentation Centre for Education in Europe, a library specialising in educational publications, is open to the public and deals with written enquiries. Over 100 conventions have been concluded by the member governments of the Council, the subjects including the equivalence of degrees and diplomas. Projects for co-operation between member governments in educational, scientific and other subjects have been in operation since the mid 1960s.

In 1987 the Council's Secretary General spoke on the Council's vocation to promote European Cultural Identity continent-wide, through action in favour, for instance, of cultural and educational research and exchanges among young people. The Council's Committee on Science and Technology in its report on European Scientific and Technical Co-operation, 1987, charted the progress that has been made towards the establishment of a closer scientific community, as was demonstrated by the EUREKA programme and the Hermes project, and called for greater co-ordination in the scientific field, for the setting up of a European scientific academy, and for the avoidance of a harmful proliferation of research organisations. Some members of the Council feel that scientific co-operation in itself is an important means of achieving European unity. The Council has called for more effective contact between the Council and OECD in relevant areas of educational and cultural co-operation.

Bibliography

A.H. Robertson, <u>The Council of Europe : Its Structure, Functions and Achievements</u> (Stevens & Sons Ltd., London, 1956; 2nd ed., 1961).

<u>The Council of Europe, 1949-1959</u> (Council of Europe, 1959).

Publications

The Council's publications include the following. It should be noted that (a) HMSO is the UK distributor for the Council; (b) Council of Europe publications are covered in <u>International Bibliography : Publications of Intergovernmental Organizations</u>, Vols. 11-, 1983- (see p.277 of this Survey); (c) the Council issues a Catalogue of Publications annually; and (d) the John Rylands University Library of Manchester holds a collection of publications of the Council, subscribing to the Parliamentary Assembly series (Documents, Order of the Day, Texts Adopted, Official Reports) and also receiving (free of charge) copies of documents chiefly in the field of international law (see <u>A Brief Guide to the Council of Europe Collection in JRULM</u>).

R.A. de Moor (rapporteur), <u>Changing Tertiary Education in Modern European Society : Report of the Working Party set up under the auspices of the Council for Cultural Co-operation, on the Diversification of Tertiary Education</u> (Council of Europe, Strasbourg, 1978)

<u>Annuaire Europeen/European Yearbook</u> (published under the auspices of the Council of Europe). Vols.1-, covering the years 1952 -
(inter alia, lists publications of the various European organisations including the Council of Europe, EC, and OECD).

<u>Forum</u> (quarterly), 1978-

<u>Catalogue of Publications</u> (annually)

<u>Reports of Parliamentary Assembly</u>

<u>Summaries of Sessions of the Parliamentary Assembly of the Council of Europe</u>

Index of Proceedings of the Assembly (1949 and later Sessions), 1951-

Cultural Co-operation in Europe : new situation and prospects, 1962.

Annual Report of the Administrative Board (First-Third), (1960-62), continued as Council for Cultural Co-operation and Cultural Fund : Annual Report 1962- (1963-).

Council for Cultural Co-operation Publications 1966-1976 : Annotated Bibliography (1977).

Education in Europe, Section 1 - Higher Education and Research (1963-); no.2 in the series is a report on the teaching of chemistry at university level by Guy Ourisson (1966) and no.3 is on the structure of university staff (1966).

Mobility of University Staff (1973).

Non-University Research Centres and their links with the Universities : a report on the situation in Europe (1967).

Permanent Education : The basis and essentials (1973).

Reforms and New Trends in Medical Undergraduate Education (1973).

Council of Europe News, 1951-.

Council of Europe : Documentation Centre for Education in Europe : Newsletter, 1968- (reports on developments in all branches and levels of education in Council of Europe member countries.)

Noel Entwistle (ed.), Strategies for Research and Development in Higher Education : Proceedings of an educational research symposium organised by the Council of Europe and the Research and Development Unit of the Office of the Chancellor of the Swedish Universities...1975 (Swets & Zeitlinger, Amsterdam, 1976).

THE EUROPEAN COMMUNITIES

Address and
contact
Commission of the European Communities,
200 rue de la Loi,
1049 Brussels,
Belgium

tel: (02) 235-11-11
telex: 21877

History
The European Communities (EC) comprise : the European Coal and Steel Community (ECSC) created in April 1951 by the Treaty of Paris; the European Economic Community (EEC), and the European Atomic Energy Community (EAEC or EURATOM) both established in March 1957 by the Treaties of Rome, the former to create a

Common Market and the latter to promote growth in nuclear industries. The common institutions of the three Communities were established by a treaty in 1965 and the three Communities have since 1967 been supervised by a single Commission. Since 1958 the three Communities have had a common parliamentary assembly, the European Parliament. Belgium, France, Federal Republic of Germany, Italy, Luxembourg, and the Netherlands were the original six members of the EC; Denmark, Eire, and the United Kingdom joined on 1 January 1973 and Greece on 1 January 1981; Portugal and Spain joined on 1 January 1986. The Single European Act (SEA), which came into force on 1 July 1987, amends the existing EC Treaties in a number of ways and commits the EC to the aim of progressively establishing a single market over a period expiring on 31 December 1992. It defines the single market as "an area without internal frontiers in which the free movement of goods, persons, services and capital is ensured". SEA also introduces a new procedure for co-operation between the Council and the European Parliament.

The ECSC Treaty provides for a financial contribution to the vocational retraining of workers. The EEC Treaty contains provisions relating to the mutual recognition of diplomas, certificates and other evidence of formal qualifications. The EAEC Treaty offers a basis for establishing schools for the training of nuclear specialists and an institution of university status. However, it was only between 1969 and 1974 that Member States of the EC abandoned a narrow legalistic approach towards Community Law on the subject of education. The Education Ministers of the Member States met for the first time in 1971 and in 1974 set up an Education Committee. In 1976 the Council and the Ministers of Education adopted an action programme covering : (i) better facilities for the education and training of nationals and the children of nationals of other Member States of the Communities and of non-member countries; (ii) promotion of closer relations between educational systems in Europe; (iii) compilation of up-to-date documentation and statistics on education; (iv) co-operation in the field of higher education; (v) teaching of foreign languages; and (vi) achievement of equal opportunity for free access to all forms of education.

The principal educational activities of the EC in the tertiary education field may be listed as:-

(i)   responsibility for the postgraduate European University Institute in Florence, founded in 1972 (the Institute beginning its academic life in Autumn 1971);

(ii)   development of a common policy on the admission of higher-education students from other member states;

(iii)   a European Community Action Scheme for the Mobility of University Students (ERASMUS) to make grants to enable university students to spend a period in another Community country (initially during 1987-89) and also to encourage the development of joint programmes between institutions of higher education to encourage academic staff mobility; and

(iv)   a programme for education and training for technology (COMETT), comprising university/industry training partnerships and exchange schemes, to be undertaken in 1986-92. An example of a COMETT programme award is that to the University of Liverpool's Institute of Medical and Dental Bioengineering in 1988 to allow the Institute to provide training courses in the UK, France, Italy, and Denmark, each course being organised in conjunction with a consortium of industrial companies within those countries.

In 1990 the EC launched two other schemes, Lingua and TEMPUS. Lingua aims to improve language teaching in higher education and training programmes in the EC. The TEMPUS programme aims to encourage the exchange and mobility of university teachers and students between EC countries and the countries of Central and Eastern Europe.

The EC also is responsible for a very large programme of research in science and technology (which includes the European Strategic Research Programme in Information Technology (ESPRIT) (financed in part by universities), research and development in advanced communications technology in Europe (RACE), and the EUREKA programme of research in advanced technology), and, to a lesser degree, in medical research. Academic institutions have also benefited from the EC's Framework research progamme (basic and applied research in the sciences). NERC, SERC, and AFRC now have an office in Brussels, monitoring the progression through the EC of applications from British scientists for EC funds, etc.

Of the twenty-three Directorates-General of the European Commission (at Brussels) are three of particular relevance : concerning Employment, Social Affairs and Education (Directorate-General V), Science, Research and Development (Directorate-General XII), and Telecommunications, Information Industries and Innovation (Directorate-General XIII), which issue their own newsletters and other publications.

The EC maintains Press Offices in the Member Countries, that in London being at 8 Storey's Gate, SW1P 3AT (tel: 071-222 8122).

Bibliography

A.H. Robertson, European Institutions : Co-operation, Integration, Unification (Stevens & Sons Ltd., London, & Matthew Bender, New York, 3rd ed., 1973). Includes sections on the Council of Europe, OECD, etc.

Sir Barnett Cocks, The European Parliament : Structure, Procedure & Practice (HMSO, London, 1973).
A work of reference which includes details of the Communities' external relations with such organisations as OECD, UN and its agencies, Council of Europe, etc.

Katharine Savage, The History of the Common Market (Kestrel Books, Harmondsworth, 2nd ed., 1976).

Anthony J.C. Kerr, The Common Market and How It Works (Pergamon Press, Oxford, 3rd ed., 1986).

Doris M. Palmer (ed.), Sources of Information on the European Communities (Mansell, London, 1979).
Includes chapters on EC material in libraries and European Documentation Centres in the UK (incorporating a list of major collections of EC documents in the UK and a select list of EC serial publications, which include European University News, Publications - European Communities, and University Studies on European Integration) and on HMSO and the E.C.

Geoffrey Parker, A Dictionary of the European Communities (Butterworths, London, 1981).

Juliet Lodge (ed.), Institutions and Policies of the European Community (Frances Pinter (Publishers), London, 1983).

David Overton, Common Market Digest : An Information Guide to the European Communities (The Library Association, London, 1983).

Ann Davison, Grants from Europe : How to Get Money and Influence Policy (Bedford Square Press of the National Council for Voluntary Organisations in association with ERICA, London, 3rd ed., 1986). Chapters on Education and Culture, Environment and Energy, etc., each chapter being subdivided into sections providing information on the key Commission department, extent of Community involvement, key contacts/people, funding, and key publications.

Stanley A. Budd, The EEC : A Guide to the Maze (Kogan Page, London, 2nd ed., 1987).

Pierre Gerbet, La Naissance du Marche Commun (Ed. Complexes, Brussels, 1987) (includes a bibliography, and a chronology from 1944 until 1987).

Steven George, The British Government and the European Community since 1984 (UACES Occasional Papers No.4, UACES, London, 1987).

European Unification : The origins and growth of the European Community (EC, Luxembourg, 1987; Periodical 2/1987 in the European Documentation series of booklets).

Francoise de la Serre, La Grande-Bretagne et la Communaute europeene (Presses Universitaire de France, Paris, 1987) Covers the historical background to British membership and provides an account of British attitudes to the EC since Britain became a member up to the agreement on the Single European Act.

David A.C. Freestone and Scott Davidson, The Institutional Framework of the European Communities (Croom Helm, London, 1988).

Gina Marks (ed.), 1992 The Facts and Challenges (The Industrial Society, London, 1988).

Butterworths Guide to the European Communities (Butterworths, London, 1989); outlines the history, institutions and policies of the Communities, citing legislation, main cases, etc., and reproducing the full amended text of the Treaty of Rome.

Peter Aspden, 'Getting to know the family', in The Times Higher Education Supplement, 2 June 1989, p.17 (report on ERASMUS and a conference on the subject).

Tony Reid (compiler), Guide to European Community Grants and Loans (UK Edition) for commerce, industry, local authorities, academic and research institutions (Eurofi plc, Newbury, Berkshire, 1990); this is a looseleaf service updated regularly for subscribers.

See too <u>Higher Education in Europe</u>, the Quarterly Review of Unesco's European Centre for Higher Education (1976-), for articles, news notes, etc. of relevance to EC countries.

<u>Publications</u>
(i) For a general introduction one may consult such works as John Jeffries, <u>A Guide to the Official Publications of the European Communities</u> (Mansell Information Publishing, London, 1978); the chapter on International Official Publications in Gavin Higgens (ed.), <u>Printed Reference Material</u> (The Library Association, London, 1980); and, in particular, Ian Thomson, <u>The Documentation of the European Communities :</u> <u>A Guide</u> (Mansell, London, 1989).

For further details of publications of the EC see the <u>Annual Catalogue</u> (available from the Office for Official Publications of the EC, Luxembourg, and from HMSO, 51 Nine Elms Lane, London, SW8 5DR) and <u>The European Community as a publisher 1989</u> (extract from the <u>Catalogue</u>; 13th ed., 1989), also the bibliographies which the EC publishes (weekly <u>Documentation Bulletin</u>, monthly <u>List of additions to the Library of the CEC</u> [Commission of the European Communities], and thrice-yearly <u>Publications and Documents of the EC received by</u> [the Commission's] <u>Library</u>). The Commission Library (based in Brussels, with a branch in Luxembourg) has a comprehensive collection of documentation of the EC, including European University Institute publications.

There are five depository libraries of EC official publications in the UK:-

British Library, London
British Library of Political and Economic Science, London
British Library, Boston Spa
Liverpool Central Library
Westminster Public Library

In addition to these major depository libraries, there are a larger number of European Documentation Centres (based in academic institutions) which receive a comprehensive range of EC documentation (though since 1987-88 some EDCs receive only a selection of EC documentaton) and European Reference Centres (usually based in academic institutions) which receive basic EC documentation. A list of all these libraries and centres is given in Appendix 6 of Ian Thomson, <u>op.cit</u>.

It should also be noted that the European Documentation Centre established in the John Rylands University Library of Manchester in 1973, until recently (as at July 1989) received a free copy of most of the Community publications; now the Centre receives only a selection of Community publications, some of them in microfilm. JRULM has online facilities for scores of the EC's own databases through ECHO, the European Commission Host Organisation.

(ii) There are a number of EC computerised databases which are available to the public. For details, see the EC's <u>Database Directory</u>; Terry Hanson's 'A survey of European Communities databases' in <u>Aslib Proceedings</u>, Vol.42 No.6, June 1990; and publications on individual host organisations, such as ECHO, which allow access to be gained to particular databases. Particular reference should be made to two databases, CELEX and SCAD. CELEX (Communitatis Europeae Lex) is a bibliographical and factual database to EC law, in the broadest sense, from 1951 to date. SCAD (Système communautaire d'accès à la documentation) provides bibliographical references to main Community instruments, official publications and documents published by the European institutions, articles from periodicals and non-EC documents dealing with the Communities, etc. The host organisation for CELEX and SCAD is Eurobases (EC host organisation, at the Commission's Brussels offices).

(iii) In addition to the Official Journal of the European Communities, the EC's publications include:-

European Communities Yearbook (7th ed., 1987).
(includes a directory of other European organisations)

General Report on the Activities of the European Communities, published annually by the Commission as required by the Treaty of 8 April 1965 establishing a Single Council and a Single Commission of the European Communities; latest report as XXIInd General Report...1988, Office for Official Publications of E.C., Luxembourg, 1989.

Bulletin of the European Communities (a monthly survey; former titles: Industry and Society, Weekly Industry Research and Technology), 1968-

European Access : The Current Awareness Bulletin to the Policies and Activities of the European Communities, 1988-to date; edited by Ian Thomson and now published by Chadwyck-Healey in association with the UK offices of the European Commission. Seeks bibliographically to record all developments re the EC; includes bibliographical review and other articles.

European University News, 1966- (issued bi-monthly by the Office for Official Publications of the EC, Luxembourg; No.154 was published in February 1988).
(includes reports on research on European studies, reports on congresses, reviews, and bibliographical notes.)

Delta (The EC's Newsletter on Further Education, latterly issued twice a year), 1982-87; title changed to ERASMUS Newsletter in 1987 and henceforth issued twice a year, reporting on developments in the ERASMUS programme.

Arnold Ebel and Brigitte Mohr (eds.), Higher Education in the European Community : Student Handbook
(1st ed., 1977; 5th ed., Kogan Page for the Office for Official Publications of the EC, London, 1988).
(later editions include sections on both the European University Institute, Florence, and the College of Europe, Bruges, which latter was founded in 1949 and is governed by an Administrative Council composed of representatives of the member states of the EC, etc.).

Edward Prosser (ed.), Higher Education in the European Community : Directory of Higher Education Institutions, Office for Official Publications of the EC, Luxembourg, 1984.

Commission of the European Communities, Thirty Years of Community Law (Office for Official Publications of the EC, Luxembourg, 1983; in The European Perspectives Series).

An Education Policy for Europe (EC, Luxembourg, 2nd ed., 1982). (includes a review of achievements and a bibliography). In the EC's European Documentation series of booklets, Periodical 4/1982.

Recognition of Diplomas and Professional Qualifications (EC, Brussels, 1984; European File 13/84).

European Centre for the Development of Vocational Training, New Perspectives in Continuing Education and Training in the European Community, Office for Official Publications of the EC, Luxembourg, 1983 (Seminar Report).

J.P. de Crayencour, The Professions in the European Community : Towards Freedom of Movement and Mutual Recognition of Qualifications, Office for Official Publications of the EC, Luxembourg, 1982.

Statistical Office of the EC, Education and Training 1970/71 - 1977/78 (1980) (a statistical publication on students and teachers in the schools and universities of Member States and on the cost of education). The former title of this publication was Education Statistics.

European University Institute: Report of activities (annual), Office for Official Publications of the EC, Luxembourg, 1976-; includes lists of EUI Working Papers (reports on research undertaken at the Institute) published during the year.

European University Institute : Academic Year...(annual prospectus), Office for Official Publications of the EC.

First report on the state of science and technology in Europe (presented by the Commission), Commission of the EC, Brussels, 1988, ref. COM (88) 647 final; Addendum to the report, 1988, ref. COM (88) 647/2 addendum final.

Records

In February 1983 the Council and the Commission of the EC decided to release the historical archives of the Communities to the public in accordance with the 30-year rule, beginning in January 1983 with ECSC records and continuing in January 1989 with EEC and EURATOM records. The intention is gradually to transfer the archives of the EC and the institutions which preceded it to the European University Institute at Florence as soon as the documents are made available to researchers under the 30-year rule. Dr. Hans Hofmann is Head of the Central Archives of the Commission of the EC in Brussels.

Dr. Klaus Jaitner is the archivist in charge of access to the EC archives which are deposited at the European University Institute (Badia Fiesolana, Via dei Roccettini 9, 50016 San Domenico di Fiesole, Firenze, Italy).

The new Archives were opened on 13 December 1985 in the Villa il Poggiolo in Florence (not far from the European University Institute) and since then documents originally produced within the EEC have been regularly sent from

Brussels and Luxembourg. As at 31 December 1987 approximately 100 shelf metres of records were held (together with 100 metres of reports of the European Parliament), the small holding for these early years being attributable to the great losses of documents during the various removals of the institutions and by their having been taken away by presidents and commissioners. The body of documents will, however, grow rapidly in coming years. Documents being accessible under the thirty years rule, to date they deal essentially with the ECSC and the preparatory negotiations for the Treaty of Rome. The individual archival holdings take their provenance from the five individual organisations of the EC: the Council of Ministers, the Commission of the European Communities, the Assembly of the European Communities (the European Parliament), the Court of Justice of the European Communities (established in 1958), and the Court of Auditors of the European Communities (established in 1977), whose officials work in Brussels and Luxembourg. It should be noted that the individual institutions have the right and the possibility of establishing and running historical archives of their own and that all technical archival tasks are also entrusted to them, the central archives in Florence having by contrast initially only the task of taking over original documents and presenting them to users.

Under the decisions reached in 1983 the archival material is normally to be made accessible in the form of copies, and personal documents, European Court of Justice documentation, and documents classified as confidential or secret are not accessible to the public. The archives of each institution are to supply each Member State with a full set of microform copies of its historical archives. In Spring 1988 the National Library of Scotland (George IV Bridge, Edinburgh, EH1 1EW) received microfiche of the EC's archives for 1952-56, which relate mainly to the European Coal and Steel Community; detailed access to the contents of the microfiche is acquired through the published Inventory of the Historical Archives (see below); the NLS was the first Library in any of the states to receive microfiche of the Archives. Microfiches of documents that individual institutions, for legal or administrative purposes, wish to retain are sent to Florence, which otherwise receives original documents from the institutions.

The European Community Historical Archive in Florence is also negotiating to receive the archives of a number of other agencies which are in part autonomous legal entities or have public-law status (like the European Investment Bank, the Joint Research Centres (ISPRA etc.), the European Schools or the European University Institute). It is negotiating with the European Space Agency for regular transmission of documents to Florence and has received the European Parliament's extensive collection of press-cuttings commencing in 1952.

For some more details see, in particular, [Hans Hofmann, ed.] Opening of the Historical Archives of the European Communities to the public (Office for Official Publications of the EC, Luxembourg, 1983) which includes chapters on the origin and history of the ECSC 1950-52, the European Communities (ECSC, EEC, EURATOM) and their institutions, and on the opening of the historical archives to the public (including details of the archives services of the institutions and other organs of the EC). Dr. Klaus Jaitner's recent unpublished paper on 'The Historical Archives of the European Communities in Florence' provides further information about the background, the foundation of the Historical Archives, the legal basis for the archives, and an outline of tasks and prospects for development; a copy has been made available to the University of Liverpool's Palaeography Library in the Department of History. A revised version of this paper, together with a summary of the documents lodged to date at the Historical Archives (from the European Parliament, Council of

Ministers, Commission of the European Communities, ECSC Consultative Committee, Deposits by private foundations, and External archives) is given by Dr. Jaitner in his paper 'The European Community Historical Archives in Florence', Journal of the Society of Archivists, Vol.9 No.4, October 1988, pp.176-180.

To date, the following volumes of inventories of the EC's archives have been published:-

Commission des Communautes europeennes, Archives generales - Inventaire des Archives historiques - Vol.1 : Dossiers de la Haute Autorite de la CECA 1952 - Discours 1952-1967 (Office des publications officielles des Communautes europeennes, Luxembourg, 1985).

Commission des Communautes europeennes, Archives generales - Inventaire des Archives historiques - Vol.2 : Dossiers de la Haute Autorite de la CECA 1953 (Office des publications officielles des Communautes europeennes, Luxembourg, 1987).

Conseil des Communautes europeennes : Inventaire des Archives historiques du Conseil - Annee 1952 - Communaute Europeenne du Charbon et de l'Acier (Secretariat General du Conseil des CE, Bruxelles, 1986) Provisional edition.

idem - Annee 1953 (Bruxelles, 1986) Ed. prov.
idem - Annee 1954 (Bruxelles, 1986) Ed. prov.
idem - Annee 1955 (Bruxelles, 1987) Ed. prov.
idem - Annee 1956 (Bruxelles, 1987) Ed. prov.

Postscript - since the completion of this text the second edition of the Guide to the Historical Archives of the European Communities (EUI, Florence, June 1990) has been published, updating the above information.

EUROPEAN UNIVERSITIES
PUBLIC RELATIONS AND INFORMATION OFFICERS

Address and
contact
Inge Knudsen,
EUPRIO Chairman,
University of Aarhus,
Nordre Ringgade 1,
DK - 8000 Aarhus C,
Denmark

tel: (45) (6) 134311

History
The association of European Universities Public Relations and Information Officers (EUPRIO), which was established in Brussels with the support of officials from the European Community on 12 May 1986 and announced to the public at a press conference of the Education Ministers of the Community in the Hague on 16 May 1986, is intended to provide a professional network of colleagues in universities throughout the Community who are engaged in the public relations, information and related tasks. EUPRIO is mounting regular

research programmes leading to pan-European conferences on matters of professional interest such as the current programme on the reporting and publication of science and technology. An annual meeting of the Steering group has been held since EUPRIO's formation. It is understood that the Community will now be funding a EUPRIO Newsletter under the terms of the ERASMUS programme. EUPRIO maintains liaison with national bodies such as SCUIO or the Association of German Press and Information Officers where they exist in the twelve member-states.

Publications
Newsletter (projected)

Directory of contact names and addresses of Information/Public Relations Officers in institutions of higher education throughout the European Community.

Press correspondents/media contacts in the fields of education, science, medicine, and finance (last updated in September 1987).

All publications are circulated only to members of EUPRIO and are not for public sale.

Records
EUPRIO has not so far taken any steps to establish a base for its records but hopes that this will soon be made possible by provision of office space in Brussels with the help of the European Commission and the ERASMUS Bureau.

Mrs. Anne Lonsdale, Information Officer at the University of Oxford, a founder-member of the Steering Committee and Vice-Chairman of the Association, kindly provided the above information about EUPRIO.

FEDERATION INTERNATIONALE DU SPORT UNIVERSITAIRE

Address and
contact
Federation Internationale du Sport Universitaire,
Rue Général Thys 12,
1050 Bruxelles,
Belgium.

tel: 010 32 2 640 68 73
telex: 64557 FISU B
Mr. Roch Campana, General Secretary.

History
The origins of the Federation Internationale du Sport Universitaire (FISU), the International University Sports Federation, date back to 1923 when a few countries held an International Sports Week in Paris. The 1923 event was organised under the auspices of the Union National des Etudiants Français (UNEF). In 1924 the Confédération Internationale des Etudiants (CIE) organised a sport-for-all event at their Congress in Warsaw, an event

repeated at the Prague CIE congress in 1925. The first "World University Games" were held in 1927 in Rome and the Games continued to be held in various countries under the auspices of CIE until 1939 and the Second World War. By 1948 this event had so grown that a formal international body (FISU) was set up to govern it. In the meantime the International Union of Students had been founded in Prague to continue the work of CIE and it planned to organise Summer and Winter Games every two years : and games were held under IUS auspices in [1947], in 1949 in Budapest, in 1951 in Berlin, and in 1954 in Budapest, but few Western athletes competed. In the West separate competitions were organised in [1947], 1949 and every second year thereafter. In 1957 both 'Eastern' and 'Western' competitors came together and joined in a World University Games and after the 1959 Universiade the IUS agreed to join FISU.

The aims of FISU are to promote the development of physical education among students of all countries and at all levels, by organising international and world university sports meetings, by exchange of information, and by promoting the value of amateur sport as a factor in the development of mankind. Members comprise national university sports bodies or national unions of students in over 60 countries. FISU is governed by a General Assembly (which meets every two years) and an Executive Committee; there are also a number of other permanent committees which cover specific areas (e.g. Committee for the Study of University Sport). Every two years FISU organises World University Games (Universiades). It also organises international university sports weeks, Winter Universiades (every two years), etc.

In recent years the Games have been held in Moscow, 1973; Rome, 1975; Sofia, 1977; Mexico City, 1979; Bucharest, 1981; Edmonton, 1983; Kobe, 1985; Zagreb, 1987; and Duisburg, West Germany (a curtailed programme), 1989; and are due to be held in Sheffield in 1991. The Sheffield Universiade will be the first time that Britain has staged the event. Nowadays the Universiade is the World's second largest sporting event, after the Olympics; in terms of countries competing, however, it is the largest.

Bibliography
Charles Wenden, 'An Outline History of the World University Summer Games', Bulletin de la Federation Internationale du Sport Universitaire, [Special Issue], September 1980, pp.6-7.

Raul Leoni and Paul Jenes, Universiadi di Atletica : I risultati completi da Torino 1959 a Zagabria 1987 (Federazione Italiana di Atletica Leggera, Rome, 1989).

In celebration of FISU's 40th anniversary, FISU intends publishing a book about its history and work in 1999.

Publications
FISU's publications are bilingual, the French and English texts appearing in parallel columns.

Bulletin de la Federation Internationale du Sport Universitaire : Special Issue, September 1980- to date (generally two issues a year have been published, a total of thirteen issues in all over the period September 1980-December 1987/March 1988). These Special Issues include illustrated accounts of the Universiades and Winter Universiades and reports on meetings of FISU's General Assemblies.

Informations, Nos. 1-, March 1980- to date (the number of issues published every year has ranged from two to five, a total of thirty-seven issues in all being published over the period March 1980-April/May 1988).

Bulletin de la FISU, Nos. [1]-4, June 1977-?1979.

FISU Bulletin, Nos. 1-11, October 1951 - 1953
            Nos. 1-9, November 1953 - June 1955
(3rd series) Nos. 1-9, October 1955 - June 1957
(4th series) Nos. 1-5, November 1957 - August 1959
(5th series) Nos. 1-3, November 1959 - February 1961
(6th series) Nos. 1-4, October 1961 - September 1962
(7th series) Nos. 1-4, March 1964 - July 1965
(8th series) Nos. 1,2, October 1965 and July 1966
(9th series) Number 1-2, June 1968

Records
The General Secretary of FISU holds the minutes of the meetings of the General Assembly and the Executive Committee of FISU and they are open to any researcher properly introduced by an academic authority.

See too entries for BSSF and BUSF.

INTERNATIONAL ASSOCIATION OF UNIVERSITIES

Address and
contact
International Association of Universities,
1, rue Miollis,
75732 Paris Cedex 15,
France.

tel: (33-1) 45 68 25 45
telex: 250615 IUB F

Dr. Franz Eberhard, Secretary-General
Miss Ann C.M. Taylor, Head of Publications Unit

History
The International Association of Universities (IAU) was formally established at the initiative of UNESCO in 1950 at an international conference in Nice attended by representatives of 150 universities. The IAU's origins may be traced to initiatives of the League of Nations which set up the Institute of Intellectual Co-operation in 1923 (within the framework of the League's International Committee of Intellectual Co-operation) and the International Bureau of University Statistics in 1933. A Permanent Higher Education Committee was created in 1939. After the Second World War, UNESCO's General Conference decided to convene a Preparatory Conference of University Representatives in 1948 and in 1949 the International Universities Bureau (IUB) was established at UNESCO's headquarters to form a documentation centre on higher education and to prepare the International Conference in Nice in 1950.

The main objectives of the IAU are to give expression to the "obligation of universities as social institutions to promote, through teaching and research, the principles of freedom and justice, of human dignity and solidarity, and to develop material and moral aid on an international level" by providing "a centre of co-operation at the international level among the universities and similar institutions of higher education of all countries, as well as among organisations in the field of higher education generally." IAU and the IUB foster and facilitate international contacts through consultancies and good offices for exchanges on an institutional level, for visits of individual scholars to foreign universities, and for the exchange of publications and material for research and teaching purposes.

Degree-conferring institutions whose main object is education and the enhancement of knowledge, whether or not they bear the name of university, may be admitted to membership of IAU. By the end of 1986 over 800 institutions in 121 countries were members. Associations of universities may be admitted as Associate Members, a status at present enjoyed by the Association of African Universities, Association of Arab Universities, ACU, Association of Southeast Asian Institutions of Higher Learning, Association des Universités partiellement ou entièrement de langue Française, International Federation of Catholic Universities, CRE, and the Union of Universities of Latin America.

A General Conference of the IAU, which meets at least every five years, determines the general policy and elects the President and members of the Administrative Board (which meets annually and supervises the activities of the IUB, which is the permanent Secretariat of the Association).

The principal activities of the IAU are in the fields of documentation and information, research, and publications. IAU organises various types of conferences, symposia, seminars, workshops, etc., in some cases such meetings being linked to the topics of specific studies and research projects. Major forthcoming meetings open to all Members include the second Mid-Term Conference of Heads of Member Institutions in Rio de Janeiro in July 1988 and the Association's Ninth Quinquennial General Conference in Helsinki in August 1990.

The Information and Documentation Centre of IUB has a specialized collection of literature and documentation on higher education systems and institutions, on higher education policies, and on research on higher education worldwide. The Library holds some 15,000 volumes and a large collection of unpublished materials and receives about 300 periodicals from all parts of the world; it also maintains a collection of some 4,000 catalogues of major higher education institutions. The Centre is currently being computerized. The IUB provides information relating to the recognition of studies, diplomas and degrees in various countries and otherwise co-operates with other bodies promoting international mobility of students, teachers, researchers, and administrators in higher education, and inter-regional exchanges.

IAU's studies and research programme focuses on issues which are either common to institutions and systems worldwide or where a comparative analysis appears particularly interesting. Topics include access to higher education; various forms of international university co-operation; the role of universities in national or regional development; and the impact of satellite communication on university teaching and research.

IAU produces a number of publications, most of them in both English and French. Apart from publishing the results of its studies and research projects and its meetings, it is responsible for three major reference works, a quarterly Bulletin, and an international journal.

IAU, as a non-governmental organization, has maintained a close associate and consultative status with UNESCO and the latter provides office space for the IUB. Since 1959 IAU and UNESCO have pooled efforts in a joint Research Programme in Higher Education. IAU also co-operates closely with its Associate Members and has established links with a number of governmental and non-governmental bodies on an international and national level.

Bibliography

International Association of Universities, International Universities Bureau, IAU/IUB, Paris, n.d. [1988] (a brochure which incorporates notes on the history, objectives, organization and activities of both bodies).

World List of Universities (18th ed., Macmillan, 1990), compiled by the IAU, includes information about the IAU and IUB.

No complete history of the IAU has been published as such. However, events in its life may be clearly followed by consulting the Administrative and General Conference Reports over the years (see below under Records).

Publications include:-

(a) Bulletin of the International Association of Universities (quarterly) Vols.1-, 1953-; temporarily suspended in 1988 but due to be resumed in a new form in 1989. See too p.298.

Higher Education Policy : The Quarterly Journal of the International Association of Universities, Vol.1 No.1-, March 1988-
(The Journal will focus on policy issues and the role of higher education in society today, and will also carry reports on relevant research being carried out in various parts of the world.)

(b) World List of Universities, and other Institutions of Higher Education, and University Organisations (published biennially; 18th ed., Macmillan for the IAU, 1990). The first edition, entitled International List of Universities...., was published in 1955. In fact, a small booklet, Universities of the World, was published by the IUB in 1950 following the International Universities Conference in Nice.

International Handbook of Universities and other Institutions of Higher Education (Macmillan Publishers Ltd., London, for the IAU; 10th ed., 1986, 11th ed., 1989). Nowadays published every two years. Excludes universities and other institutions of higher learning in the USA and the Commonwealth, which have their own Handbooks. Includes 'A Note' on the IAU and its Permanent Secretariat.

World Guide to Higher Education : A Comparative Survey of Systems, Degrees and Qualifications, 2nd ed., The UNESCO Press, Paris, 1982; compiled by the IAU for UNESCO.

(c)   Papers of the IAU include:-

    2.   Health at the University (1954)
    3.   Student Mental Health (1958)
    6.   The Expansion of Higher Education (1960)
    8.   The Administration of Universities (1967); includes papers on the
          university administrative systems of the UK, France, USA, Federal
          Republic of Germany, Latin America, and the USSR.
    15.   The Right to Education and Access to Higher Education (1978)
    18.   The Future of University Education (1983)
    19.   Universities and Regional Development (1985); the French version
          (Cahiers 19), Les Universites et le developpement regional, was
          published in 1984.

(d)   Studies and Reports include:-

    The Staffing of Higher Education (1960)

    Some Economic Aspects of Education Development in Europe (1961)

    Report of the International Conference of Universities, Nice, December
          1950 (1951)

    Reports of Proceedings of the Second and Third General Conferences of
          the IAU, 1955 and 1960 (1956,1961)

    Reports of the General Conferences of the IAU, covering the Fourth -
          Eighth General Conferences, 1965-85 (1966-86)

    Administrative Reports of the International Association of Universities
          : 1951-1954 (1955), 1955-1959 (1960), 1960-1964 (1965), 1965-1969
          (1970), 1970-1974 (1975), 1975-1979 (1980), and 1980-1984 (1985).

(e)   Joint UNESCO - IAU Research Programme in Higher Education include:-

    The International Study of University Admissions : Vol.I Access to
          Higher Education by Frank Bowles (1963) and Vol.II National
          Studies (1965).

    Higher Education and Development in South-East Asia : Summary Report
          (1965).

    Lifelong Education and University Resources (1978) (joint publication of
          UNESCO and IAU).

    New Trends and New Responsibilities for Universities in Latin America
          (1980).

    Universities and Environmental Education (1986).

See too the List of Publications issued by IAU.

Records

The Administrative Reports of IAU (see above under Publications (d)), which include details of meetings of the Administrative Board, have been published each five years since 1955.

The Reports of the General Conferences since 1950 have also been published (see above under Publications (d)).

These publications may (also) be consulted by anyone wishing to visit the IAU's Reference Library and Documentation Centre.

INTERNATIONAL ASSOCIATION OF UNIVERSITY PROFESSORS AND LECTURERS

Address and contact

International Association of University Professors and Lecturers,
18 rue du Docteur Roux,
F-75015 Paris,
France.

tel: 783. 31.65
Prof. L.-P. Laprevote, Hon. Secretary-General

History

The International Association of University Professors and Lecturers (IAUPL) was founded in 1944 as an amalgamation of the International University Conference (founded in 1934) and the Association of University Professors and Lecturers of the Allied Countries in Great Britain (founded in 1942). The International University Conference sought to co-ordinate the efforts of the teaching staff of universities; its first meeting was a Congress at Oxford in 1934 which was organised by the AUT, and later congresses were held at Grenoble, Heidelberg, and in Switzerland. The Association of University Professors and Lecturers of the Allied Countries in Great Britain was founded by Professor S. Glaser (then President of the Association of Polish Professors in Great Britain) in collaboration with university professors and scientific researchers, with various objects including the reconstruction of the universities of the occupied countries after the War and developing academic fraternity between university professors and researchers of the Allied Countries who were refugees in Great Britain. The Association's first general meeting was held in May 1942 at the Polish Institute in Great Britain when the members of the first Executive Committee were elected and the Association's objects were debated. It was during a conjoint meeting of the Association and the International University Conference in September 1944 that the IAUPL was constituted. In 1947 IAUPL was added to the list of UNESCO's non-governmental organisations and in 1966 it was admitted as a member of the Conference of Non-Governmental Organisations having consultative status with the Economic and Social Council of the UN.

The objects of IAUPL are the development of academic fraternity amongst university teachers and research workers; the protection of independence and freedom of teaching and research; the furtherance of the interests of all university teachers; and the consideration of academic problems. It has 186,000 members in thirty-five countries. It is governed by a Central Council (which normally meets every two years, at international conferences) and by an Executive Committee.

IAUPL organised sixteen university congresses over the period 1945-72, three seminars on the condition of university research over the period 1965-69, and nine meetings of the European Liaison Committee of IAUPL over the period 1974-83. The Association has organised three Round Tables, in 1979 (with a theme of the attacks on the university of today), 1986 (with the theme being the functions and tasks, condition and status of a university professor in advanced societies), and 1987, and in October 1988 was due to organise in liaison with UNESCO a Round Table in Malta on the theme of the international responsibilities of university professors : the Pax Academica.

Bibliography

L'Essentiel sur l'Histoire et les Travaux de l'IAUPL, n.d. [1987] (Provides a note on IAUPL's origins, lists of IAUPL's Presidents and Secretaries-General, lists of meetings etc. organised by the Association, and list of themes of various declarations, motions, adopted texts, etc.)

Publications

Professor Hacquaert, The Recruitment and Training of University Teachers (1967).

Communication, Nos.1-, 1944- (nowadays five issues a year).

Educational Conference, May 11, 1943 : The Function of a University in a Modern Community... (Basil Blackwell, Oxford, 1943).

Second Education Conference, April 15, 1944 : Some Comparisons between Universities... (Basil Blackwell, Oxford, 1944).

University Degree Systems : A report presented by Professor R.C. McLean on behalf of the International Association of University Professors and Lecturers to the International Conference of Universities, Nice, 4th - 9th December, 1950... (International Universities Bureau, Paris, 1952).

The principal documents of reference of the Association are three Declarations:- on academic freedom (1969), on the university professor (1979), and on the rights and basic duties of academic freedom (1982).

Records

In his Guide to the Archives of other international inter-governmental organizations and non-governmental organizations (UNESCO, 1985), Mr. Mabbs states that few archives before 1969 have survived and that from 1969 there are minutes of meetings and miscellaneous publications.

Permission to consult the archives may be obtained from the Secretary-General.

INTERNATIONAL FEDERATION OF UNIVERSITY WOMEN

<u>Address and</u>
<u>contact</u>
International Federation of University Women,
37, Quai Wilson,
CH-1201 Geneve,
Switzerland.

tel: 022-31 23 80
Executive Secretary: Mrs. Dorothy Davies
Office Manager: Rosemary Scott-Woods

<u>History</u>
The International Federation of University Women (IFUW) was founded in 1919 by a group of graduates from Canada, Great Britain, and the USA. According to its Constitution, the purposes of IFUW are to promote understanding and friendship among the university women of the world, irrespective of their race, nationality, religion, or political opinions; to encourage international cooperation; to further the development of education; to represent university women in international organisations; to encourage the full application of their knowledge and skills to the problems which arise at all levels of public life, whether local, national, regional, or worldwide; and to encourage their participation in the solving of these problems.

Any woman who has an approved qualification, usually a degree, from a recognised university or institution of comparable academic standing can become a member of IFUW by joining the national federation or association of university women, affiliated to or in association with IFUW, that exists in her country. If none exists she can apply to become an "independent member". National federations and associations are active in over fifty countries, including Great Britain (affiliated with IFUW in 1919), USA (affiliated in 1919), Ireland (affiliated in 1924), France (affiliated in 1920), and the Federal Republic of Germany (Germany originally affiliated in 1926). Since 1953 the number of affiliates has doubled as national federations and associations in Asia, Africa and Latin America have joined. The British, Danish, and Indian federations have residences which IFUW members may use, the British one being Crosby Hall, Cheyne Walk, London, SW3 5AZ.

The supreme authority of IFUW is vested in the triennial Conference, the 22nd Conference being held in New Zealand in 1986. The executive body is the Council which meets at each Conference and at least once between Conferences. Maintaining the efficient functioning of IFUW is the Board of Officers (elected at the Conference), which usually meets twice a year. The Board is assisted by the Advisory Group, composed of the conveners of committees, the representatives to intergovernmental organisations and the two assistant treasurers. The Standing Committees deal with the award of international fellowships, finance, status of women and cultural relations, and membership.

In addition to triennial conferences, IFUW organises Councils and Regional Meetings (stress being placed on more Regional Meetings being organised). Each triennium a Study and Action Programme suggests a common basis of endeavour and work for the national federations and associations : for 1986 to 1989 this Programme is outlined as Women, Leadership and Development : (a) the environment, (b) bio-technology and the future of humanity, and (c) women and the promotion of peace.

IFUW undertakes studies and compiles reports dealing with the legal, social, economic, and educational status of women. Individual federations and associations undertake a wide variety of activities, for example literacy projects, adult education, self-help training for rural women, child care, secondary school and university scholarships, environment projects, and seminars. IFUW also awards international fellowships and grants to assist individual members further their studies and careers.

As an international non-governmental organisation, IFUW enjoys consultative status with UNESCO, UNICEF, and ECOSOC. It also co-operates with other such international organisations, in particular through Project Five-O, a project involved in the provision of non-formal education in developing countries which brings together five organisations : the Associated Country Women of the World, the International Council of Women, the International Federation of Business and Professional Women, Soroptimist International, and IFUW.

Since 1972 IFUW Headquarters has been based in Switzerland.

Nowadays the federations and associations of university women of 51 nations are members of IFUW, numbering some 230,000 women.

Bibliography
Edith C. Batho, A Lamp of Friendship (London, [1969]) (A short history of the Federation.) A sequel has not as yet been written.

Publications include:-
(a)   News Letter, later Newsletter, 1951- to date (annual).

        Communiqué, [by] 1972 - to date (annual). The earliest copy IFUW holds in its archives was published in 1972 but the Federation thinks it must have been published before, when the Headquarters was in London.

        Triennial Report 1920-, Yearbook 1920-, and Bulletin 1920- have been amalgamated for economic reasons; nowadays one publication is issued every three years and takes the form of a Conference Report or Blue Book which covers the activities of IFUW over the triennium. The IFUW's archives include a complete set of these publications, in English or French, since 1920.

(b)   Occasional Papers Nos.1-, 1922- and Pamphlets Nos.1-, 1920- appear to have ceased in the 1930s; neither series is nowadays published.

(c)   Triennial Study and Action Programme booklet.

(d)   A List of International Fellowships for Research (London, 2nd ed., 1934).

        Lexique international des Termes Universitaires ([London], 1939). Covers 31 countries in all. Details are given for each country under the following headings: introduction, academic institutions, governing and administrative bodies, administrative and academic staff, students and students' associations, examinations degrees and diplomas, general academic terms, and university extension. Thus serves as both a glossary of academic terms and a useful introduction to the university life of the country concerned.

[Germaine Cyfer-Diderich], The Position of the Woman Graduate Today: a
        Survey, 1956-1965 (London, [1966]).

Report of the Seminar on International Understanding, Berne and Geneva,
        11th to 21st August, 1955 (London [? 1956]). This seminar was
        organised by IFUW.

(e)   International Federation of University Women (leaflet, updated every
        three years, giving history, purposes, IFUW leadership, etc; the
        current edition covers the period 1986-89.)

Records
The principal records of the Federation commence in 1919 and bona fide
researchers would be allowed access to them.

As noted above, the Federation's headquarters also holds copies of its
publications.

See too the entry for the British Federation of University Women.

INTERNATIONAL FEDERATION OF
WORKERS' EDUCATIONAL ASSOCIATIONS

Address and
contact
International Federation of Workers' Educational Associations,
c/o International Department,
Histadrut,
93 Arlosoroff Street,
Tel Aviv 61002,
Israel.

tel: 03-262335, 431782
Mr. David Faran-Frankfurter, Secretary - General

History
The International Federation of Workers' Educational Associations (IFWEA) was
founded in October 1947 to promote co-operation between national non-
governmental bodies concerned with adult and workers' education, through
clearing-house services, exchange of information, conferences, publications,
etc. The idea of an international federation of WEAs was born during the
Second World War. At an exploratory conference in London in October 1945,
convened by the UK's WEA and to which representatives from workers'
educational organisations in all countries were invited, it was decided to set
up a formal international body to promote co-operation between the
organisations for workers' education. Ernest Green, then General Secretary of
the UK WEA, became first President of IFWEA and Harry Nutt (also of the UK
WEA) General Secretary, the Secretariat being established at the WEA's central
office in London; Mr. Nutt served as General Secretary until 1968. The
Secetariat moved to Vienna in 1974 and to London in 1977, where it remained
for the next ten years before it moved to its present office in Tel Aviv.

The IFWEA aims to increase the opportunity for workers to improve the quality of their intellectual, cultural, social and economic lives, and seeks to achieve this by : international conferences and seminars on adult and workers' education; the exchange of literature and information; the publication of a series of bulletins and newsletters; promoting new organisations for workers' education where appropriate movements do not already exist; and representing the interests of workers' education in relation to other international organisations. The General Conference decides IFWEA's general policy and elects an Executive Committee which is responsible for the work of the Federation between General Conferences.

In June 1977 the IFWEA's General Conference agreed to arrangements for its secretariat to return to London, with an honorary part-time General Secretary. The WEA provided half-time and subsequently full-time secretarial assistance etc. for the IFWEA, the latter paying for the same. This 'holding' operation lasted for ten years, until the transfer of the secretariat to Israel, to be accommodated in the offices of the Histadrut, a member organisation, and to be provided with a full-time General Secretary. In the meantime, however, there was an intensive drive for the development of the IFWEA which resulted in an increase in the number of member organisations from twenty-six to thirty-nine (particularly in the greater membership in the Mediterranean countries and improved contacts in Africa); the increased use of French and the development of Spanish among the Federation's working languages; the widespread distribution of an International Charter of Workers' Education; the increasing recognition by, and representation in, UNESCO, the International Labour Organisation (ILO), and non-governmental labour organisations; and increasing contact with educators in trade unions and cooperative movements of the developing countries.

Bibliography
The Story of IFWEA (IFWEA, London, [1980]); with a foreword by Hubert Hermans, President; appendices include lists of general conferences, Presidents, Vice-Presidents, General Secretaries, IFWEA seminars and summer schools, and IFWEA publications.)

Publications
A list of publications of IFWEA, [1947]-1979 appears as Appendix 7 of The Story of IFWEA [1980].

The publications include:-
International Bulletin of Workers' Education (later entitled IFWEA Bulletin), 1951-

IFWEA - IVA - FIAET (leaflet outlining the Federation's aims and activities, with names and addresses of member organisations; periodically updated.)

Constitution

Reports of Proceedings at Second (1950) and later General Conferences with Reports of the Secretariat and Executive Committee for the three years up to the year of the General Conference in each case.

G.D.H. Cole, Independent Voluntaryism in Workers' Education (1953)

David and Helen Kimble, Adult Education in a Changing Africa : a report on the inter-African seminar held in the Gold Coast... (IFWEA, London, 1956).

The Relationship between Vocational and Non-Vocational Adult Education : Report of a seminar held with the co-operation of the I.L.O. and UNESCO at the International Labour Office, Geneva... (IFWEA, London, 1959).

Report of a Seminar on Adult Education and the Disadvantaged, Oxford, 1975.

Report of a Seminar on the Role of Adult Education and Cultural Organisations in Europe, Stockholm, 1975.

International Charter of Workers' Education (IFWEA, London, [1980]) (adopted at the 12th General Conference, 1980).

Paid Educational Leave - A New Social Right : A Report of an International Seminar in Dublin, November 1981 (IFWEA, London, [c.1982]).

IFWEA IVA FIAET : Executive Committee News, Nos. [1]-, September 1987 - to date. An annex to No.3, May 1988, lists educational publications of IFWEA's member organisations and received at the Federation's Secretariat.

Copies of IFWEA publications may be found in certain Continuing Education Libraries in UK universities, e.g. in the Adult Education section of the Education Library, University of Liverpool, which holds an incomplete set of the Bulletin.

Records
The principal records which survived the changing location of the Secretariat are the Minutes and Decisions of the Executive Committee's meetings, commencing in 1976; some publications such as Paid Educational Leave [c.1982], news letters, conference reports; and miscellaneous.

Unfortunately, the archives of IFWEA which had been located at the WEA National office in Lisbon were destroyed.

INTERNATIONAL UNION OF STUDENTS

Address and
contact
International Union of Students,
POB 58,
17th November Street,
1101 Prague 01,
Czechoslovakia.

tel: 231 28 12
telex: 122858

History
The International Union of Students (IUS) was founded in 1946. Its objects are to defend the rights and interests of students; to strive for peace, national

independence, academic freedom, and democratic education; and to unite the student movement in furtherance of these objects. It comprises over 100 organisations from over 100 countries.

The IUS' activities include conferences, award of scholarships, travel and exchange, and sporting and cultural events.

Publications include:-
World Student News (Vol.7 No.1 was published in 1953).

Newsletter

Secretariat Reports (monthly)

Records
In his Guide to the Archives of other international inter-governmental organizations and non-governmental organizations (UNESCO, 1985), Mr. Mabbs states that no details were provided of archives from 1946 but that some of the archives (unspecified) are available for research.

Chris Cook (compiler), Sources in British Political History 1900-1951 Vol.6 First Consolidated Supplement (Macmillan, 1985) states that a collection of records re the IUS 1946-69 is housed in the International Institute of Social History at Amsterdam. The records were brought together mainly by the International Student Conference and include a file from the NUS on the origins and early history of the IUS.

INTER-UNIVERSITY COUNCIL FOR HIGHER EDUCATION OVERSEAS AND THE BRITISH COUNCIL'S HIGHER EDUCATION DIVISION

Address and
contact
The British Council,
65 Davies Street,
London,
W1Y 2AA

tel: 071 389 7521
Miss Victorine Martineau, Archivist
Miss Elizabeth Steward, Chief Registrar

History of the IUC
The Inter-University Council for Higher Education Overseas (IUC), which was until 1955 entitled the Inter-University Council for Higher Education in the Colonies, was established in March 1946 by the universities in the United Kingdom, at the invitation of the British Government, to assist the advancement of higher education in developing countries in the Colonies (later in the Commonwealth) and to encourage co-operation between universities in those countries and universities in the United Kingdom. The establishment of the IUC had been advocated in the Report of the Commission on Higher Education in the Colonies (the Asquith Commission), 1945 (Cmd.6647). The Asquith Commission had also recommended that a separate body, a Colonial University

Grants Advisory Committee (CUGAC) should be set up to advise on the allocation of all funds except those for salary supplementation for overseas service (for which the IUC should be responsible), and the IUC was to work closely with the CUGAC.

In 1946 two universities (in Malta and Hong Kong) existed within the IUC's geographical purview. By 1970 the IUC was associated with thirty-two universities within the Commonwealth and three outside (in Ethiopia, Liberia and the Sudan). Until 1963 the IUC had been formally confined to helping countries of the Commonwealth which had been dependent in 1946, though it had also been initially authorised to help the Sudan; after 1963 its activities were extended to other developing countries.

In 1968 the IUC was reorganised and became able to handle government funds, taking over the functions of the Committee on University Secondment in respect of those universities with which the IUC was associated. In October 1970 the IUC was incorporated as a limited company and from April 1971 it disposed of greatly increased funds from the Ministry of Overseas Development. Latterly IUC's activities were almost wholly financed by the Overseas Development Administration (of the Foreign and Commonwealth Office) but involved organising forms of academic collaboration which, to a degree, overlapped with the British Council's activities. As announced in the Report on Non-Departmental Public Bodies (Cmnd.7797, HMSO, 1980), the position of the IUC was accordingly examined, in the light of Ministerial decisions on the future of the British Council. In 1978-79 the IUC employed 60 persons and spent a gross £2.5m, all funded by the Government.

The IUC ceased to exist on 31 March 1981 and was merged with the British Council to form the Council's Higher Education Division, guided by the Committee for International Co-operation in Higher Education (CICHE). CICHE meets six times a year and guides the Council's work in higher education. A new and autonomous body, the Inter-University and Polytechic Council for Higher Education Overseas, was also formed in April 1981; it meets twice a year and nominates the representitive members of CICHE. The Annual Report and Accounts of the British Council are presented to Parliament.

The British Council was established in 1934 and incorporated by Royal Charter in 1940. Its aim is to promote a wider knowledge and appreciation of Great Britain in other countries through cultural, educational, and technical co-operation. A good deal of the work directed towards this aim consists of visits by individuals and groups from overseas to study or to meet their counterparts in Britain; in 1985/86 24,000 people were in Britain for educational or professional reasons on schemes run by the Council. In addition to its overseas offices and cultural centres, the Council has offices in fifteen university towns in Great Britain. The Council is currently (in 1988-89) represented in 82 countries; it has established in Brussels a dedicated EC Unit on behalf of British universities and polytechnics. The Council is an independent statutory body whose objectives and priorities are informed and guided by those of the Foreign and Commonwealth Office. As the Government stated in 1987, the Council is viewed as the principal instrument of its cultural diplomacy (other instruments being the BBC's External Services and the Central Office of Information); but apart from cultural goals, Britain's cultural diplomacy "helps to make Britain and British standards better known and understood, so that we may pursue British interests more effectively" (Fourth Report of the [House of Commons] Foreign Affairs Committee Session 1986-87: Cultural Diplomacy : Observations by the Government, Cm 231, HMSO, 1987). The Council's annual programme of activity is worth over £250m. The Council is funded by grants from the British Government, fees paid by Government agencies and international development organisations for work the Council does on their behalf, and money earned from teaching, consultancies and other services. The Council administers the new Academic Links Projects for both Hungary and Poland which are funded by the Overseas Development Administration through the Joint Assistance Unit located in the Foreign and Commonwealth Office. The Council publishes an Annual Report and Accounts.

The IUC furthered inter-departmental links between universities in the UK and overseas; assisted with staff recruitment at the request of overseas universities under secondment or contract arrangements; supported local staff development programmes, including training programmes in the UK; supported a large number of annual short-term visits to the associated overseas universities by senior staff from UK universities; and, inter alia, supported a number of lectureships in tropical medicine.

The main constitutional body of the IUC was the Council, composed of representatives from all British universities, ex officio and nominated members, and a number of co-opted members. The Council was assisted by an Executive Committee which was responsible for day-to-day decisions, the Executive Committee meeting six times a year or more frequently if there was need. The Council met three times a year. The Executive Committee received reports from its sub-committees and working groups, as well as reports from individuals or teams returning from overseas visits. In addition there were territorial and functional sub-committees and working groups, committees making training awards to overseas personnel, and anything up to two hundred advisory selection committees (helping to recommend staff for overseas appointments) could also be operating in any one year.

The Territorial groups were:-
    The West Africa Working Group
    The East and Central Africa Working Group
    The Caribbean and South Pacific Working Group
    The South East Asia Working Group

The functional sub-committees were:-
    The Rural Development Working Group
    The Manpower and Training Committee (renamed the Academic Policy Committee in 1970)
    The Finance Committee.

Bibliography of the IUC

I.C.M.Maxwell, Universities in Partnership: The Inter-University Council and the growth of higher education in developing countries 1946-70, Scottish Academic Press, Edinburgh, 1980. Based on the IUC's archives and the memories of people who took part, this book records those events and trends which seemed, from the central vantage point of the IUC, to be significant in the unfolding pattern of university development overseas and sets the development of the several universities in their international perspective.

Sir A.M.Carr-Saunders, New Universities Overseas, George Allen & Unwin, London, 1961.

Eric Ashby, Universities: British, Indian, African, Weidenfeld and Nicolson, London, 1966.

Martin Kolinsky, 'The Demise of the Inter-University Council for Higher Education Overseas: A Chapter in the History of the Idea of the University' in Minerva, A Review of Science, Learning and Policy, Vol.XXI No.1, Spring 1983, pp.37-80. (In fact this paper traces not only the demise of the IUC but also its establishment, development, and funding, and its relationship with the Ministry of Overseas Development and the British Council.)

See too the reports presented to Parliament by the Secretary of State for the Colonies:

Cmd.7331 (1948)
Cmd.7801 (1949)
Colonial No.273 (1951)
Cmd.9515 (1955)

Bibliography of the British Council

A.J.S.White, The British Council: The First 25 Years 1934-1959, The British Council, London, 1965.

Francis Donaldson, The British Council: The First Fifty Years, Jonathan Cape, London, 1984.

The THES reports on developments in the work of the Council, in particular more recently on its declining resources and its current restructuring plan, as in the issue of 27 April 1990, p.9.

Records (etc.) of the IUC

(a)   The IUC's records, 1946-81, have been transferred to the Public Record Office, Kew and form Class BW90. There is a full list of BW90 together with two alphabetical indexes - to IUC university and geographical files, and to IUC subject files. The subject index covers organisations with which the IUC had dealings, files on subjects under instruction, and specific topics of importance, and the IUC's own Secretariat and 'domestic' files. The index to IUC university and geographical files includes a section on Great Britain, links between the UK and overseas universities, and UK universities and overseas development, as well as references to individual UK universities, e.g. University of Liverpool: H 25, the list description of which is:-

(i)   BW90/2446 1978-1980   University of Liverpool   Former Ref
                                link in mathematics with   H25/38/810
                                University of Khartoum

(ii)   BW90/2447 1974-1980   Ditto: Link in veterinary   H25/57/810
                                sciences with University
                                of Khartoum

(iii) BW90/2448 1978-1979   Ditto: Link with Biomedical   H25/69/826
                                Engineering Unit, University
                                of Lagos College of Medicine

(iv)   BW90/2449 1978-1980   Ditto: Link in Tropical   H25/101/810
       (closed for 30 years)   Paediatrics with University
                                of Khartoum.

The vast majority of the papers (including agenda and minutes of the Council and the Executive Committee) are open without restriction. Some papers (for instance IUC members' personal correspondence files) are closed for 50 years or until 2018, though the majority of closed papers are closed for 30 years.

(b)   The records of the Technical Education and Training Organisation for Overseas Countries (TETOC), whose management was also taken over by the British Council, have also been deposited by the British Council in the Public Record Office, Kew, reference Class BW91. There is a list of these records (121 pp.), a copy of which is also held by the National Register of Archives (ref. NRA No. 29293).

(c)   Photographs accumulated by the IUC were transferred to the Royal Commonwealth Society, where they will be catalogued and made available for consultation in the Library.

(d)   The IUC's reference library was broken up on 1981, some of the material from it being transferred to Rhodes House Library, South Parks Road, Oxford, OX1 3RG.

(e)   A few Colonial Office papers re the IUC are to be found among the educational papers of the Office in the Public Record Office, Kew. They may be traced by using the Social Services correspondence registers, PRO ref. C.O.965, files coded 12001 onwards (from 1946 onwards).

Records of the British Council

Selected records of the Council, up to 1954, have been transferred to the Public Record Office, Kew, and form the BW Group. They include Minutes, Registered Files, and Country Files. There is an almost complete list of the BW Group.

ORGANISATION FOR ECONOMIC CO-OPERATION AND DEVELOPMENT

Address and contact

Organisation for Economic Co-operation and Development,
2, rue André-Pascal,
75775 Paris Cedex 16,
France

tel: 45-24-82-00
telex: 620160
telefax: (33-1)45 24 85 00
Mr. Thierry Monnier, Head of the External Relations Division

History

The Organisation for Economic Co-operation and Development (OECD) was set up under a Convention signed in Paris, 14 December 1960. The three main objectives laid down in the Convention were:-

1. to achieve the highest sustainable economic growth and employment and a rising standard of living in member countries, while maintaining financial stability, and thus to contribute to the development of the world economy;

2. to contribute to sound economic expansion in member as well as non-member countries in the process of economic development; and

3. to contribute to the expansion of world trade on a multi- lateral, non-discriminatory basis in accordance with international obligations.

The OECD replaced the Organisation for European Economic Co-operation (OEEC), which had been created by a Convention signed on 16 April 1948 by Austria, Belgium, Denmark, Eire, France, Greece, Iceland, Italy, Luxembourg, Norway, Netherlands, Portugal, United Kingdom, Sweden, Switzerland, and Turkey and the commanders in chief of the zones of occupation in Germany of France, United Kingdom, and the USA. The Federal Republic of Germany succeeded the allied occupation authorities in October 1949 and Spain joined in July 1959. OECD replaced OEEC because of the radical economic changes which had taken place in the late 1950s, including the failure to establish a Free Trade Area embracing all Western Europe (the EEC being set up by six countries, another seven countries setting up a Free Trade Association, EFTA); the need to give aid to the less-developed countries; the need to increase scientific and technical potential through international co-operation had become pressing; and the realisation that governments could not manage their affairs efficiently unless their general economic policies were better co-ordinated between all the leading industrial democracies.

OECD now has over twenty member countries, including Australia, France, Federal Republic of Germany, Eire, Italy, the UK, and the USA. The governing body of OECD is the Council, assisted by the Executive Committee, and by other committees, etc. The main bodies include the Education Committee and the Committee for Scientific and Technological Policy.

OECD's special programmes include the Programme for Educational Building and the Centre for Educational Research and Innovation (CERI). CERI was set up in 1968 and all member countries of OECD together with Yugoslavia are members. CERI is also responsible for OECD's Programme on Institutional Management in Higher Education (IMHE). IMHE, which was established in 1969, today has over 100 institutions of higher education in nineteen OECD countries as active participants. Member institutions of IMHE are invited to send representatives to meetings, which include workshops, training seminars and general conferences. IMHE has produced a series of Studies in Institutional Management in Higher Education which OECD has published and the Programme also produces the journal, Higher Education Management (which includes reports on meetings and research) (see too p.300). CERI's current mandate expires at the end of 1991.

Bibliography
Though so far there is no published history of OECD in existence, on the occasion of its 20th anniversary in 1980 the following two works were published:-

Organisation for Economic Co-operation and Development 1960 [-] 1980 (OECD, Paris, 1980).
(an album of photographs which records some of the major events in the history of OECD)

From Marshall Plan Through 20 Years of OECD (OECD Information Service, Paris, 1980)
(a short historical chronology)

Jean-Pierre Puissochet, 'Organisation de Cooperation et de Developpement Economiques : L'institution, les objectifs généraux et la structure de l'O.C.D.E.', Juriclasseur Périodique, Fascicule 160-A, OECD, 1983. (includes a bibliography of both OEEC and OECD).

Jean-Pierre Puissochet, 'Organisation de Cooperation et de Developpement Economiques : Les principales activités de l'O.C.D.E.', Juriclasseur Périodique, Fascicule 160-B, OECD, 1983; and sections updating sections of the 1983 account, published in the same series in 1987 (9, 1987(1)).

Publications
OECD's publications include the following. It should be noted that its publications are covered in International Bibliography... Vols.11-, 1983- (see p.277 of this Survey). The John Rylands University Library of Manchester is one of the libraries in the UK which has a standing order for all OECD publications; the JRULM's collection is fairly comprehensive.

(a)   The OECD Observer, etc., 1962-

(b)   Education and Development : Technical Reports, 1965-

(c)   Higher Education Management (formerly entitled International Journal of Institutional Management in Higher Education), Vols.1-, 1977-

(d)   The OECD has published the following volumes in its Reviews of National Policies for Education series, each volume having a section on higher education provisions:-

Australia - The Transition from School to Work or Further Study in Australia (1977)
Austria (1970)
Austria - Higher Education and Research (1976)
Canada (1976)
Denmark (1980)
England and Wales (1975)
Finland (1982)
France (1971)
Germany (1972)
Greece (1982)
Iceland (1987)
Ireland (1969)
Italy (1969)
Italy - Educational Reforms in (1985)
Japan (1971)
Netherlands (1970)
Netherlands - Contours of a Future Education System (1976)
New Zealand (1983)

Norway (1976)
Portugal 1984)
Spain (1987)
Sweden (1969)
Sweden - Educational Reforms in (1981)
United States (1971)
United States - Federal Policies for Education for the Disadvantaged (1981)
Yugoslavia (1982)

(e) Learning Opportunities for Adults series of publications:-
    Vol. I   -   General Report (1977)
    Vol. II   -   New Structures, Programmes and Methods (1979)
    Vol. III   -   The Non-Participation Issue (1979)
    Vol. IV   -   Participation in Adult Education (1977)
    Vol. V   -   Widening Access for the Disadvantaged (1981)

(f) Higher Education and the Demand for Scientific Manpower in the United States (1963).

Seymour E. Harris (ed.), Economic Aspects of Higher Education (1964).

Agricultural Education at University Level (1965).

Development of Higher Education, 1950-1967 (2 vols., 1970-71).

Interdisciplinarity : Problems of Teaching and Research in Universities : ... Report... based on the results of a Seminar... organised by CERI in collaboration with the French Ministry of Education (1972).

Leonard M. Cantor, Recurrent Education : Policy and Development in OECD Member Countries : United Kingdom (CERI, 1974).

Policies for Higher Education (General report on Conference on 'Future Structures of Post-Secondary Education') (1974).

Education in OECD Developing Countries : Trends and Perspectives (1974).

The Educational Situation in OECD Countries... (1974).

Maurice Kogan, Education Policies in Perspective : An Appraisal (1979).

Future Educational Policies in the Changing Social and Economic Context (1979).

Educational Statistics in OECD Countries (1981).

The Future of University Research (1981).

The University and the Community : the Problems of Changing Relationships (1982).

D. Porter and J.S. Padley (eds.), Training University Administrators in Europe (Gower, Aldershot, 1982).
Published in association with the OECD's Programme on

Institutional Management in Higher Education and the Working Group on Recurrent Education of the German Universities' Chancellors Speakers' Group.

Policies for Higher Education in the 1980s (Intergovernmental Conference, OECD, 12-14 October 1981) (1983).

Educational Trends in the 1970s : A Quantitative Analysis (1984).

Industry and University : New Forms of Co-operation and Communication (1984).

Adults and Higher Education (survey report of OECD and CERI, published by OECD, 1987).

Universities under Scrutiny (1987); a report reviewing the problems and dilemmas confronting universities in OECD countries.

Post-Graduate Education in the 1980s (1987).

Changing Patterns of Finance in Higher Education (1989); a report by Professor Gareth Williams.
(see, too, the report on the conference at Barcelona University, 'The missions and means of the university : issue and prospects for the financing of the European university system', in THES, 15 September 1989, p.9.)

(g)   OECD publications are obtainable from HMSO, 49 High Holborn, London (personal callers) or HMSO, P.O. Box 276, London, SW8 5DT (postal orders only). OECD publishes a Catalogue of Publications on Sale.., the latest being that ..'as at 1st January 1987'.

Records
(i)   The Acts (Decisions, Resolutions, Recommendations) adopted by the OEEC Council up to 1954 have been derestricted and it is possible that a similar decision may be taken in the future concerning Acts adopted by the Council subsequent to 1954.

(ii)   The minutes of meetings of the Council of OECD and of all the main bodies of the Organisation - which includes CERI - are classified as restricted and cannot be made available to outside sources.

STANDING CONFERENCE OF RECTORS, PRESIDENTS, AND VICE-CHANCELLORS OF THE EUROPEAN UNIVERSITIES

Address and
contact
Dr. Andris Barblan,
Secretary General,
Standing Conference of Rectors, Presidents, and Vice-Chancellors
of the European Universities,
10, Conseil-Général,
CH-1211 Genève 4,
Switzerland.
tel: (41) (22) 29-26-44 and 29-22-51
telex: 428 380

History

The origins of the Standing Conference (CRE), which records its foundation in 1959, may be traced back to 1948.

In the Brussels Treaty of 1948, signed by Belgium, France, Luxembourg, the Netherlands, and the United Kingdom it was, inter alia, agreed that they would make every effort in common "to lead their peoples towards a better understanding of the principles which form the basis of their common civilisation". This was the origin of that part of the work of the Brussels Treaty Organisation (BTO) which was entrusted to its Cultural Committee. In September 1953 a meeting was organised by the BTO in The Hague attended by a number of university Rectors and Vice-Chancellors, as well as by others concerned with university administration in the five BTO countries and by observers from the other countries of the Council of Europe. This meeting recommended that a full Conference of University Rectors should be convened in the Summer of 1955 and preparations for this first conference were made at a meeting of Rectors, Vice-Chancellors and experts at Clermond-Ferrand in 1954. In 1954, the five-power BTO was widened in scope, by the accession of West Germany and Italy, to form an association of seven countries, known as the Western European Union. In the planning of this first conference and the establishment of the Standing Conference, the Vice-Chancellor of the University of Liverpool, Sir James Mountford, played an important role and the University Archives, Liverpool holds his correspondence etc. with the BT Permanent Commission, The British Council, Western European Union, etc.

At the first conference of European Rectors and Vice-Chancellors, convened by the Western European Union and held at Cambridge 20-27 July 1955, a number of resolutions were adopted by the full conference on the balance between specialisation and general culture, the autonomy and independence of universities, the selection, training and welfare of students, the university and the community, and on the convening of similar conferences in the future. The conference considered "that regular meetings of Rectors and Vice-Chancellors of universities lead to fruitful personal contacts and discussions, likely to promote the improvement and development of universities and establishments for higher education and their adaptation to the needs of a rapidly changing world" and recommended that "similar conferences by convened periodically, and that in the intervening periods an organising committee chosen from amongst the members of the present conference will be given the task of collecting documentation concerning university education in the countries represented at this conference, to prepare future conferences, and to ensure thus the permanence of relations between the universities." The participants at this first conference were drawn from Belgium, Federal

Republic of Germany, France, Italy, Luxembourg, the Netherlands, and the United Kingdom and from the following Council of Europe countries: Denmark, Eire, Greece, Iceland, Norway, Saar, Sweden, and Turkey.

Following the 1955 conference a permanent European Universities Committee was created by the Western European Union, as a sub-committee of the Committee of Cultural Experts of the WEU. The Committee in turn established a Bureau (which meets between plenary sessions of the Committee) and a Publications (Sub-)Committee. The second Conference was held in Dijon in 1959, and subsequent Conferences have been held in 1964 and 1969 and subsequently every five years. The title of the Standing Conference was changed from the Standing Conference of Rectors and Vice-Chancellors of the European Universities to its current title in the 1970s.

The objective of CRE (the agreed acronym) is to promote co-operation among European universities. Its functions include: to provide a forum for inter-European discussions and informal meetings; to inform members and other interested parties about developments in university policy throughout the continent; to reflect on the role of the university in European society both now and in the past; and to represent the university's point of view to bodies concerned with higher education in Europe. To fulfil these four major functions, the CRE arranges meetings, publishes, and encourages research projects.

The CRE's General Assembly (as the CRE's Conference, held every five years, is now entitled) is open to all members and to observers from national and international bodies of inter-university co-operation. The latest (9th) General Assembly to be held was at Durham in September 1989; its theme was 'The University and the Community'. In the Summer of 1986 CRE's membership was drawn from 365 universities and equivalent institutions of higher education in 22 European countries, but at the General Assembly held at Durham it was decided to enlarge the membership of the Conference to include 21 eastern European universities and some higher technological institutes and also 20 English and Welsh polytechnics together with Paisley College of Technology.

Between General Assemblies, the CRE organises bi-annual conferences, limited to some 80-100 members, which promote regular contacts between university executive heads. A specific theme of topical interest is discussed at these conferences. The 29th bi-annual conference was held, in Belgrade, in October 1985; the previous bi-annual conference was devoted to the impact of new information techniques on European universities. In 1986 the first mid-term conference was held, the bi-annual conference of the quinquennium being enlarged to include more executive heads than is customary. Between conferences the work of CRE is organised by the Secretary General from headquarters which since 1964 have been at the University of Geneva. The everyday work of CRE is overseen by a Permanent Committee, which held its 58th session in Belgrade in October 1985.

CRE also organises (a) occasional seminars on a consultancy basis at the request of national rectors'/vice-chancellors' conferences, and (b) academic seminars supported by outside funding, linked to joint university research projects sponsored by CRE. CRE has decided to supplement the general debate by encouraging in-depth studies on specific themes. Already a pilot project has been launched to examine the social identity of the European university through the ages and to determine the relevance of past developments for the present. Scholars in forty member universities, as well as an editorial board, are engaged on this project, the aim being to produce a series of publications on 'The history of the European university as an institution in society'. It is intended that there will be four volumes (covering the Middle Ages, from the Reformation to the French Revolution, from the French Revolution to the Second World War, and from 1945 to the present day) and that the English language edition of the first volume will be published by Cambridge U.P. in 1990, with a German edition following in 1991.

Bibliography

L'Europe des universités. Historique de la Conférence permanente des recteurs et vice-chanceliers des universités européenes, 1948-1962 (Westdeutsche Rektorenkonfenz, Bad Godesberg, 1964).

CRE Information, N.S., No.47, 1979, is largely given over to a series of papers (in French and English) on the origins and history of CRE, principally up to 1969.

Reports on CRE's activities are published as General Assembly proceedings every five years.

Publications include:-

CRE Information, Vols.1 onwards followed by New Series Nos.1-, 1965- (A quarterly bulletin which publishes the proceedings of the conferences etc. of CRE and reports on developments in individual countries. A particularly valuable recent number is No.75, 3rd Quarter 1986, which is devoted to an account of university systems in Europe with sections on Austria, Spain, Federal Republic of Germany, France, Malta, Netherlands, Norway, Sweden, Switzerland, and the United Kingdom. No. 69, 1st Quarter 1985, comprises accounts of the development of universities in Austria, England, France, Germany, Norway, Poland, Spain, and Sweden. No.71, 3rd Quarter 1985, includes a list of CRE members.) At the end of March 1988 CRE Information is to be replaced by CRE Action.

CRE Newsletter (an occasional publication, not issued on a regular basis, the first issue being published in 1980).

CRE Yearbook (Yearbook of the European universities), 1972-73; replaced by the CRE Directory which is issued every two years as a special bulletin in CRE Information.

Proceedings of the General Assemblies

Lubor Jílek (ed.), Historical Compendium of European Universities [1984]. A bilingual (English and French) reference work, providing a chronology of more than 600 institutions.

Records

Permanent Committee minutes date back to 1960 (in respect of the Dijon meeting) and copies are distributed to Committee members twice a year, the Committee meeting on a bi-annual basis. Bona fide researchers may also consult these minutes in the CRE's office.

UNITED NATIONS EDUCATIONAL, SCIENTIFIC AND CULTURAL ORGANISATION

<u>Address and</u>
<u>contact</u>
UNESCO,
7, Place de Fontenoy,
F-75700 Paris,
France.

tel: 45-77-16-10
telex: 270002, 204461

<u>History</u>
The United Nations Educational, Scientific and Cultural Organisation (UNESCO), one of the United Nations' nineteen specialized inter-governmental agencies, was established in November 1946 'for the purpose of advancing, through the educational, scientific and cultural relations of the peoples of the world, the objectives of international peace and the common welfare of mankind'. The United Nations itself was established in 1945 and amongst its principal organs is the Economic and Social Council which is responsible, under the General Assembly, for carrying out the United Nations' functions with regard to international economic, social, cultural, educational, health, and related matters. To support it in its work, UNESCO has a number of Regional Offices for Education and also Regional Offices for Science and Technology, together with such institutes as the European Centre for Higher Education (CEPES) at Bucharest, Romania; the International Bureau of Education (IBE) at Geneva, which was founded in 1925 and was incorporated into UNESCO in 1969 as an international centre of comparative education; and the International Institute for Educational Planning (IIEP) at Paris, which was founded by UNESCO in 1963. In 1963 UNESCO launched its Development of Higher Education series of publications (some of which have been published jointly with IAU) and in 1971 began work on a long-term programme to promote new trends in higher education. UNESCO has an overall policy of regarding education as a lifelong process; an increasing priority is now given to pre-primary training and adult education.

In 1984 the USA left UNESCO and Britain left a year later, at the end of 1985, complaining of excessive bureaucracy, financial extravagance, political hostility to Western nations, and insufficiently practical programmes. Britain, however, continues to support a wide range of scientific organisations whose parent organisation is UNESCO : the Inter-Governmental Oceanographic Commission (IOC), the International Geological Correlation Project, the World Heritage Convention, etc. Britain's financial assistance will mainly come from the Overseas Development Administration (which was responsible for Britain's funding of UNESCO) but be channelled through such bodies as NERC. The House of Commons Foreign Affairs Committee has reported on the UK's membership of UNESCO in Sessions 1984-85 (HC 461) and 1989-90 (HC 255). In response, the British Government, which had been reviewing its withdrawal from membership, has most recently (1990) decided not to rejoin but to look forward to the day when it "can join a reformed organisation." The USA has also decided not to rejoin.

Bibliography

Thomas Hovet and Erica Hovet (eds.), Annual Review of United Nations Affairs : A Chronology and Fact Book of the United Nations 1941-1985 (Oceana Publications Inc., New York, 7th ed., 1986).

Evan Luard, A History of the United Nations : Vol.1, The Years of Western Domination, 1945-1955 (Macmillan, London, 1982) and Vol.2, The Age of Decolonization, 1955-1965 (Macmillan, Basingstoke, 1989).

In the Minds of Men : UNESCO 1946-1971 (UNESCO, Paris, 1972).

Richard Hoggart, An Idea and Its Servants : UNESCO from within (Chatto and Windus, London, 1978).

David Pitt and Thomas G. Weiss (eds.), The Nature of United Nations Bureaucracies (Croom Helm, Beckenham, 1986). Includes a case study of UNESCO, 'A Secretariat under Fire'.

Julian Behrstock, The Eighth Case : Troubled Times at the United Nations (University Press of America, 1987).

Peter Lengyel, International Social Science : the UNESCO Experience (Transaction Books, 1987).

Everyone's United Nations (UN, New York, 10th ed., 1986; includes details of the work of UNESCO, etc; 1st edition published in 1948).

Douglas Williams, The Specialized Agencies and the United Nations : the System in Crisis (Hurst & Co. (Publishers) Ltd., London, 1987).

Clare Wells, The United Nations, UNESCO and the Politics of Knowledge (Macmillan Press, London, 1987).

Graham Hancock, Lords of Poverty : The free-wheeling lifestyles, power, prestige and corruption of the multi-billion dollar aid business (Macmillan, London, 1989).

The World of Learning 1989 (39th edition, 1989), pp.1-4.

House of Commons Foreign Affairs Committee : First Report, UNESCO, Vol. I : Report, Vol. II : Minutes of Evidence with Appendices, HC 1989-90, 255-I and II, HMSO, 1990. Vol. II includes memoranda submitted by UNESCO, the Foreign and Commonwealth Office, NERC, the Royal Society, etc.

Publications

UNESCO's publications include the following. It should be noted that its publications are covered in International Bibliography..., Vols.1-, 1973- (see p.277 of this Survey), and that the UN has a network of depository libraries all over the world. A list of these libraries is available from the Public Inquiries Unit, Office of Publication Information, United Nations, New York. Only the two main UN libraries (at Geneva and at UN Headquarters, New York) have complete collections of all documents of the UN system as some documents are not on release even to depository libraries. The British Library's holdings of UN publications are nearly comprehensive. Much of the information about the UN is now available on computer databases which can be searched on-line (see the Advisory Committee for the Co-ordination of Information Systems' Directory of United Nations Databases and Information Systems.)

(a) Bibliography of Publications issued by UNESCO or under its auspices : the First Twenty-Five Years : 1946 to 1971 (Unesco, 1973).

Unesco List of Documents and Publications, Vols. 1-, 1972-

(b) Educational Documentation and Information (1971-), previously (1927-70) entitled Bulletin (of the) International Bureau of Education (quarterly), 1927-

Unesco Monitor (official publication), 1947-

The Courier, formerly The UNESCO Courier (monthly), 1948-

International Yearbook of Education (Unesco and the International Bureau of Education) 1949-

Statistical Yearbook

Bibliographical Newsletter of the Libraries Division of Unesco, 1952-

World Survey of Education, Vol. IV : Higher Education (Unesco, 1966). (UNESCO first publishd the World Handbook of Educational Organization and Statistics in 1952; later entitled World Survey of Education).

UNESCO News (twice monthly, giving official information, articles on Unesco's programme, etc; originally UNESCO Chronicle, commencing publication in 1955).

Unesco Handbook of International Exchanges, 1965-

Prospects-Quarterly Review of Education, formerly Prospects in Education, 1969-

Higher Education in Europe : Quarterly Review of the European Centre for Higher Education (CEPES, Unesco), Vols. 1-, 1976-.

(c) World Guide to Higher Education : A Comparative Survey of Systems, Degrees and Qualifications (The Unesco Press, 1st ed., 1976, 2nd ed., 1982).

The International Study of University Admissions : Access to Higher Education, Vol.I Director's Report by Frank Bowles and Vol.II National Studies (1963, 1965). Published by UNESCO and the International Association of Universities. The joint UNESCO-IAU Research Programme in Higher Education was instituted in 1959.

The Development of Higher Education in Africa (report of a conference) (Unesco, 1963; in Development of Higher Education series).

The Teaching of Sciences in African Universities (Unesco, 1964; in Development of Higher Education series).

<u>A survey of the teaching of physics at universities</u> (Unesco, 1966).

<u>Unesco Statistical Digest : A Statistical Summary of Data on Education, Science and Technology, Culture and Communication, by Country</u> (Unesco, 1987).

Gareth Williams, <u>Towards Lifelong Education : a new role for higher education institutions</u> (Unesco, Paris, 1977; in Development of Higher Education series).

<u>Promoting Equity, Excellence and Efficiency in Higher Education : Implications for Policy, Planning and Management</u> (UNESCO, 1987).

R.S. Adams and D. Battersby, <u>Pedagogical Staff Development in Higher Education</u> (UNESCO, 1987); an analysis of issues, problems, and trends.

The United Nations Organisation has an Information Centre at its London office, Ship House, 20 Buckingham Gate, London, SW1E 6LB (tel: 071 630 1981). A number of UNESCO (and UN, etc.) publications are obtainable by post from HMSO, PO Box 276, London, SW8 5DT.

<u>Records</u>
The Archives Section of the UNESCO Library, Archives and Documentation Services Division (LAD/ARC) is, in principle, responsible for all the archives of UNESCO.

At the time (1984) of the publication of the <u>Guide to the Archives of International Organizations I. The United Nations System</u> (UNESCO, Paris, 1984) edited by Lowell H. Hattery, the archives comprised principally those of the International Institute of Intellectual Cooperation (created in 1922 by the Council of the League of Nations and officially inaugurated in January 1926, and closed at the end of 1946), the Conference of the Allied Ministers of Education (which met, in London, 1942-45), the Preparatory Commission of UNESCO (which met, in London later in Paris, 1945-46), the International Relief Union (founded in 1927), and UNESCO.

The records of UNESCO itself which are described (together with a note on finding aids) in the <u>Guide</u> cover those of:-

The Secretariat (Archive group 8)

Archives of field units (Archive group 9); the greater part of the archives of UNESCO Regional Offices are preserved in these offices (which are listed in an annex).

Printed archives (Archive groups 4-7: documents of the General Conference, the Executive Board, the Secretariat, and publications of UNESCO).

Microcopies (Archive group 11)

Audio-visual archives (Archive group 12)

The <u>Guide</u> also provides an administrative history of UNESCO and its Secretariat, and a bibliography.

Unesco documents and field mission reports, Unesco publications and Unesco-licensed publications are freely accessible in the reading room of the Archives Section, unless they are marked restricted or confidential (in which case the prior agreement of the relevant unit of the Secretariat has to be obtained to consult them).

Secretariat records, correspondence and administrative files are generally open for consultation after thirty years. Certain types of materials may be consulted before thirty years have elapsed and certain materials (e.g. exceptionally sensitive information on relations between Unesco and the United Nations, intergovernmental and non-governmental organisations) only after fifty years. In 1986 a relaxation of access to UNESCO records was under consideration, following the UN Secretariat's rule of twenty years time limit, but until any changes are made the thirty year rule applies. It should be stressed that access to archives within the open period can be refused if they are "unmistakably of confidential nature still" and exceptions "to a paper or file that is not yet in the open period may be made by the Chief Archivist" after some provisions are fulfilled. The Chief Archivist is currently Dr. Markku Järvinen.

(The rules governing access by outside persons to Unesco Archives, 1977, are published as an appendix in Marie Charlotte Stark, Development of Records Management and Archives Services within United Nations Agencies : A RAMP Study with Guidelines, PGI-83/WS/26, UNESCO, Paris, 1983 and also on pp. 138-9 of the Guide to the Archives of International Organizations I. The United Nations System, UNESCO, 1984. An update on the access situation is contained in Bodil Ulate Segura, Access to the Archives of United Nations Agencies : A RAMP Study with Guidelines, PGI-86/WS/24, UNESCO, Paris, 1987. References are made to UNESCO in Marilla B. Guptil, Archival Appraisal of Records of International Organizations : A RAMP Study with Guidelines, PGI-85/WS/4, UNESCO, Paris, 1985.)

WORLD UNIVERSITY SERVICE

Address and
contact
World University Service,
5 Chemin des Iris,
1216 Geneva,
Switzerland.

tel: 022 988711
telex: 27273 WUS CH

History
World University Service (WUS) originated as International Student Service (ISS) in 1920. Its name was changed to World University Service in 1951.

The aims of ISS were to act as a permanent relief organisation, a school of international affairs, and as a social service. In the later 1930s, in particular, ISS raised vast sums of money on behalf of the Chinese universities and for the relief of students driven from Austria, etc. and awarded many Training Scholarships. It organised conferences on international questions. In the social work field it aimed to study student conditions and prospects of future employment and to stimulate students to an awareness of social problems and to enable them to play an active part in current social activities. Many universities had co-operating and other committees of staff and students supporting ISS' work.

By the mid 1950s WUS could be described as a fellowship of over thirty national committees co-ordinated by the international secretariat in Geneva. Relief was given to every student of any nationality who was in need of assistance by means of the distribution of books, food, clothes, etc. Students were recruited for overseas conferences, study tours and courses, travel bursaries being made available. It sought to encourage hospitality for foreign students in Britain and to develop the interest of British students in University life abroad. Research was conducted into such problems as university entrance and health.

WUS' concerns have come to embrace education in its widest sense, with participation in literacy programmes and support for 'appropriate' education. It has provided study grants for more than 1,000 refugees in the UK, over the past ten years, from Latin America, Africa, and the Middle East. At present WUS has programmes for Central American, Ethiopian and Etritrean, South African and Namibian refugees, both in the UK and in the region. Support is given for non-formal and literacy projects particularly in the Horn of Africa and for community libraries and resources. The success of WUS' Southern African Campus Scholarships Campaign has permitted forty Southern Africans currently to study at universities and polytechnics through fee waivers etc. In Central America particular help has been given in El Salvador (particularly during the military occupation of its university, 1980-84) and in Nicaragua. WUS is the only campaigning organisation in the UK to concentrate on the role of education in the advancement of women, especially in the Third World, producing reports, a campaigning pack, etc. WUS makes grants or small awards to a number of refugee groups in the UK and has set up an advice service, open to all refugees in the London area, to give guidance on courses available and English language training. It also runs an advice and training service for advisers outside London.

The WUS' UK office is at 20/21 Compton Terrace, London, N1 2UN.

WUS is an independent, non-governmental, non-political organisation, composed of committees of students and staff in post-secondary institutions in, nowadays, 60 countries. It finances and administers post-secondary scholarships for political refugees and those denied equal educational opportunities and supports development programmes linking the human and technical resources of universities to social and economic development.

Publications include:-
WUS Bulletin (monthly)

WUS News (every two months)

Annual Report, 1959- (earlier reports are included in WUS Year Book)
        Reports on conferences, seminars, and research.

The British Journal of International Student Service, new series (1946),
        continued as ISS Review (1946-50), continued as ISS Year Book, 1951,
        continued as WUS Year Book, 1952-

Overseas Students : the dramatic decline : the WUS report (WUS UK, London,
        1981).

Issues. A mid-term commentary on international university affairs, 1948-?

Frank D. Squire (ed.), <u>Student Health and Sport in the University</u> (ISS, Geneva, 1940).

R. Oxtoby (ed.), <u>Staff-Student Relation : Report on a conference organised by the United Kingdom Council of World University Service...London...1967</u> (London, 1967).

Eve Hall (ed.), <u>A Handbook for Refugees in the United Kingdom</u> (WUS, London, 1980).

Valerie Shawcross, Kate Grosser, and Jane Goldsmith, <u>Women in Mind : The Educational Needs of Women Refugees in the UK</u> (WUS, London, 1987).

<u>Where Education is a Crime</u> (WUS, London, 1990); a report on the continuing closure of Palestinian universities and colleges in the territories occupied by Israel and the effects of closure.

Records
It should be noted that individual universities' Students' Unions may retain minute books of local branches of the ISS/WUS and references to their activities etc. may be found in the Unions' publications. For instance, the University Archives Liverpool holds the minutes of the University of Liverpool branch of ISS/WUS 2 Dec. 1947 - 18 June 1963 (ref. A.027/17) and successive editions of the University of Liverpool <u>Students' Handbook</u> which refer to ISS/WUS.

While it is hoped that it will prove possible to produce a second, revised edition of this survey, or perhaps rather a supplement, in several years time, incorporating corrections, additional information, and entries for bodies not covered in the main text of this first edition, it may be useful to note some of the bodies not so far 'fully' covered:

(a) UK Government Departments
Department of Education and Science

The DES is responsible for all aspects of education in England, and for Government policy towards universities throughout England, Wales, and Scotland, and for Government support for fundamental or long-term civil science. An account of the DES' work is contained in William Pile, The Department of Education and Science (George Allen and Unwin, London, 1979) and in such journal articles as Maurice Kogan, 'The DES and Whitehall', Higher Education Quarterly, Vol.41 No.3, 1987, pp.225-240.

The Branches of the DES which deal with university matters are based at the DES' offices, Elizabeth House, York Road, London, SE1 7PH (tel. 071 934 9000). They are the Further and Higher Education Branches 1-3, and also the Science Branch. FHE Branch 1 is composed of four Divisions of which Division A is concerned with universities' policy and finance, liaison with the UFC, etc., Division B is concerned with the management and structure of polytechnics and colleges of higher education, liaison with NAB, CNAA, etc., and Division D provides the secretariat for the Computer Board for Universities and Research Councils. FHE Branch 2 has three Divisions of which Division A is concerned with information technology in higher education, the EC's COMETT Programme, etc. FHE Branch 3 has three Divisions of which Division A is concerned with adult and continuing education (including the WEA, etc.), Division B is concerned with the government of universities, grants to the British Academy, European University Institute, the OU, etc., and Division C is concerned with general student support policy. The Science Branch is concerned with the policy and funding for basic civil science, the ABRC, the Royal Society, the Fellowship of Engineering, etc. For further details, see the Education Year Book 1991 (Longman, 1990).

DES publications currently in print published by HMSO are listed in the periodically revised HMSO Sectional List No.2; a number of DES publications (including its Statistical Bulletins) are not published by HMSO but by the Department itself. The DES' Annual Report, published by HMSO (and presented to Parliament pursuant to the Education Act 1944), includes sections on post-16 education in colleges and universities (which incorporates reports on the work of the National Advisory Body for Public Sector Higher Education (NAB), the Computer Board for Universities and Research Councils, and the Unit for Development of Adult Continuing Education (UDACE)); on civil science (which incorporates reports on the work of ABRC and the five research councils); and on finance. The appendices to the Annual Report include lists of the Department's publications for the year. Annual Reports were published by the DES and its forebears between 1839 and 1985. In 1988 the Annual Report was replaced by the first in a list of DES publications, DES Publications 1986: A list of publications and selected Press Notices compiled by the DES Library (DES, 1988).

The Kew branch of the Public Record Office holds a number of records relating to universities amongst the records of the DES and its predecessors. They include:-

ED 10   General Education: General Files, 1872-1945, which include

ED 10/207	1918-28	Appointments of Returning Officers for university constituencies under the Representation of the People Act, 1918; suggestion by Sir Oliver Lodge that the Vice-Chancellor of Birmingham University undertakes duties in respect of Combined Constituency.
ED 10/264-9	1938-44	National Service - Release of teachers and members of local authority staff for Forces... Positions of university and other students and lecturers.

ED 24   Private Office Papers, Series I, 1851-1935, which include

ED 24/1340-1346	1919-21 n.d.	Higher Education: Scheme for Ex-Service Students - proposed administrative organisation of the scheme and grant regulations, report on history and administration of scheme, etc.
ED 24/511-528, 1937-1999	1903-34	University Education : General
e.g.ED 24/515	1905-11	House of Commons Questions and Answers
/1961	1917-19	Papers with statistics urging increased grants to medical students.
/1977	1919-34	UGC : papers
/1982	1920-21	Liverpool University: papers (printed)
ED 24/2000-2001, 529-566	1903-20	Imperial College of Science and Technology : Correspondence, etc.
ED 24/2002-2023	1912-35	London University, including establishment of School of Oriental Studies.
ED 24/567-569	1910-11	Unification of Grants to Universities : Correspondence, minutes, etc.

ED 24/77-81, 82A	1889-1902	University Colleges: Grant - House of Commons Returns (printed)
ED 24/570-575, 2024-2029	1904-22	University of Wales

ED 25   External Relations : Universities Bureau of the British Empire and British National Committee on Intellectual Co-operation Papers (minutes, reports, correspondence, etc.), 1922-46.

ED 39   Legal Endowments : Endowment Files : Universities and Colleges, 1854- 1944.
Arranged alphabetically by counties under England and Wales.
Cover Fellowships, Lectureships, Exhibitions, Scholarships, etc.

e.g. ED 39/83-87	1876-1903	Liverpool University. (includes: Roger Lyon Jones Charity - correspondence concerning payment of legacy, 1876-79)
ED 39/308	1884-95	School of Medicine and Surgery, Sheffield - sale of property and application of proceeds.

ED 71   Awards : State Scholarship University Committee : files, 1920-44
(Concern England and Wales)

e.g. ED 71/8	1920-33	Liverpool University Committee
ED 71/13	1920-39	Sheffield University Committee

ED 72   Awards : University Examining Bodies : files, 1920-44
(re state scholarship scheme)

e.g. ED 72/1	1920-35	Bristol University Examinations Committee
ED 72/5	1920-35	Northern Universities Joint Matriculation Board
ED 72/12	1936-44	Northern Universities Join Matriculation Board

ED 73   Further Education : Adult Education : Tutorial Classes Files, 1921-69. These files, which relate to England and Wales, include HM Inspectors' reports and annual reports or financial statements submitted by the 'Responsible Bodies'.

e.g. ED 73/15	1928-35	Liverpool University, Department of Extra-Mural Studies
ED 73/64	1936-45	Liverpool University Joint Committee
ED 73/107	1946-55	Liverpool University, Department of Extra-Mural Studies
ED 73/40	1927-35	WEA, West Lancashire and Cheshire District
ED 73/84	1936-44	WEA, N.W. District

| | ED 73/152 | 1949-55 | The National Institute of Adult Education |

ED 76   Further Education : Adult Education : Vacation Course Files, 1928-55. (England and Wales)

| | e.g. ED 76/11 | 1929-55 | Liverpool University Tutorial Classes Joint Committee |
| | ED 76/21 | 1945-55 | WEA, Headquarters |

ED 81   Teachers : University Training Department Files, 1931-61. (England, Wales, and Northern Ireland)

| | e.g. ED 81/6 | 1935 | Liverpool University Training Department |
| | ED 81/28 | 1945-55 | University of Liverpool Department of Education : general |

ED 112   Expired Commissions : Durham University, 1926-37 (records of and re Royal Commission appointed in 1934 and records of earlier independent inquiry)

ED 116   Committee on Higher Education (Robbins Committee, 1961-63) : Agenda and Minutes

ED 118   Committee on Higher Education (Robbins Committee, 1961-63): Surveys and Evidence

ED 119   Universities and University Colleges : files, 1874-1967 (England and Wales)
(comprise reference by Privy Council to Education Department and subsequently the Board of Education about university statutes and charters; also concern award of grant originally undertaken by the Treasury and subsequently distributed by the Board of Education prior to setting up of the UGC.)

	e.g. ED 119/25	1903-10	Liverpool University
	ED 119/26	1915-17	Liverpool University
	ED 119/98	1944-50	Liverpool University

ED 121   External Relations : General Files, 1871-1960 and later.
(include files re British Council : Training of Overseas Students, Congress of Universities of the Empire, Conference of Allied Ministers of Education 1942-45, UNESCO, and the Imperial Institute later the Commonwealth Institute.)

The above details are based on the entries in the PRO's Current Guide (which is being continuously updated and which may be consulted in both branches of the PRO) and in individual lists. Part 3 (Index) of the Current Guide provides references to over a dozen ED classes which, inter alia, relate to universities. Microfiche copies of the PRO Current Guide part 2 (Class Descriptions) and Index may be purchased. Orders should be directed to the Museum Section, Public Record Office, Chancery Lane, London, WC2A 1LR; copies may also be purchased at the museum counter there. A microfiche edition of the whole of the Current Guide together with the class lists of records housed at the Kew branch of the PRO (i.e. the class lists of 'modern government departments', excluding those of records held at the Chancery Lane branch) has recently (1988) been published by HMSO. See too the PRO's Information No.78, 1986, on 'Education : Records of Teachers', and Information No.80, 1987, on 'Records relating to technical and further education'.

Scottish Education Department

The Scottish Education Department (New St.Andrew's House, St.James Centre, Edinburgh, EH1 3SY; tel: 031-556 8400) is responsible for the administration of public education in Scotland (except universities), youth and community services, social work services, the arts, libraries, museums, galleries, and sport. The annual report of the Department for the last thirty or more years has been entitled Education in Scotland in... [year concerned]. The reports for the period up to 1975 are more comprehensive than those subsequently published and provide details of Further Education provisions. SED publications currently in print published by HMSO are listed in the periodically revised HMSO Sectional List No.36.

The centenary history of the Scottish Office (John S. Gibson, The Thistle and the Crown : A History of the Scottish Office, HMSO, Edinburgh, 1985) contains a number of references to the SED. Walter M. Humes, The Leadership Class in Scottish Education (John Donald Publishers Ltd., Edinburgh, 1986) includes a chapter on the SED and a section on the structure and management of tertiary education. See too Andrew McPherson and Charles D. Raab, Governing Education: a Sociology of Policy since 1945 (Edinburgh U.P., 1988).

The Scottish Record Office (SRO) holds (in its West Register House, Charlotte Square, Edinburgh repository) a number of records relating to higher and further education in Scotland amongst the records of the Department, including:

ED. 8 — Advisory Councils on Education in Scotland files, 1920-61 (Between 1920 and 1967 eight Advisory Councils on Education in Scotland were appointed for periods of from three to five years. The subjects considered by these Councils included:-
1st Advisory Council (1920-24) - changes in regulations for the training of teachers; conditions of entrance to the Scottish universities.
2nd Advisory Council (1924-29) - adult education.
6th Advisory Council (1942-46) - adult education; technical and continued education; training of teachers.
7th Advisory Council (1947-51) - further education; higher technological education.
8th Advisory Council (1957-61) - supply of teachers.

ED.26 — Higher and Formal Further Education Files 1826-1981

ED.27 — Informal Further Education Files 1901-82

ED.34 — Reports of the Committee of the Privy Council on Education in Scotland (1839-1922) and of the Secretary of State on Education in Scotland (1945-), 1839-1979.

ED.35 — Educational Research Files, 1927-85.
(These files deal generally with research in education and particularly with the activities of the Scottish Council for Research in Education incorporated in 1932 inter alia to promote, support and prosecute all forms of educational

research and development relating to education, including curricula in universities, and to found, endow, and maintain research fellowships.)

ED.51   Training and Supply of Teachers Files, 1900-85.

(Details as at March 1988. It should be noted that periodic transmissions of non-current records are made by the SED to the SRO and thus further and later records in most of the above classes can be excepted to be deposited in the SRO in the future.)

It should be noted that the SRO has a number of records relating to Scottish universities apart from those in the ED classes, e.g. records of the Carnegie Trust for the Universities of Scotland (ref. GD.1/464). The SRO has published a Source List (No.17) on Material on Education in the SRO and has a Source List on the Scottish Universities in preparation. A new Guide to the Scottish Record Office, edited by Dr. John Imrie, is in preparation (1989), to replace M. Livingstone, Guide to the Public Records of Scotland (1905).

Department of Health and Social Security

The DHSS was created in November 1968 through the merger of the Ministry of Health (set up in 1919 under the Ministry of Health Act 1919 and taking over the powers and duties of the Local Government Board and the National Health Insurance Commissions for England and Wales) and the Ministry of Social Security (set up in 1966 and taking over most of the functions of the Ministry of Pensions and National Insurance and the National Assistance Board, though by 1951 the Ministry of Health was concerned almost exclusively with national and local health, medical and hospital services, other functions having been transferred in the meantime to other departments). In April 1969 health and welfare functions relating to Wales were transferred to the Welsh Office. On 25 July 1988 the split of the DHSS into a Department of Social Security and a Department of Health was announced.

For the Health Services see in particular the various annual reports and handbooks published by HMSO for the DHSS and Charles Webster, The Health Services since the War : Volume I, Problems of Health Care : The National Health Service before 1957 (HMSO, 1988); the second volume of Dr. Webster's history will cover the period 1957 to 1979.

The Kew branch of the Public Record Office holds a number of records relating to medical education and research, etc., including:-

MH 58   Public Health and Poor Law Series : General Health Questions, 1910-66, being files of correspondence and minutes on policy and individual cases. Includes:

General Series: ...Medical Research Council
Medical Education : postgraduate hospitals, medical schools and courses, Postgraduate Medical Education Committee 1925-30, Athlone Committee on postgraduate education 1920-21, proposed international academy.

Medical Research Council, 1924-34 (MH 58/260, 262)

Tropical diseases : schools and hospitals.

(the above details are based on the <u>Guide</u> to the Public Record Office and the list of MH 58)

Department of Education, Welsh Office

The Further Education Division of the Department of Education of the Welsh Office (Cathays Park, Cardiff, CF1 3NQ) is responsible, inter alia, for the supply and training of teachers, advanced and non-advanced further education, adult education, and liaison with the University of Wales.

The Welsh Office was formally constituted in 1965. In April 1969 it took over responsibility for the health and welfare services in Wales from the DHSS. In April 1978 it took over functions in relation to further education and to the training and supply of teachers for primary and secondary education in Wales from the DES. Since 1965 provision has been made by the UGC for consultation with the Welsh Office in the case of universities and colleges in Wales (the UGC remaining responsible for grants throughout Great Britain).

Provisions are made for the deposit of records of the Welsh Office at the Public Record Office, where those selected for preservation are generally available for consultation at the Kew branch of the P.R.O. after thirty years has elapsed from the date of the file etc. in question.

Department of Education for Northern Ireland

The Department of Education for Northern Ireland (Rathgael House, Balloo Road, Bangor, County Down, BT19 2PR) is responsible for the development of primary, secondary, and further education, including higher education, community and adult education, teacher training, etc. It has a Higher Education and Teacher Training; Scholarships and Postgraduate Awards Division.

The Public Record Office of Northern Ireland (66 Balmoral Avenue, Belfast, BT9 6NY) holds the following records relating to higher education:

ED 17	c.30 'HE' Higher Education files relating largely to the financial assistance given by the Government to Magee University College, Londonderry and to Queen's University of Belfast, 1922-1958.
ED 39	3 files of the Lockwood Committee on Higher Education which include minutes of committee meetings, a summary index of the evidence submitted and correspondence, 1963-64.
FIN 58	9 files of the Lockwood Committee on Higher Education which contain minutes of the working party set up in preparation for the Committee, the minutes of the Committee itself, a series of verbatim reports, papers submitted in evidence and miscellaneous correspondence, 1962-72.

Other Departments of State, etc.

Apart from the records of the DES and the DHSS, it should be noted that the Public Record Office holds a large number of other records emanating from other Departments of State etc. which relate to the development of universities and research councils in this country and overseas. They include:-

Treasury: Supply Files, ref. T.161 - include files on higher education, universities, adult education, education grants, etc.

Development Commission: Correspondence and Papers, 1910-81, ref. D.4 - include files on fishery research, scientific research and veterinary research.

Ministry of Agriculture, Fisheries and Food : Agricultural Education and Research Correspondence and Papers, 1888-1963, ref. MAF 33 - include files on universities, colleges and institutes, training, grants, scholarships, veterinary education and research, etc.

e.g.	MAF 33/27	1911-43	Oxford University: Capital Grant, Visit and Report, etc.
	MAF 33/247-8	1933-56	Liverpool University School of Veterinary Science: capital grants and Veterinary Education Committee investigation.
	MAF 33/749-764	1919-48	Agricultural Research Council: minutes of meetings, reports, etc.

For accounts of the Ministry's history and work, see Sir John Winnifrith, The Ministry of Agriculture, Fisheries and Food (George Allen and Unwin, London, 1962) and Susan Foreman, Loaves and Fishes, an illustrated history of the Ministry of Agriculture, Fisheries and Food 1889-1989 (HMSO, 1989).

Privy Council Office: nowadays, the contacts between the Privy Council and universities mainly relate to the grant of charters to universities and the amendment of these charters' statutes. However, in addition, in the pre-2nd World War period, committees of the Privy Council were responsible for state sponsorship of scientific research. These committees included the future Department of Scientific and Industrial Research (set up in 1915 as a Committee; a separate Department, 1916-65) and the Medical Research Committee (set up in 1913 and answerable to the Minister for National Health Insurance until it became the Medical Research Council, incorporated by charter, in 1920) and the records of such departments and departmental bodies are mainly to be found in the Kew branch of the Public Record Office.

Admiralty : Royal Greenwich Observatory Board of Visitors Papers (1827-1964), ref. ADM 190 - includes minutes, warrants of appointments, and correspondence concerning visits to the Observatory (responsibility for which was transferred to what is now SERC in 1965, when the Board of Visitors was dissolved).

(now the Universities Funding Council)
Aeronautical Research Council: see entry in the Survey (pp.17-19).

University Grants Committee: see entry in the Survey (pp.173-83).

(b) Adult Education in H.M. Forces

1. Central Advisory Council for Adult Education in H.M. Forces, later Central Committee for Adult Education in H.M. Forces, later The Committee for University Assistance to Adult Education in H.M. Forces.

A Central Advisory Council for Education in H.M. Forces was in existence by January 1940 and in August 1940 arrangements were made for the work to be financed from Service funds. On the Council's initiative, regional committees to organise this work were established in extra-mural areas all over the country, each Regional Committee being based on a university area. By the winter of 1943-44 more than 4,000 meetings per week were being arranged. In 1948 most universities agreed to accept responsibility for civilian assistance for adult education in the Forces, setting up special committees. The Central Advisory Council was at the same time replaced by a Central Committee for Adult Education in H.M. Forces (which included representatives of the universities, local education authorities, WEA, and the Services) and a peak of activity was reached by the Committee about 1954-56. The decision to end conscription for national service was a factor which led to a further reorganisation in 1960 whereby the Central Committee was replaced by a Committee for University Assistance to Adult Education in H.M. Forces and universities were asked to accept responsibilities only for work of an extra-mural character. With the end of national service, the emphasis in the work of university extra-mural departments for the Services was more towards vocational education. In 1966 the Ministry of Defence established a scheme for Higher Defence Studies independently of the existing scheme of collaboration with university extra-mural departments, the new scheme initially causing much difficulty in the relationships between universities and the Services. Coming under the auspices of the Ministry of Defence, the Committee was finally wound up in 1980, following a review of non-Departmental public bodies (Cmnd. 7797, HMSO, 1980).

The history of the successive bodies is provided in N.S. Wilson, Education in the Forces, 1939-46: The Civilian Contribution (Evans Brothers Ltd., London [1949]); C. Lloyd, British Services Education (Longmans, Green for the British Council, London, 1950); and Thomas Kelly, A History of Adult Education in Great Britain (2nd ed., Liverpool U.P., 1970).

The records of the Committee and its predecessors are classified as public records : as yet they have not been transferred to the Public Record Office.

2.   Regional Committees for Adult Education in H.M. Forces.

Regional Committees for Adult Education in H.M. Forces were established, mainly in late 1939 and in 1940, in twenty-three university extra-mural areas all over the country. The titles and functions of these committees changed over time in line with developments in the work of the Central Advisory Council for Adult Education in H.M. Forces and its successors. For instance, the Liverpool Regional Committee for Adult Education in H.M. Forces (which functioned from December 1939 and whose Hon. Secretary was the University's Director of Extra-Mural Studies) was replaced in 1949 by the Liverpool Regional Committee for Education in H.M. Forces, a committee which, while sponsored by the University of Liverpool, remained constitutionally independent; the Committee's composition was further changed in 1955 and in 1960 it was reconstituted on a smaller scale and, in response to the decline in activities sponsored by the Committee, at the end of Session 1970-71 the Committee was wound up, though assistance continued to be given to the Forces by the University's Institute of Extension Studies.

It is believed that of the twenty-three Regional Committees that existed, the records (including minute books and correspondence files) of only about a half a dozen have been retained by the universities which provided the Secretaries of the Regional Committees: they include Cambridge, Exeter (records in Adult Education Department), Leeds (records in University Central Filing Office), Liverpool (records in University Archives), Nottingham (records in University Library Department of Manuscripts), and Oxford.

It should be noted that not all the Regional Committees' Secretaries were drawn from members of staff of universities. However, even in those cases where the Committees' records do not apparently survive, one might still expect to find a section of the annual report of the university and/or of its department covering the subject of work for H.M. Forces.

Mr. Paul MacKenzie of St.Antony's College, Oxford, who is currently working on a D.Phil. thesis on 'Morale and the Politics of Army Education, 1917- 1949' kindly reported to me on the survival of Regional Committee records and also mentioned that PRO sources that might be of use include: WO 32/12432 - Central Advisory Council for Education in HM Forces, future of, 1946-48, and WO 32/12438 - Army Educational Advisory Board, 1946-50.

(c)   Councils, Committees and Groups

1.   Committee of Heads of University Chemistry Departments

The current Chairman is Professor J.A. McCleverty, Department of Chemistry, University of Birmingham, P.O. Box 363, Birmingham, B15 2TT.

2.   Committee of Heads of University Geoscience Departments (CHUGD)

The Committee may be contacted through its Secretary, Dr. M.R. Dobson, Department of Geology, University College of Wales, Aberystwyth.

Reference is made to this Committee in the UGC's response in September 1987 to the report, Strengthening University Earth Sciences ('Oxburgh Report'), whose proposed three-tiered hierarchical organisation for geology departments was greeted with wide opposition in the geoscience community.

3.   Committee of Heads of University Law Schools

The current Chairman is Professor Graham J. Zellick, Faculty of Laws, Queen Mary College, Mile End Road, London, E1 4NS.

4.   Committee of Professors in Operational Research

The current Chairman of the Committee (COPIOR) is Professor K.B. Haley, School of Engineering Production, University of Birmingham, P.O. Box 363, Birmingham, B15 2TT.

5.   Committee of Professors of Statistics

The current Chairman is Professor John B. Copas, Department of Mathematics, University of Birmingham.

6. Committee of University Professors of Food Science and Technology.

The current Chairman is Professor W.M. Waites, Department of Applied Biochemistry and Food Science, University of Nottingham, School of Agriculture, Sutton Bonington, Loughborough, Leicestershire, LE12 5RD.

7. Council for Industry and Higher Education

The Council for Industry and Higher Education is an independent body made up of twenty-six heads of large companies and eleven vice-chancellors, polytechnic directors and heads of colleges. The Council was established in January 1986 and aims to encourage industry and higher education to work together and to represent their joint thinking to government. The Council's Director has been reported as being hesitant about formulating a permanent existence for the Council in view of the increasing collaboration between industry and higher education (THES, 24 June 1988, p.5). The chairman is the Rt.Hon.Lord Prior, Chairman of the General Electric Company (GEC), and the Director of the Council is Mr. Patrick Coldsteam. The Council's office is at 100, Park Village East, London, NW1 3SR.

The Council has so far published two papers, Towards a Partnership: Higher Education-Government-Industry (1987) and Towards a Partnership : The Company Response (1988). The articles on 'Industry and Higher Education' in the THES, 2 September 1988, include one which refers especially to the Council. In 1989 HMSO commenced publication of a series of booklets on collaboration between business and higher educa-tion which has the support of the Department of Trade and Industry and the Council for Industry and Higher Education. The titles so far pub-lished in the series are Policy and Strategy for Companies (1989), Policy and Strategy for Higher Education (1989), Getting Good Graduates (1990), Continuing Education and Training (1990), Organisation and Management in Higher Education (1990), and Research and Development (1990).

In 1989 the CIHE initiated a scheme known as the Partnership Awards Scheme for commending innovation in teaching and learning in higher education.

8. Council of University Classical Departments

The current Chairman is Professor P. P. Wiseman, University of Exeter, Department of Classics, The Queens Gate, Exeter, EX4 4QT. The Council organises a biennial conference. In 1990 the Council published a study of employers' attitudes, Ann Hughes Hallett and James Lapsley, Classics in the Market Place.

9. Council of University Management Schools

The Chairman of the Council of University Management Schools (CUMS) from 28 September 1990 to September 1993 will be Professor David Ashton, The Management School, University of Lancaster, Gillow House, Lancaster, LA1 4YX; the Administrator and secretariat of CUMS will also operate from this address.

10. Council of Validating Universities and Conference of Validating Universities.

The Conference of Validating Universities started life, in the late 1970s, as an informal gathering and did not adopt a formal constitution. The Conference normally meets once a year. Each university in the UK which is involved in validating higher education awards in institutions other than itself is entitled to send at least one representative. The Conference has no formal powers. Conference produces reports, but not minutes, of its proceedings and these are regarded as confidential to the universities involved in validation.

The Council of Validating Universities was established by the Conference in May 1982 and the Council subsequently adopted a constitution. The objects of the Council are "to keep under review the validation concerns of universities and to support and assist universities in their validation work." The Council's functions include the organisation of the Conference. The Council does not produce formal minutes: these are regarded as confidential to members. The Secretary (currently Mr. J.H.E. Wood, Secretary, School of Education, University of Lancaster, University House, Lancaster, LA1 4YW) holds the minute books dating from the Council's inception.

Neither Conference nor Council has any publications to its credit. Papers are produced for internal circulation (only).

11. Education Librarians Group, Library Association

It is understood that librarians working in universities have been/are members of this Group and have served on its committee, etc. Records of the Group, covering the period 1961-86, have recently been deposited in the Modern Records Centre, University of Warwick Library, ref. MSS.274. See too p.104.

12. Examining Groups

Examining Boards and Groups are not covered, with the sole exception of the Joint Matriculation Board (pp.98-9).

13. Joint University Council for Social and Public Administation

The Council was established in 1918 and consists of representatives of universities and polytechnics in Great Britain and Ireland which provide courses of study for training in social work, social administration and public administration.

The Conference Officer is Mrs. Dorothy Parry, Joint University Council for Social and Public Administration, Regent's College, Inner Circle, Regent's Park, London, NW1 4NS.

14. National Committee for Philosophy

The National Committee for Philosophy (NCP) was founded at a meeting of a Philosophical Action Committee in December 1985; concern had been expressed for some years at the effects of UGC cuts on philosophical studies in UK universities and the Action Committee's members represented a number of societies etc. with interests in philosophy. The NCP is representative of the philosophical profession in the UK, its purpose being to promote and foster all aspects of the teaching and study of philosophy at all levels in the UK. The NCP convenes an annual conference of professional philosophers, known as the Standing

Conference of Philosophers (SCP); all departments or sections teaching degree-level philosophy in UK universities, polytechnics, and colleges are eligible for membership of the SCP. The first SCP took place in July 1986. The NCP has made a number of representations and submissions to the UGC, the NAB, individual universities, etc.

The chairman of the NCP, Mr. George MacDonald Ross (Department of Philosophy, The University, Leeds, LS2 9JT), is the author of a type-script account of the NCP's 'Origins and Activities', August 1988.

15. National Council for Modern Languages in Higher and Further Education

The current Secretary is Dr. P. Gold, Department of Business and Languages, Sheffield City Polytechnic, Totley Hall Lane, Sheffield, S17 4AB.

16. National Universities Committee of the National Association of Local Government Officers

This Committee comprises elected district representatives who negotiate the terms and conditions of service and pay of clerical and related staffs in universities. The Committee's Secretariat is provided by NALGO, NALGO House, 1 Mabledon Place, London, WC1H 9AJ (tel: 071-388 2366).

Amongst the circulated minutes of committees, agendas, reports and related papers of NALGO committees etc. which Mr. Peter Morgan has deposited in the Modern Records Centre, University of Warwick Library (ref. MSS.262) are such papers for NALGO's National Universities Committee, 1973-85.

17. Standing Committee of University Drama Departments

The current Chairman is Professor David H. Bradby, Department of Drama and Theatre Studies, Royal Holloway and Bedford New College, Egham Hill, Egham, Surrey, TW20 OEX.

18. Standing Committee of University Professors and Heads of Archaeology Departments (SCUPHA)

The current Chairman is Professor Malcolm Todd, Department of History and Archaeology, Queen's Building, University of Exeter, Exeter, EX4 4QJ.

In early 1987 the Standing [Committee] submitted a report on the teaching of archaeology in Britain to the UGC. Inter alia, according to the THES, 6 March 1987, the report suggested that some departments should be merged to create a stronger science and wider geographical spread in the regions and called on the UGC to collaborate with the universities in planned restructuring of the subject.

19. Standing Committee of University Teachers of Turkish

Reference is made to the Committee in a letter (about the importance of modern Turkish studies) from its chairman, Professor C.H. Dodd, Middle East Centre, School of Oriental and African Studies, Malet Street, London, published in The Times, 19 November 1987.

20.   Standing Committee on Modern Greek in the Universities.

The current Chairman of the Committee is Dr. Peter A. Mackridge, Lecturer in Modern Greek, St.Cross College, Oxford, OX1 3LZ; the only other officer is the Secretary, Dr. D.W. Holton, Selwyn College, Cambridge.

21.   Standing Committee on University Studies in Africa.

The current Chairman of the Committee is Mr. Richard Rathbone, Department of History, School of Oriental and African Studies, University of London, Malet Street, London, WC1E 7HP.

22.   Standing Conference of Professors of Physics

The current Chairman of this Conference (SCPP) is Professor Brian Rainford, Department of Physics, University of Southampton.

23.   Universities and Industry Joint Committee

In 1970-72 the Confederation of British Industry published Industry, Science and Universities: Report of a Working Party on Universities and Industrial Research to the Universities and Industry Joint Committee and its two appendices, Replies from Industry... and Replies from Universities...

The CBI's archives have been deposited at the Modern Records Centre, University of Warwick Library, with additions periodically made since the initial deposit in 1979.

24.   Universities' Committee on Integrated Sandwich Courses

This committee organised a National Conference on Degree Sandwich Courses at the University of Bath 15-17 April 1975 and its [proceedings] were published by Bath U.P. in 1976.

25.   University Group on Defence Policy

The British Library's Catalogue reveals that this Group published pamphlets nos. 1 [etc.], London, 1959-?

(d)   Associations, Conferences, Consortia

1.   Association of Clinical Professors
The Secretary of the Association is Professor C.L. Berry, Department of Morbid Anatomy, The London Hospital Medical College, The London Hospital, London, E1 1BB.

2.   Association of Professors of Modern Languages at Technological Universities
The post of Chairman of the Association changes annually. The current (as at June 1990) Chairman is Professor A. Easson, Department of Modern Languages, University of Salford, Salford, M5 4WT.

3.   Association of Dutch Language Teachers
(Secretary : Dr. Colin Wimpory, Teeside Polytechnic Management Centre, Flatts Lane, Normanby, Cleveland, TS6 OQS)

In common, it is believed, with other Associations of language teachers (e.g. the Association of Teachers of Italian), the Association of Dutch Language Teachers (ADuLT) includes lecturers and students in universities amongst its membership.

The Association was founded in 1977 to promote contact among teachers of Dutch in all sectors of education and others interested in the teaching and study of Dutch in the United Kingdom. Contact between members is maintained through occasional thematic workshops, a two-day biennial conference (during which a General Meeting is held which elects the Committee of ADuLT), and the ADuLT Newsletter (which is published two or three times a year, and some of whose articles are written in Dutch).

Dutch is not a language normally taught at secondary schools like French or German and so there is no typical ADuLT member. Membership of ADuLT (currently around one hundred) consists partly of teachers of Dutch in secondary and higher education, together with adult education tutors and lecturers, teachers at the British or American Schools in The Hague, administrators, publishers, and translators in several countries, and those who are interested in the Low Countries or in studying Dutch.

ADuLT is a member of the Joint Council of Language Associations (JCLA), a national body that organizes a major conference on foreign language teaching each year. ADuLT is also represented on the National Congress on Languages in Education (NCLE), the National Council for Modern Languages in Higher and Further Education (NCML), and the Festival of Languages and Young Linguist of the Year Competition (FOLYLC). ADuLT also makes use of the services of the Centre for Information on Language Teaching and Research (CILT) and has links with the Internationale Vereniging voor Neerlandistiek (IVN; International Association for Dutch Studies) and the Nederlandse Taalunie (Dutch Language Union) whose work is comparable to that of the British Council.

4. Association of Student Counselling

The current Secretary is Mr. John Jenkinson, Student Services Centre, Plymouth Polytechnic, Drake Circus, Plymouth, PL4 8AA. The Association covers universities, polytechnics, and further education and other higher education institutions with student counsellors.

5. Association of University Departments of Theology and Religious Studies

The current Chairman is Professor J.D.G. Dunn, University of Durham, Department of Theology, Abbey House, Palace Green, Durham, DH1 3RS.

6. Conference of Agricultural Professors

The current Chairman is Professor John Prescott, Wye College, Ashford, Kent, TN25 5AH.

7. Conference of Professors of Accounting

The current Chairman is Professor A.M. Bourn, Department of Accounting and Management Economics, University of Southampton, Southampton, S09 5NH.

8. Conference of Professors of Applied Mathematics

The current Chairman is Professor S. Barnett, Department of Mathematics, University of Bradford, Richmond Road, Bradford, West Yorkshire, BD7 1DP.

9. Conference of Professors of Computer Science

The current Chairman is Professor F.H. Sumner, Department of Computer Science, University of Manchester, Manchester, M13 9PL.

10. Consortium of University Research Libraries

This Consortium (CURL) was formed in 1983 by the librarians of the seven universities in the UK with more than 10,000 students (Cambridge, Edinburgh, Glasgow, Leeds, London, Manchester, and Oxford). Reference is made to it in Alan F. Taylor (ed.), <u>Proceedings of the 72nd Annual Conference of the Scottish Library Association: In Search of Excellence, Peebles 1986</u> (Scottish Library Association, Motherwell, 1987).

CURL has established a database for bibliographic records at the University of Manchester Regional Computing Centre; the prime objective of this pilot project (which has been funded by the UGC for two-three years) is to pool the bibliographic record resources of the existing member libraries. It is intended that the database should become available to library users through JANET in due course.

At present (May 1990) CURL is seeking funding for the long term database (which is currently open to staff at all university libraries in the UK).

The Chairman of CURL is Mr. D. Cox, c/o University Library, Leeds, LS2 9JT.

11. Engineering Professors Conference

The current Secretary of the Conference (EPC) is Professor A.N. Bramley, Department of Mechanical Engineering, University of Bath, Claverton Down, Bath, BA2 7AY.

12. Heads of Geography Departments Conference
(formerly entitled Conference of Heads of Departments of Geography in Universities of the British Isles)

Jointly with the Human Geography Committee of SSRC published <u>Geography Departments of Universities and Polytechnics in the British Isles, theses in preparation, theses completed</u>, [1981].

The Secretary of the Conference is Dr. Colin Pooley, Department of Geography, University of Lancaster, Lancaster, LA1 4YB.

13. Heads of Physiology Departments

The current Chairman is Professor N.R. Saunders, School of Biochemical and Physiological Sciences, University of Southampton, Highfield, Southampton, SO9 5NH.

14. Heads of University Departments of Mathematics and Statistics

The current Chairman is Professor Ian Roxburgh, Department of Mathematical Sciences, Queen Mary and Westfield College, Mile End Road, London, E1 4NS.

15. National Association for Tertiary Education for the Deaf

Announcement in THES, 19 February 1988, of an open meeting after its annual meeting in London on 23 April 1988, with further information being available upon sending a SAE to Chris Green, Rivendell, Brookside, Bakewell, Derbyshire.

16. National Association of University Music Staff

The current Chairman of the Association (NAUMS) is Professor Sebastian Forbes, Department of Music, University of Surrey.

17. Professors and Heads of University Departments of Sociology

The current Chairman is Professor John R. Urry, Department of Sociology, University of Lancaster, Lancaster, LA1 4YW.

18. Standing Conference of Directors of Latin American Studies Centres

The current Chairman is Professor Leslie Bethell, Institute of Latin American Studies, 31 Tavistock Square, London, WC1H 9HA.

19. Standing Conference of Heads of Schools of Architecture

The current Chairman of the Conference (SCOSA) is Professor Michael Brawne, School of Architecture and Building Engineering, University of Bath.

20. Universities' Power Engineering Conference

The aim of the conference is to provide a forum for all aspects of electric power engineering, with contributions from a wide range of universities, polytechnics, and industry. The 24th conference was due to be held in September 1989 at The Queen's University of Belfast. The Chairman and Conference Organiser changes from year to year, the current holder (1989) being Dr. A. Refsum, Department of Electrical and Electronic Engineering, The Queen's University of Belfast, Ashby Building, Stranmills Road, Belfast, BT9 5AH, Northern Ireland.

21. University Hospitals Association (England and Wales)

The Executive Secretary of the Association is Professor D.R. Wood, c/o Department of Pharmacology, Worsley Building, University of Leeds, LS2 9JT.

(e) Political Associations

1. Conservative Collegiate Forum

Formed in January 1987, the Forum took over the functions of the Federation of Conservative Students. Covers Conservative Associations in

universities and polytechnics. The CCF may be reached c/o Conservative Central Office, 32 Smith Square, London, SW1P 3HH.

As part of its attack on the National Union of Students, CCF has published reports, Perestroika on Campus : Can Students Escape their Closed Shop? (1989) and A Long March into Obscurity (1990).

2. Federation of Conservative Students

The Federation was founded in May 1930 as the Federation of University Conservative and Unionist Associations, changing its name to the Federation of Conservative Students (FCS) in 1967. The FCS was disbanded in November 1986 and its functions were shortly afterwards taken over by a new body, the Conservative Collegiate Forum.

The aims of the FCS were to encourage the formation and maintenance of active student Conservative associations in all institutions of higher education; to provide assistance and information to such associations; to express the students' viewpoint to the Conservative Party; to recruit active and able party members; to provide a common platform for political discussion; and to speak as a representative body of Conservative students.

According to Chris Cook et al., Sources in British Political History 1900-1951 Vol.1 (1975), p.290, the FCS's Committee minutes for the post-war years, and in some cases dating from 1930, were (and it is believed still are) preserved at Conservative Central Office, 32 Smith Square, London, SW1P 3HH.

3. National Association of Conservative Graduates

A report on a meeting of the Association in London, July 1975, appeared in The Times, 16 July 1975, under the heading 'Universities' freedom is under threat, Tory spokesman says'.

The NACG may be reached c/o Conservative Central Office, 32 Smith Square, London, SW1P 3HH. The current Chairman is Mr. Paul Branigan (113 Vale Road, Chesham, Bucks., HP5 3HP).

4. The University Labour Federation

Membership of the Federation was acquired through membership of the Socialist Society of a university or college, or, if not at a university, by becoming a subscribing member. The Federation was based at 22 Key Street, Cambridge, by the 1940s.

Its publications included:-

University Forward (the organ of ULF, issued twice termly), 1935-43

The People's Education (ULF Pamphlet No.11) [1943]

Songs of the People [? by 1943]

and the following, all published by c.1943: Students in Action, Medicine and Socialism, Science and Socialism, and Why Socialism?

(f) Religious and Humanist Bodies

In addition to the Universities and Colleges Christian Fellowship and the Student Christian Movement, which are covered in the survey, a number of university-related bodies may be located by reference to denominational directories, etc., including:-

1. Catholic Student Council

   The Council's aim is to encourage and develop the commitment of Catholic students in higher education to the Church's mission in the world today. The Council (which was established in 1974) is the successor body to the Union of Catholic Students. The office of the Council is at 186 St.Paul's Road, Balsall Heath, Birmingham, West Midlands, B12 8LZ.

2. International Catholic Movement for Intellectual and Cultural Affairs, and the International Movement of Catholic Students

   The address of the General Secretariat of the International Catholic Movement for Intellectual and Cultural Affairs (ICMICA), whose members are graduates, and of the International Movement of Catholic Students, whose members are undergraduates, is Boite Postale 1062, 1701 Fribourg, Switzerland (tel: 937-26-26-49). The current Secretaries are Victor Karunan (ICMICA) and Etienne Bisimwa respectively. The Bureau de Coordination of the International Movement of Catholic Students is at 171 Rue de Rennes, 75006 Paris, France.

3. The Churches Commission on Overseas Students

   Established in 1975 with an invitation by the British Council of Churches to member churches, missionary societies and other Christian organisations, the Commission seeks to communicate current concerns regarding overseas students and to assist churches to respond to those concerns. The Commission's office is at 2 Chester House, Pages Lane, London, N10 1PR.

4. Union of Jewish Students of the United Kingdom and Ireland (formerly the Inter-University Jewish Federation of Great Britain and Ireland, established in 1919) Hillel House, 1/2 Endsleigh Street, London, WC1H ODS.

5. United Society for the Propagation of the Gospel

   The USPG was formed in 1965 by the merger of the Society for the Propagation of the Gospel (which had been in existence since 1701) and the Universities' Mission to Central Africa (founded in response to Livingstone's call in 1857); the Cambridge Mission in Delhi (1877) merged in 1968. The USPG is a voluntary society based in the Church of England and serving Anglican and united churches in mission in about 40 countries (including the United Kingdom and Eire). For the earlier history of the Universities' Mission to Central Africa, see George Herbert Wilson, The History of the Universities' Mission to Central Africa (UMCA, London, 1936).

6. University Catholic Federation of Great Britain

A consultative body to discuss problems in the fields of university and higher education, whose current Secretary is Dr. P.J. Aggett, 3 Emmanuel Court, Westbourne Avenue, London, W5 6JP (Catholic Directory 1987).

At a meeting of the Federation in 1942 the Newman Association was founded. The Association is a member of the International Catholic Association for Intellectual and Cultural Affairs and its Hon.Secretary is Miss Brenda Tweed, 22 Cortayne Road, London, SW6 3QA (Catholic Directory 1988). An entry for the Association appears in Chris Cook et al., Sources in British Political History 1900-1951, Vol.1, 1975, p.205.

7. University Humanist Federation

Established in c.1959, holding annual conferences (some of whose Proceedings have been published) and commencing publication of a Bulletin, Ethic, in 1959. The Federation was later transformed into the Students Humanist Federation but has since lapsed. However, two Humanist student groups have recently been established, at Cambridge (Cambridge University Humanist Workshop, including non-University students) and at Swansea, both of which are affiliated to the British Humanist Association, 13 Prince of Wales Terrace, London, W8.

(g) The University of the Third Age

L'Université du Troisième Age has existed in France since 1973, the concept spreading to other European countries and being introduced in the United Kingdom in 1981, the University of the Third Age in Cambridge becoming the basis for a variety of local developments. In the UK the University is an association of autonomous bodies; there is a national liaison committee, and a national Third Age Trust (a registered charity) to which local groups may be affiliated.
For further information one can read the papers on U3A in Britain in Universities Quarterly, vol. 38 no.1, 1984, and, more generally, Eric Midwinter (ed.), Mutual Aid Universities (Croom Helm, Beckenham, 1984), and contact the University's office, 6 Parkside Gardens, London, SW19 5EY. Also, as regards the background, see A Fresh Map of Life : The Emergence of the Third Age (Weidenfeld and Nicolson, 1989) by Peter Laslett, one of the founders of U3A.

(h) Councils, Associations, etc. in Scotland and Northern Ireland

There are a number of bodies in Scotland and Northern Ireland which should appear in the survey, in addition to those few which are covered in this first edition. They include:-

1. Northern Ireland Council for Continuing Education

The Northern Ireland Council for Continuing Education, established in 1974, was reconstituted in 1982 with a wider advisory role and further reconstituted in 1987. The future of the Council is currently (1989) under review. The Secretary of the Council is Miss S. Pidduck, Department of Education for Northern Ireland, Rathgael House, Balloo Road, Bangor, County Down, BT19 2PR.

2. Northern Ireland Council for Postgraduate Medical Education

    Established in 1970 by the Department of Health and Social Services for Northern Ireland. Offices at 5 Annadale Avenue, Belfast, BT7 3JH.

3. Scottish Institute of Adult and Continuing Education

    30 Rutland Square
    Edinburgh
    EH1 2BW

    Its members comprise all the Regional and Island Education Authorities, the three Districts of the WEA in Scotland, the Scottish universities, the OU in Scotland, many colleges, etc., and individuals. It organises conferences, operates an information and documentation centre, and its publications include Scottish Journal of Adult Education and Scottish Handbook of Adult and Continuing Education : A comprehensive directory and guide... (current edition, 1986).

4. Scottish Universities Council for Studies in Education

    The current Chairman of the Council is Professor Nigel Grant
    Department of Education
    University of Glasgow
    G12 8QQ

5. Scottish Universities Council on Entrance

    12 The Links
    St.Andrews
    Fife
    KY16 9JB

    Established in 1969, replacing the former Scottish Universities Entrance Board. The Council consists of representatives of all the Scottish universities. It publishes an annual Compendium of Information.

6. Scottish Universities Physical Education Association

    The current (March 1988) Secretary is Mr. William Hunter
    Director of the Department of Physical Education and Recreation
    University of Strathclyde and the Treasurer is Mr. Alan Francis
    Department of Physical Education and Sports Science
    University of Glasgow
    77 Oakfield Avenue
    Glasgow
    G12 8LT

7. Scottish Universities Research and Reactor Centre

    Birniehill
    East Kilbride
    Glasgow

    The Scottish Universities Research and Reactor Centre (SURRC) was established in 1963 to provide facilities for research and teaching in nuclear science and its application in a wide variety of subjects. The

Centre is operated by a consortium of the Universities of Edinburgh, Glasgow and Strathclyde, with the Universities of Aberdeen and St.Andrews as associate members. It is funded by earmarked contributions to each university's recurrent grant from the UGC, with additional support from the Research Councils, government, and industrial contracts. It publishes an annual report.

8.   Standing Committee of the Scottish Universities

The current Chairman and Secretary of the Standing Committee are Professor George McNicol, Principal of the University of Aberdeen, and Mr. N.R.D. Begg, Secretary of the University of Aberdeen, respectively, their address being University of Aberdeen, Regent Walk, Aberdeen, AB9 1FX, Scotland; the term of office of the Chairman and Secretary is two years. Until 1988, when it was restructured, the Committee was known as the Annual Conference of Courts of the Scottish Universities.

9.   Universities Council for Adult and Continuing Education (Scotland)

c/o Mr. C. George
Director of Adult Education and Extra-Mural Studies
University of St.Andrews
Mansefield
3 St.Mary's Place
St.Andrews
Fife
KY16 9UY

(i)   Bodies which upon further investigation were found not to cover tertiary education

Amongst these bodies are:-
1.   The Asbestosis Research Council (ARC), which was established in 1957 by private arrangement between the major UK asbestos manufacturing companies.

2.   the Conference for Independent Further Education which was founded in 1973 and is a professional association of Principals which aims to share information and exchange ideas in order to maintain the highest professional standards in independent colleges in Britain preparing students for the GCE examinations and university admission. It publishes a comprehensive handbook, Your Choice (ed. Robin Bellerby; 1982), and a List of Members and Guide to Courses.

(j)   Bodies whose current existence, etc. cannot be established

British Universities Society of Arts

Reference is made to this Society in the 5th edition (1977) of G.P. Henderson and S.P.A. Henderson (eds.), Directory of British Associations... (CBD Research Ltd., Beckenham, Kent) where it is noted that it was founded in 1959 by F.E. Baker (who was its Chairman); that its headquarters was at 32 Shaftesbury Avenue, London, W.1; that it had branches in Tokyo, Hong Kong, Bangkok, Johannesburg, and Nairobi; that it had 3,000 individual members in the UK and 2,500 in Japan; that its object was educational exchanges between persons following a recognised course of study in Arts or Science beyond secondary education; and that its publications comprised an Annual Report and Newsletter and List of possible employers and institutions. Consultation of more recent reference works, telephone directories, etc. has failed to reveal its existence nowadays or where its records (if any survive) might be found.

(k) <u>Bodies and pressure groups established in the last few years, in response to pressures on higher education</u>

1. Committee of University Autonomy, later the Council for Academic Autonomy

The Committee of University Autonomy was established in early 1988 with the launch of a petition opposing "the current threat to our universities and colleges and to their intellectual liberties" posed by the Education Reform Bill. The Committee aimed to monitor implementation of the Bill once it had been enacted, and in the meantime pressed the Government to accept amendments to the Bill. The Secretary of the Committee was Dr. Anthony Smith, Department of Sociology, London School of Economics and Political Science, Houghton Street, London, WC2A 2AE.

The Committee became the Council for Academic Autonomy later in 1988, Dr. Smith becoming Secretary of the Council's Steering Committee. According to press reports, the Council is concerned to monitor all cases of infringement of academic freedom in British universities and colleges; it will monitor the activities of the university commissioners who will be amending university charters and statutes.

2. Higher Education for the Labour Party (HELP)

A Labour Party sponsored campaign launched with an advertisement in <u>The Guardian</u>, 9 June 1986, which appeared above the names of a large number of persons working in and concerned with higher education. Donations were invited and were to be sent to Mr. Giles Radice, M.P., London, SW1 OBR.

3. History at the Universities Defence Group

Referred to by the President of the Historical Association in the Association's magazine, <u>The Historian</u>, no.9, Winter 1985/86.

The Group is not under the auspices of the Historical Association but works in conjunction with it. Correspondence for the current Convenor and the current Secretary of the Group may be addressed c/o The Historical Association, 59a Kennington Park Road, London, SE11 4JH, who will forward it.

For a background article on the plight of History at the universities see Huw Richards, 'Dating game fades to grey', in <u>The Times Higher Education Supplement</u>, 28 April 1989, p.9. <u>THES</u>, 27 October 1989, includes a report on the Group's annual plenary meeting.

4. Save British Science

A pressure group launched in January 1986 with support among university and research council scientists. Its aim is to put across the case for more research funding in Britain. In SBS' report, <u>Science Strategy for</u>

the 1990s (1989), seven major policies are proposed, relating to schools, higher education, the brain drain, Europe, research and development, industry, and science-industry collaboration. For the background, see John Mulvey and Denis Noble, 'Saving British Science', AUT Bulletin, No.165, 1989, pp.6-7.

For information contact John Mulvey, the Hon. Secretary, Save British Science Society, Box 241, Oxford, OX1 3QQ.

5.   University Museums Group

Formed on 30 April 1987, in response to the crisis situation in university museums, to which reference was made in several papers delivered at the Museums Association's Annual Conference in July 1986, the papers of Mr. Alan Warhurst and Professor Frank Willett on the subject being published in Museums Journal, vol.86 no.3, December 1986, pp. 137-144. In her report on university museums in Scotland, A World of Learning : University Collectons in Scotland (HMSO, 1990), Laura Drysdale proposes the establishment of direct links between the Group and the UFC.

The Hon. Secretary of the Group is Mr. Alan Warhurst, Director, The Manchester Museum, The University, Manchester, M13 9PL.

(1)   Royal Colleges, etc.

Whilst in the interim report submitted to the Specialist Repositories Group's Forum in 1980 a brief entry appeared for the Royal Society, it should be noted that entries for the Royal Society of London and for the majority of the Royal Colleges (etc.) appear in Janet Foster and Julia Sheppard, British Archives : A Guide to Archive Resources in the United Kingdom (Macmillan, 2nd ed., 1989).

(m)   University Constituencies

The Representation of the People Act, 1918 (7&8 Geo.5 c.64) made provision for a university franchise, the university constituencies being:-

England and Wales:

University of Oxford	2
" " Cambridge	2
" " London	1
" " Wales	1

Universities of Durham, Manchester,
Liverpool, Leeds, Sheffield, Birmingham,
and Bristol ('Combined English
Universities Constituency')   2

Scotland:

Universities of St.Andrews, Glasgow,
Aberdeen, and Edinburgh   3

The franchise was granted, initially to men only, to those who, inter alia, had received a degree (other than an honorary degree) at any university forming, or forming part of, the constituency, or in the case of the Scottish universities was qualified under the Representation of the People (Scotland) Act, 1868 (or in the case of the University of Dublin had received a degree, other than an honorary degree, at the University or had obtained a Scholarship or Fellowship in the University).

The governing body of every university forming, or forming part of, a constituency had to keep a register of persons entitled to vote, but it was not necessary to prepare an absent voters list. At a contested election for a university constituency where there were two or more members to be elected, any election of the full number of members was according to the principle of proportional representation, each elector having one transferable vote.

Almost the whole of the 1918 Act was repealed by the Representation of the People Act 1948 (11 & 12 Geo. 6 c.65) : the university constituencies were abolished.

Records of the Combined English Universities Constituency

The University Archives, Liverpool holds (a) copies of the printed lists of electors of the University of Liverpool entitled to vote for the Constituency for the following dates: 1918, 1921-27, 1929-39, 1944-45 (each entry providing number, Christian name and surname, postal address, first degree (B.A. etc.) and year of admission to first degree) (ref. S.2560- 2562), and (b) a University of Liverpool Parliamentary Registration Receipt Book, 1928-47 (ref. S.2087).

The Special Collections Department, Sydney Jones Library, University of Liverpool holds the papers of Miss Eleanor Rathbone (1872-1946) who was M.P. (Independent) for the Combined English Universities Constituency 1929- 46, the papers including election addresses, correspondence etc. (ref. Rathbone Papers XIV).

Sheffield University Archives hold some papers comprising correspondence, election addresses and official papers for elections and by-elections in the Constituency.

See too entry for the Congress of University Convocations and Graduate Associations (p.81-3).

(n) Holiday Companies etc.

University Holidays Limited

Incorporated as a company on 15 December 1972 (no. 1,087,019); dissolved on 20 December 1983; latterly had offices at 8 Herbal Hill, London, EC1R 5JB.

University Students Abroad Limited

Incorporated as a company on 30 December 1963 (no. 786,191), its offices are now at Lowlands, Chorleywood Road, Rickmansworth, Hertfordshire, WD3 4ES. The Companies Registration Office has received the company's annual returns including the most recent (for year to 30 September 1988).

(o) Overseas bodies

Mr. A.W. Mabbs in his Guide to the Archives of International Organisations, Part III: Archives of other international inter-governmental organisations and non-governmental organisations (UNESCO, 1985) includes details for two such organisations in the university field, the International Association of University Professors and Lecturers and the International Union of Students. This current survey includes these and a dozen or so additional other international organisations but reference to the Year Books etc. referred to in the Bibliography indicates that there are a number of additional bodies, some covering a particular continent and others covering several continents, such as the International Association of Technological University Libraries (IATUL) whose eleventh biennial conference was held in Oxford in April 1985, and the United Nations University (sponsored jointly by the UN and UNESCO), which has its headquarters in Tokyo and which works through collaborating institutions in different parts of the world and which has over thirty Associated Institutions.

The list of organisations in the USA which have CUA correspondents (see p.280-1) gives some slight indication of the range and number of national organisations in the tertiary education field which one can expect to find overseas.

BIBLIOGRAPHY

This brief bibliography aims to provide (1) a list of reference works (through the use of which the reader can obtain further information about a particular institution, society, etc.); (2) a select list of guides to information sources and repositories (principally archives); (3) a reference to the wealth of information to be derived from Government and Parliamentary publications; (4) a short list of books and articles on the history of university education in the UK which complements references to specific books and journal articles in the individual entries for each body covered in the main text; and (5) a list of (and an introduction to) the principal indexing and abstracting journals and also the journals which cover higher education.

1 (a) Bibliographies, (b) Directories, (c) Year Books

(a) Bibliographies

John P. Powell (compiler), Universities and University Education : A Select Bibliography, (The National Foundation for Educational Research in England and Wales, Occasional Publication No.14, Slough, 1966).

Primarily a guide to the British university system and the published literature associated with it, though a section devoted to higher education in the USA is included.

John P. Powell (compiler), Universities and University Education : A Select Bibliography 1965-70 and supplement (to the above guide) (The National Foundation for Educational Research in England and Wales, Slough, 1971).

John P. Powell (compiler), Higher Education : A Select Bibliography Vol.3: 1970-75 and supplement to Vol.1 (Higher Education Research and Development Society of Australasia, Sydney, Australia, 1977).

Harold Silver and S. John Teague, The History of British Universities 1800 - 1969, excluding Oxford and Cambridge : a bibliography (Society for Research into Higher Education, London, 1970).

Thomas Kelly (ed.), A Select Bibliography of Adult Education in Great Britain including works published to the end of the year 1972 (National Institute of Adult Education, London, 1974). The first and second editions, covering works published up to the end of 1961, were published by the National Institute in 1952 and 1962 respectively.

J.E. Thomas and J.H. Davies (eds.), A Select Bibliography of Adult Continuing Education in Great Britain including works published to the end of the year 1981 (National Institute of Adult Continuing Education, Leicester, 1984).

J.H. Davies and J.E. Thomas (eds.), A Select Bibliography of Adult Continuing Education (National Institute of Adult Continuing Education, 5th ed., revised and updated, 1988); contains references to material published up to the end of 1987.

P.H.J.H. Gosden, Educational administration in England and Wales: a bibliographical guide (University of Leeds Institute of Education, 1967; Paper No.6).

D.A. Howell, A bibliography of educational administration in the United Kingdom (NFER Publishing Co.Ltd., [1978]).

Michael Berry, Teacher Training Institutions in England and Wales : a bibliographical guide to their history (Society for Research into Higher Education Ltd., London, 1973).

C.W.J. Higson (ed.), Sources for the History of Education : a list of material (including school books) contained in the Libraries of the Institutes and Schools of Education, together with works from the Libraries of the Universities of Nottingham and Reading (The Library Association, London, 1967); also C.W.J. Higson (ed.), Supplement to Sources for the History of Education...(The Library Association, London, 1976).

James Craigie, A Bibliography of Scottish Education before 1872 (University of London Press Ltd., 1970) and A Bibliography of Scottish Education 1872-1972 (University of London Press Ltd., 1974).

R.R. Bilboul and F.L. Kent (eds.), Retrospective Index to Theses of Great Britain and Ireland, 1716-1950 (European Bibliographical Center (Clio Press), Oxford, 1975-77); Vol.1 Social Sciences and Humanities, Vol.2 Applied Sciences and Technology, Vol.3 Life Sciences, Vol.4 Physical Sciences, and Vol.5 Chemical Sciences.

Index to Theses accepted for Higher Degrees in the Universities of Great Britain and Ireland and [Vol.18,1970, to date] the Council for National Academic Awards, Vols.1 (for 1950-51, published 1953)- to date, published by Aslib, London. The scope of this publication was extended from Vol.35, 1987, onwards to provide, additionally, Abstracts of theses as the changed and current title (Index to Theses with Abstracts accepted...) notes. The contents of the volumes are ordered according to a subject classification and the volumes have subject indexes.

Victor F. Gilbert and Colin Holmes (compilers), Theses and Dissertations on the History of Education, presented at British and Irish universities between 1900-1976 (History of Education Society, 1979; No.6 in the Society's Guides to Sources in the History of Education series). Covers theses and dissertations concerning the history of education in many countries, including the U.K. There are separate sections devoted to Higher education: universities, Adult and workers' education, etc. There are indices to persons, places, subjects, and authors.

The Society for Research into Higher Education's publications include a Register of Research into Higher Education...mainly in the United Kingdom (first published in 1975) and a Register of Research into Higher Education in Western Europe (first published in 1973). The Society is based at the University of Surrey, Guildford.

<u>Current Research in Britain</u>, published annually (since 1985) by the British Library (in place of <u>Research in British Universities, Polytechnics and Colleges</u>, which has been produced by the British Library since 1979), appears in four volumes : <u>Physical Sciences, Biological Sciences, Social Sciences</u>, and <u>The Humanities</u>. Each volume includes separate indexes of names, study areas, and keywords. The volume on <u>The Humanities</u> is published biennially, the other volumes in the series annually.

John M. Fletcher (ed.), <u>The History of European Universities: Work in Progress and Publications: 1 1977 -5 1981</u> (Department of Modern Languages, University of Aston in Birmingham, 1978-82).

Volumes VII (1988) onwards of the annual international journal <u>The History of Universities</u> will include a bibliography for the penultimate year of works relating to the history of universities, and update the material previously published in <u>Work in Progress and Publications</u> and add items omitted for the period 1977-85.

Philip G. Altbach, David H. Kelly, and Jan Kluczynski, <u>Higher Education in International Perspective : A Survey and Bibliography</u> (Mansell Publishing Limited, London and New York, 1985).

Philip G. Altbach, <u>Higher Education in Developing Countries : A Select Bibliography</u> (Centre for International Affairs, Harvard University, 1970; Occasional Papers in International Affairs No.24).

Robert L. Collison (editor-in-chief), <u>World Bibliographical Series</u> (Clio Press, Oxford, Santa Barbara, and Denver, 1978-). This series will eventually cover every country in the world; a separate volume is devoted to each country. Each volume comprises annotated entries on published works dealing with, inter alia, education in the country concerned.

Th.D. Dimitrov (compiler and editor), <u>World Bibliography of International Documentation</u>, 2 vols. (UNIFO Publishers Ltd., New York, 1981). Vol.I covers International Organisations, Activities, etc. and Vol.II covers Politics and World Affairs, Periodicals, Conferences, and includes indexes.

<u>International Bibliography, Information, Documentation; Publications of the United Nations system</u>, Vols. 1-10, 1973-82, published by Bowker, New York; continued as <u>International Bibliography: Publications of Intergovernmental Organizations</u>, Vols. 11- , 1983- , published quarterly by UNIPUB, Lanham, Maryland, U.S.A. (includes publications of the Council of Europe, OECD, United Nations, and UNESCO; the subject classifications employed include Education, with sub-divisions for Adult Education, Higher Education, International Education, etc.)

<u>Saggio Bibliografico per un servizio di documentazione dell' amministrazione universitaria : Serie prima</u> (L'archivio storico dell' Universita, Bologna, 2nd ed., 1987). As part of its 900th anniversary celebrations in 1988, the University of Bologna is presenting a new library conceived for the collecting and exhibiting of all literature published by universities of the world on their history : the University has contacted universities

throughout the world seeking copies of such works. The works collected will form the basis of a catalogue which will be published. Saggio Bibliografico...Serie prima lists 868 works published in Italy, France, USA, UK, etc., with separate indexes of universities (and international associations, etc.), authors, and subjects.

(b) Directories

principally relating to Great Britain and Ireland

C.A.P. Henderson (ed.), Current British Directories : a guide to directories published in the British Isles (C.B.D. Research Ltd., Beckenham, Kent, 11th ed., 1988).

G.P. Henderson and S.P.A. Henderson (eds.), Directory of British Associations and Associations in Ireland (C.B.D. Research Ltd., Beckenham, Kent; 9th ed., 1988).

Lindsay Sellar (ed.), Councils, Committees & Boards : a handbook of advisory, consultative, executive & similar bodies in British public life (C.B.D. Research Ltd., Beckenham, Kent; 7th ed., 1989).

Lindsay Sellar (ed.), Centres & Bureaux : a directory of concentrations of effort, information and expertise (C.B.D. Research Ltd., Beckenham, Kent, 1987).
Includes entries for the Central Bureau for Educational Visits and Exchanges (established in 1948 by the British Government and UNESCO) and the Scottish Universities Research and Reactor Centre (SURRC; established in 1963).

Patricia Millard (ed.), Trade Associations and Professional Bodies of the United Kingdom (Pergamon Press, Oxford, etc., 8th ed., 1987).

Whitaker's Almanack
An annual publication which presents a wealth of information about public affairs, government, industry, finance, commerce, social usage and the arts; with a full index. Includes an Education Directory (covers the universities, polytechnics, etc. of Great Britain) and an alphabetically arranged directory of the 'principal' British and Irish societies and institutions (name, year of foundation, address, and names of chairman and/or secretary).

Ellen M. Codlin (ed.) Aslib Directory [of] Information Sources [in the United Kingdom]: Volume 1: Science, Technology and Commerce (Aslib, London; 5th ed., 1982) and Volume 2 : the Social Sciences, Medicine and the Humanities (Aslib, London; 5th ed., 1984).

Alphabetically arranged, each entry identifying the organisation concerned: its address and telephone number, nature of the organisation, subject coverage, special information service, and publications.

Ellen M. Codlin (ed.), <u>Shorter Aslib Directory of Information Sources in the United Kingdom</u> (Aslib, London, 1986).
Alphabetically arranged, each entry identifying the organisation concerned : its address and telephone number, nature of the organisation, subject coverage, special information service, special or rare collections held, and publications.

Andrew Pates, Martin Good, and Alastair Thomson (eds.), <u>The Education Factbook : An A-Z Guide to Education and Training in Britain</u> (Macmillan Press, London, 1983).

<u>Scottish Education Directory</u> (Carrick Publishing, Ayr, 1987). The first edition of a new directory dealing with all sectors of Scottish education.

<u>Voluntary Organisations : An NCVO Directory 1985/86</u> (Bedford Square Press of the National Council for Voluntary Organisations, London, 1985).

<u>Public Bodies</u> (HMSO, for the Management and Personnel Office of the Cabinet Office).

An annual publication (<u>Public Bodies 1987</u>, etc.), this book provides brief details about public bodies for which Ministers have a degree of accountability. It includes non-departmental public bodies but excludes central government departments. For each body, the details include number of staff employed, expenditure, and how the body's annual report may be obtained. Covers the Research Councils, British Council, CNAA, ABRC, Computer Board for Universities and Research Councils, Scottish Tertiary Education Advisory Council, and Welsh Committee for Postgraduate Medical and Dental Education. Alphabetical index.

international

<u>The World of Learning</u> (Europa Publications Ltd., London). Now published (annually) in one volume, previously in two volumes. Lists principal learned societies and professional associations, (as well as universities etc.) of each country, each entry providing address, date founded and purpose, and titles of annual publications. The bodies covered include, in the case of the UK, the Royal Society, the Royal Colleges, the CVCP (with references to the associated bodies serviced from the Committee's Secretariat such as SCUE, UAP, UCNTS, and the Clinical Academic Staff Salaries Committee), and the UGC. Includes international organizations (with separate Education Section). Full alphabetical index (of institutions). 40th ed., 1989. First ed., 1947.

<u>International Handbook of Universities and other Institutions of Higher Education</u> (Macmillan Publishers Ltd., London, for International Association of Universities; 11th ed., 1989). Covers universities and other institutions of higher learning in over 110 countries excluding the USA and the Commonwealth which have their own handbooks (see elsewhere in this section). First published in 1959. Published every two years.

<u>World List of Universities</u> 18th ed., Macmillan, 1990).
   Compiled by the International Association of Universities, Part I lists establishments alphabetically by country and Part II is a guide to the principal international and regional organisations concerned with higher education and student affairs.

<u>World Guide to Higher Education : A Comparative Survey of Systems, Degrees and Qualifications</u>, 2nd ed., The UNESCO Press, Paris, 1982; compiled by the IAU for UNESCO.

R.W. Adams (ed.), <u>Directory of European Professional & Learned Societies</u> (C.B.D. Research Ltd., Beckenham, Kent, 4th ed., 1989).

   This directory does not include international or pan-European associations (most of which are listed in <u>Pan-European Associations</u>, C.B.D. Research Ltd., <u>Europa Year Book</u>, Europa Publications Ltd., London, etc.), nor associations in the UK and the Republic of Ireland (covered by the <u>Directory of British Associations...</u>).

J. Cameron, R. Cowen, B. Holmes, P. Hurst, and M. McLean (eds.), <u>International Handbook of Education Systems</u> (John Wiley & Sons, Chichester, etc.):-

   Vol.I   <u>Europe and Canada</u> (Brian Holmes, ed.), 1983
   Vol.II   <u>Africa and the Middle East</u> (John Cameron and Paul Hurst, eds.), 1983
   Vol.III <u>Asia, Australasia and Latin America</u> (Robert Cowen and Martin McLean, eds.), 1984.

<u>American Universities and Colleges</u> (Walker de Gruyter, New York and Berlin, for the American Council on Education, Washington, USA; 1st ed., 1928; 12th ed., 1983).

<u>Correspondents with overseas organisations: a note</u>

The <u>Newsletter</u> of the Conference of University Administrators (CUA) publishes (normally annually, in one of its issues) a list of CUA Correspondents with overseas organisations. The organisations listed in the July 1987 <u>Newsletter</u> (No.59) which have CUA correspondents are:-

(a) <u>USA</u>

   American Association of Collegiate Registrars and Admissions Officers (AACRAO)
   American Association of University Administrators (AAUA)
   American Council on Education (ACE)
   Association of College and University Housing Officers (ACUHO)
   Association of Institutional Research (AIR)
   Association of Physical Plant Administrators (APPA)
   Council for the Advancement and Support of Education (CASE)
   International Educational Exchange Liaison Group (IEELG)

International Education Research Foundation
National Association of College and University Business Officers
(NACUBO)
National Association of College and University Food Services
(NACUFS)
National Association of Foreign Student Affairs (NAFSA)
Society for College and University Planning
(SCUP)

(b) Canada

Canadian Association of University Business Officers (CAUBO)

(c) Australia

Australian Institute of Tertiary Education Administrators
(AITEA)

(d) Belgium

The Vlaamse Universitaire Raad

(e) France

Groupe Permanent des Secrétaires Généraux d'Universités

(f) Netherlands

UNIDOEL

The Newsletter also lists CUA Correspondents for overseas countries
without identified organisations. The CUA Newsletter also, in its
International News section, has reports etc. on the activities of the
above and 'other' bodies (such as the periodic International Meeting of
Tertiary Educational Administrators, which is organised by the CUA's
International Committee, the fifth such meeting being held in Sydney,
Australia, 26 July - 1 August 1987).

(c) Year Books

Education Year Book (Longman, Harlow)

Of more relevance to secondary education. Includes Government Education
Departments (listing, for instance, the responsibilities of the various
Divisions of the Further and Higher Education Branches of the DES).
Includes lists of the GCE Examining Boards (on which universities are
represented, e.g. the Southern Universities' Joint Board for School
Examinations, drawn from the Universities of Bath, Bristol, Exeter,
Reading, Southampton, and Surrey), CSE Examining Boards, and research
and advisory bodies, such as the Advisory Council for Adult and
Continuing Education, the Council for Tertiary Education (Scotland), the
Schools Council, the Standing Conference on University Entrance, UCCA,
and the Scottish Universities Council on Entrance, and the Research
Councils.

Year Book of Adult Continuing Education (National Institute of Adult Continuing Education, Leicester)

The Directory section includes Broadcasting (authorities, etc.), Education Journals, Local Education Authorities, Ministry of Defence, Polytechnics, Professional Associations (including NIACE Council members), Regional Adult Education Organisations, Regional Advisory Councils (for Further Education), Universities, WEA (including District Offices and Secretaries), Additional Organisations (e.g. British Association of Settlements and Social Action Centres), sections on Adult and Continuing Education in Scotland and Northern Ireland, and Overseas Contacts.

Commonwealth Universities Yearbook (Association of Commonwealth Universites) (see entry for the ACU)

The Europa Year Book : A World Survey (First published in 1926; since 1960 it has appeared in annual two-volume editions).

1987 edition (Europa Publications Ltd., London, 1987) :
Vol. I	(International organizations - including the United Nations, and its commissions, bodies, and agencies, the Commonwealth, the Council of Europe, the European Communities, Organisation for Economic Co-operation and Development, Association of African Universities, Association of Arab Universities, Association of Caribbean Universities and Research Institutes, Association of Partially or Wholly French-Language Universities, Association of South-East Asian Institutions of Higher Learning, International Association of Universities, International Association of University Professors and Lecturers, International Federation of Catholic Universities, International Federation of University Women, Organization of the Catholic Universities of Latin America, Standing Conference of Rectors and Vice-Chancellors of the European Universities, and Union of Latin American Universities; also Afghanistan- Jordan).
Vol. II	Kampuchea - Zimbabwe.

Union of International Associations (ed.), Yearbook of International Organizations (K.G. Saur, Munchen, New York, London, and Paris):

Vol.1 :	Organization descriptions and index. 24th ed., 1987/88, published 1987.
Vol.2 :	Geographic Volume; International Organization Participation; country directory of secretariats and membership (5th ed., 1987/88, published 1987).

2.   Guides to Information Sources and Repositories

Published sources of information principally relating to the United Kingdom

Gavin Higgens (ed.), <u>Printed Reference Material</u> (The Library Association, London, 1980; 2nd ed., 1984).

A volume in the Handbooks on Library Practice series, the chapters include those on the subjects of Periodicals and Serials, Government Publications, Subject Bibliographies, On-Line Information Retrieval Systems, and International Official Publications.

N. Roberts (ed.), <u>Use of Social Sciences Literature</u> (Butterworths, London, 1977).

Includes chapters on 'The literature and sources of education' and 'Exploiting the official publications of the United Kingdom'.

In the same series published by Butterworths are L.T. Morton and S. Godbolt (eds.), <u>Information Sources in the Medical Sciences</u> (1984); E.H.K. Dibden and J.C. Tomlinson (eds.), <u>Information Sources in Education and Work</u> (1981); Pietro Corsi and Paul Weindling (eds.), <u>Information Sources in the History of Science and Medicine</u> (1983); C.P. Auger (ed.), <u>Use of Reports Literature</u> (1975); and edited individual volumes on the Use of Biological, Chemical, Earth Sciences, Economics, Engineering, Physics etc. Literature; and more recent edited volumes on Information Sources in the Life Sciences, Physics, Science and Technology, Engineering, and Law, etc., some of these latter volumes being second editions of volumes in the earlier 'Use of...Literature' series.

Margaret A. Clennett, <u>Key guide to Information Sources in Dentistry</u> (Mansell Publishing Ltd., London, 1985).

<u>Key guides to Information Sources</u> are also available in the subjects of Agricultural Engineering, Archaeology, Food Science and Technology, etc. Each volume provides an account of the history and scope of the subject, outlining the structure of the literature and the relationships between various information sources; an annotated bibliography of reference sources; and a directory of selected organisations from whom information may be obtained.

Sheila Dale and Joan Carty, <u>Finding Out About Continuing Education : Sources of Information and their Use</u> (Open U.P., 1985)

Includes chapters on Bibliographical tools and on Organizations and Associations.

James G. Olle, <u>A Guide to Sources of Information in Libraries</u> (Gower Publishing Co.Ltd., Aldershot, 1984)

Ann Harrold (ed.), <u>Libraries in the United Kingdom and the Republic of Ireland 1986</u> (The Library Association, London; 12th ed., 1986). Includes libraries of universities, selected government, national and special libraries.

R.T. Adkins (ed.), <u>Guide to Government Department and other Libraries 1988</u> (The British Library Board, London, 1988).

Stephen Richard (compiler), Directory of British Official Publications: A Guide to Sources (Mansell Publishing Ltd., London and New York, 2nd ed., 1984).
(includes the establishments and divisions of government departments, the units, institutes etc. of the research councils, etc.)

James L. Hall, Online Bibliographic Databases : A Directory and Sourcebook (Aslib, London; 4th ed., 1986)
(Describes 250 bibliographic databases 'likely to be of use to librarians and information searchers dealing with day-to-day enquiry work'. Includes sample records for all the databases described (which include ERIC: Educational Resources Information Center).

Archive sources in Britain

Janet Foster and Julia Sheppard, British Archives: A Guide to Archive Resources in the United Kingdom (Macmillan Publishers Ltd., 1982, paperback edition 1984; 2nd ed., 1989).
(Information, per record repository etc., arranged under the following headings: address, telephone number, enquiries to, opening hours, access, historical background, acquisitions policy, archives of organisation, major collections, non-manuscript material, finding aids, facilities, and publications. A more comprehensive coverage of repositories, etc. than is provided by Record Repositories in Great Britain.)

The Royal Commission on Historical Manuscripts, Record Repositories in Great Britain, HMSO, 8th ed., 1987.
(Covers national, local government, university, and special repositories. Information, per repository, provides address, telephone number, name of person in charge, opening hours, reprographic and other facilities, and details of published guide.)

Michael Jubb, Guide to the Records relating to Science and Technology in the British Public Record Office : A RAMP Study, (1984; PGI-84/WS/9; UNESCO, Paris).
In three sections covering Civil Government (including Scientific and Industrial Research, Agriculture, Fisheries and Food, Medical Services, Social and Economic Sciences, etc.); Defence; and Overseas. (see, too, Guide to the contents of the Public Record Office, 3 vols., HMSO, 1963 and 1969; and the copies of the Current Guide, including index, available for consultation at the Public Record Office and also available on microfiche. Microfiche copies of the Current Guide part 2 (class descriptions) and index are available for purchase from the PRO's Chancery Lane branch (see p.252 of this Survey). Microfiche copies of the Current Guide and of the PRO's Class Lists of those records that are held at the Kew branch may be purchased from HMSO (who have advertised the microfiche edition as 'Kew Lists'). The records held at the Kew branch come from the modern departments of state and are principally of 19th and 20th century date : they include the records of almost all departments of state concerned with education, health, etc., the records at the Chancery Lane branch being principally medieval records, State

284

Papers before 1782, and modern legal records.

Chris Cook, with Philip Jones, Josephine Sinclair, and Jeffrey Weeks, Sources in British Political History 1900-1951: Vol.1: A Guide to the Archives of Selected Organisations and Societies, Macmillan, London, 1975.

Chris Cook, Sources in British Political History 1900-1951: Vol.6: First Consolidated Supplement, Macmillan, London, 1985.
Covers the British Association for the Advancement of Science, the British Council, the Society for the Protection of Science and Learning Ltd., and the Workers' Educational Association amongst other organisations.

Dr. Cook (North London Polytechnic) is currently working upon a second consolidated supplement to Sources in British Political History 1900- 1951.

Brenda Swann and Maureen Turnbull, Records of Interest to Social Scientists 1919 to 1939 : Introduction (HMSO, 1971; Public Record Office Handbooks No.14)
Includes records of Ministry of Health, Department of Education, UGC, etc.

Richard Storey and Alistair Tough, Consolidated Guide to the Modern Records Centre, University of Warwick Library, University of Warwick Library Occasional Publications No.14, Coventry, 1986.

Part 1 provides summary entries on all the Centre's holdings (which include the records of the ATTI, AUT, the British Educational Research Association (minutes from 1974, conference papers, subject files, ref. MSS.268), Committee for Research into Teacher Education (subject and correspondence files 1969-76, ref. MSS.269), and the World Federation of Scientific Workers (minutes, reports, circulars, journals etc., 1946-85, ref. MSS.270) and Part 2 describes in more detail accessions mid 1981 to April 1986; index to Part 2.

Reference should also be made to the Consolidated Guide's predecessors, the Guide (1977) and Supplement (1981), both also published as University of Warwick Library Occasional Publications. The Consolidated Guide may be updated by reference to the Centre's regular Information Bulletin and annual Report.

John Bennett (compiler), Richard Storey (editor), Trade Union & Related Records (University of Warwick Library Occasional Publications No.5, 5th edition, 1988). A basic guide to deposited sources for labour history.

John Orbell, A Guide to Tracing the History of a Business (Gower Publishing Co., Aldershot, etc., for the Business Archives Council, 1987).
(Of particular use as regards those educational bodies which are registered as companies.)

Colleges of Education : A checklist of archives (History of Education Society, [1980]).
  Arranged alphabetically per college. Lists the main categories of materials relating to each college and also published or typescript histories, etc.

International published and archival sources

International guide to educational documentation (UNESCO, Paris; 1st edition, covering works published 1955-60, published in 1963; 2nd edition, covering works published 1960-65, published in 1971).

Eugene P. Sheehy (ed.), Guide to Reference Books (American Library Association, Chicago and London, 10th ed., 1986).

Barbara L. Bell, An Annotated Guide to Current National Bibliographies (Chadwyck-Healey Inc., Alexandria, USA, 1986). The UK entries include details of British National Bibliography (1950-), The Bibliography of Scotland (covers period 1976/77-, published by HMSO), Bibliotheca Celtica (covers period 1909-, published by National Library of Wales), and Irish Publishing Record (covers period 1967-, published by University College, Dublin).

D.H. Borchardt and J.D. Thawley (compilers), Guide to the Availability of Theses (1981), and G.G. Allen and K. Deubert (compilers), Guide to the Availability of Theses : II Non-University Institutions (1984), both compiled for the Section of University Libraries and other General Research Libraries of the International Federation of Library Associations and Institutions (IFLA Publications Nos. 17 and 29) and published by K.G. Saur, München, New York, etc.

Guide to the Archives of International Organizations (UNESCO, Paris, 3 vols., 1984-85):-
  Part I Lowell H. Hattery (editor), The United Nations System (1984; Documentation, libraries and archives : bibliographies and reference works : 8).
  Part II Peter Walne (compiler), Archives of international organizations and their former officials in the custody of national and other archival and manuscript repositories (1985; PGI-85/WS/18). (As regards the U.K. repositories, there are entries for the Public Record Office, the Imperial War Museum, and the Bodleian Library, Oxford.)
  Part III A.W. Mabbs (compiler), Archives of other international inter-governmental organizations and non-governmental organizations (1985; PGI-85/WS/19).
  As regards the United Nations system, see too Bodil Ulate-Segura, L'Acces aux Archives des Organismes des Nations Unies (1988; PGI-86/WS/24), also published by UNESCO, Paris; available in English version too.

University of Oxford Development Records Project : Universities in Africa Draft Archival Guide (1981).
  Covers A. The Colonial Office and its ancillary bodies (including the Colonial Research Committee, Colonial Social Science Research Council, Overseas Research Council, Council for Technical Education and Training Overseas (TETOC), Commission on Higher Education in East Africa (De La Warr Commission or Makerere

286

Commission), Commission on Higher Education in the Colonies (Asquith Commission); **B.** Other Institutions and Conferences (Association of Commonwealth Universities, British Council, Fabian Colonial Bureau, Inter- University Council, International Association of Universities, Royal Commonwealth Society, UNESCO, and the Dulverton Trust); **C.** Universities (in Great Britain; and papers of African universities which are deposited in Britain); and **D.** Papers of individuals (deposited in Great Britain and overseas).

Directory of Archives and Manuscript Repositories in the United States (The Oryx Press, Phoenix, Arizona, on behalf of the National Historical Publications and Records Commission; 2nd ed., 1988).

3. Government and Parliamentary publications

Vladimir M. Palic, Government Publications: A Guide to Bibliographic Tools, incorporating Government Organization Manuals: A Bibliography (Pergamon Press, Oxford, etc. [1977])
Covers international, national and state publications.

Frank Rodgers, A Guide to British Government Publications (The H.W. Wilson Company, New York, 1980).

Michael Argles, British Government Publications in Education during the 19th century (History of Education Society, 1971; No.1 in the Society's Guides to Sources in the History of Education series).

Michael Argles and J.E. Vaughan, British Government Publications concerning Education during the 20th century (History of Education Society, 4th ed., 1982; No.7 in the Society's Guides to Sources in the History of Education series).

P. and G. Ford, Select list of British Parliamentary Papers, 1833-1899 (Blackwell, Oxford, 1953).

P. and G. Ford, A breviate of Parliamentary Papers, 1900-1916 (Blackwell, Oxford, 1957); the same authors also produced breviates of Parliamentary papers covering later periods: 1917-1939 (Blackwell, Oxford, 1951), 1940-1954 (Blackwell, Oxford, 1961); with Diana Marshallsay they were the authors of Select list of British Parliamentary Papers, 1955-1964 (Irish University Press, 1970). Finding aids to later Parliamentary papers are: Diana Marshallsay and J.H. Smith (eds.), Ford list of British Parliamentary Papers, 1965- 1974 (KTO Press, Nendeln, Liechtenstein, 1979).

HMSO publishes a very large number of titles on behalf of the Parliament of the United Kingdom and of government departments and also distributes in the UK a number of publications on behalf of various major national and international organisations (including the European Communities, UNESCO, and the World Health Organization). HMSO's catalogues of publications include:

(a) <u>Monthly</u> and <u>Annual Catalogues</u> of Parliamentary and non-Parliamentary publications : on Agriculture, Forestry and Fisheries; Education; Medicine and Health; Reference; Schools, Statistics; and Veterinary; etc.

(b) <u>Sectional lists</u> of current publications based mainly on the divisions of responsibility between UK government departments, including 1. Agriculture, Fisheries and Food, 2. Department of Education and Science, 11. Department of Health and Social Security, and 24. British National Archives.

HMSO's bibliographic database has been mounted on the British Library's online information service (BLAISE-LINE) and also on DIALOG, the largest online host in the world.

It should be noted that many British government publications are published directly by government departments and institutions and not published and listed by HMSO. Likewise, a number of non-Parliamentary publications (including <u>some</u> reports of committees, Green Papers, and White Papers) are not published by HMSO.

The principal series of Parliamentary publications (including the Journals, Official reports of the Parliamentary debates ('Hansard'), Bills, and Papers of both Houses of Parliament, and Command Papers presented to Parliament) are published by HMSO.

Reference is made in the appropriate section of this survey to the publications of or about individual bodies, but an indication of the range of more general Parliamentary and non-Parliamentary publications which have a bearing on university education may be given by the following list of some more recent publications:-

<u>Government Response to Second Report from the Education, Science and Arts Committee Session 1982-83 : Further and Higher Education in Northern Ireland</u>, Cmnd. 9278, HMSO, 1984.
(The reference for the report of the House of Commons' Committee referred to is HC (1982-83) No.180.)

<u>Academic Validation in Public Sector Higher Education : The Report of the Committee of Enquiry into the Academic Validation of Degree Courses in Public Section</u> (sic) <u>Higher Education</u> (Chairman : Sir Norman Lindop), Cmnd. 9501, HMSO, 1985.

Includes chapters on the historical background to public sector validation, university validation of public sector courses, and improvements to this validation.

<u>The Development of Higher Education into the 1990s</u> [Green Paper], Cmnd. 9524, HMSO, 1985.

<u>Future Strategy for Higher Education in Scotland : Report of the Scottish Tertiary Education Advisory Council on its Review of Higher Education in Scotland</u> (Chairman : Mr. Donald M. McCallum, CBE), Cmnd. 9676, HMSO, 1985.

Treaty Series No.21 (1986) : Convention on the Recognition of Studies, Diplomas and Degrees concerning Higher Education in the States belonging to the Europe Region, Paris, 21 December 1979, Cmnd. 9762, HMSO, 1986.

(The objectives of the Convention, which entered into force for the UK on 22 November 1985, are the promotion of the mobility of persons and the exchange of ideas, knowledge, and scientific and technological experience.)

Civil Research and Development : First Report of the House of Lords Select Committee on Science and Technology Session 1986-87, HL 20, HMSO, 1986.
3 vols. - Vol. I Report (72pp.) Vol. II Oral Evidence (594pp.), and Vol. III Written Evidence (292pp.).

The report claimed that research and development in the UK were underfunded and that neither government nor industry was spending enough at current levels to restore the UK's industrial position in world markets. Inter alia it recommended that a Council on Science and Technology should be established, under the chairmanship of the Prime Minister, to oversee the whole of scientific and technological endeavour, absorbing ACARD.

Second Report from the Foreign Affairs Committee Session 1985-86 : UK - Soviet Relations : Observations by the Government, Cmnd. 9842, HMSO, 1986.
(in a section on Cultural Relations and Education, this refers to the role of universities, UGC, and ESRC, and the support of Soviet and East European studies and Russian Language teaching.)

The Future of the Science Budget : The Government Response to the First Report from the Education, Science and Arts Committee, Session 1984- 85, Cmnd. 9849, HMSO, 1986.
(includes references to the roles of ABRC, ACARD, etc.)

The Government Response to the Second Report of the House of Lords Select Committee on Science and Technology, 1985-86 Session : Marine Science and Technology, Cmnd. 9861, HMSO, 1986.
(Includes paragraphs on 'Research Institutes and Universities' which refer to NERC, SERC, and UGC).

Treasury Minute on the Thirty-Second to Forty-Ninth Reports from the Committee of Public Accounts Session 1985-86, Cmnd. 9917, HMSO, 1986.
(pp.12-14 concerns the 41st Report : Department of Education and Science : Redundancy Compensation Payments to University Staff, HC (1985-86) 179.)

National Audit Office : Report by the Comptroller and Auditor General : Department of Education and Science : Postgraduate Awards, HC (1986- 87) 368, HMSO, 1987.

First Report from the Education, Science and Arts Committee Session 1986-87: Student Awards, together with Proceedings of the Committee, the Minutes of Evidence and Appendices, HC (1986-87) 28, HMSO, 1986.

Higher Education : Meeting the Challenge, Cm.114, HMSO, 1987.
    (White Paper)
    Announces changes in the funding and national planning of
    polytechnics and colleges in England, a revised policy on access
    to higher education, the Government's initial response to the
    Croham Report (Cm.81, HMSO, 1987), and a renewed emphasis on the
    need for quality and efficiency.

Civil Research and Development : Government response to the First Report
    of the House of Lords Select Committee on Science and Technology,
    1986-87 Session, Cm.185, HMSO, 1987.

Education Reform Bill, House of Commons Bill 53, 50/1, HMSO, 1987.
    This Bill inter alia provides for the establishment of
    corporations to conduct polytechnics and other higher education
    institutions maintained by local education authorities and
    establishes a Universities Funding Council (in place of the
    University Grants Committee) and a Polytechnics and Colleges
    Funding Council (which takes over from the National Advisory Body
    for Public Sector Higher Education), and introduces new
    arrangements in relation to academic tenure (providing for
    University Commissioners to be appointed to amend where necessary
    the statutes of universities to permit dismissal of staff). The
    provisions relating to universities extend to England and Scotland
    and Wales.

Education Statistics for the United Kingdom, 1987 edition (HMSO, for the
    Government Statistical Service).

Education Reform Bill : DES [Press Release] 343/87, 20 November 1987
    (a factual summary of the Bill is attached)

Top-up Loans for Students, Cm.520, HMSO, 1988; The Education (Student
    Loans) Act 1990 implements most of the White Paper's proposals
    and a Student Loans Co.Ltd. has been formed, with offices in
    Glasgow, to administer the scheme in association with the
    universities, etc.

Aspects of higher education in the United States of America: a
    commentary by Her Majesty's Inspectorate, HMSO for DES, 1989.

Social Trends 20, HMSO for the Central Statistical Office, 1990.
    (Social Trends, an annual publication which was first published in
    1970, includes a chapter on Education (including Higher
    Education), providing statistics of full- and part-time students,
    destination of first degree graduates, etc.)

House of Commons Committee of Public Accounts: First Report: Financial
    Problems at Universities, HC 1989-90, 136, HMSO, 1990.

Malcolm Rigg, Peter Elias, Michael White and Steve Johnson, An Overview
    of the Demand for Graduates, HMSO for the Policy Studies Institute
    and the Institute for Employment Research, 1990.

4. <u>Short list of books and articles on the history of university education in the United Kingdom.</u>

This list is intended to complement references to specific books and articles in the individual entries for each body covered in the main text.

J.W. Adamson, <u>English Education 1789-1902</u> (Cambridge U.P., 1930, reprinted 1965).

W.S. Angus, 'University Administrative Staff', <u>Public Administration</u>, Vol.51, 1973, pp.17-39.

Lord Annan, 'British Higher Education, 1960-80: A Personal Retrospect', <u>Minerva : A Review of Science, Learning and Policy</u>, Vol. XX Nos. 1-2, 1982, pp.1-24.

W.H.G. Armytage, <u>Civic Universities : Aspects of a British Tradition</u> (Ernest Benn, London, 1955).

Eric Ashby, <u>Technology and the Academics : an Essay on Universities and the Scientific Revolution</u> (Macmillan, London, 1958).

Eric Ashby, <u>Adapting Universities to a Technological Society</u> (Jossey-Bass Publishers, San Francisco, 1974).

Christopher Ball (Dorma Urwin ed.), <u>Fitness for Purpose : Essays in Higher Education</u> (Society for Research into Higher Education and NFER-Nelson, 1985).
(Mr. Ball became first Chairman of what is now known as the National Advisory Body for Public Sector Higher Education).

Tony Becher (ed.), <u>British Higher Education</u> (Allen and Unwin, 1987).

R. E. Bell and A.J. Youngson (editors), <u>Present and Future in Higher Education</u> (Tavistock Publications, London, 1973).

Robert O. Berdahl, <u>British Universities and the State</u> (Cambridge U.P., 1959).

A.M. Carr-Saunders and P.A. Wilson, <u>The Professions</u> (Oxford U.P., 1933; reprinted by Frank Cass, London, 1964).

John Carswell, <u>Government and the Universities in Britain : Programme and Performance, 1960-1980</u> (Cambridge U.P., 1985).
(Mr. Carswell was, for some time, head of the universities branch in the new DES; later, 1974-77, he served as Secretary of the UGC.)

<u>The Future of Higher Education in Northern Ireland : Report of the Higher Education Review Group for Northern Ireland</u> (Chairman : Sir Henry Chilver), Department of Education for Northern Ireland, HMSO, Belfast, 1982.
(includes individual chapters on the universities and polytechnic of Northern Ireland).

Derman Christopherson, <u>The University at Work</u> (SCM Press Ltd. for the University Teachers' Group, London, 1973).

Ngaio Crequer, 'The Passing of the Education Reform Act', <u>Higher Education Quarterly</u>, Vol.43 No.1, 1989, pp.3-19.

<u>Review of the University Grants Committee : Report of a Committee under the Chairmanship of Lord Croham, GCB</u>, Cm 81, HMSO, 1987.

E.G. Edwards, <u>Higher Education for Everyone</u> (Spokesman, 1982). (includes useful background information)

John Fielden and Geoffrey Lockwood, <u>Planning and Management in Universities : A Study of British Universities</u> (Chatto and Windus for Sussex U.P., 1973). (Includes details of relevant organisations, recent research, and a bibliography).

Peter Gosden, <u>The Education System since 1944</u> (Martin Robertson, Oxford, 1983). (Includes chapters on the Supply and Training of Teachers, on the Universities, and on Further Education.)

V.H.H. Green, <u>The Universities</u> (Penguin Books, Harmondsworth, 1969) (an historical introduction).

Sir Hector Hetherington, <u>The British University System, 1914-1954</u> (Oliver and Boyd, Edinburgh and London, for the University of Aberdeen, 1954; reprinted from <u>Aberdeen University Review</u>).

Konrad H. Jarausch (ed.), <u>The Transformation of Higher Learning 1860-1930: Expansion, Diversification, Social Opening, and Professionalization in England, Germany, Russia, and the United States</u> (University of Chicago Press, 1983).

Elie Kedourie, <u>Diamonds into Glass : the Government and the Universities</u> (Centre for Policy Studies, London, 1987).

Thomas Kelly, <u>A History of Adult Education in Great Britain</u> (Liverpool U.P., 1962, 2nd ed. 1970).

Thomas Kelly, <u>For Advancement of Learning : the University of Liverpool 1881-1981</u> (Liverpool U.P., 1981).
Of wider interest and value, placing as it does developments in a national as well as a local context. Its full notes on Sources refer to government and other publications, etc.

Maurice Kogan and David Kogan, <u>The Attack on Higher Education</u> (Kogan Page, London, 1983).

John Lawlor (editor), <u>The New University</u> (Routledge and Kegan Paul, London, 1968).
(a series of essays relating to British, American, Australian, and New Zealand universities).

John Lawlor (editor), <u>Higher Education : Patterns of Change in the 1970s</u> (Routledge and Kegan Paul, London, 1972).

G. Lockwood, 'The Role of the Registrar in today's University', <u>Higher Education</u>, Vol.8 No.3, 1979, pp. 299-320.

Geoffrey Lockwood and John Davies [and other contributors], Universities : the Management Challenge (Society for Research into Higher Education and NFER-Nelson, Windsor, 1985). (see too entry under Fielden and Lockwood above).

Higher Education in Northern Ireland : Report of the Committee appointed by the Minister of Finance, Cmd. 475, HMSO, 1965 (Chairman : Sir John Lockwood).

Stuart Maclure, Education Re-formed : A Guide to the Education Reform Act 1988 (Hodder and Stoughton, London, 1988)

Angus Mitchell and George Thomson (eds.), Higher Education in Scotland (University of Edinburgh, 1987).

Sir Walter Moberly, The Crisis in the University (SCM Press Ltd., London, for the Christian Frontier Council, 1949)

Graeme C. Moodie and Rowland Eustace, Power and Authority in British Universities (George Allen and Unwin, London, 1974).

Max Morris and Clive Griggs (eds.), Education : the Wasted Years?, 1973-1986 (Falmer Press, London, 1988)

Sir James Mountford, British Universities (Oxford U.P., 1966).

W. Roy Niblett, Universities Between Two Worlds (University of London Press Ltd., 1974).

R.D. Osborne, R.J. Cormack, and R.L. Miller (eds.), Education and Policy in Northern Ireland (Policy Research Institute, Belfast, 1987).

H.J. Perkin, New Universities in the United Kingdom (Organisation for Economic Co-operation and Development, 1969).
(the first volume to be published in the OECD's Case Studies on Innovation in Higher Education).

Harold Perkin, The Rise of Professional Society : England since 1880, (Routledge, London, 1989).

David Phillips (ed.), Oxford Review of Education, Vol.14 No.1, 1988, a special issue on 'The Legacy of Robbins'.

Nicholas Phillipson (ed.), Universities, Society, and the Future, A Conference held on the 400th Anniversary of the University of Edinburgh, 1983 (Edinburgh U.P., 1983).

Higher Education : Report of the Committee appointed by the Prime Minister under the Chairmanship of Lord Robbins 1961-63, Cmnd. 2154, HMSO, 1963.
(together with six volumes of appendices - Appendices 1. The Demand for Places in Higher Education; 2. Students and their Education; 3. Teachers in Higher Education; 4. Administrative, Financial and Economic Aspects of Higher Education; and 5. Higher Education in Other Countries : covering Australia, Canada, France, Federal Republic of Germany, The Netherlands, New Zealand, Sweden, Switzerland, U.S.A., and U.S.S.R.).

Lord Robbins, <u>Higher Education Revisited</u> (Macmillan, London, 1980).

Michael Sanderson, <u>The Universities and British Industry 1850-1970</u> (Routledge and Kegan Paul, London, 1972).

Michael Sanderson (ed.), <u>The Universities in the Nineteenth Century</u> (Routledge and Kegan Paul, London, 1975).

Peter Scott, <u>The Crisis of the University</u> (Croom Helm, Beckenham, 1984).

Paul Seabury (ed.), <u>Universities in the Western World</u> (Collier Macmillan Publishers, London, 1975).

Peter R. Sharp, <u>The Creation of the Local Authority Sector of Higher Education</u> (The Falmer Press, Lewes, 1987).

Michael Shattock (ed.), <u>The Structure & Governance of Higher Education</u> (Society for Research into Higher Education, Guildford, 1983). Includes chapters on CNAA and on the NAB, and passages on the UGC, CVCP, etc.

Maurice Shock, <u>A Time of Trial</u> (Liverpool University Press, 1989). (The text of Sir Maurice Shock's Whelan Memorial Lecture delivered at the University of Liverpool in November 1987. The lecture was concerned with the relationship between universities and the Government over the last decade.)

Renate Simpson <u>How the Ph.D. came to Britain : a century of struggle for postgraduate education</u> (Society for Research into Higher Education, Guildford, Surrey, 1983; the Society's Monograph no. 54.)

Michael D. Stephens and Gordon W. Roderick (eds.), <u>Universities for a Changing World : The Role of the Universities in the later Twentieth Century</u> (David and Charles, Newton Abbot, 1975).

Peter Venables, <u>Higher Education Developments : The Technological Universities 1956-1976</u> (Faber and Faber, London, 1978).

Geoffrey Walford, <u>Restructuring Universities : Politics and Power in the Management of Change</u> (Croom Helm, Beckenham, 1987). An account of some of the major changes that occured in the 1980s, both nationally and at the University of Aston in Birmingham.

Gareth Williams and Tessa Blackstone, <u>Response to Adversity : Higher Education in a Harsh Climate</u> (Society for Research into Higher Education, Guildford, 1983).

5. <u>Journals</u>

The following is a list of the principal (a) indexing and abstracting journals and (b) journals which make reference to developments in higher education in Great Britain (etc.). For a full list of journals, their publishers and prices, etc., one should consult the latest edition of <u>Willing's Press Guide</u> (an annual publicaton, first published in 1874). In addition, the following are amongst the reference works to which one can usefully turn:-

David P. Woodworth and Christine M. Goodair, <u>Current British Journals: A bibliographical guide</u>, 4th ed., The British Library Document Supply Centre in association with the UK Serials Group, 1986.

> Titles are listed in UDC order. Each entry includes title, date of first issue of current title, previous titles, publisher, index (availability and approximate publication frequency), etc. There is both an alphabetical title index and a subject index.

<u>Ulrich's International Periodicals Directory</u>, 1989-90   28th ed., R.R.Bowker Company, New York and London, 1989.

> 3 vols.; with indices to titles and to publications of international organisations, etc. 27th edition incorporates <u>Irregular Serials and Annuals</u>, a separate publication which commenced publication in 1967. The 27th edition is updated by <u>Ulrich's Update : A Quarterly Supplement to Ulrich's International Periodicals Directory</u>.

James D. Stewart with Muriel E. Hammond and Erwin Saenger (eds.), <u>British Union - Catalogue of Periodicals, A Record of the Periodicals of the World, from the Seventeenth Century to the Present Day, in British Libraries,</u> 4 vols., Butterworths Scientific Publications, London, 1955-58; together with <u>Supplement to 1960</u> (1962), <u>New Periodical Titles 1960-1968</u> (1970), and <u>New Periodical Titles</u> published annually from 1969 until ceasing publication in 1980, all published by Butterworths, London.

<u>Contents Pages in Education</u>, Vol.1 No.1-, 1986-

> A computer-based, international current awareness service that shows the contents pages of over 600 of the world's education journals. Contents pages are arranged alphabetically by journal title. Issued monthly, each issue includes about 170 contents pages of the latest issues of these journals, author and subject indexes, and a full list of all journals covered by the service (with subscription address, ISSN, and frequency of publication). Published by Carfax Publishing Company.

J.E.Vaughan, <u>British Journals Concerning Education: a list for research workers and others</u>, British Educational Research Association, 1983.

> Although the information in this list requires updating to take account of changes in title and of publisher of some journals listed, etc., it remains a useful concise list which, inter alia, provides the year in which each journal first appeared.

It should be noted that papers on an aspect of university education may well appear in a journal which is not included in this list or in a journal in which one might not expect to find such papers. For instance, Vol.29 No.1 (Feb 1987) of <u>Educational Research: The Journal of the NFER</u> (National Foundation for Educational Research) includes a paper 'Towards graduation: students' views about the alternative way', though this journal is principally devoted to papers on primary and secondary education, training of teachers, etc.

The titles of some journals do not accurately reflect the subject matter of the contents. One journal which is excluded from this list is the NUT Education Review (1987-to date) which originated as the Higher Education Journal (1937-70), serving the interests in fact of NUT members in "the academic secondary schools", changing its title to Secondary Education (1970-78), then to Secondary Education Journal (1979-86) before adopting its current title.

(a)   indexing and abstracting journals

British Education Index, Vols.1-, 1954-

Three termly issues and an annual cumulation.   Covers about 230 British titles, with subject and author indexes.   Note changes in indexing style in 1976 and again in 1981.

The Brotherton Library, University of Leeds, Leeds, LS2 9JT, is currently transferring the British Education Index from the British Library's Blaise to Dialog and it is expected that on-line access using Dialog will be available from June 1988. This will cover the British Education Index from 1976 - to date and also the British Education Theses Index. Further details about the service will be available from the British Education Index in the Brotherton Library.

Current Index to Journals in Education, Vols.1-, 1969-

Monthly, with annual and semi-annual cumulations.   Covers 700 publications.
In four main sections:-

1.   Subject index under terms derived from the Thesaurus of ERIC Descriptors. (ERIC is an acronym for Educational Resources Information Center, a national organisation, supported financially by the U.S. Office of Education, which acquires, abstracts, indexes, stores, retrieves, and disseminates the most significant educational research documents.)
2.   Author index.
3.   Journal contents index.
4.   Main entry section: full references with short abstracts in ERIC EJ number order.

Education Abstracts, Vols.1-16, 1949-64.

This UNESCO publication was issued four times a year, with each issue devoted to one aspect of education.

Educational Administration Abstracts, Vols.1-, 1966-

Published three times a year.   Covers 95 journals.   Abstracts arranged under subject headings, with author index.   No cumulations.

<u>Research into Higher Education Abstracts</u>, Vols.1-, 1967-

Quarterly.   Author and subject indexes in each issue, with an annual cumulation.   Covers journals and books relevant to higher education. Aims to provide a comprehensive coverage of sources pertaining to British higher education and to offer a selective coverage of sources relating to higher education elsewhere.

<u>Resources in Education</u>   (vols.1-11, 1966-76, entitled <u>Research in Education</u>), Vols.12-, 1977-

A monthly abstracting journal.

<u>Review of Educational Research</u>, Vols.1-, 1931-

Published four times a year by the American Educational Research Association.

(b)   <u>journals</u>

<u>Adult Education</u>, Vols.1-, 1926-

Published by the National Institute of Adult Continuing Education (England and Wales), 19B, De Montfort Street, Leicester.
It is concerned with the development of all aspects of adult continuing education.   There is a <u>Cumulative Index</u> to Vols.1-51, 1926- 79, published in [c.1979]; this index includes Universities in its headings.

<u>Annals of Science: An International Review of the History of Science and Technology from the Thirteenth Century</u>, Vols.1-, 1936- (initially subtitled <u>A Quarterly Review of the History of Science since the Renaissance</u>; the current subtitle, signalising an extension of the period covered, was adopted in January 1976 with Vol.33).

An index to Vols.1-25, 1936-69, was published [in c.1970].
On occasion this journal includes a paper on an aspect of university and higher education in the 19th and 20th centuries (e.g. P.K.Hoch, 'The Reception of Central European Refugee Physicists of the 1930s: U.S.S.R., U.K., U.S.A.' in Vol.40, No.3, 1983, pp.217-246, and S.T.Keith, 'Scientists as Entrepreneurs: Arthur Tindall and the Rise of Bristol Physics' [on the University's Physics Department] in Vol.41 No.4, 1984, pp.335-357), though the majority of papers deal with pre 19th century subjects (e.g. Natural Philosophy at the University of Paris 1600-1740 in Vol.38, 1981) or with pre-university developments (e.g. G.Kitteringham, 'Science in Provincial Society: The Case of Liverpool in the early Nineteenth Century', in Vol.39, 1982, pp.329- 348)

<u>British Educational Research Journal</u>, Vols.1-, 1975-

British Journal of Educational Studies, Vols.1-, 1953-

British Journal of Educational Technology, Vols.1-, 1970-

British Journal of Sociology of Education, Vols.1-, 1980-

This journal publishes academic articles from throughout the world which contribute to theory and empirical reseach in the sociology of education. Though most articles are concerned with primary and secondary education, there is occasionally an article concerned with higher education, e.g. 'The Cuts in British Higher Education: a symposium' (Vol.5 No.2, 1984, pp.167-181) and Kevin McCormick, 'The Search for Corporatist Structures in British Higher Technological Education: the creation of the National Advisory Council on Education in Industry and Commerce (NACEIC) in 1948' (Vol.7 No.3, 1986, pp.293- 317).

Bulletin of the International Association of Universities, Vols.1-, 1953-

A quarterly publication published with the financial assistance of UNESCO. Includes reports on developments in individual countries and in national and international organisations concerned with university and higher education, including the Association of Universities and Colleges of Canada (AUCC), the Association des Universités partiellement ou entièrement de Langue Française (AUPELF), the Federation Internationale des Universités Catholiques (FIUC), the Union des Universités d'Amerique Latine (UDUAL), Association of Southeast Asian Institutions of Higher Learning (ASAIHL), Union Internationale des Etudiants (UIE), Association of European University Public Relations and Information Officers (EUPRIO), the ACU, CRE, United Nations Development Programme (UNDP), UNESCO, Council of Europe, European Community, etc.

Also includes a list of the IAU's own publications.

Comparative Education, Vols.1-, 1965-

An international journal of educational studies, with a number of papers on higher education.

Compare: a journal of comparative education, Vols.1-, 1971-

An international journal which seeks to serve the needs of teachers and research workers in comparative and international education and related areas of study. Includes papers on higher education (e.g. Guy Neave, 'Visions of Mortality: some views on entrances and exits from higher education in Western Europe', Vol.16 No.2, 1986, pp.167-173).

Critical Quarterly, Vols.1-, 1959-

Educational Review, Vols.1-, 1948-

Thirty Year Subject and Author Index to Vols.1-30, 1948-78, (which indicates that over 40 articles on some aspect of university education appeared over this period, and subsequent volumes include articles on higher education, e.g. Vol.33 No.2, June 1981, is devoted to Teacher Education for the 1990s, and Vol.33 No.3, November 1981, includes a paper on 'Student Perspectives in Higher Education: some implications for future university planning').

Educational Studies, Vols.1-, 1975-

Principally concerned with the social sciences, this journal occasionally includes a paper on an aspect of higher education (e.g. 'Employer Sponsorship of Undergraduate Engineers: a student perspective', in Vol.11 No.3, 1985, pp.189-202).

European Journal of Education: research, development and policies, Vols.14-, 1979-

This journal (successor to Paedagogica Europaea) "devotes its attention to educational reforms and general developments in Western and Eastern Europe, and in particular to policy implications and the issues they pose." It is the official journal of the European Cultural Foundation's European Institute of Education and Social Policy (Paris/Brussels). (Passing reference may be made here to the European Institute for the Media (EIM), established within the University of Manchester in 1983 and working in connection with the European Cultural Foundation; the EIM maintains an extensive library.)

A complete list of the contents of Vols.1-14, 1965-79, together with a combined author index, was published in Vol.14 No.4, 1979.

Each issue concentrates on a particular theme, e.g. 'Review of New Trends in European Higher Education', 'Government Policies for the Teaching Profession', 'Postgraduate Education', and 'The Role of the National Inspectorate in European Education Systems' in Nos.1-4 respectively of Vol.21, 1986.

Higher Education: the international journal of higher education and educational planning, Vols.1-, 1972-

This major journal publishes "authoritative overview articles, comparative studies and analyses of specific problems." It follows education in universities, polytechnics, technical colleges, adult education institutes, etc. throughout the world.
Vol.10, 1981, includes a title index and an author index to Vols.1-10 (1972-81).

<u>Higher Education in Europe</u>, Vols.1-, 1976-

A quarterly review (originally a bi-monthly bulletin) published in English, French, and Russian by the European Centre for Higher Education (CEPES) of UNESCO. It "covers problems of higher education" in "the Europe Region (which includes, besides all the countries of Europe, Canada, Israel, and the United States of America)."

The principal themes of papers in recent issues include the changing roles and needs of students in higher education (Vol.X No.1, January- March 1985), the impacts of new information technologies on higher education (Vol.X No.4, October-December 1985), and reforms of higher education systems (Vol.XII No.3, 1987).

<u>Higher Education Management</u> (formerly entitled <u>International Journal of Institutional Management in Higher Education</u>; Vols.1-, 1977-88), Vols.1-, 1989-

Published by the Organisation of Economic Co-operation and Development. Vol.2 No.1 (1990) includes Gordon Macnair's account of 'The British Enterprise in Higher Education Initiative', the Enterprise in Higher Education Initiative (EHE) being a Government initiative to produce more enterprising students through processes of curriculum change which commenced operation in October 1988 and is under the direction of the Department of Employment's Training Agency, Moorfoot, Sheffield, S1 4PQ.

<u>Higher Education Policy</u>, Vols.1-, 1988-

The quarterly journal of the International Association of Universities. The journal is to focus on policy issues and the role of higher education in society today, and will also carry reports on relevant research being carried out in various parts of the world.

<u>Higher Education Quarterly</u>, (first published as the <u>Universities Quarterly</u>, Vols.1-29, 1946-75; changed title with the Autumn 1975 issue to become the <u>New Universities Quarterly: Culture, Education and Society</u>, Vols.30-, 1975-82; in 1982 'New' was dropped from the title and so it became <u>Universities Quarterly: Culture, Education and Society</u>, Vols.37-40, 1982-86; current title adopted in 1987 when it came under the auspices of the Society for Research into Higher Education), (1946)-

An account of the <u>Universities Quarterly</u>'s evolution 1946-86, by the editor, Boris Ford, appeared in Vol.40 No.4, 1986, pp.331-343.

Vol.41 No.1, 1987, of <u>Higher Education Quarterly</u> includes articles on central government and higher education planning 1965-86, on university financing 1979-86, and on the Scottish dimension.

Vol.44 No.1, 1990, includes an article on the funding of UK higher education in the 20th century.

The Society for Research into Higher Education publishes a Bulletin, an International Newsletter, and some forty other titles including Studies in Higher Education and Research into Higher Education Abstracts, in addition to Higher Education Quarterly.

Higher Education Review, Vols.1-, 1968-

(Published three times a year, by Tyrrell Burgess Associates Ltd.) An international journal of policy and practice in post school education; "the radical academic journal for all sectors of higher education."
Vol.21 No.2, 1989, includes C. Mar Molinero, 'A multidimensional scaling analysis of the 1986 rankings of universities in the UK'.

History of Education, Vols.1-, 1972-

The journal of the History of Education Society. Includes papers on university education in the U.K. and overseas.

For instance, Vol.16 No.3, September 1987, includes papers on 'the student movement in England and Wales during the 1930s' (by Brian Simon) and on 'the reform of higher education in 1986' (by Lord Annan).

History of Education Society Bulletin, Nos.1-, 1967-

Includes some papers which cover the history of university education (and its precursors) e.g. G. W. Roderick and M.D.Stephens, 'Merseyside Scientific Societies during the Nineteenth Century: their Educational Role' in No,21, 1978, pp.2-18, and J.B.Thomas, 'University College, London, and the training of teachers' in No.37, 1986, pp.44-49. The Bulletin includes a section listing 'Recent literature of the History of Education.'

History of Science, Vols.1-, 1962-
(originally subtitled An Annual Review of Literature, Research and Teaching, now subtitled A review of literature and research in the history of science, medicine and technology in its intellectual and social context).

Contains a number of papers and reviews of value on the background to the history of higher education, e.g. the papers and reviews on the subject of the history of Biochemistry and on aspects of the professionalization of Psychology in early 20th century Britain in Vol.18, 1980, and on sources for the history of Histology, on science and the universities, and on prosopography in the history of science in Vol.15, 1977.

The History of Universities, Vols.1-, 1981-

As the preface to Vol.1, 1981, noted The History of Universities will publish material concerned mainly with the history of European and American universities before the outbreak of the Second

World War; nowadays the period covered by the journal is from the Middle Ages to 1945. Up to Vol. VI, 1986-7, (1987) inclusive History of Universities tended to concentrate on the period before the establishment and growth of civic universities in the 19th century. The subsequent volumes give greater weight to the post-1800 period and also include the bibliographical section of The History of European Universities : Work in Progress and Publications the last number (No.5) of which was published in 1982.

Vols. I - III published by Avebury Publishing Co., Amersham, subsequent volumes published by Oxford University Press. Each annual issue includes reviews as well as articles.

Industry and Higher Education, Vols.1-, 1987-

An international journal, published, four times a year, by Butterworth Scientific Ltd., which focuses on the economic, organisational, political, social and legal aspects of industry - higher education collaboration.

Journal of Educational Administration and History (formerly entitled The Journal of Educational Administration),Vols.1-, 1963-

Published under the auspices of the School of Education of the University of Leeds, the journal aims to "publish work and stimulate interest in the fields of the administration and history of education."

Journal of Further and Higher Education (including Education for Teaching), Vols.1-, 1977-

This journal is published by the National Association of Teachers in Further and Higher Education (NATFHE). It includes a number of papers relating to university education, e.g. Hywel Thomas, 'The Demand for Higher Education: Problems and Possibilities' in Vol.7, 1983, pp.36- 46, and Christopher Allinson, 'Management Education and the Universities', in Vol.11, 1987, pp.19-22, in addition to papers on further education, higher education in the public sector, teacher training, etc.

Journal of Higher Education, Vols.1-, 1930-

(Published by Ohio State University Press in association with the American Association for Higher Education)

Journal of Sources in Educational History, Vols.1-, 1978-

Minerva: a review of science, learning and policy, Vols.1-, 1962-

(Published four times a year by the International Council on the Future of the University, 745, Fifth Avenue, New York City 10022). Includes a number of papers on university higher education and the history of the same, such as Geoffrey L. Price, 'The expansion of British universities and their struggle to maintain autonomy, 1943-46' in Vol.16 No.3, 1978, pp.357-381, Michael Shattock, 'Higher Education and the Research Councils' in Vol.27 Nos.2-3, 1989, pp.195-222, and Cyril S. Smith and Otto N. Larsen, 'The Criterion of "Relevance" in the Support of Research in the Social Sciences: 1965-1985' in Vol.27 No.4, 1989, pp.461-482.

NATFHE Journal, Vols.1-, 1908-

(Published by the National Association of Teachers in Further and Higher Education).

Nature, Vols.1-, 1869-

Nowadays an international weekly journal covering all the sciences. Issues include review articles, articles, news and views, and book reviews.

On occasion, an issue features a supplement or a number of articles on the state of science in a particular country, including the role of universities, e.g. on Israel (issue of 18-24 June 1987), the U.S.S.R. (issue of 29 Oct. - 4 Nov. 1987), and the Nordic countries (issue of 26 Nov. - 2 Dec. 1987).

Oxford Review of Education, Vols.1-, 1975-

This journal's object is "to advance the study of education" and it publishes papers on the theory and practice of education from scholars throughout the world. Includes a number of papers reflecting on the history and future of higher education, e.g. Helen Patrick, 'From Cross to CATE [Council for the Accreditation of Teacher Education, established in 1984]: the universities and teacher education over the past century' in Vol.12, 1986, pp.243-261, and Geoffrey Caston, 'Planning, Government and Administration in Two University Systems: California and the United Kingdom' in Vol.5, 1979, pp.183-194. Vol.14 No.1, 1988, is a special issue on 'The Legacy of Robbins'.

Paedagogicia Europaea, Vols.1-13, 1965-1978; the forerunner of the European Journal of Education which continues the numbering of the series of volumes.

Paedagogicia Historica: International Journal of the History of Education, Vols.1-, 1960-

Includes a few papers on aspects of the history of universities. Includes, on a regular basis, lists of dissertations in progress.

Research in Education, Nos.1-, 1969-

This journal on occasion includes a paper on an aspect of university education, e.g. J.P.Powell, 'Student Evaluation of University Teaching: A Survey of Research' in No.8, 1972, pp.1-15 (based upon a report prepared at the request of the AUT) and Alan Woodley, 'The Older the Better?. A study of mature student performance in British universities' in No.32, 1984, pp.35-50 (based in part on data provided on the 1972-74 intakes of all U.K. universities).

Scottish Educational Review, formerly entitled Scottish Educational Studies, Vols. 1-, 1969-

Published by the Scottish Academic Press, Edinburgh, in association with the Scottish Educational Research Association. Includes papers and reviews of books on higher education in Scotland, e.g. Albert Pilliner and Gerda Siann, 'A Survey of Undergraduate Assessment at the University of Edinburgh' in Vol.5 No.1, 1973, pp.35-45; Dougal Hutchison, 'Regionalism in Scottish Universities' in Vol.8 No.1, 1976, pp.36-40; Ronnie Carr and Bob Glaister, 'Information Paper 7: The Open University in Scotland' in Vol.13 No.1, 1981, pp.58-61; and David Elliot, 'Information Paper 13 : The Scottish Examination Board' in Vol.16 No.1, 1984, pp.51-53.

Scottish Journal of Adult Education, Vols.1-, 1973-

Published, twice a year, by the Scottish Institute of Adult and Continuing Education. (The separate journal, Scottish Adult Education, ceased publication in 1968.) Includes a number of articles on universities and adult and continuing education, e.g. 'Review of Higher Education in Scotland' (an edited account of evidence submitted to the Scottish Tertiary Education Advisory Council by the SIAE) in Vol.7 No.1, 1986, pp.26-31, and 'Scottish Universities as a Community Resource', by Tony Graham and Valerie Wilson and 'Part-time Undergraduate Courses in Scottish Universities: A Guide to Provision', by Leslie D. Simpson, both in Vol.7 No.3, 1986, pp.4-13 and 24-31 respectively.

Studies in the Education of Adults, formerly entitled Studies in Adult Education, Vols.1-, 1969-

Published, twice a year, by the National Institute of Adult Continuing Education (England and Wales) (NIACE), Leicester, jointly with the Universities Council for Adult and Continuing Education (UCACE) and the Standing Conference on University Teaching and Research in the Education of Adults (SCUTREA).
Includes a number of papers on the history of the subject, e.g. in Vol.15, 1983, there are papers on 'The Ideology of English Adult Education Teaching 1925-50' by Roger Fieldhouse (pp.11-35) and on 'Further Education Pressure Groups: the Campaign for Adult Education in 1944', by Brendan Evans (pp.92-103), amongst others.

Studies in Higher Education, Vols.1-, 1976-

Published, three times (formerly twice) a year, by Carfax Publishing Company for the Society for Research into Higher Education. The primary focus of this journal is on teaching in higher education and papers cover developments overseas as well as in the U.K.; its "central aim is to illuminate those factors which contribute to effective course design and efficient teaching and learning in higher education." A number of papers are based on surveys and on data provided by inter- and supra-university bodies, e.g. Malcolm Tight, 'The Provision of Part-time First Degree Courses in the United Kingdom', (pp.173-188), Jim Taylor, 'The Employability of Graduates: differences between universities', (pp.17-17), George Brown and Madeleine Atkins, 'Academic Staff Training in British Universities: results of a national survey', (pp.29-42), and Alan Smithers and Alice Griffin, 'Mature Students at University: entry, experience and outcomes' (based in part on an analysis of applications submitted to the Joint Matriculation Board for the period 1975-80), all in Vol.11, 1986.

The Times Higher Education Supplement, Nos.1-, 1971-

Published weekly (on a Friday).

Year Book of Adult Education, 1961-

Published by the National Institute of Adult Continuing Education, Leicester.
A directory of organisations with an index. The organisations covered include the DES, polytechnics, and universities, WEA (including list of district offices and secretaries), Ministry of Defence, regional advisory councils, and professional associations (including AUT, NATFHE, and NUS).

Abbreviations and Acronyms: A Glossary

A formidable array of abbreviations, initials and acronyms nowadays confronts readers not only of the specialist professional literature but also of publications directed at a wider public (such as the 'quality' newspapers, such weekly publications as New Scientist and the Times Higher Education Supplement, and government publications). To assist in their elucidation there are dictionaries, including:-

A.C. Montgomery (ed.), Acronyms and Abbreviations in Library and Information Work : a reference handbook of British usage (The Library Association, London; 3rd ed., 1986).

Joan V. Marder (ed.), Acronyms and initialisms in education : a handlist (Librarians of Institutes and Schools of Education; 3rd ed., 1986).

James C. Palmer and Anita Y. Colby (compilers and editors), Dictionary of Educational Acronyms, Abbreviations, and Initialisms (Oryx Press, Phoenix, U.S.A., 1982).

Lesley Roberts, List of Common Abbreviations in Training and Education (The New Opportunities Press Ltd., London, 1986).

F.A. Buttress, World Guide to Abbreviations of Organizations (Blackie & Son Ltd., Glasgow; 8th ed., 1988, revised by H.J. Heaney)

R. de Sola, Abbreviations Dictionary (Elsevier, New York; 7th ed., 1985). Over 250,000 definitions are given in this international edition.

Council of the European Communities Multilingual Glossary of Abbreviations (Office of Official Publications of the European Communities, Luxembourg, 1983).

In some cases, the same abbreviation or initials are used by several different bodies. For instance, ARA stands not only for Associate of the Royal Academy but also for Alternative Information Service (Liverpool, UK), according to one of the reference works listed above, not to mention the fact that it also stands, by coincidence, for the initials of the author of this survey! For such reasons and to assist users of this survey, the following is a select list of abbreviations etc. more commonly encountered in the higher education context particularly in the UK.

AACE	Association for Adult and Continuing Education
AAU	Academic Audit Unit
ABRC	Advisory Board for the Research Councils
ACACE	Advisory Council for Adult and Continuing Education
ACARD	Advisory Council for Applied Research and Development
ACOST	Advisory Council on Science and Technology
ACSP	Advisory Council for Scientific Policy
ACU	Association of Commonwealth Universities (formerly AUBC)
ADuLT	Association of Dutch Language Teachers
AFRC	Agricultural and Food Research Council
AGCAS	Association of Graduate Careers Advisory Services
AGR	Association of Graduate Recruiters
AIR	Association of Institutional Research

AISEIT	Association of Institute and School of Education In-Service Tutors
ALBSU	Adult Literacy and Basic Skills Unit (of NIACE)
AOE	Admission Officers Conference
APA	Association of Polytechnic Administrators
APW	Association of Principals and Wardens of University Halls
ARC	Aeronautical Research Council; Agricultural Research Council (later became AFRC)
ASAIHL	Association of South-East Asian Institutes of Higher Learning
ATCDE	Association of Teachers in Colleges and Departments of Education
ATTI	Association of Teachers in Technical Institutions
AUAO	Association of University Accommodation Officers
AUBC	Association of Universities of the British Commonwealth (later became ACU)
AUPELF	Association des Universités partiellement ou entièrement de langue Française
AUPF	Association of University Professors of French
AUT	Association of University Teachers
AUTGP	Association of University Teachers of General Practice
AUT (Scotland) or AUT(S)	Association of University Teachers (Scotland)
AUUC	Association of Universities and Colleges of Canada
BAAP	British Association of Academic Phoneticians
BAS	British Antarctic Survey
BASSEES	British Association for Soviet, Slavonic and East European Studies
BCSA	British Colleges Sports Association
BCCU	British College Christian Union
BFUW	British Federation of University Women
BPSA	British Polytechnics Sports Association
BSSF	British Students Sports Federation
BTO	Brussels Treaty Organisation
BUAC	British Universities' Accommodation Consortium
BUAS	British Universities Association of Slavists
BUFC	British Universities Film Council Ltd. (became BUFVC)
BUFVC	British Universities Film and Video Council (formerly BUFC)
BUIRA	British Universities Industrial Relations Association
BUSF	British Universities Sports Federation
CACGS	Computer-Aided Career Guidance System
CASSC	Clinical Academic Staff Salaries Committee
CAUBO	Canadian Association of University Business Officers
CCF	Conservative Collegiate Forum
CCNTS	Central Council for Non-Teaching Staffs in Universities
CCTUT	Co-ordinating Committee for the Training of University Teachers
CCW	Curriculum Council for Wales
CEC	Commission of the European Communities
CELEX	Communitatis Europeae Lex
CEPES	(Unesco) European Centre for Higher Education
CERI	Centre for Educational Research and Innovation

CEST	Centre for Exploitable Areas of Science and Technology/ Centre for the Exploitation of Science and Technology
CFTC	Commonwealth Fund for Technical Co-operation
CHEST	Combined Higher Education Software Team
CHUGD	Committee of Heads of University Geoscience Departments
CICHE	Committee for International Co-operation in Higher Education
CIHE	Council for Industry and Higher Education
CILT	Centre for Information on Language Teaching and Research
COMEC	Council of Military Education Committees of the Universities of the United Kingdom
CNAA	Council for National Academic Awards
COMETT	Community Programme for Co-operation between the Universities and Industry in the field of Training for Technology
COPIOR	Committee of Professors in Operational Research
CORAL	Conference of Teachers of Regional and Local History in Tertiary Education
COUP	Conference on University Purchasing
COUPA	Conference of University Personnel Administrators
CP	Council of Principals
CRE	Standing Conference of Rectors, Presidents, and Vice-Chancellors of the European Universities
CRS	Conference of Registrars and Secretaries
CSC	Commonwealth Scholarship Commission
CSP	Council for Scientific Policy
CST	Council for Science and Technology
CSU	Central Services Unit for University and Polytechnic Careers and Appointments Services
CTES	Council for Tertiary Education in Scotland
CTI	Computers in Teaching Initiative
CTISS	Computers in Teaching Initiative Support Service
CUA	Conference of University Administrators (formerly MUAAS)
CUC	Conference of University Convocations
CUGAC	Colonial University Grants Advisory Committee
CUMS	Council of University Management Schools
CURL	Consortium of University Research Libraries
CVCP	Committee of Vice-Chancellors and Principals of the Universities of the United Kingdom
DAFS	Department of Agriculture and Fisheries for Scotland
DES	Department of Education and Science
DHSS	Department of Health and Social Security
DPO	Data Processing Officer(s)
EC	European Communities
ECHO	European Commission Host Organisation
ECOSOC	United Nations Economic and Social Council
EEC	European Economic Community
EHE	Enterprise in Higher Education Initiative
EIM	European Institute for the Media
EPC	Engineering Professors Conference
ERASMUS	European Community Action Scheme for the Mobility of University Students

ESPRIT	European Strategic Programme for Research in Information Technology
ESRC	Economic and Social Research Council (formerly SSRC)
ETA	Educational Television Association (formerly NECCTA)
EUDISED	European Documentation and Information System in Education
EUPRIO	Association of European Universities Public Relations and Information Officers
EUREKA	European Research C(K)o-ordinating Agency
FCS	Federation of Conservative Students
FICU	Fonds International de Cooperation Universitaire
FISU	Federation Internationale du Sport Universitaire
FIUC	Federation Internationale des Universites Catholiques
FOLYLC	Festival of Languages and Young Linguist of the Year Competition
FSSU	Federated Superannuation Scheme for Universities
HEIST	Higher Education Information Services Trust
HELP	Higher Education for the Labour Party
HUDG	History at the Universities Defence Group
IAU	International Association of Universities
IAUPL	International Association of University Professors and Lecturers
IBE	International Bureau of Education
ICMICA	International Catholic Movement for Intellectual and Cultural Affairs
IEELG	International Educational Exchange Liaison Group
IIEP	International Institute for Educational Planning
IFUW	International Federation of University Women
IFWEA	International Federation of Workers Educational Associations
IMHE	Programme on Institutional Management in Higher Education
INSET	In-Service Education of Teachers programme
IOC	Inter-Governmental Oceanographic Commission
IOS	Institute of Oceanographic Sciences
ISS	International Student Service
IUB	International Universities Bureau
IUC	Inter-University Council for Higher Education Overseas
IUCC	Inter-University Committee on Computing
IUPC	Inter-University and Polytechnic Council for Higher Education Overseas
IUS	International Union of Students
IUSO	Institute of University Safety Officers
IVN	Internationale Vereniging voor Neerlandistiek (International Association for Dutch Studies)
JANET	Joint Academic Network
JMB	Joint Matriculation Board

LISE	Librarians of Institutes and Schools of Education
MAFF	Ministry of Agriculture, Fisheries and Food
MECs	Military Education Committees
MRC	Medical Research Council
MUAAS	Meeting of University Academic Administrative Staffs (became CUA)
NAB	National Advisory Body for Public Sector Higher Education
NACG	National Association of Conservative Graduates
NAFSA	National Association of Foreign Student Affairs
NASEES	National Association of Soviet and European Studies
NATFHE	National Association of Teachers in Further and Higher Education
NAUMS	National Association of University Music Staff
NCC	National Curriculum Council
NCLE	National Congress on Languages in Education
NCML	National Council for Modern Languages in Further and Higher Education
NCP	National Committee for Philosophy
NECCTA	National Educational Closed Circuit Television Association (became ETA)
NERC	Natural Environment Research Council
NFER	National Foundation for Educational Research in England and Wales
NIACE	National Institute of Adult Continuing Education (England and Wales)
NSDTU	National Staff Development and Training Unit
NUS	National Union of Students
OECD	Organization for Economic Co-operation and Development
OEEC	Organisation for European Economic Co-operation
OTC	Officers Training Corps
PBI	Plant Breeding Institute
PCAS	Polytechnics Central Admissions System
PCFC	Polytechnics and Colleges Funding Council
PEPC	Pay and Employment Policy Committee
PICKUP	Professional, Industrial and Commercial Updating programme
PRO	Public Record Office
RACE	Research in Advanced Communications Technologies for Europe
SARIS	Scottish Agricultural Research Institutes
SBS	Save British Science (Society)
SCAD	Système Communautaire d'Accès à la Documentation
SCASS	Standing Conference of Arts and Social Sciences

SCASSU	Standing Conference of Arts and Social Sciences in Universities
SCDC	School Curriculum Development Committee
SCM	Student Christian Movement
SCOEG	Standing Conference of Employers of Graduates
SCONUL	Standing Conference of National and University Libraries
SCOSA	Standing Conference of Heads of Schools of Architecture
SCP	Standing Conference of Philosophers
SCPP	Standing Conference of Professors of Physics
SCUE	Standing Conference on University Entrance
SCUIO	Standing Conference of University Information Officers
SCUPHA	Standing Committee of University Professors and Heads of Archaeology Departments
SCUTREA	Standing Conference on University Teaching and Research in the Education of Adults
SEA	Single European Act
SEAC	School Examinations and Assessment Council
SEC	Secondary Examinations Council
SED	Scottish Education Department
SERC	Science and Engineering Research Council
SFMU	Students' Foreign Missionary Union
SRHE	Society for Research in Higher Education
SSRC	Social Science Research Council (became ESRC)
STEAC	Scottish Tertiary Education Advisory Council
SUAC	Scottish Universities Accommodation Consortium
SUPC	Southern Universities' Purchasing Consortium
SURRC	Scottish Universities Research and Reactor Centre
SUSF	Scottish Universities Sports Federation
SUSOC	Student Union Senior Officers Conference
SVMU	Student Volunteer Missionary Union of Great Britain and Ireland
TCA	Training College Association
TCS	Teaching Company Scheme
TETOC	Technical Education and Training Organisation for Overseas Countries
THES	The Times Higher Education Supplement
UACES	University Association for Contemporary European Studies
UAP	University Authorities Panel
UAU	Universities Athletic Union
UCAE	Universities Council for Adult Education (became UCACE)
UCACE	Universities Council for Adult and Continuing Education (formerly UCAE)
UCCA	Universities Central Council on Admissions
UCCF	Universities and Colleges Christian Fellowship
UCET	Universities Council for the Education of Teachers
UCNS	Universities Committee for Non-Teaching Staffs
UCOC	University Catering Officers Conference
UDAL	Union des Universites d'Amerique Latine
UFAW	Universities Federation for Animal Welfare
UFC	Universities Funding Council
UGC	University Grants Committee
UIE	Union Internationale des Etudiants

UKCOSA	United Kingdom Council for Overseas Student Affairs
ULF	University Labour Federation
UNDP	United Nations Development Programme
UNESCO	United Nations Educational, Scientific and Cultural Organisation
UNICEF	United Nations Children's Fund
UREF	Universite des Reseaux d'Expression Francaise
USA	Universities' Safety Association
USR	Universities Statistical Record
USS	Universities Superannuation Scheme Limited
UWAU	University of Wales Athletic Union
U3A	University of the Third Age
WEA	Workers' Educational Association
WEO	Welsh Education Office
WIVAB	Women's Inter-University Athletic Board
WSCF	World Student Christian Federation
WUS	World University Service

INDEX

American Council on Education 280
Amnesty International 140
Amsterdam, International Institute of Social History 230
Anglo-Australian Telescope 132
Annual Conference of Courts of the Scottish Universities 270
Antarctica 121
Area Training Organisations 101
Argentina 140
Army Educational Advisory Board 258
Art Students' Christian Union 153,155
Arts Council 14
Asbestosis Research Council 270
Asia 120,148,175,198,205,225,280
ASLIB 52,147,212,276
Asquith Commission on Higher Education in the Colonies 230,287
Associated Country Women of the World 226
Association d'études linguistiques interculturelles africaines 203
Association des Universités partiellement ou entièrement de Langue Française
        201-4,220,282,298
Association for the Study of German Politics 189
Association for the Study of Modern and Contemporary France 189
Association for the Study of Modern Italy 189
Association of Accommodation and Welfare Officers 34
Association of African Universities 220,282
Association of Arab Universities 220,282
Association of Caribbean Universities and Research Institutes 282
Association of Clinical Professors 262
Association of College and University Housing Officers 280
Association of Commonwealth Universities 58,60,61,63,73,165,198-201,204,
        206,220,282,287,298
Association of Dutch Language Teachers 262-3
Association of European Documentation Centres Librarians 190
Association of European University Public Relations and Information Officers
        298
Association of German Press and Information Officers 217
Association of Graduate Careers Advisory Services 22-25,26,57
Association of Graduate Recruiters 24,25-26,82
Association of Heads of Psychology Departments 26-27
Association of Institute and School of Education In-Service Tutors 28
Association of Institutional Research 280
Association of Inter-Varsity Clubs 29-30
Association of Phoneticians of the (British) Commonwealth 43
Association of Physical Plant Administrators 280
Association of Polish Professors in Great Britain 223
Association of Polytechnic Administrators 75
Association of Principals, Wardens and Advisers of University Women Students
        31-32
Association of Principals and Wardens of University Halls 31-32
Association of Professors of Modern Languages at Technological Universities
        262
Association of Scientific, Technical and Managerial Staffs 165
Association of South-East Asian Institutions of Higher Learning 220,282,298
Association of Student Counselling 263
Association of Teachers in Colleges and Departments of Education
        108,110,112,169
Association of Teachers of Italian 263
Association of Teachers of Russian 46
Association of Teachers in Technical Institutions 108,109-11,285

Association of Universities and Colleges of Canada 298
Association of Universities of the British Commonwealth 60,198-9
Association of University Accommodation Officers 33-4
Association of University Departments of Theology and Religious Studies 263
Association of University Lecturers 36
Association of University Lodgings Wardens and Officers 33
Association of University Professors of French 34-5
Association of University Professors and Lecturers of the Allied Countries in
    Great Britain 223
Association of University Teachers 35-9,40,60,82,84,108,117,192,223,285,
    304,305
Association of University Teachers (Scotland) 36,37,39-40
Association of University Teachers of Economics 7,40
Association of University Teachers of General Practice 41-2
Association to Promote the Higher Education of Working Men 194
Aston in Birmingham, University of 92,126,164,294
Athletic Unions 55
Athlone Committee on Postgraduate Education 254
Australasia 198,280
Australia 235,236,292,293
Australian Institute of Tertiary Education Administrators 281
Austria 235,236,241,246

B

Bangkok 270
Bangladesh 140
Bangor, University College of North Wales 68,126,164,197
Barcelona 238
Bath, University of 65,143,164,262,264,265,281
Bedford College of Higher Education 71
Belfast 31,79,255,269
Belfast, Queen's University 64,90,138,164
Belgium 111,202,206,209,235,239,281
Belgrade 240
Berlin 218
Berne 227
Beveridge, Lord 140
Biafra 140
Bidston Observatory 121
Birmingham 31,36,49,56,150,152,155,267
Birmingham, University of 34,67,81,90,98,100,126,164,182,250,258,272
Bithell correspondence 81
Board of Education 102,103,173,182,183,252
Board of Longitude 134
Bologna University 277-8
Bradford, University of 124,164,264
Brazil 140
Breul correspondence 81
Bristol 31,64,177
Bristol Polytechnic 65
Bristol, University of 45,67,68,81,110,142,143,164,182,251,272,281,297
British Academy 140,249
British Antarctic Survey 121,122,123
British Association for the Advancement of Science 285
British Association for Soviet, Slavonic and East European Studies 45-7
British Association of Academic Phoneticians 5,43

British Association of Health Services in Higher Education 5,43-5
British Association of Settlements and Social Action Centres 282
British Broadcasting Corporation 231
British College Christian Union 151
British Colleges Sports Association 48,49,56
British Council 46,74,114,155,156,200,230-4,252,263,279,285,287
British Council of Churches 153,267
British Education Index 103
British Educational Research Association 101,285,295
British Federation of University Women 47-8
British Film Institute 14,50-1
British Geological Survey 121
British Humanist Association 268
British Institute in Paris 35
British Institute of Adult Education 113-6
British Library 3,18,52,94,103,147,161,196,212,243,262,277,283,295,296
British Museum (Natural History) 10
British National Committee on Intellectual Co-operation 251
British Olympic Association 158
British Polytechnics Sports Association 48,56
British Records Association 51
British Student Health Association 43-5
British Student Health Officers Association 43
British Students Sports Federation 48-9,56
British Universities' Accommodation Consortium 49-50
British Universities Association of Slavists 46-7
British Universities Film Council 50-3
British Universities Film and Video Council 50-3
British Universities Industrial Relations Association 53-5
British Universities Physical Education Association 56
British Universities Society of Arts 270
British Universities Sports Board 139
British Universities Sports Federation 48,49,55-6,139
British Youth Council 153
Brunel University 90,142,143,149,164
Brussels Treaty Organisation 239
Brynmor Jones Committee 51
Bucharest 218,242
Buckingham, University of 73,159
Budapest 218
Business and Technician Education Council 108

C

Cabinet Office 15,16
California 303
Cambridge 21,123,162,239,266,268
Cambridge Group for the History of Population and Social Structure 92
Cambridge Mission in Delhi 267
Cambridge, University of 11,29,31,35,36,53,67,81,82,92,132,134,143,
    164,174,182,193,194,258,262,264,272,275
Canada 198,204,225,236,280,293,300
Canadian Association of University Business Officers 281
Cardiff 41,78,114,185,255
Cardiff, Medical School 182
Cardiff, University College 67,68,164,183
Caribbean 120,198,202,204,205,232

Department of Environment 15,34
Department of Health, and Ministry of Health 104,105,254,285
Department of Health and Social Security 10,187,254-5
Department of Scientific and Industrial Research 18,131,256
Department of Social Security 254
Department of (Trade and) Industry 15,17,24,132,259
Development Commission 256
Dijon 240,241
Dijon, University of 74
Diploma in Management Studies 87
Dublin 31,69,229
Dublin, University of 273
Dublin, University and Trinity Colleges 69,77
Duisburg 218
Dulverton Trust 287
Dundee College of Education 135
Dundee, University of 39,82,136,137,139,145,164,193
Dunfermline College of Physical Education 135
Durham 3,31,78,240
Durham, University of 67,81,124,164,252,263,272
Dutch Language Union 263

E

East Anglia, University of 5,53,83,84,137,143,164
Eastern Europe 148
ECHO 212
Economic and Social Council (UN) 226,242
Economic and Social Research Council 4,10,91-4,169,289
Edinburgh 31,36,39,78,134,136,138,139,151,215,253,269
Edinburgh, University of 41,46,49,68,77,81,90,136,137,139,164,184,193,264,
    270,272,293,304
Edmonton 218
Education and Science, Department of see under Department of Education and
    Science
Education Librarians Group of the Library Association 260
Educational Resources Information Center 284,296
Educational Television Association 95-6
Edwards Report on University Physics 181
Eire see under Ireland
El Salvador 247
Employment, Department of see under Department of Employment
Endsleigh Insurance Services Ltd. and other Endsleigh companies 118,119
Energy, Department of see under Department of Energy
Engineering Professors Conference 264
Enterprise in Higher Education Initiative 300
Environment, Department of see under Department of Environment
Equal Opportunities Commission 120
ERASMUS 209,211,213,217
ERICA 211
Eritrea 247
ESPRIT 132,210
ESRC Data Archive 92-3
Essex, University of 92,142,143,164
Ethiopia 140,231,247
Ethnic Relations Unit 93

G

H

Hong Kong   231,270
Hull   31
Hull, University of   124,164
Humane Slaughter Association   171
Humberside College of Higher Education   70,71-2
Hume, Major Charles W.   170,172
Hungary   140,232
Hurstmonceux   132

I

Iceland   235,236,240
Imperial College of Science and Technology   67,250
Imperial Institute   252
Imperial War Museum   286
India   225
Industrial Relations Research Unit   92
Industrial Training Boards   24
In-Service Education of Teachers Programme   28,175
Institute for Marine Environmental Research   121
Institute Laue-Langevin   132
Institute for Animal Health   20
Institute for Grassland Research and Animal Production   20
Institute of Animal Disease Research   20
Institute of Animal Physiology and Genetics Research   20
Institute of Arable Crops Research   20
Institute of Engineering Research   20
Institute of Food Research   20
Institute of Geological Sciences   121
Institute of Horticultural Research   20
Institute of Housing   34
Institute of Hydrology   121
Institute of Information Scientists   147
Institute of Intellectual Co-operation   219
Institute of Manpower Studies   25
Institute of Oceanographic Sciences   121,123
Institute of Plant Science Research   20
Institute of Terrestrial Ecology   121
Institute of University Safety Officers   184
Institute of Virology   121
Institutes of Education   28,100-4,168,276
Institutes of Higher Education   27,108
Interdisciplinary Research Centres   4,11,132
Inter-Governmental Oceanographic Commission   242
International Agency for Research on Cancer   105
International Association for Dutch Studies   263
International Association of Technological University Libraries   274
International Association of Universities   202,219-23,242,244,279-80,282,287,
    298,300
International Association of University Professors and Lecturers   223-4,274,
    282
International Bureau of Education   242,244
International Bureau of University Statistics   219
International Catholic Association/Movement for Intellectual and Cultural
    Affairs   267,268
International Committee of Intellectual Co-operation   219
International Committee of UK University Administrators   73,79

Joint Matriculation Board   98-9,251,305
Joint Steering Committee of Convocation   81
Joint University Council for Social and Public Administration   260
Jones, Roger Lyon, Charity   251
Jordan   282

K

Kampuchea   282
Keele, University of   126,137,164,193
Kent, University of   143,164
Keyworth   123
Khartoum, University of   233
King's College London   68,189
Kobe   218

L

Labour Party   271
Lagos, University of, College of Medicine   233
Lampeter, St.David's College   164
Lancaster, University of   71,77,90,126,164,259,260,264,265
La Palma Observatory   132
Latin America   222,225,247,280
Laurie, Professor R. Douglas   36,37,38
League of Nations   219,245
Leeds,   University of   31,45,47,67,68,75,81,98,124,125,144,164,168,182,
      194,258,261,264,265,272,296,302
Leicester   2,31,113,114,162
Leicester, University of   81,100,124,164
Liaison   Committee   for   Professional   Occupational   Health   and   Safety
      Organisations   184
Liberia   231
Leverhulme Trust   156
Librarians of Institutes and Schools of Education   100-4
Library Association   101,102,103,147,211,276,283
Library Association, Education Librarians Group 104
Library Association, Colleges, Institutes and Schools of Education Section
      101
Liege   203
Lindop Report on Academic Validation in Public Sector Higher Education
      87,88,288
Lingua   210
Lisbon   229
Lister Institute of Preventive Medicine   106
Liverpool   7,120,151,157,187,196,212,297
Liverpool Association of University Women   47
Liverpool, University of   3,7,8,11,31,36,38,67,78-9,80,81,83,98,125,126,127,
      132,154,159,164,182,193,194,197,209,215,229,233,239,248,250,251,252,
      256,257,258,272-3,292,294
Local Government Board   254
Lockwood Committee on Higher Education   255,293
Lockwood Report on School Curricula and Examinations   129
Lodge, Sir Oliver   194,250

London   2,5,9,14,25,26,29,31,35,36,42,43,48,58,63,64,65,68,71,78,86,93,107,
        114,117,118,123,127,139,146,150,151,155,156,157,164,168,171,173,177,
        189,191,194,197,198,204,206,210,225,226,227,228,230,245,247,249,252,
        260,261,262,265,266,267,268,270,271,273
London, King's College   68,189
London School of Economics and Political Science   68,92,271
London School of Hygiene and Tropical Medicine   92
London, School of Oriental (and African) Studies   250,262
London, University College   5,80,148-9,301
London, University of   31,44,46,47,68,76,80-1,90,97,109,137,145,164,182,185,
        193,194,250,258,261,264,265,272
London, University of, Institute of Education 92,101,131,170
Lords, House of   15,21,122,289-90
Loughborough, University of   124,164
Luton College of Higher Education   95
Luxembourg   206,209,215,235,239,240
Lyons   203

M

McCallum Report on Higher Education in Scotland   135-6,288
Mackenzie Report on General Practice in Medical Schools   42
McNair Report on the Supply, Recruitment and Training of Teachers and Youth
        Leaders   100
Magee University College, Londonderry   255
Majut correspondence   81
Makerere Commission on Higher Education in East Africa   286-7
Malta   224,231,241
Manchester   36,41,54,57,65,81,100,152,157,158
Manchester, University of   27,31,38,40,68,72,73,81,98,126,158,164,182,194,
        207,212,236,264,272,299
Manchester, University of, Institute of Science and Technology   58,126,164
Manpower Services Commission   4,25,114,134
Mansbridge, Albert   113,194,195
Marine Biological Association of the United Kingdom   121
Marrakesh   202,203
Marshall Scholarship Programme   198
Matriculation Examination   98
Medical Research Committee   104-7,256
Medical Research Council   4,10,92,104-7,254,256
Medical Students   250
Meeting of University Academic Administrative Staffs   72,75
Merrison Report on the Support of University Scientific Research   12,93
Merseyside   5,301
Mexico   218
Middle East   247,280
Military Education Committees   85-6
Ministry of Agriculture, Fisheries and Food see under Agriculture, Fisheries
        and Food, Ministry of
Modern Universities Conference   152
Montreal   201
Montreal, University of   201,202,204
Moray House College of Education   135
Morris Report   11,12
Moscow   218

Mountford, Sir James 239,293
Munster, University of 74
Museums Association 272

N

Nairobi 204,270
Namibia 247
National Advisory Body for Public Sector Higher Education 108,134,145,249,
    290,291,294
National Advisory Committee on the Training and Supply of Teachers 170
National Advisory Council on Education in Industry and Commerce 298
National Association for Tertiary Education for the Deaf 265
National Assistance Board 254
National Association of College and University Business Officers 281
National Association of College and University Food Services 281
National Association of Conservative Graduates 266
National Association of Foreign Student Affairs 281
National Association of Local Government Officers 165
National Association of Soviet and East European Studies 46-7
National Association of Teachers in Further and Higher Education 6,82,107-
    12,169,302,303,305
National Association of University Music Staff 265
National Audit Office 289
National Board for Prices and Incomes 192
National Committee for Philosophy 260-1
National Congress on Languages in Education 263
National Council for Diplomas in Art and Design 87,89
National Council for Modern Languages in Higher and Further Education 261,
    263
National Council for Technological Awards 87,89
National Curriculum Council 127,128
National Educational Closed Circuit Television Association 95-6
National Film Archive 51
National Foundation for Adult Education 113-6
National Foundation for Educational Research 169,275,295
National Health Insurance Commissions for England and Wales 254
National Health Service 44,60,105
National Incomes Commission 192
National Institute for Medical Research 105,106
National Institute of Adult Continuing Education (England and Wales) 7,13,
    113-6,167,275,282,297,304,305
National Institute of Adult Education 113-6,252,275
National Institute of Economic and Social Research 92
National Institute of Oceanography 121
National Library of Scotland 215
National Physical Laboratory 17
National Register of Archives 141,197,234
National Seed Development Organisation 21
National Service 250
National Staff Development and Training Unit 59
National Union of Public Employees 165
National Union of Students 6,7,34,56,60,82,84,117-20,230,266,305
National Union of Teachers 108,110,112,296
National Universities Committee of NALGO 261
Natural Environment Research Council 4,10,21,65,120-3,210,242,243,289

P

Pacific   198
Page Report on Veterinary Manpower and Education   181
Paisley College of Technology   240
Paris   158,202,217,219,223,234,245,267
Paris, University of   297
Parliament   61,106,137,171,174,183,249,250,287-90
Parliament, Members of   60,81,145,271,272-3
Parliamentary Constituencies   81,83,250,272-3
Pay and Employment Policy Committee   60,165,192
Pensions and National Insurance, Ministry of   254
PICKUP Programme   175
Plant Breeding Institute   21
Plymouth Polytechnic   263
Poland   140,232,241
Polish Institute in Great Britain   223
Polytechnics (general)   10,23,26,27,51,54,57-8,70,71,80,87-8,92,94,95,108,
        110,118,121,132,145,147,152,162,175,184,189,190,231,240,247,249,259,
        260,261,263,264,265,266,277,278,282,290,291,299,305
Polytechnics and Colleges Funding Council   9,145,290
Polytechnics Central Admissions System   160
Portugal   139,209,235,237
Postgraduate Medical Education Committee   254
Prague   117,218,229
Principals and Wardens of Men's Colleges and Halls of Residence   31-2
Privy Council Office   9,91,104-5,121,173,252,256
Privy Council, Committee on Education in Scotland   253
Professors and Heads of University Departments of Sociology   265
Programme for Educational Building   235
Programme on Institutional Management in Higher Education   235,237-8
Property Services Agency   143
Proudman Oceanographic Laboratory   121
Public Record Office and Public Records   4,5,7,12,14,17,18,22,66-7,89,94,
        106-7,123,131,133,134,147,181-3,233-4,249-53,255-6,257,284,285,286
Public Record Office of Northern Ireland   255

Q

Queen's University Belfast   64,90,138,255,265

R

RACE   210
Rathbone, Miss Eleanor, M.P.   83,273
Reading   194,196
Reading, University of   31,68,83,103,142,143,164,182,276,281
Records of Achievement   98
Reynard, Miss   31
Regional Committees for Adult Education in HM Forces   257-8
Regional Examining Boards   98
Religious and Theological Students' Fellowship   163
REPLAN   114,116

S

Scottish Council for Research in Education 253-4
Scottish Council of Churches 153
Scottish Education Department 134-6,186,253
Scottish Examination Board 304
Scottish Educational Research Association 304
Scottish Home and Health Department 10
Scottish Institute of Adult and Continuing Education 269,304
Scottish Joint Committee for Diplomas in Management Studies 87
Scottish Library Association 264
Scottish Marine Biological Association 121
Scottish Record Office 7,253-4
Scottish Tertiary Education Advisory Council 134-6,279,288,304
Scottish Universities Accommodation Consortium 136-7
Scottish Universities Campus Hotels 136-7
Scottish Universities Council for Studies in Education 269
Scottish Universities Council on Entrance 269,281
Scottish Universities Entrance Board 269
Scottish Universities Management Services and Efficiency Unit 137-8
Scottish Universities Physical Education Association 269
Scottish Universities Research and Reactor Centre 269-70,278
Scottish Universities Safety/Security Officers 184
Scottish Universities Sports Board 139
Scottish Universities Sports Federation 55,138-9
Sea Mammal Research Unit 121
Secondary Examinations Council 60,98-9,128,130
Secondary Heads Association 60
Secondary Schools Examination Council 127,130,131
Secretaries Committee of the Scottish Universities 138
Senegal 202
Sheffield 218,261,300
Sheffield School of Medicine and Surgery 251
Sheffield, University of 31,33,49,59,68,81,83,92,98,124,137,144,150,164,182,
    193,194,251,272,273
Silverman, Miss Marguerite 171
Simeone, Mr. R.N. 29
Slade Film Hitory Register 51,52
Smith, A.L. 194
Social and Applied Psychology Unit 92
Social and Community Planning Research 92
Social Science Research Council 91-4,148,264
Social Security, Department of see under Department of Social Security
Society for Animal Welfare in Israel 171
Society for College and University Planning 281
Society for the Propagation of the Gospel 267
Society for the Protection of Science and Learning 139-42,285
Society for Research into Higher Education 6,45,75,199,275,276,291,293,
    294,300-01,305
Society of Archivists 2,5,7,147
Sofia 218
Solihull 112
Soroptomist International 226
South Africa 120,140,247
South East Asia 232
South Pacific 232
Southampton 41,72
Southampton, University of 31,33,34,43,68,79,85,142,143,164,182,262,263,
    264,281
South-East Asia 222

T

U

W

Y

Z